PENGUIN BOOKS

THE EDIFICE COMPLEX

Deyan Sudjic has been the architecture critic of the *Observer* newspaper in London since 2000. He was the editor of the Italian magazine *Domus* and the director of the Venice Architecture Biennale. He recently took up a new role as Director of the Design Museum in London. He is the author of many previous books on architecture.

Praise for *The Edifice Complex*

"Intellectually robust."   —*Kirkus Reviews*

"Provocative . . . lively and sharp."   —*Publishers Weekly*

"Sudjic is an elegant stylist, and his architectural descriptions are clear and precise."   —*National Post* (Canada)

"A new book worth reading."   —*Cincinnati CityBeat*

"Captivating . . . The reader need not share the author's tastes to enjoy it."   —*The New York Sun*

"Deyan Sudjic: probably the most influential figure in architecture you've never heard of."   —Slate.com

"Deyan Sudjic's new book is as compelling a read as a popular novel. . . . At times, it is as though the worlds of academe and the gossip column collide. . . . Sudjic is incredibly adept at taking us behind the scenes. . . . Fascinating."   —Norman Foster

"Sudjic proceeds energetically (and often very funnily). . . . The conventional wisdom that despots and their architects inhabit a hermetic milieu . . . is subtly overturned. . . . A thrilling and passionately indignant trawl through vanity's most polluted depths."
                    —*The Times* (London)

"[This] is a book against type. . . . *The Edifice Complex* is essential reading for anyone who cares about the physical world around them, for architecture is the most overwhelming of cultural forms. . . . Fascinating . . . evocative . . . this is an honest book."
                    —*The Independent*

THE
EDIFICE
COMPLEX

HOW THE RICH AND
POWERFUL—AND THEIR
ARCHITECTS—SHAPE THE WORLD

DEYAN SUDJIC

PENGUIN BOOKS

PENGUIN BOOKS

Published by the Penguin Group

Penguin Group (USA) Inc., 375 Hudson Street, New York, New York 10014, U.S.A.
Penguin Group (Canada), 90 Eglinton Avenue East, Suite 700, Toronto,
Ontario, Canada M4P 2Y3 (a division of Pearson Penguin Canada Inc.)
Penguin Books Ltd, 80 Strand, London WC2R 0RL, England
Penguin Ireland, 25 St Stephen's Green, Dublin 2, Ireland (a division of Penguin Books Ltd)
Penguin Group (Australia), 250 Camberwell Road, Camberwell,
Victoria 3124, Australia (a division of Pearson Australia Group Pty Ltd)
Penguin Books India Pvt Ltd, 11 Community Centre, Panchsheel Park, New Delhi – 110 017, India
Penguin Group (NZ), cnr Airborne and Rosedale Roads, Albany,
Auckland 1310, New Zealand (a division of Pearson New Zealand Ltd)
Penguin Books (South Africa) (Pty) Ltd, 24 Sturdee Avenue,
Rosebank, Johannesburg 2196, South Africa

Penguin Books Ltd, Registered Offices:
80 Strand, London WC2R 0RL, England

First published in the United States of America by The Penguin Press,
a member of Penguin Group (USA) Inc. 2005
Published in Penguin Books 2006

1   3   5   7   9   10   8   6   4   2

Selections reprinted from Philip Johnson Papers 1908–2001,
Research Library, The Getty Research Institute, Los Angeles (980060)

THE LIBRARY OF CONGRESS HAS CATALOGED THE HARDCOVER EDITION AS FOLLOWS:
Sudjic, Deyan.
The edifice complex : how the rich and powerful shape the world / Deyan Sudjic.
p. cm.
Includes index.
ISBN 1-59420-068-8 (hc.)
ISBN 0 14 30.3801 X (pbk.)
1. Power (Social sciences)   2. Public architecture.   I. Title.
JC330.S83 2005
725'01—dc22   2005048943

Printed in the United States of America

ACKNOWLEDGMENTS

The author would like to thank, for their varied help, advice, and encouragement, Steve Featherstone of Llewellyn-Davies; Peter Murray of Wordsearch; Zhang Xin and Yung Ho Chang; Alex Linklater; Clair Paterson and Tina Bennett of Janklow and Nesbit; Charles Jencks; Stefan McGrath and Will Goodlad at Penguin UK; and Emily Loose and Alexandra Lane at Penguin Group (USA). And, in their unique ways, Sarah Miller and Olivia Sudjic.

CONTENTS

CHAPTER 1

WHY WE BUILD

I USED TO KEEP A PHOTOGRAPH TORN FROM A TABLOID PINNED UP over my desk. Through the blotchy newsprint you could make out the blurred image of an architectural model the size of a small car jacked up to eye level. Left to themselves, architects use noncommittal shades of gray for their models, but this one was painted in glossy lipstick colors, suggesting it was made to impress a client with an attention span shorter than most.

Strips of cardboard and balsa wood had been used to represent a mosque with a squat dome fenced in by concentric circles of spiky minarets. The gaudy shapes and the reduction of an intricate decorative tradition to a cartoon, not much different from a hundred other attempts at having it both ways, tried—and failed—to be simultaneously boldly modern and respectfully rooted in the past. The questionable architectural details weren't what made it such an unsettling image. What really grabbed my attention was the glimpse of the darker aspects of building that the picture captured.

None of the uniformed figures clustered respectfully around the model looked like the architects who usually feature conspicuously in this kind of picture, but there wasn't much doubt about the identity of the thickset man with the heavy moustache, looking disorientingly like a World War II British army major in his vintage khaki sweater and beret, or the unblinking fascination with which he was gazing so adoringly at his model.

Saddam Hussein, like many authoritarians, was an enthusiastic patron of architecture. Unlike Napoleon III, whose fastidious tastes are still clearly visible in the parade-ground tidiness of the boulevards of Paris, or Benito Mussolini, with his contradictory passions for modernism and Caesar Augustus, Hussein had no obvious preference for any specific architectural style. He did, however, have an instinctive grasp of how to use architecture to glorify himself and his regime and to intimidate his opponents.

From the moment of its conception, the Mother of All Battles Mosque had a very clear purpose: to claim the first Gulf War as a victory for Iraq. Hussein was humiliated in that war. His army was expelled from Kuwait. Its desperate flight home left the highway disfigured by the grotesque train of incinerated Iraqi conscripts, trapped in their burnt-out plundered cars, the roadside strewn with loot. Hussein wanted to build his own reality to try to wipe out that image of defeat, just as the Kuwaitis used their tame parliament—designed by Jørn Utzon, architect of the Sydney Opera House, no less—to suggest that they were a Scandinavian democracy rather than a Gulf oligarchy. Building anything at all while Iraq struggled with the deprivations brought by Hussein's manipulation of United Nations sanctions was a calculated gesture of defiance. And the mosque itself came loaded with an iconography that made this defiance all the more explicit.

The message of the newspaper picture of Hussein's mosque is unambiguous. Architecture is about power. The powerful build because that is what the powerful do. On the most basic level, building creates jobs that are useful to keep a restless workforce quiet. But it also reflects well on the capability and decisiveness—and the determination—of the powerful. Above all, architecture is the means to tell a story about those who build it.

Architecture is used by political leaders to seduce, to impress, and to intimidate. Certainly those were the underlying reasons for Saddam Hussein's building campaign. His palaces and monuments were tattooed all over Iraq, less indelibly than he would have liked, in an attempt to present the entire country as his personal property, both to his external and to his internal foes.

In the south, outside Basra, lines of bronze effigies ten feet tall follow the shoreline. They depict Iraqi officers killed in the meat-grinder war against Iran. The sculptures point across the Gulf toward the old enemy—an enemy with its own taste for monument building in the days of the Shah, the product of a failed attempt to construct a pedigree for the Pahlavi dynasty.

On the edge of central Baghdad, a pair of notorious outsize crossed swords span the highway, gripped by giant bronze hands modeled on Hussein's own but cast in the quintessentially English suburb of Basingstoke. In Saddam's day, nets filled with shoals of captured Iranian helmets dangled from the two sword hilts. Such monuments, kitsch as they are, are universal. They date from the victory memorials of the Peloponnesian Wars and the triumphs Imperial Rome granted its favored generals. The same ritual celebration of the defeat of an enemy is reflected in the monumental sculptures cast from captured Napoleonic cannon that adorn the centers of London and Berlin.

The idea of the crossed swords was filched without acknowledgment from Mike Gold, an architect based in London, who originally proposed it, minus the helmets, as an innocuously whimsical civic landmark for a motorway in Saudi Arabia. In Iraq, its meaning was completely transformed. Gianni Versace's inflammatory caricature of sex and money could be worn with a sense of irony in Milan, but not in Slobodan Milosevic's Belgrade, where the bandit classes took the glitter and leopard-skin look at face value. And in Baghdad, a piece of ironic postmodernism became the most literal kind of architectural propaganda.

But Hussein had an objective wider than celebrating his questionable victories and intimidating his enemies. His mosque-building campaign can be seen as an overcompensation for the essentially secular nature of his regime; it demonstrates his credentials as a devout defender of the faith, despite his taste for whisky and murder.

Yet architectural propaganda is not the exclusive domain of those commissioning a building. As the United States dispatched two more aircraft carriers toward Iraq at the end of 2002, *The New York Times* published a photograph of Saddam Hussein's Mother of All Battles Mosque on its front page. Here, four years after the design was first unveiled, was the completed building. Without a hint of skepticism, the *Times* baldly repeated the conventional media wisdom that the minarets—an outer ring of four and an inner, slightly shorter group of four more—are representations of, respectively, Kalashnikov assault rifles and Scud missiles. This assertion existed mainly in the minds of the western media, and their taxi drivers, and might be a little more convincing if the minarets had tail fins, or were decorated with olive drab camouflage paint rather than white limestone embellished with blue mosaic. Nor does the outer ring come equipped with gun sights or the distinctive curved magazine and walnut stock of a Kalashnikov. They look much less martial—and much less elegant—than the pencil-slim Ottoman minarets of Istanbul, which certainly do look like rockets.

The *Times* reporter sounded disappointed after his tour of the mosque: "Where once visitors were told what seems obvious, how the cylinders of the inner minarets slim to an aerodynamic peak, like a ballistic missile tapering at the nose cone, they are now assured that no such references were ever in the architects' minds." But by then America already felt itself at war, and such a bombastic interpretation of the mosque was too much of a propaganda gift.

Although the mosque does not use literally militaristic metaphors, its underlying message is hardly reassuring. The image of the exterior is less a howl of defiance than a conventional piece of labored Gulf hotel glitz, looking more like a police academy in drag than a national monument. More telling was the paper's photograph of the glass showcase at the heart of the mosque, which contains a 650-page transcription of the Koran. According to the *Times,* the mosque's imam, Sheik Thahir Ibrahim Shammariu, claimed that the calligrapher used Hussein's own blood, donated over a period of two years at the scarcely believable rate of a pint every fortnight, to fill his pen. Another photo accompanying the article showed the reflecting pool that encircles the mosque, allegedly shaped like a map of the Arab world. At one end a blue mosaic plinth juts out of the water to form an island. The *Times* claimed that this irregular mound took the shape of Hussein's thumbprint. The paper didn't go into how it could be so sure that it had correctly identified the thumb as Hussein's own. If true it carries a message that could not be clearer. The mosque's imam was disappointingly reluctant to confirm the warlike iconography of the mosque to the *Times,* but he was obligingly ready to spell out some of its more occult meanings. The outer minarets are 43 meters high, he pointed out, supposedly for the 43 days of bombing at the start of the first Gulf War. The four minarets of the inner ring, representing April, the fourth month, are 37 meters high, for the year 1937. The 28 water jets in the pool symbolize the 28th day of the month. Together they spell out April 28, 1937, Hussein's birthday.

In the flesh, the mosque is not a particularly effective way of demonstrating Iraqi defiance. And since Hussein's purpose was to present himself as a devout Muslim, it seems unlikely that he would have used the Christian calendar to do so. This emphasis on the power of numbers, if it really is intentional, was uncomfortably echoed in some of the seven finalists in the competition to rebuild the World Trade Center, revealed in New York in the same week that this story appeared. Richard Meier and

Peter Eisenman's plan featured a tower 1111 feet high, presumably on the basis that a mere 911 feet would have been too short to attract enough attention. Daniel Libeskind famously went for 1776 feet.

One interpretation of Hussein's enthusiasm for building could be to see him simply as following in the tradition common all over Asia and the Middle East of employing fashionable western architects to design prestige projects to demonstrate how up-to-date he was. Indeed, Baghdad had a history of planning gargantuan architectural monuments throughout much of the twentieth century. In 1957 King Faisal II commissioned Frank Lloyd Wright to design an opera house in the manner of Moscow's unbuilt Palace of the Soviets. A colossal thirty-story-high memorial sculpture of Iraq's greatest caliph, Haroun al-Rashid, grandson of Baghdad's founder, took Lenin's place as its centerpiece. It would have been a piece of nation building on an epic scale by an Iraq still emerging from British colonial rule. A commission for Walter Gropius to design a university actually was built. Le Corbusier also secured a commission in Baghdad from Faisal in 1956, designing an arena completed only long after Le Corbusier's death in 1965; it was then named the Saddam Hussein Sports Center.

Hussein wanted to do more than look modern. He was also attempting to co-opt a much older heritage of monument making that stretched back five thousand years to Ur and the first urban civilizations on the Euphrates. He initiated a series of damaging "restorations" of Iraq's ancient sites, not flinching from reconstructing the Hanging Gardens of Babylon using materials more commonly found in a suburban subdivision. He had each brick stamped with his own name in the manner of the ancient emperors, to demonstrate that he was their natural successor. He even posted guards in period costume, equipped with spears, at his version of Ishtar's gate in his Babylonian theme park.

Hussein's determination to use architecture as a propaganda tool to glorify his state and consolidate his hold on it was clear enough. Even though it was hardly effective, when measured against his objectives, architecture stands clearly incriminated for the part it played in his brutal regime. But what can you say about those commissioned to execute his ideas?

The mosque is certainly a banal piece of architecture. And those who designed it are guilty of a lack of imagination, but does the use to which Hussein has put it neccessarily implicate the architect in anything worse?

Architecture has an existence independent of those who pay for it. Simply because the architect of the mosque worked for one of the more brutal of recent leaders, there is no reason to assume that he is himself culpable, as we did of Albert Speer when he was convicted by the Nuremberg war crimes court. The mosque is not itself committing an act of violence; its architectural forms need not in themselves be the embodiment of a dictatorship.

Whether architecture can project an inherent meaning at all is still an open question, though one that is often asked. Are there, in fact, such things as totalitarian, democratic, and nationalistic buildings? And if they do exist, what is it that gives architecture such meanings? Can classical columns or glass walls really be described, as some have claimed, as the signs of fascist or democratic buildings? Are these fixed and permanent meanings, or can they be changed over time?

If Saddam Hussein had shown the wit, or the cunning, to invite Zaha Hadid, the most celebrated woman architect in the world, and herself born in Baghdad, to design that mosque, we might have been distracted enough to see his regime in a different light. If Hadid had accepted, we would certainly see her differently: at best a political innocent, at worst a naïve compromiser. Certainly her chances of getting to build anything in America would have been dramatically diminished.

A Hadid mosque would have sent another kind of message: still a glorification of Hussein's state, still an act of defiance, but a claim of the cultural high ground too. It would have suggested a regime more sophisticated than the one that countenanced the cold-blooded murder of

Hussein's two sons-in-law and the gassing of thousands of its own citizens. But would Hadid—in the unlikely event that she had been asked, and the even more unlikely event that she had accepted—have been seen as playing a part in reasserting a more civilized Iraq? Or would she have been condemned as a pawn in a game of state, prepared to subordinate every other consideration in the pursuit of the chance to build?

It is not only architects who are driven by the overwhelming urge to build at any cost. Saddam Hussein's obsession with building raises a series of questions about the psychology that motivated him. To explore the question of why he, and others like him, invested so much in building, we need to consider whether architecture is an end in itself, or a means to an end.

WE BUILD FOR EMOTIONAL AND PSYCHOLOGICAL PURPOSES, AS well for ideological and practical reasons. The language of architecture is used to project power, as much by software billionaires endowing a museum in return for naming rights as by sociopathic dictators. When Michael Eisner, who was obsessed by architecture, set about building Euro Disney on the outskirts of Paris, he recruited every famous architect he could get his hands on and had a detailed opinion about every aspect of what they proposed. It was a characteristic that infuriated Aldo Rossi, the leading Italian architect of his generation, who ended up pulling out of the commission. "I am not personally offended, and can ignore all the negative points that have been made about our project at the last meeting in Paris," he wrote to Eisner. "The cavalier Bernini, invited to Paris for the Louvre project, was tormented by a multitude of functionaries who continued to demand that changes be made to the project. It is clear that I am not the cavalier Bernini. But it is also clear that you are not the King of France."

Architecture has been shaped by the ego, and by the fear of death, as well as by political and religious impulses. And it in turn serves to give

them shape and form. Trying to make sense of the world without acknowledging architecture's psychological impact on it is to miss a fundamental aspect of its nature. To do so would be like ignoring the impact
of warfare on the history of technology and vice versa. Unlike science
and technology, which have conventionally been presented as being free
of ideological connotations, architecture is both a practical tool and an
expressive language, capable of carrying highly specific messages.

Yet the difficulty in establishing the precise political meanings of
buildings and the elusive nature of the political content of architecture
have led today's generation of architects to claim that their work is au-
tonomous, or neutral. Conversely, they may believe that if there is such
a thing as overtly "political" architecture, it is confined to an isolated
ghetto, no more representative of the concerns of high-culture architecture than a shopping mall or a Las Vegas casino. It is a flawed assumption. There may be no fixed political meaning to a given architectural
language, but that does not mean that architecture lacks the potential to
assume a political aspect. Few successful architects can avoid producing
buildings with a political dimension at some point in their career,
whether they want to or not. And almost all political leaders find themselves using architects for political purposes. It is a relationship that re-
curs in almost every kind of regime and appeals to egotists of every
description. That is why there are photographs of Tony Blair, François
Mitterrand, and Winston Churchill (not to mention countless mayors,
archbishops, chief executives, and billionaire robber barons) bowed over
their own, equally elaborate architectural models, looking just as narcissistically transfixed as the beatific Hussein beaming over his mosque.
This is not to equate George Bush the Elder's presidential library, or
Tony Blair's Millennium Dome or his Wembley Stadium or any Olympic
arena that Britain will build for the 2012 games, with Hussein's mosque.
To maneuver at the court of an elected prime minister to secure the
chance to build involves an altogether less corrosive kind of compromise
than the potentially lethal survival dance demanded by a dictatorship.

But democratic regimes are just as likely to deploy architecture as an instrument of statecraft as totalitarians.

Versailles was built as Louis XIV's court whose architectural splendor and physical location were meant to neutralize the power base of the nobility in the French provinces. Two centuries later, Napoleon III was once more using architecture as an instrument of political power when he engaged Georges Eugène Haussmann to rebuild Paris on a monumental scale. He was attempting not so much to curb the power of the Parisian mob as to legitimize his questionable claims to an imperial title. And François Mitterrand saw a Paris adorned by a transformed Louvre and the Grande Arche at La Défense as an essential part of his strategy to make Paris the undisputed capital of a modern Europe. For all three rulers, how those monuments looked was as much part of the strategy as what they contained. Mitterrand adopted an aggressive architecture of simplified geometric forms in steel and glass to symbolize French commitment to modernity, just as the Sun King made Versailles a temple to a royal cult to demonstrate the divine right of kings.

I STARTED TO COLLECT IMAGES OF THE RICH AND POWERFUL LEANing over architectural models in a more systematic way after I suddenly found myself in the middle of one, invited as an observer. The elder statesman of Japanese architecture, Arata Isozaki, had leased an art gallery in Milan owned by Miuccia Prada for a presentation to an important client. Outside, two black Mercedeses full of bodyguards were parked on either side of the entrance, alongside a vanload of *carabinieri.* Inside was another of those room-size models. Isozaki described it as a villa. In fact it's a palace for a Qatari sheik, who at the time was his country's minister for culture. And the palace has to do rather more than accommodate the sheik, his family, his collection of rare breed animals, his Ferraris, his Bridget Rileys, and his Hockney swimming pool, as well as his Richard Serra landscape installation. It is a deliberate effort to inject a sense of cultural depth into a desert sheikdom with little urban tradition. Each piece of the building has been allocated to an individual architect or designer. And Isozaki's assistants are marshaling them for an audience with the sheik to present their projects. The architects wait, and they wait, drinking coffee and eating pastries dispensed by waiters in black tie until the sheik finally arrives, almost two hours late. Here is the relationship between power and architecture in its most naked form, a relationship of subservience to the mighty as clear as if the architect were a hairdresser or a tailor. (In fact the villa never got built, and the last that I heard of the sheik was when the British newspapers reported that he was under house arrest and summarily removed from his ministry, where he was responsible for the purchase of millions of dollars' worth of art on behalf of the government.)

We are used to discussing architecture in terms of its relationship to art history, or as a reflection of technological change, or as an expression of social anthropology. We know how to categorize buildings by the shapes of their windows or the decorative detail of their column capitals. We understand them as the products of available materials and skills. What we are not so comfortable with is coming to grips with the wider political dimensions of buildings: why they exist in fact, rather than how. It's an omission that is surprising, given the closeness of the relationship between architecture and power. Architecture has always been dependent on the allocation of precious resources and scarce manpower. As such, its execution has always been at the discretion of those with their hands on the levers of power rather than of architects. Pharaonic Egypt did not devote the surplus from its harvests to the construction of the pyramids, rather than to road building or abolishing slavery, because of any creative urge of the pharaoh's architects.

Despite a certain amount of pious rhetoric about architecture's duty to serve the community, to work at all in any culture the architect has to establish a relationship with the rich and the powerful. There is nobody else with the resources to build. And it is the genetically predetermined destiny of the architect to do anything he can to try to build, just as it is the mission of migrating salmon to make one last exhausting upriver trip to spawn before expiring. The architectural profession can be seen then, not as well-meaning herbivores, but as ready to enter into a Faustian bargain. It has no alternative but to trim and compromise with whatever regime is in power.

Every kind of political culture uses architecture for what can, at heart, be understood as rational, pragmatic purposes, even when it is used to make a symbolic point. But when the line between political calculation and psychopathology breaks down, architecture becomes not just a matter of practical politics, but a fantasy, or a sickness that consumes its victims.

There is a psychological parallel between making a mark on the landscape with a building and the exercise of political power. Both depend on the imposition of will. Certainly, seeing their worldview confirmed by reducing an entire city to the scale of a doll's house in an architectural model has an inherent appeal for those who regard the individual as of no account. Even more attractive is the possibility of imposing their will in the physical sense on a city by reshaping it in the way that Haussmann did in Paris.

Architecture feeds the egos of the susceptible. They grow more and more dependent on it to the point that architecture becomes an end in itself, seducing its addicts as they build more and more on an ever larger scale.

Building is the means by which the egotism of the individual is expressed in its most naked form: the Edifice Complex.

On balance, Haussmann's Paris steered clear of megalomania. Ceauşescu's Bucharest did not. In both these cities, demolition was almost as essential a part of the process of transformation as new building. And destruction and construction can be seen as closely related. Whatever else it was, the assault on the Twin Towers, driven by visceral hatred, was a literal acceptance of the iconic power of architecture, and an attempt to destabilize that power even more forcefully through erasure. The fact that one of the hijackers at the controls of the airliners was himself an architecture graduate serves only to underline the point.

This book is an exploration of what it is that makes individuals and societies build in the way that they do, what their buildings mean, and the uses to which they are put. It looks in some detail at a selection of buildings, architects, billionaires, politicians, and dictators, mostly from the twentieth century, in the belief that understanding the nature of their shared obsessions can help us protect ourselves from their more malevolent ambitions.

Architecture has the ability to modify weather and light. In that it has power. Stone and steel last longer than flesh and blood. Over time architecture takes on the patina and the resonance of the events that have taken place inside it, and of the people who have occupied it. Buildings are historical markers that show the passing of time, and the changes of regimes; no wonder that the totalitarians were so keen about erasing those buildings that challenged their vision of what a country should be. No wonder that it is architectural imagery that underpins the otherwise banal cult of Freemasonry, with its great architect and its dividing-compasses symbol.

What an architect can offer a Hussein—or an Eisner, for that matter—is in part the sense that together they are making a place in which there is some sense of meaning and purpose. This includes a sense of belonging to a wider world, but at the same time celebrating the individual and his or her place in that world.

The nature of the relationship between the architect and the patron is complex and critical. For many architects it has been an act of faith to maintain that great architecture depends on a great client, the strong individual. This is of course a somewhat self-serving concept, calculated to flatter the patron, and is fundamentally just as unsatisfactory as the idea that great architecture depends on a single architectural genius. The latter concept results in the cult of celebrity, reducing the complex creative process to a caricature.

There certainly are individuals who commission an architect and, whether from vanity or the controlling instinct, see every decision as being essentially theirs. But it is not the only model for the relationship.

The appeal of construction lies in the special kind of pleasure that is to be had in the process of building, and in the transformation of an idea into a physical reality—sometimes slow and steady, sometimes in large steps. That pleasure is hard to replicate in the daily experience of a completed building. And it may explain why so many individuals, once they have built once, try to repeat the experience again and again.

But there is more to it than the process of watching a wall rise, or a space take shape. The appeal of architecture to those who aspire to political power lies in the way that it is an expression of will. To design a building, or to have a building designed, is to suggest that this is the world as we want it. This is the perfect room from which to run a state, a business empire, a city, a family. It is the way to create a physical version of an idea or an emotion. It is the way to construct reality as we wish it to be, rather than as it is.

In its scale and its complications, architecture is by far the biggest and most overwhelming of all cultural forms. It literally determines the way that we see the world, and how we interact with one another.

For the patron, it is a chance to exert a sense of control over events. And for a certain kind of architect it offers the possibility of control over people. It allows the architect to indulge in the *Gesamtkunstwerk*, the total work of art, so mocked by Adolf Loos in his parable of the poor rich man in which the client has become just another part of the furniture:

> Once it happened that he was celebrating his birthday. His
> wife and children had given him many presents. He liked
> their choice immensely and enjoyed it all thoroughly. But soon

the architect arrived to set things right, and to take all the decisions in difficult questions. He entered the room. The master
greeted him with pleasure, for he had much on his mind. But
the architect did not see the man's joy. He had discovered
something quite different and grew pale.

"What kind of slippers are these you have got on?" he
asked painfully.

The master of the house looked at his embroidered slippers. Then he breathed a sigh of relief. This time he felt quite
guiltless. The slippers had been made to the architect's original designs. So he answered in a superior way.

"But, Mr Architect, have you already forgotten? You yourself designed them!"

"Of course," thundered the architect, "but for the bedroom! They completely disrupt the mood here with these two
impossible spots of color. Can't you see that?"

Some rather similar questions were explored more sympathetically
by the Milanese architect Ernesto Rogers in his belief that the values
and the aspirations of a culture, when expressed by architecture, could
be distilled in such an intense way that it would be possible to deduce
from the simplest of objects produced by a society, even a spoon, the
nature of its largest artifact, the city.

Architecture is intimately concerned with the instinct to control. To
order, to categorize, to shape life as it will be lived in a space, to choreo-
graph every activity within every space, demands a certain view of the
world, one in which humility is unlikely to figure very large. There is a
deep-rooted belief that the architect has succeeded in his task only if he
has managed to finesse the clients into building not just something that
they don't understand, but something that they don't want. It is a view
of the world that is the product of an architectural profession that has
constructed a sense of itself as constituting a priesthood, defined by its

arcane language, but also its sense of inferiority about its relative status with other cultural forms.

Architecture of course is about life as well as about death. It shapes the way we live our lives, even if not quite so directly as some architects imagine. It does have a practical purpose, but it is also pursued for its own sake, as a metaphor for something else. It is about control because of the possibility it gives of being entirely in command of our personal environment, and the people that we are sharing it with, if even only for a brief moment. Architecture has the power to frame the world, canceling out the things that the architect or patron doesn't want you to see, concentrating on those that he does. It directs light, it creates the relationship between where you eat and where you prepare food. Of course any sensible architect makes this a loose fit. You can write in the kitchen, you can eat in the bath, you can sleep in the study. But the architecture has created a grain and a texture that you can go with, and which you can choose to ignore.

It's the mind-set demonstrated by the German architect Frei Otto, who named his children in alphabetical order. It's the experience of taking a drive in the backseat of Norman Foster's chauffeur-driven Range Rover, on the way to his private jet, to find that both seat pockets are filled with pristine sketchbooks and freshly sharpened pencils (as well as a mobile telephone), just in case something should occur to the great architect in transit and be lost to the world because he is lacking paper and pen to record it before it passes across his field of consciousness and vanishes forever.

It's the idea that design can be an instrument for control, as it is for the German modernist Dieter Rams. So distressing does he find the idea of visual disorder that he used to claim that he took a large paper bag with him on country walks to collect the rubbish. His own office is a study in neutrality, the Switzerland of the design world, the kind of room in which a single fingerprint on the wall or a paper out of place has the impact of a visual landslide. He designed everything in it, the furniture, the products on the shelves, the clock, the radio, the storage system, and the only color comes from the orange cigarette packet, permanently in Rams's hands.

Rams devotes enormous effort and patience to designing perfect objects that defeat fashion and cancel out the passing of time by defying visual redundancy. He made the ideal calculator, with the most carefully considered rounded corners, and the perfect buttons, and the clearest sequence of operating functions, only to find the entire category of objects "calculators" had become redundant. He designed the most beautiful, the most functional record player, and the same thing happened. Not only have records all but vanished, so have the tapes that replaced them. And the compact discs that replaced them are rapidly on their way out too, leaving Rams and his attempts at control and order looking like the hopelessly deluded activities of a Canute, attempting to prevent the tide from washing away the grains of sand on a beach.

Architecture has its roots in the creation of shelter in a physical sense, but it has become an attempt to construct a particular view of the world, whether it is an individual house, a complex of streets and apartments, or a city plan. There is a very different kind of connection between an architect and the mayor who invites him to build a new housing complex, and the relationship between that architect and the individuals who will actually live in it. Architecture is still shaped by the powerful, and not the many. But that does not make it any less significant.

CHAPTER 2

THE LONG MARCH TO THE LEADER'S DESK

ADOLF HITLER WENT TO PARIS ONLY ONCE IN HIS LIFE. HE FLEW there in the wake of the French army's collapse as the victorious leader of the Third Reich that he had created, stretching from the Atlantic to the Soviet frontier to wash away Germany's humiliation at Versailles. He landed at Le Bourget just before dawn on June 23, 1940, and it was not generals or party leaders who sat closest to him on his personal plane. Extraordinarily, Hitler chose to savor his greatest moment of military triumph by sharing it with two architects, Albert Speer and Hermann Giesler, along with Arno Breker, the regime's sculptor in chief. He skipped the obvious political sites. Instead of the Elysée Palace and the National Assembly, he took them to see Charles Garnier's Opéra. Hitler spent more than an hour testing his memories of the plans he had studied so obsessively in his days of poverty in Vienna. He knew the building well enough in his mind that, as they toured the grandiloquent marble corridors, he could smugly point out a blocked door that had once led to a room lost in later alterations.

One of the twentieth century's most unforgettable photographs was taken on the steps of Les Invalides later that day. It's an image that is key to understanding the nature of Hitler's pursuit of power. Hitler, the former corporal with a lifelong passion for architecture, had lingered over Napoleon's tomb, and on the way out had entrusted Giesler with the task of designing something even more impressive, when the time came. As the group emerge into the sunshine, Hitler of course is in the center, wearing a long white overcoat. Everybody else is dressed from head to foot in black, in an eerie precursor of the universal taste for Commes des Garçons suits among architects of the early years of the twenty-first century. Most of them are soldiers; a couple belong to Hitler's political entourage, led by Martin Bormann. But the uniformed man on Hitler's immediate right, pointing into the camera, is Speer. At a respectful distance to his left stand Giesler and Breker, the sculptor in his Nazi forage cap.

Here is the leader surrounded by his architectural acolytes. He is a magic figure radiating light, like the Sun King hemmed in by lesser mortals lost in darkness. It is a scene as carefully designed as one of Speer's party rallies, just as pregnant with meaning, and, in theory, as astonishing a tableau as if George W. Bush had decided to tour Baghdad in the company of Philip Johnson, Jeff Koons, and Frank Gehry. The dictator is demonstrating his priorities and making his intentions manifestly clear: Hitler, the great architect, is ready to redesign the world. And yet, somehow, we never entirely got the message; he wanted to be seen not as a military leader or a political figure, but as an artist. For so many leaders architecture represents simply a means to an end. There is the real possibility that for Hitler at least, it was always an end in itself.

BY THE TIME THAT EMIL HÁCHA FINALLY NEGOTIATED THE SECOND of the two pairs of outsize bronze gates forming the ceremonial entrance to the Reich Chancellery on Wilhelmstrasse, it was well after midnight. The Czech president had made the short drive through the empty streets of Berlin from his suite at the Adlon Hotel sitting beside Hitler's foreign minister, Joachim von Ribbentrop. A tiny crowd, no more than fifty people, waited in the rain to see them sweep by on the way to the most difficult three hours of Hácha's life.

This was a brutal time to be embarking on a state visit, but March 15, 1939, was one of the more desperate days in European history. Hitler had reoccupied the Rhineland, annexed Austria, and seized the Sudetenland without firing a shot. If he could, he was determined to secure control of the rest of Czechoslovakia in the same way. The first and only president of the second Czechoslovak republic traveled to Berlin in a despairing and futile attempt to snatch his country back from oblivion. Czechoslovakia had already lost the Sudetenland, with its carefully prepared lines of pillboxes and fortifications on the frontier with Germany, in the betrayal of the Munich conference. Now Hitler wanted to destroy the beleaguered state altogether. Encouraged by Germany, the Hungarians and the Russians were moving to scoop up slices of Czech territory, leaving the rest to Hitler as a protectorate of the Reich. At the same time, the Slovaks prepared to secede to create their own satellite state, allowing Hitler a free run to attack Poland, his next target in the search for *lebensraum.*

Hácha had no cards but his dignity left to play. His officials had been telephoning Berlin for the last three days pleading for an audience with the Führer. By the time Hitler finally agreed to a meeting, 200,000 German soldiers were mobilized to move across the frontier.

In fact, the special train bringing Hácha, his daughter, his foreign minister, and a small entourage of other Czech officials was more than an hour late arriving in Berlin, delayed by troop transports moving south and east. Hácha's position as a supplicant was made immediately clear. A guard of honor met the president at Anhalt Station, fulfilling diplomatic protocol to the letter, but the reception party numbered only insultingly junior functionaries and the German bandmaster skipped Czechoslovakia's national anthem. Hácha must have wished that he had stayed in Prague and ordered his troops into action.

The negotiating process had started without the Czechs knowing it, and they had already lost the first round. Hácha went to his hotel, while his foreign minister, Frantisek Chvalovsky, called on Ribbentrop at the German foreign office. The terms they took to Hácha at the Adlon were so brutal that the Czechs at first refused to leave the hotel. Ribbentrop left them thinking it over for more than an hour while he went to see Hitler alone. According to one account, he passed the time watching a film with the Führer before finally returning to collect them.

Hácha had become president when his predecessor Edvard Beneš went into exile following Neville Chamberlain's 1938 refusal to back his stand against Hitler's territorial demands, and his acquiescence to the dismemberment of the first Czechoslovak republic. Hácha was a respected jurist and the head of the Czechoslovak Supreme Court, but he had little political experience and even less stomach for a fight. Whether his readiness to accommodate Hitler was an attempt to save his own skin or to spare his country from futile bloodshed remains a sharply contested issue. He was to die in disgrace in 1945 in the hospital of the Prague prison where he was held as a collaborator after the Allied liberation of the German protectorate of Bohemia and Moravia. Whatever his intentions, he would have needed real courage to sustain himself as he entered the Chancellery's Court of Honor on that Berlin night six years earlier.

Albert Speer had designed this courtyard, a prelude to the Chancellery itself, as a world within a world, from which there was no way out except on Hitler's terms. Its blank, floodlit walls shut out the city to create a hollow space open to the sky in which Hitler's guards drilled back and forth, casting giant shadows against the background of its superhuman proportions. The void of the courtyard was filled by shouted orders and the sound of marching boots on stone. Here was a practical demonstration of the expression of political power through building, its symbolic quality put to use for highly specific purposes.

Fewer than one hundred miles away, a well-equipped Czech army with modern artillery, technologically advanced aircraft, and Skoda tanks was waiting for Hácha's order to defend its country. In Berlin, however, the president was being made to feel helpless, transfixed by Speer's floodlights on an architectural stage set, meticulously designed to demonstrate to him that he was at the mercy of the most powerful man in the world.

Hácha reviewed his second honor guard of the night, to the musical accompaniment of another military band, and ascended the steps up from the courtyard to the tall, narrow entrance to the Chancellery, flanked by a pair of Arno Breker's fifteen-foot-high bronzes. They depicted prominently muscled naked Teutonic giants. The one on Hácha's left held a drawn sword to represent the Wehrmacht, while his comrade on the other side, symbolizing the National Socialist party, grasped a burning torch. Above Hácha's head, set into the German stone of which the whole Chancellery was built, a bronze eagle took wing, gripping a swastika in its claws. Four monolithic columns dominated the steps. Hácha was a short man in his late sixties with thinning and receding hair and prominent eyebrows; he suffered from a weak heart. His ascent—under the gaze of the SS guards in steel helmets and white gloves, bayonets fixed to their rifles—left him out of breath. The steps demonstrated to visitors that ascending to the Führer's higher plane was a privilege, but they also created a windowless ground floor, reflecting the defensive planning of a building linked to three levels of underground bunkers, below and behind the Chancellery. Hácha was white faced, anxious, and dizzy as he made his way across the entrance lobby, completed just eight weeks earlier. He was exactly the kind of visitor the Chancellery was designed for. If ever architecture had been intended for use as a weapon of war, it was here. The grandeur of the Chancellery was an essential part of Hitler's campaign to browbeat Hácha into surrender. Beyond the courtyard, itself a kind of summation of the Nazi state, was an elaborate sequence of spaces inside the Chancellery, carefully orchestrated to deliver official visitors to Hitler's presence in a suitably intimidated frame of mind. After a quarter-mile walk, visitors were left in no doubt of the power of the new Germany. This was architecture that was very much a means to an end.

"I have an urgent assignment for you," Hitler had told Speer at the beginning of 1938. "I shall be holding extremely important conferences in the near future. For these I need grand halls and salons that will make an impression on people, especially on the lesser dignitaries." Bismarck, of course, was able to orchestrate German unification without the need for any such ego-boosting props. He had worked in the relatively modest surroundings of the old Chancellery, which was swallowed up by Speer's work. But then Bismarck had never wanted to be an architect.

Past the chancellery guards and out of the way of the floodlights, Ribbentrop ushered Hácha across the porch and into a windowless hall beyond, its walls inlaid with the pagan imagery of mosaic eagles grasping burning torches garlanded with oak leaves, its floors slippery with marble. There was no furniture, nor even a trace of carpet to soften the severity of the hall. A clouded glass ceiling floated over the marble, electrically lit from within to cast a shadowless light, in an inescapably modern, almost art deco gesture. Even Hitler could not shut out every trace of the contemporary world. This was the space that Breker described as "permeated with the fire of political power." And it had no other purpose than to impress.

Under the hovering glass and the massive marble walls, the bronze doors at the far end of the hall shimmered and beckoned and threatened. Visitors were propelled down its length as if being whirled through a wind tunnel. As Hácha walked, he was aware of his heart accelerating in rapid fluctuating beats.

Moving through the next set of doors, Ribbentrop led Hácha across the floor of a circular room topped with a dome. Speer designed it in an ineffectual attempt to conceal the fact that even the inexorable march of his triumphal axis toward Hitler's presence, for the time being at least, still had to adapt itself to the random accidents of the geometry of Berlin's street plan and surviving architectural fragments. Beyond this room,

Hácha found another echoing marble hall. At 450 feet, it was almost twice the length of the Hall of Mirrors at Versailles. Hitler and Speer never tired of repeating the point as they reeled off endless lists of the record-breaking architectural statistics to which they laid claim with the Chancellery.

In the far-off distance Hácha could see yet another space, the reception hall to which Hitler had summoned the Berlin diplomatic corps for the Chancellery's inauguration that January. As he had said then, "on the long walk from the entrance to the reception hall, they will get a taste of the power and grandeur of the German Reich." But this was not where Ribbentrop was leading Hácha. The hall that they walked through was thirty feet high. On the left a parade of windows looked out over Voss Strasse, and on the right were five giant doorways, each seventeen feet high. They stopped at the central pair of double doors, guarded by two more SS men in steel helmets. On a bronze scroll above the door case were the initials AH. This was Hitler's study, which he called his workroom, though "theater" was a more appropriate description. Hácha might perhaps have recognized the eighteenth-century tapestries hanging on either side of the door from his days as a law student on holiday in Vienna. They were taken from the Kunsthistorisch Museum and depicted Alexander the Great's conquest of what was then considered to be the world.

The room dissolved into a coffered ceiling high overhead. In the far corner stood Adolf Hitler, his desk positioned against one of five floor-to-ceiling windows. Sprawling over 4000 square feet, this was hardly just a room. To walk from the door to the desk took a nerve-wracking full minute. Hácha may have missed the significance of Alexander's exploits on the tapestry outside, but the marquetry inlay showing Mars with his sword halfway out of its scabbard on the front of Hitler's desk could not have sent a more obvious message on this of all nights. It was a message amplified by the blood-red marble walls, the giant globe on a stand next to the marble table by the window, and the carpet woven with a swastika motif. A bust of Bismarck sat by the desk. Hácha would not have known that this was one of Speer's conjuring tricks. The original had been smashed during the building of the Chancellery. Speer had kept what he took to be a bad omen secret, and asked Breker to make a copy. "We gave it some patina by steeping it in tea," he later claimed.

Far away on the other side of the room, over a fireplace set between twin doors, hung Franz von Lembach's portrait of Bismarck. In front of the fire was a sofa as big as a lifeboat, occupied by Joseph Goebbels and Hermann Göring. Air Marshal Göring began to describe the effortless slaughter his Stukas could inflict on Prague. They would start with the destruction of Prague Castle and move across the city, quadrant by quadrant. Hácha suddenly collapsed under the pressure. He rallied, but three-quarters of an hour after his arrival, before the treaty putting the Czechs under German protection could be signed, he fainted again, and Hitler's own doctor was called.

"I had so belabored the old man that his nerves gave way completely, he was on the point of signing, then he had a heart attack," Hitler told Speer later. "In the adjoining room Dr. Morell gave him an injection, but in this case it was too effective. Hácha regained too much of his strength, revived, and was no longer prepared to sign."

It wasn't until 4:00 A.M. that Hácha's spirit broke, and he finally agreed to put his name to a document that spelled out Czechoslovakia's abject capitulation, declaring that he had entrusted the fate of the Czechs to the hands of Hitler and the Reich. Czechoslovakia had ceased to exist, and Hácha was reduced to the status of figurehead, a humiliation that he had ample time to reflect on during his endless walk back through the marble and mosaic halls of the Chancellery.

SPEER'S ARCHITECTURE HAD APPARENTLY DONE ALL THAT HITLER had expected of it, dealing a near fatal blow to the Czech president and helping Germany overrun an entire country unopposed. Speer had made every piece of stone, every decorative rug, every piece of furniture, every light switch, and each twist and turn in the floor plan serve to reinforce the message of Germany's inherent superiority.

Speer was passionate about his determination to use real stone, rather than a cosmetic veneer of the material, to create buildings that would have a dignity even as ruins. But in spite of this gesture toward authenticity, at a deeper level his was an architecture of sleight of hand rather than substance. Germany was not the most powerful state in the world. Hitler was not Caesar Augustus. Speer's buildings pretended that they were. But perhaps all architecture depends on the creation of an illusion of one kind or another.

The Chancellery was a long, thin building, much of it just one room and a corridor wide, running the whole quarter-mile length of Voss Strasse. Speer created a symmetrical stone façade for the corridor that faced across the street to address the back of Wertheim's department store.

To give this façade a certain palatial quality, he divided it into three, with a set-back central section and two projecting wings, each with its own column-flanked entrance. Taken at face value, the gigantic façade, which implied a massive palace extended behind it, and the reality, which consisted of just one room plus a hallway, were an absurd mismatch. Official visitors, misled by the expansive grandiloquence of Voss Strasse and arriving at the wrong door, needed to be ushered around the corner, to the sliver of stone that contained the main entrance for admission, even as the logic of Speer's architecture suggested it was the palace's back door. Otherwise, they would miss the whole charade. Skip all those grand entrances, courtyards, and halls, and they would be able to stride across the corridor straight to Hitler's desk.

There were actually four levels aboveground in the Chancellery, but the façade was designed to make it look as if there were just three, making the proportions so massive that the sills of the lowest windows, supposedly on the ground floor, were twelve feet above the pavement.

Pedestrians facing this gigantic stone object found themselves confronted with cold hostility.

The message of the architecture could not be made more obvious: this was a place reserved for giants, even if the building served as nothing more than an impressive wrapping for the single most essential element in the design, the triumphal route to Hitler's desk. Hácha experienced it like a spelunker, moving from one giant underground cavern to another, never sure exactly where he would find himself, or what he would have to confront next, as an intimidating and bewildering sequence of spaces unfolded in front of him.

Even the process of building the Chancellery was presented as a demonstration of German technical and organizational superiority over other races. Speer and Hitler conspired a little misleadingly to suggest that the whole project took just a year to complete, from start to finish. They announced the scheme to build a new chancellery only in January 1938, when Speer had already started buying houses on Voss Strasse and was preparing to demolish them to clear the site. Much was made of the thousands of workers brought in from all over the Reich to work on the project, and the Führer's munificence in accommodating them in Berlin's hotels.

The role of the concentration camp for political prisoners at Flossenburg in upper Bavaria in supplying the white granite to be used in the building of Hitler's new Berlin was less publicized at the time, but it and other camps had an intimate connection with Speer's architecture. The SS had established the German Earth and Stone Works Company in 1938 to provide the building materials for the new Germany, forcing their prisoners to work themselves to death in order to pay for the system that imprisoned and tortured them.

The Flossenburg and Mauthausen camps were carefully sited close to stone quarries so as to serve Speer's needs for his monumental building projects, in not just Berlin but Nuremberg, Munich, and Linz too. The camps and the monuments were part of a single system, and each

made the other possible. With their stone watchtowers and their tur-
reted walls, the camps themselves represented a certain architectural
ambition. Hundreds of Spanish Republican prisoners died building
them. Two more camps were established at Oranienburg to supply
bricks. Later, when Speer became Hitler's armaments minister, he used
the camps as a threat to intimidate those workers he called "slackers"
from claiming sickness to avoid war work. He was also intending to use
slave labor, guarded by the SS, on Berlin's construction sites.

Architecture, as Speer practiced it, was primarily a means to an end.
Aside from its role in supporting the concentration camps, and defining
the Nazi state, that end was personal aggrandizement. The more that he
could please his patron the Führer, the greater the rewards. And the
more that his work helped to make complete the victory of Nazi Germany over the world, the greater would be the resources from which
those rewards could be made. The details of what Speer built were less
significant to him than the fact that he was building what the Führer
wanted. Speer had studied architecture at Berlin's Polytechnic University but failed to secure the place that he wanted in Hans Poelzig's master class—because, said Speer with elaborate and unconvincing humility,
his drawing failed to make the grade. So he studied under Poelzig's mirror opposite, Heinrich Tessenow, instead.

Poelzig was an expressionist with a following among left-wing students. Tessenow was an austere classicist, and though never a Nazi himself, he attracted the right-wing nationalist students who dominated the
Polytechnic. Despite his earlier preferences, Speer was diligent enough
in learning the mannerisms of his master for Tessenow to employ him as
an assistant. Later Speer was ready to accommodate Hitler's own far
more flamboyant tastes. No doubt if Hitler had demanded architectural
abstraction, Speer would still have been happy to oblige. But Hitler
wanted ancient Rome, and Speer did his best to provide it.

Speer first succumbed to the sinister glamour of National Socialism when he heard Hitler speak in December 1930. After what he described as an initial period of softening up by his students, and watching the Weimar's police force break up a column of brownshirts, he went to a Nazi student rally in Berlin. He came away mesmerized. Hitler gave a polished performance rather than the harangue that Speer had been expecting. He decided to apply for party membership in January 1931. It was a move with an immediate impact on his professional life. Speer's architectural career was based entirely on Nazi commissions. Using Bauhaus wallpapers, he redecorated for the party a villa in the Grunewald, just outside Berlin. Then he remodeled a building on Voss Strasse in the heart of the government district that the Nazis took on in the period before the election of 1933. It was a large and impressive structure in a smart area, near the Chancellery, deliberately selected for its confident, respectable image. Afterward Karl Hanke from the party's propaganda department gave Speer the chance to change the course of history when he showed him the ideas he was working on for the staging of a Nazi festival. "I saw the sketches on Hanke's desk. The designs outraged both my revolutionary and my architectural feelings." Speer promptly volunteered his services to produce something rather more glamorous. He choreographed the May Day party rally in 1933 at Berlin's Tempelhof airfield, and outdid himself at the same event the following year at the zeppelin field in Nuremberg when he designed its huge flags and its searchlights raking the sky like a Busby Berkeley musical.

Speer was not without competitors. Hitler worked with a whole series of architects and was particularly close to three: Speer, Giesler, and Paul Ludwig Troost from Bavaria, who had specialized in fitting out transatlantic liners and for whom he expressed the most respect. Hitler was introduced to Troost in Munich at the end of the 1920s and displayed a remarkable deference to him, even after the Nazi seizure of power. Troost's architecture demonstrated Munich's place at the center of the Nazi movement: he built the Brown House, Hitler's headquarters, the party shrine, and the House of German Art. Hitler called Troost

Germany's greatest architect since Schinkel and asked him to remodel a Berlin mansion for use as the chancellor's official residence. Only when Troost's health began to fail was Speer appointed as the executive architect, charged with managing the successful completion of the project. During one of Hitler's site tours in 1933, the Führer got talking with Speer, and invited the elegant young architect to lunch with a group of senior party figures. Joachim Fest, Speer's collaborator on his memoirs, claims that there was an unacknowledged erotic aspect to Speer and Hitler's relationship. He reads a great deal into the way that Hitler gave a jacketless Speer his own coat, complete with gold party lapel pin, to keep warm on the way to that first lunch.

Troost's early death left the way open for Speer to assume his position as the preeminent Nazi architect. But he still had to contend with Hermann Giesler, who worked for Hitler in Weimar, Munich, and Linz. Such ideologues as Christian Schultze-Naumburg also expected their violent opposition to modernism in general, and the Bauhaus in particular, to be translated into positions of influence.

Nonetheless, on the strength of his easy personal relationship with Hitler, Speer began work on a series of other commissions that reflected the aspirations of a new regime attempting to make its mark. He redecorated the German embassy in London. He was asked to add a balcony to the Weimar-era Chancellery in Wilhelmsplatz as a suitable setting for Hitler's public harangues. There were a lot more rallies to design, the Olympics to coordinate, and then the vast party rally grounds in Nuremberg to plan.

Hitler treated Nuremberg as a test for Speer, and when he liked what he saw of Speer's reviewing stand and his confident marshaling of the various elements of the rallying grounds, he appointed him as Germany's inspector general for buildings. His principal task was the rebuilding of Berlin. Speer was just thirty-one years old when Hitler established him in the Arnim-Boitzenburg Palace on the Pariser Platz, next to the Brandenburg Gate, evicting the Prussian Academy of Arts to make way for his protégé. Speer was paid a salary higher than that of the mayor of Berlin, granted a budget to recruit his own staff, and given constant access to the most powerful man in Germany.

The gardens behind the palace had been taken over to create an elaborate sequence of exhibition galleries in the nineteenth century. It was here that Speer kept all the models that rapidly accumulated as the biggest project of his career took shape: the design of Germania (as the new Berlin would be called), the epicenter of Hitler's empire. The Berlin office was supplemented by a specially built studio at the Berchtesgaden, so that Speer could continue to work when called on to attend Hitler at his mountain retreat. In just five years, he had gone from being an obscure teaching assistant to presiding over the transformation of Berlin into the capital of the world.

IN HIS MEMOIRS, SPEER PAINTED A PICTURE OF HIS RELATIONSHIP with his most important client that will sound familiar to any architect. He was called to meetings with Hitler by functionaries, simply because the Führer had not seen him for a while. He complained of being forced to cut short his holiday in France to fly back to one meeting, only to discover on his arrival that it had been canceled.

Speer understood the importance of publicity and presentation. He lavished as much care on designing himself as he did on the buildings he produced. He always claimed—in the face of much photographic evidence to the contrary—to prefer not to wear party uniforms. Matthias Schmidt's 1982 book, *Albert Speer: The End of a Myth*, shows the lengths to which Speer would go to present his place in history in the most favorable light possible. Even after he emerged from Spandau Prison, he was ready to tamper with the Bundesarchiv, by substituting a sanitized version of the journal he had kept as inspector general of buildings. When his deception was in danger of being exposed, he asked Rudolph

Wolters, his friend and architectural collaborator, to put back a photocopy of the original.

Speer always tried hard to show that he wasn't actually in the room when Heinrich Himmler was talking about liquidating the Jews. There is no question, however, that he played his own personal part in the Final Solution. Speer confiscated 23,765 Jewish homes in Berlin, and expelled upwards of 75,000 people who had lived in them from the city. The archives of Speer's buildings inspectorate also contained neatly filed and officially stamped demolition permits authorizing the destruction of scores of synagogues.

Speer was a tirelessly energetic servant of Hitler. But in the hands of the American army in 1945, he was quick to try to impress his interrogators George Ball and John Kenneth Galbraith by suggesting how useful he could be to the Allies. "He kept presenting himself as an outstanding technician and organizer. He could assume that his enemies would admire a good mind, and a technological talent," Galbraith remembers. Despite his best efforts, the Americans declined the implied offer of his services. Instead they shipped Wernher von Braun from his V-2 rocket testing grounds across the Atlantic. Ballistics, it seemed, could safely be disentangled from political ideology in a way that architecture could not.

IT WASN'T ONLY POLITICALLY ENGAGED ARCHITECTS LIKE SPEER who made buildings with a political significance. Far from it. Politically committed architects of lackluster ability are rarely as effective at producing politically significant buildings as are gifted agnostics. Ludwig Mies van der Rohe, though the director of the Bauhaus, the radical modernist school of architecture and art, was neither a Marxist nor a Nazi. Despite such lapses of judgment as signing a call urging Germany to vote for Hitler in the referendum of 1934 that legitimated the Nazi seizure of power, he presented himself as an apolitical figure. But he did manage to build with equal conviction a haunting memorial to the Spartacist revolutionaries Rosa Luxemburg and Karl Liebknecht, who were murdered in 1919 as they tried to set up a German Soviet (it was eventually destroyed on Hitler's orders), and to produce a design for the new headquarters of the Reichsbank in Berlin, which might so easily have been the first landmark of the Nazi regime.

Mies was asked to build the Luxemburg memorial when, at a dinner, he mocked the conventional design that the Spartacist party organization had in mind and, like Speer in the Nazi party propaganda office, suggested that he could do better. Mies's design took the form of a stack of unstable brick cubes, restlessly pulling and pushing one another from behind a five-pointed cast bronze star with the hammer and sickle pinned to it. Mies had to hoodwink a foundry owner, who was reluctant to manufacture such provocative insignia, by commissioning them piece by innocuous piece. The bricks, salvaged from burnt-out demolition sites, were scarred and pockmarked. "Just a brick wall," said Mies of the design. "Like the one they were put up against and shot."

In later life he gave every impression of not being much concerned whether Luxemburg and Liebknecht had lived or died, which can hardly have endeared him to his client. Although perhaps that was an inevitable stance for a newly American Mies, looking to impress the State Department in the hope of an official commission. Even if neither Mies nor the Spartacists fully supported the objectives of the other, the memorial had brought benefits for both sides. Mies offered Berlin's revolutionary left the chance to use contemporary architecture as a weapon of cultural propaganda. In the 1960s the Catholic hierarchy used Le Corbusier and Alvar Aalto in much the same way to help them build churches that expressed the continuing cultural relevance of their faith to contemporary life. The French Communist party asked Oscar Niemeyer to design its headquarters in Paris for similar reasons. As for Mies, he got the chance to ingratiate himself with Germany's progressive elite in the hope of further commissions, albeit of a less provocative kind.

THE FACT THAT SOME MODERN ARCHITECTS SUCH AS HANNES Meyer, Mies's predecessor as Bauhaus director, were socialists while Hitler loved the classical pantheon turned architecture into a political argument. For a time, there was a misleadingly literal presumption that abstraction and a free plan were the badges of progressive politics and that classicism was the physical expression of right-wing authoritarianism.

In a series of absurd oversimplifications, political ideologues characterized the classical orders as both an unmistakable symbol of fascist or reactionary politics and an expression of the values of the Soviet proletariat. Long after the defeat of the Nazis, reputable German architects could publicly condemn the English architect and D-day veteran James Stirling's design for an art museum in Stuttgart, because it has a classical plan.

Leon Krier, Albert Speer's foremost apologist, suggests that "Speer's projects continue, not unlike sex for the virgin, to be the object of pseudo-embarrassment for architects. . . . The inability to deal with the problem today in an intelligent manner reveals nothing about Nationalist Socialist architecture, but tells us a great deal about the moral depravity of a profession which, on the one hand claims against all odds that modernist architecture is better than it looks, and on the other, that Nazi architecture is profoundly bad, however good it may look." But Krier, a professional iconoclast, never followed the logic of his position to its obvious conclusion by entirely divorcing the form of a building from the values of those who created it. Nor did he extend his no doubt polemical admiration of Speer's work to acknowledge Hitler's own architectural talents, which were so important in shaping Speer's buildings.

If classical architecture was, as Krier claims, "implicitly condemned by Nuremberg to an even heavier sentence than Speer," the flat roof, the white wall, and the aesthetics of the machine have more often been presented as the personification of democratic or progressive regimes. Oppo-

nents of this architectural language from both right and left have represented it as the mark of the "rootless cosmopolitan," the code words both
Hitler and Stalin used to describe Jews. There is a famous photomontage
of Stuttgart's Weissenhof Siedlung, the permanent exhibition of modern
housing planned by Mies, depicted as an alien Semitic encampment on
German soil to prove the point. But exactly the same signifiers—the flat
roof, the bare white wall, and the imagery of the machine—were put to
very different uses in the service of Mussolini. Indeed, Mies and his great
American apologist, Speer's contemporary and counterpart Philip Johnson, did their best to persuade Hitler and those close to him that architectural abstraction could be used to glorify the Reich. It was Mies van der
Rohe's great good fortune that they did not succeed.

As it happens, Speer and Mies were both ready to work for the most
odious national leader of modern times. The difference between them
was that Speer devoted himself entirely to realizing the architectural
ambitions of his master, while Mies, although he would bend and compromise on political issues, was unyielding about architecture. For Mies
architecture was an end in itself, even though he was prepared to allow
others to use his work for their own political purposes. Speer, on the
other hand, is now as well known for his political life as for his architecture, and indeed for a brief moment he genuinely believed that he could
become Hitler's successor. After the war, Speer attempted to detach his
work from a political message. He claimed when he became a Nazi cabinet minister that "the task that I am about to perform is unpolitical.
I have felt very good about my work so long as both I and my work
were evaluated purely on the basis of my professional performance."
If he could say this about his role building weapons for the Third Reich,
he was hardly likely to be any less generous in his own verdict on his
architecture.

In the end Speer never had the creative resources to become an architectural innovator or even to find his own voice. He would rather have
been Poelzig's student, but expediently took on the color of Tessenow,

and then spent most of the rest of his architectural career trying to interpret Hitler's ideas.

How much Hitler himself was against the modern architecture that Mies embraced is not quite so clear-cut. Nazi propaganda embraced both the idealized thatch and half timber of the German peasant cottage— the style used, for example, as a model for the barracks for the troops guarding the Berchtesgaden—and at the other extreme, the simple unadorned steel and glass of the Luftwaffe's building program. Hitler was always ambivalent about the precise nature of his architectural preferences. In the 1920s in the Munich beer cellars, he was declaiming that "a strong Germany must have a great architecture since architecture is a vital index of national power and strength" and that "out of our new ideology and our political will to power we will create stone documents."

There were certainly some architects, such as Schultze-Naumburg, who hated the success and the prestige of the Bauhaus architects and who wanted to use the Führer as a battering ram to destroy their rivals. To present them as Marxists, Bolsheviks, and Jews was part of the standard rhetoric of the time. "Tear down the oriental glass palace of the Bauhaus," demanded the *Anhalter Tage Zeitung* in 1932. In fact, when the Bauhaus became a school for party leaders after the Nazi takeover, a pitched roof was added, presumably in the interests of making it look more German.

In 1932 the *Völkischer Beobachter* raved, "The Bauhaus, that was the cathedral of marxism, a cathedral however which damned well looked like a synagogue." By this time, the school had already moved from Dessau to Berlin, where the apolitical Mies tried to purge it of its reputation as a hotbed of leftist radicalism, to the bitter protests of those students who were members of the Communist party. Mies had no sympathy for Nazi ideology, but with no desire to leave Germany, he was looking for ways to work under the new regime.

Hitler could sound like a Miesian himself: "To be German means to be logical, and above all to be truthful. Germanness equals clarity." Mies was ready to take him at his word. In 1934, he tried to seek an accommodation with Hitler, rather than face exile. His competition design for the German pavilion at the Brussels World's Fair was clearly related to his famous temple to modernity, the 1929 Barcelona pavilion. However, there was the conspicuous addition of a swastika on the roof, a gesture that did not keep it from ending up on the floor of Hitler's study with all the other rejects.

The language of architectural debate in Germany was extraordinarily violent. "No prison camps parading as workers housing subsidized by public funds! Get compensation money from those criminals who enriched themselves with these crimes against national culture!" wrote Bettina Feistl Rohmeder in *Im terror des Kunstbolschewismus*, published in Karlsruhe in 1938. Nevertheless, Mies, Poelzig, and Gropius were all invited to take part in the Reichsbank competition—but not Erich Mendelsohn, who was Jewish—which suggested that the Nazi regime had not yet decided that modern architecture was incompatible with National Socialism. It's possible that Philip Johnson, who characterized Mies's work as German, and Bruno Werner, the art critic of the *Deutsche Allgemeine Zeitung* (who in 1933 wrote that Poelzig and Mies were not Bolshevists), were part of a coordinated strategy to appeal to the wing of the Nazi party led by Goebbels, who claimed to be interested in modernity.

Hitler himself suggested, "There is a danger that we might relapse into a senseless and soulless imitation of the past. The architect will not hesitate to use modern building materials."

Mies could perhaps fight off doubts about the appropriateness of his architecture in a National Socialist state. But as the author of the Luxemburg monument, he could not afford a second question over his political reliability at the same time. While Mies was working on his design for the Reichsbank, the Gestapo raided the factory in the Berlin suburbs that he had leased for the Bauhaus, locking out the students and putting armed guards at the gate. This might have been a deliberate act of cultural terror. However, the closure was more likely to have been the result of low-level spite and petty factional struggles spilling out of Dessau into Berlin than a decision from the highest levels of the leadership. Nevertheless, it was a dangerous development.

Mies showed real courage in confronting the Gestapo in his attempt to have the school reopened. He went to see Alfred Rosenberg, the culture minister, to appeal against the closure. He was told that there was no fundamental Nazi objection to the Bauhaus. But Mies's courage may have been tinged with more expedient motives. Perhaps the episode of the Bauhaus was not quite the titanic struggle between ideologies that it was later represented to be. His decision to go to Rosenberg's office was an act that, as the historian Elaine Hochman suggests, was intimately connected with Mies's own struggle to remain in contention for the Reichsbank competition, the first big architectural project mooted in Berlin after Hitler came to power. Mies must have seen a possibility of finding a way to continue to work in Germany without having to temper his architectural language to the new regime, by doing just enough politically to avoid being blacklisted but not so much as to lose his self-respect. This would explain why he was ready to fight to have the closure order on the Bauhaus rescinded, lifting a potentially dangerous black mark on his record as the director of an institution that had been judged subversive. But then, when the conditions for reopening involved the replacement of those faculty members considered racially or politically undesirable by the Gestapo, he shut it down of his own volition.

MIES'S HOPE OF BUILDING FOR THE NAZIS WAS BASED ON THE ambiguous nature of Hitler's architectural pronouncements. The usual view of Hitler's promiscuous inability to present a unified view of what he regarded as Nazi architecture is to suggest that his inconsistencies reflected merely the inherent incoherence of his worldview. Undoubtedly there was a lack of consistency in a philosophy (if it can be so called) that sought to modernize Germany with autobahns and mass motoring but also had followers who believed in the desperate necessity to save the German *volk* from the evils of the modern city by returning to a preindustrial past. But there is another explanation for Hitler's inconsistent aesthetic attitudes in the mechanisms of power itself. Hitler's authority, as that of any dictator, depended on retaining control. The classicism favored by Speer and Hitler had apparently nothing in common with the cottage-style housing built for party followers or the Miesian modernism of the Reich's aircraft factories, but Hitler was ready to tip from one to the other. If choosing different styles for different projects was pragmatism, it nonetheless ensured that no one faction could assume an unchallenged hold on the architecture of Germany. All of them had to rely on their relationship with Hitler in their intrigues and jostling for position against their rivals.

Even so, while Hitler was prepared to toy with the rhetoric of modernity, he undoubtedly had a genuine antipathy to the modern movement. The fact that it had been described as the international style can hardly have endeared it to an ideologue who looked for a racial aspect to every cultural form and placed the greatest emphasis on the construction of a powerful national identity for Germany. In the end, however, his objections to exposed steel, flat roofs, and strip windows seem to be rooted as much in personal aesthetic preferences as in politics.

MORE THAN ONCE, HITLER ACTIVELY CONSIDERED BECOMING AN architect, suggesting that his attitudes toward the subject were based on his own tastes. After his rejection from the painting course at the Vienna Academy of Fine Arts, he thought about applying to the academy's architecture school, or failing that, embarking on an architectural apprenticeship. After his mentor's death, he was invited to take over the practice by Gerde Troost, Paul's widow. The quality of Hitler's surviving architectural drawings, the photographs of him sketching on squared graph paper with a pencil, and the fluency of his plans suggest that this could have been an entirely serious proposition. In his book on Hitler, Heinrich Hoffman recalls asking the man he called his friend why he hadn't become an architect, to be told: "I decided to become the master builder of the Third Reich." Hitler's followers were in no doubt that is exactly what happened. At a professional conference in Munich in 1937, party architect Franz Moraller announced, "Architecture shows everywhere the great hand of our leader. From him come the greatest impulses for the creation of and the search for new ways. In this way, architecture too has a political and cultural role to play."

Hitler wasn't the only senior Nazi figure with a personal bias toward architecture. Alfred Rosenberg, a Baltic German and editor of the *Völkischer Beobachter*, graduated in architecture from the University of St. Petersburg. Perhaps it is a coincidence, and architecture should not be held guilty by association with such figures—architects after all come from each end of the political spectrum. Stalin's loathsome, sadistic secret policeman Lavrenty Beria was also trained as an architect. But just as it is as well to keep a careful eye on those political leaders with a taste for writing poetry, such as Stalin himself in his early days, or Radovan Karadzic, the war criminal who presided over the butchery of Bosnia's Muslims, or Daniel Ortega, the Sandinista dictator of Nicaragua with the droopy moustache, so an enthusiasm for architecture is a sinister characteristic when present in a certain kind of political figure.

It would be reassuring to believe that Hitler's version of architecture has just as little to do with the real thing as the doggerel of tyrants has with authentic poetry. The conventional argument—that Hitler could not in fact have been a real architect—centers on his lack of interest in detail or technique. Yet these are all issues that could just as well be raised against any one of a dozen of the most famous architects in the world practicing today. Speer claimed after the war that Hitler would have been a competent if not a brilliant designer—not a view he was in the habit of expressing when the Führer was still alive—and there is no reason to doubt him.

More telling a criticism is the fact that Hitler had no interest in the architectural culture of his times. In Vienna, he seems not to have noticed that this was a city in cultural ferment as Adolf Loos, Otto Wagner, and Josef Hoffmann were shaping a revolutionary new direction for architecture, one that was synonymous with modernity. All he could see were the banal gingerbread hulks of the Ringstrasse and the baroque monuments of the past. This was hardly an appreciation of architecture as a living cultural form. His interest in building had more to do with the attempt to construct his idea of the world, and it was that obsession as much as his limited talent as a designer that left him unable to create an authentic work of architecture.

It is significant that Hitler failed to engage with architects of genuine creative ability throughout his life. His relationship with Speer and Giesler would suggest that he instead looked for those who were malleable and suggestible to carry out his will and build his vision.

Hitler did not have a sense of what a Nazi building should look like, in terms of how the structure expressed a clear ideology, but a tight definition of a coherent architectural ideology is not really the issue. The point of being a dictator is to have the power and authority to be able to say that the architecture of the regime is whatever the leader says it is. An art historian might bring a cool detachment to an examination of the Doric order to define its characteristics. But even a baroque building is defined as much by interpretation and suggestion as by any single coherent set of signifying features.

SPEER DESIGNED THE CHANCELLERY BY USING THE LANGUAGE OF Greek and Roman architecture and imbued it with an unmistakable sense of menace. But the building had to do more than intimidate foreigners. It was there to impress Germans too, both by its size and with the mythology that it embodied. Hitler was engaged in the creation of a political system, and he needed a leadership myth to go with it. In his hands, leadership was no longer presented as a bureaucratic and bloodless function of shared responsibilities, cabinet papers, civil service briefs and pragmatic day-to-day politics. In Hitler's fantasies, the Reich was government as it had been in the days of the Roman Empire, in the time of the Germanic chieftains, and in the era of the Prussian kings, all transformed into modern dress. In fact he was making things up as he went along, as if he were devising a board game, or refining the rules of a sport. And his buildings were used to test out rules and rituals, ludicrous though many of them were.

The Chancellery was a court, designed to personify and make clear Hitler's assumption of absolute power. Under fascism, Germany's parliament was an irrelevance, and Hitler's cabinet not much less of one. Although Speer's design for the Chancellery included a wood-paneled cabinet room, with a private corridor from the leader's study that would have allowed him to appear and disappear at will, Hitler rarely used the room. Speer records taking ministers on special tours, gazing at the blue leather desk blotters, with their names embossed on them in gold letters. All that counted in the state that Hitler built was its supreme leader, and the architecture that represented his position.

Buildings by themselves were not enough. To fill all those rooms, so optimistically named on the architect's drawings as reception halls and cabinet rooms, they needed to be animated by rituals that reflected their role in the running of the state. Mature states have evolved those rituals over generations. Germany in 1939 was anything but a mature state, and Hitler's grasp on power depended not just on force, but on his ability to invent a convincing state choreography. He needed ceremonies, salutes, protocols, and a timetable of daily rituals, just as he needed the uniforms, flags, and insignia to which he devoted so much mesmerized care and attention. To try to instill some sense of purpose to the Chancellery in between the irregular performances staged to overawe visiting heads of state, Hitler relied on the ancient idea of the feudal hall and the feast. He created an entourage of personal followers, making a chorus that formed the background for his daily routine. Speer recalls a floating court of between forty and fifty people, most of them politically unthreatening party members from the early days in Munich who needed only to telephone the Chancellery's chief steward to secure a place at the Führer's table for lunch, scheduled for two o'clock every afternoon. In Speer's words, hard to take at face value though they are, these were dreary events, to which Hitler was reluctant to admit the army hierarchy for fear of revealing to the Wehrmacht's meritocrats just how unimpressive his inner court really was. In the evening there were private film screenings, which at least excused participants from the burden of conversation.

Paul Troost had already built a party headquarters in Munich. One room, furnished with leather upholstered seats drawn up in a U and hung with tapestries, was designated as the party's Senate Hall to conjure the idea of the wise old men of the movement, meeting to deliberate issues of state. But no such senate ever existed, and Hitler allocated the space to his deputy Rudolf Hess for his office. Evidently, Hitler himself could tire of some of his games even before he had started them.

Hitler could not stop himself from building, but he had to keep coming up with convincing new uses to fill each new building he started. No sooner had Speer completed the Chancellery, with all of its 163,000 square feet, than he was set to work on designing a colossal new palace for Hitler. And Hess was once more earmarked to take over the Führer's castoffs; he would be expected to move into Voss Strasse after Hitler left. Hitler's palace was to be situated at the heart of the new Berlin, unencumbered by the constraints of existing streets—or budgets. With its gardens and palm houses and courtyards, it sprawled over 2.5 million square feet. Diplomats would have been obliged to trudge three-tenths of a mile from the ceremonial entrance to Hitler's desk. By that time, there would be no more diplomacy, just the rendering of tribute to the supreme leader of the world from his vassals.

Speer's first Chancellery was perhaps the biggest and the most complete of all the ever larger architectural models that he made for Hitler's pleasure. It was the diagram for the huge new city that Hitler wanted to build where Berlin had stood. Architectural models were everywhere in Hitler's world, just as they would figure large in Saddam Hussein's. A huge one, a hundred feet long, of Berlin's new north–south axis, was on permanent display in Speer's studio. It came in sections raised up to chest height, so they could be pulled apart to offer Hitler a closer look at the façades, and allow him to explore the effect from pavement level of different lighting conditions. The model was painted to suggest the materials that would have been used, and marching ranks of lead toy soldiers set the mood. Hitler would lead expeditions of dinner guests with flashlights across the garden of the Chancellery and through a specially built rear entrance to the studio to see it late at night. There were more detailed models of individual buildings. And much bigger models of Hitler's two personal designs: a triumphal arch and a great hall.

As preparations for building began to get under way, life-size replicas of sections of the façades were commissioned by Speer and installed on an outdoor site at Treptow, on the edge of Berlin, to give Hitler an idea of what to expect. Hitler was clearly not a man with a liking for unpleasant surprises. He wanted as lifelike a representation of a design as possible before it was built. Speer even constructed a full-size timber and concrete slice of the gigantic 400,000-seat stadium that he had designed for Nuremberg. Fragments of the foundations on a Bavarian hillside still survive and are a highlight on the dubious pilgrimage route followed by enthusiasts for the architectural relics of the Third Reich.

LIKE THE CHANCELLERY, THE NEW CAPITAL OF GERMANIA WAS based on a monomaniacal dependence on two primary axes. The north–south axis would have stretched for almost four miles, with a railway station at each end, a primitively obvious restatement of the idea of a city gate. It's surprising only that Speer did not go as far as suggesting the creation of an all-embracing city wall, a move that was left to Walter Ulbricht.

The Chancellery's miniature version of the north–south axis bisected the marble hall looking over Voss Strasse, ran through the center of Hitler's study, sliced the garden at the rear looking toward the Pariser Platz in half, and finally terminated in Hitler's greenhouse. The city's east–west axis co-opted the Unter den Linden and the Brandenburg Gate, running from the ceremonial entrance and the Court of Honor, to the Chancellery's reception room. These cross axes can be seen as having their origins in the planning of the Roman cities that so obsessed Hitler, or Louis XIV's bedroom at Versailles, positioned at the crossing point of two of the most important roads in France.

The grand avenue forming Germania's north–south axis would have had a distinct character in different sections and was studded with monuments, squares, and circles along its length. Hitler's monstrous great hall, like the circular vestibule in the Chancellery, was needed to deal with a change of direction in the axis. It would have acted as a hinge to shift the great boulevard to the west as it crossed the Spree on its way to its northern pole. Even Speer's paired wall lights, used everywhere in the Chancellery, were closely related to the streetlights that he was already beginning to install on Berlin's triumphal new east–west route, from the Lustgarten to the Unter den Linden and the Tiergarten. The parallels between the Chancellery and Berlin itself suggest that Hitler and Speer saw them as being a representation of the same authoritarian ideas about power.

Hitler was one of the most accomplished exponents of the art of corporate identity that the world has ever seen, and he used architecture as a primary tool to manipulate it. His plans for the rebuilding of Germany's cities and for the construction of party and state institutions in Berlin, Munich, and Nuremberg were intended to strengthen the aura of authority and invincibility around the Nazis, just like the black leather greatcoats adopted by the SS but on an infinitely larger scale. Even more significantly, Hitler used architecture to define and make possible his idea of what a totalitarian state should be. Hitler's Berlin would have been a communal hive for his swarm of black and brown uniformed workers and soldiers, with the engorged leader queen at its center. The individual counted for less than nothing.

Hitler was using architecture as a means to further his grip on power, but at the same time, as he revealed on the steps of Les Invalides, he clearly understood it to be an end in itself:

> Our big cities of today possess no monuments dominating the city picture which might somehow be regarded as the symbols of the whole epoch. This was true in the cities of antiquity, since nearly every one possessed a special monument in which it took pride. The characteristic aspect of the ancient city did not lie in private buildings, but in the communal monuments which seemed made not for the moment but for eternity, because they were intended to reflect not the wealth of the individual owner, but the greatness and wealth of the community.
>
> Only if we compare the dimensions of the ancient state structures with contemporary dwelling houses can we understand the overpowering sweep and force of its emphasis on the principle of giving first place to public works. The few still towering colossuses which we admire in the ruins and wreckage of the ancient world are not former business palaces but temples and state structures, in other words, works whose owner was the community. Even in the splendor of late Rome, first place was not taken by the villas and palaces of individual citizens, but by the temples and baths, the stadiums, circuses, aqueducts, basilicas, etc., of the state and hence of the whole people.

It was exactly these "community" monuments that Hitler wanted to build in Germany. They were designed to secure the future for the Nazis and to be a weapon in their campaign against the democratic present. He wrote:

> How truly deplorable the relation between state buildings and private buildings has become today! If the fate of Rome should strike Berlin, future generations would some day admire the department stores of a few Jews as the mightiest works of our era, and the hotels of a few corporations as the characteristic expression of the culture of our times. Just compare the miserable discrepancy prevailing even in a city like Berlin, between the structures of the Reich and those of finance and commerce. Even the sum of money spent on state buildings is usually laughable and inadequate. Works are not built for eternity, but at most for the need of the moment. And in them, there is no dominant higher idea. Our cities of the present lack the outstanding symbol of national community, which we must therefore not be surprised to find, sees no symbol of itself in the cities. The inevitable result is a desolation, whose practical effect is the total indifference of the big city dweller to the destiny of his city.

As with the Chancellery, Hitler's plans for rebuilding Berlin were driven by a mix of strategic calculation, a morbid fascination with the manipulation of people and places, and the sheer relish of building on a gigantic scale. "Our enemies will guess it, but our own followers must know it. New buildings are put up to strengthen our new authority," proclaimed Hitler in his Party Day speech in 1937.

For Hitler, architecture was a propaganda tool, to be used to inspire his followers and oppress his enemies. "The great building program is a tonic against the inferiority complex of the German folk. He who would educate a folk must give to it visible grounds for pride. This is not to show off but to give self confidence to the nation. A nation of 80 million has the right to own such buildings, our enemies and followers must realize that these buildings strengthen our authority."

The sheer scale and size of what Hitler and Speer were planning for Berlin were so vast and so intimidating that we understand it now only as a malevolent and feverish fantasy. The gigantic dome that would have dominated Berlin had begun as a sketch that Hitler had carried with him everywhere he went since 1925, along with his dream of a German Arc de Triomphe. It was the starting point for what Speer tried to realize in stone, glass, steel, and concrete. The dome would have accommodated 180,000 people, and stood one thousand feet high. Even today, nothing in Europe would match its scale. "That a monument's value resides in its size is a belief basic to mankind," wrote Hitler.

The models have gone. Apparently an attempt to move some of them out of Berlin in April 1945 failed when a convoy carrying cases of models from the Chancellery was attacked by Russian infantry. The designs exist as a series of photographs and sketches, and some carefully delineated large-scale plans housed in the Library of Congress in Washington that chart the streets that had been demolished to make way for Hitler's boulevard. They seem to show a city overwhelmed by an alien sea monster descended from another galaxy sucking the life out of old Berlin. Hitler's monstrous dome is far larger than any other structure in the city, disrupting and perverting its fabric. But this unsettling image, hanging over Berlin like a bad dream, was more than a fantasy. Site investigations had been carried out to see that the load-bearing capabilities of Berlin's soil were sufficient for the dome's weight. Contracts had been signed with Norwegian, Swedish, and Italian quarries for the granite to build it. A start had been made on building barracks for the slave labor force that would work on it. Speer had 10,000 Soviet prisoners handed over to his custody to work on the Berlin project, and he persuaded Reinhard Heydrich to provide him another 15,000 Czechs for the same purpose. In return he advised Heydrich on how to realize his plan to rebuild Prague. Speer had also secured the services of the SS to guard his slaves. A completion date of 1950 had been set for the new Berlin, in time for a world's fair in the city.

Germania was the work of far more than a solitary fantasist. It represented the efforts of scores of architects, of government departments and the armed forces, of Germany's largest companies and its universities and hospitals. A relatively modestly scaled capital of four million was to be inflated into a metropolis on the order of London or Paris, and its population doubled.

Speer's strategy, following ideas already explored by Berlin's planners in the 1920s, was to create a new focus for the city well to the west of the existing center. This was not the first time that Berlin had considered such a scheme, but Hitler was certainly the first political leader to treat the project so seriously and to inject monumental architecture into the mix. He was the first to see the project as a political issue rather than a technical one. He was determined to ignore the existing Berlin, or rather to subjugate it, to an extent that disturbed even the Nazi mayor Julius Lippert, who attempted to thwart the plan. Germania would have turned its back on the royal palace, the Protestant cathedral, and the Lustgarten, which made up the old center, and created an entirely new ceremonial, government, and business quarter. Germania was notable too for the number of monuments that Hitler wanted it to have. No leader can have devoted so much thought, so far in advance, to planning his victory monuments, not just before the victories had been won, but before he had a country or even an army. To mark Hitler's fiftieth birthday, Speer had given him a model of the triumphal arch large enough to stand up inside. If built, the real thing would have formed a landmark 386 feet high, more than twice as tall as Napoleon's Arc de Triomphe. It was to be situated close to one end of the Berlin axis. The Great Hall, positioned at the other end of the axis, was another of Hitler's ideas. Less attention appears to have been paid to how the grand boulevard, with three rows of trees on either side and a green 250-foot-wide median, would have functioned when it wasn't full of ranks of marching soldiers. As a huge, unbridgeable chasm of traffic, it would have cut Berlin in two.

The base of the Great Hall was to be a stone cube, a third of a mile square, with its south face sliced open by a gigantic colonnade, gaping open like a rectangular mailbox. The dome oozed out of this base like a monstrously inflated tumor and was itself topped by a lantern—strictly a baroque rather than a Roman motif.

Hitler changed his mind several times about the shape of the lantern, as he did about almost everything else, but in the end he opted for a version that was surmounted by a globe that itself carried an eagle, its wings open, its claws bared. From the gigantic Konigsplatz hundreds of feet below, the masses could have looked up and, at the right spot, caught a glimpse of Australia and New Zealand rendered in outline in the lower quadrant of the globe. Northwestern Europe would have been visible only from the skies, or to visitors poring over the model in Speer's offices. Time and again Hitler was photographed with it, his face looming over the model of Berlin, like a distant mountainous landscape overwhelming the city.

The eastern side of the square in front of the hall would have been formed by the old Reichstag. Though it was once a landmark, Hitler would have turned it into a toy, dwarfed by the monuments of Nazi Germany arranged in tidy ranks all around it. The army high command and Hitler's new palace would have made up the other two sides. As it happens, this square was positioned close to the site of the Chancellery built for the newly reunited Germany in the 1990s.

The axes would not have been a single straight line, but were made up of a series of segments, hinged around gigantic spaces and vast monumental buildings. Speer and Hitler selected the crossing point between the two axes to position the prodigious new Chancellery, which would have occupied the most privileged site in the whole city.

Whether the plan was genuinely an attempt to design a real city, rather than create a parade ground realized at the scale of a city, is open to question. Certainly Speer had no obvious expertise or experience in urban planning before he began the project.

The axis would have spanned the Spree, curving around the dome, and the old Reichstag, with a new bridge. Beyond that was a vast rectangular artificial lake, three-quarters of a mile long, which would have formed a reflecting pool for the dome, and the setting for another group of public buildings: the city hall on one side of the water, designed by German Bestelmeyer from Munich in a manner derived from Stockholm's town hall; the admiralty on the other. The latter was designed by Paul Bonatz, who, despite securing a number of prominent commissions from the Nazis, considered it expedient to leave Germany for Ankara in 1942. Beyond were the offices of the regional administration, the police headquarters, and, in pride of place, the northern railroad station. Behind the regular façades of the waterfront buildings, pierced by a series of picturesquely placed towers, Speer's team drew up studies for a second rank of structures, including barracks for the guard regiments and the war college.

Speer placed Göring's palace, designed on a scale, if it is possible, even more inflated and theatrical than Hitler's, just south of the Chancellery and the Tiergarten. The Führer's palace was planned around that long diplomatic walk. At the heart of Göring's was a great flight of stairs, rising through four floors, whose empty rhetoric was so grandiloquent that it provoked one of Mussolini's architects to exclaim, "Now, they really have taken leave of their senses."

There is something faintly comic about the prospect of Speer shuttling back and forth from Führer to Marshal, planning ever larger, ever more elaborate headquarters for these two sinister arrested adolescents conspiring over the spoils of a future that was not yet theirs, asking their architect for yet more sumptuous interiors as if they were a couple talking to their decorator with a sheaf of cuttings torn from the pages of *Architectural Digest*. For his part, Göring was so impressed by the stairs, which switched back and forth propelling visitors in a zigzag past endless expanses of blank walls, that he commissioned a portrait bust of Speer to stand in the hall, which would have served mainly as the most elaborate elevator lobby the world had yet seen. "In tribute to this the greatest staircase in the world, Breker must create a monument to the inspector general of buildings; it will be installed here to commemorate forever the man who so magnificently shaped this building," Göring proclaimed.

A photograph survives of Speer posing for his bust in the studio that he designed for Breker. He is standing looking heroic and gazing into the middle distance, dressed in tweed, with a crewneck sweater revealing just a patch of tie. Only the party badge on his lapel suggests his political affiliations. Breker, a short man in a smock, is bent reverentially over his chisel, rendering his handsome patron and friend as a creative, but above all decisive figure.

AFTER HE WAS RELEASED FROM PRISON, SPEER PURPORTED TO BE particularly horrified by his design for Göring's palace. "This was a decisive step in my personal development, away from the neoclassicism I had first espoused and which was perhaps still to be seen in the Chancellery, to a blatant nouveau riche architecture of prestige."

Certainly Göring's palace represented the architecture of excess. All the halls and stairways and salons took up more space than the offices. There was a ballroom, an open-air summer theater with 240 seats, and a lavish private apartment. The roof was designed to carry a layer of soil thirteen feet deep, supposedly as an air defense measure. But it would have been used for a garden dotted with swimming pools, tennis courts, fountains, ponds, colonnades, pergolas, and refreshment rooms.

To the south of Göring's building, the axis opened out into a traffic circle, where construction was well advanced on the German House of Tourism, designed by the firm of Dierksmeier and Rottcher, at the time of Germany's defeat. To the dismay of Speer's enthusiasts, this section, part of the western sector of the city after the end of the war, was demolished to create West Berlin's Kulturforum, making way for Mies van der Rohe's New National Gallery, and Hans Scharoun's concert hall and library.

As the axis moved southward, the ministries would have given way to cinemas, shops, and corporate headquarters. "We had of course recognized that lining the new avenue solely with public buildings would lead to a certain lifelessness and had therefore reserved two thirds of the length of the street for private buildings," Speer claimed. "With Hitler's support, we fended off efforts by various government agencies to displace the business buildings. We had no wish for an avenue consisting solely of ministries." However, the axis was too wide ever to have become a genuine street. In this section, cohesion broke down altogether, and Speer's boulevard became an aimless sea of isolated landmarks, as if it were a piece of modernist tabula rasa planning. Among the elements that Speer wanted to include were a Roman bathhouse, two cinemas (one seating five thousand), an opera house, a concert hall, and a twenty-one-story hotel designed by Casar Pinnau, along with a congress center and a law-court complex.

Albert Speer was a man who always liked to tell people what he thought that they wanted to hear. When he wrote his autobiography, he assumed that his readers, delivered from the nightmare of a world ruled by Adolf Hitler, wanted to be told how dismal the architecture that he and Hitler had planned really was:

> Nowadays, when I leaf through the numerous photos of models of our one time grand boulevard, I see that it would have turned out not only crazy, but also boring. Even these varied parts of the avenue strike me as lifeless and regimented. When on the morning after my release from imprisonment, I passed one of these buildings on the way to the airport I saw in a few seconds what I had been blind to for years, our plan completely

lacked a sense of proportion. We had set aside block units of between 500 and 660 ft. A uniform height limit had been imposed. Skyscrapers were banished from the foreground, thus
we deprived ourselves of all the contrasts essential for animat-
ing and loosening the pattern. The entire conception was
stamped by a monumental rigidity that would have counter-
acted all our efforts to introduce urban life into this avenue.

The fact that this judgment is mostly accurate does not mean that Speer
actually believed it. To judge by the lavishly produced volumes of his
buildings and projects he published in 1978, Speer never disowned his
work. In front of a sympathetic audience, he was ready to defend his creation rather than to denounce it: "There were quiet interior courtyards,
with colonnades and small luxury shops. Electric signs were to be employed profusely: the whole avenue was conceived by Hitler and me as a
continuous sales display of German goods, which would exert a special
attraction upon foreigners."

One of Germany's most famous architects and several of its most
powerful corporations became involved in this part of the plan. Peter
Behrens himself, for whom Le Corbusier, Walter Gropius, and Mies van
der Rohe had all worked, designed offices for AEG that would have been
built just south of the House of Tourism. Nestler designed Agfa's headquarters next to the Allianz insurance giant.

Speer involved as many architects as he could in the project, provided that they were ready to work in what he could broadly describe as
a German style. Speer needed the support of the many architects more
mature than he was, who designed the individual buildings. Their experience supplemented his strictly limited repertoire. Wilhelm Kreis, for
example, was twice Speer's age and had been the president of the architects' guild before the Nazis came to power. As a figure closely connected
to the Weimar regime, the Nazis sidelined him, but Gerde Troost spoke
up for him and he was commissioned to design some of the most promi-

nent monuments for Berlin. It was Kreis who turned yet another of Hitler's sketches into a design for the Soldiers Hall, in which it was planned to carve the name of every German soldier killed in battle since 1914, more than 1,800,000 of them. The building would have also housed, once it was captured from the French, the railway carriage in which Germany had agreed to the armistice of World War I. That only a fraction of the names would have been legible to visitors—or that there might be 10,000 Johannes Schmidts, carved indistinguishably one after the other—was of no concern to a state in which the individual had ceased to matter. Speer went ahead and signed contracts with the SS to use white flecked granite from the Flossenburg concentration camp's quarry to build it.

Speer staged a whole series of architectural competitions for the major individual buildings, but in effect, every entry was the same: symmetrical, classical, with a central colonnade, and faced in solid stone. The National Socialists made a fetish of the material, which they represented as a means of binding buildings with the soil from which it emerged.

Pinnau tried a couple of times to design skyscrapers with specifically German characteristics. They ended up as a model for the East Germans when they built Stalin Allee, dominated by domed stone turrets. But the bulk of the new Berlin would have been in uniform blocks, five floors below the cornice, and an attic level above.

At the south end of the axis, Berlin's second railway station formed the entrance to a plaza more than half a mile long. Lined with captured tanks and field guns, the plaza culminated in Hitler's own Arc de Triomphe. In the distance, you would have seen the dome of the great hall three miles away, rising above everything.

Speer was particularly proud of the design for the four-level station—bigger, of course, than New York's Grand Central Terminal. "Our happiest concept, comparatively speaking," he suggested; its "steel ribbing, showing through sheathings of copper and glass would have handsomely offset the great blocks of stone." Arriving dignitaries would have descended by a large outside staircase as soon as they stepped out of the station; they would be overwhelmed, or rather stunned, by the urban scene and thus by the power of the Reich.

The east–west axis was, by comparison, more modest. It took up the line of the Unter den Linden, stretching all the way from east of the Museum Island, west through the Tiergarten. Speer moved a nineteenth-century victory column, wrapped with guns captured in campaigns against Denmark, Austria, and France, from in front of the burnt-out hulk of the Reichstag to the center of a vast circle in the Tiergarten. On the Museum Island Hitler wanted to build a clutch of new museums. Hans Dustmann, Walter Gropius's former assistant, designed a museum of ethnology. Wilhelm Kreis worked on a museum of the nineteenth century, a museum of Egyptology, and a German museum. This is where Speer planned to create the Mussolini Platz, and where IG Farben was going to build its headquarters.

From 1937 onward, Speer began widening the east–west axis, reducing the number of intersections, and cutting down trees that obstructed the view. Plans were drawn up to relocate the Polytechnic and to demolish the Charite hospital to make way for the Great Hall. In April 1941, negotiations to build it began with a consortium made up of a group of Germany's leading construction firms. That August the consortium to build the triumphal arch—Bauwerk T, as it was called in Speer's office— was appointed and contracts drawn up to build the Soldiers Hall. But very soon, as the war turned against Germany, construction slowed, and then stopped, even though twenty-five thousand properties standing in the way of the north–south axis had been demolished, and the railway yards at the Anhalt, Potsdamer, and Lehrter Stations had been torn up in preparation for building the Great Hall. Design work continued until 1942.

INSTEAD OF A CITY OF POSSIBILITIES, A PLACE OF INDIVIDUAL choice, Speer's Berlin would have been capable of just one interpretation. There would have only been one way to understand it: as a celebration of the power that had built it. Hitler spoke of his determination to make a city that would impress "the farmer from the provinces who travels to the Great Hall and is moved by what he sees."

Why do we find the idea of Hitler building his own Rome so disturbing? It is perhaps the sense that if he had managed to finish it, he would have succeeded in what he really wanted, making his mark on history in a way that would preempt judgment or dissent. Destroying his Berlin would have been all but impossible; even if every single building were totally erased, the axis would have left its unmistakable trace. No matter how oppressive or lifeless or maladroit his architecture, the sheer size and scale would have left us if not convinced by its message, then hard put to explain exactly why we admire the Romans enough to want to preserve every surviving fragment of their cities, and not Hitler's.

To imagine the completion of Germania is to imagine the victory of Adolf Hitler. The one could not have happened without the other. It was an attempt to intimidate the rest of the world, a propaganda campaign on an unprecedented scale designed to glamorize and celebrate the regime, to bind Hitler's followers to his idea of what Germany should be. His architecture expressed his hunger for power and for submission in others. "If all the documents were to disappear, the historians would still read Hitler's plan to dominate the world in the buildings of the Third Reich," wrote Speer.

By the time the war ended, Speer's hubris about the ruin value of the Reich's architecture, which he had evoked to justify the use of such costly "genuine" materials as solid granite and marble, looked hollow and empty. Riddled with shell fire and Allied bombs, the bronze doors long since stripped away for salvage, the Chancellery's Court of Honor was anything but a noble ruin. It was littered with ammunition boxes and the detritus of a field kitchen; it had seen summary executions and the alcohol-dulled debauched oblivion of the remains of Hitler's court as it waited for the last days. Speer even claimed to have explored the possibility of turning his creation into a weapon against the Führer, with a plan (which may or may not have existed) to poison the air supply to the bunker.

After the German defeat, Allied leaders made pilgrimages to the ruins of the Chancellery to see the death throes of Hitler's regime for themselves. Before the Russians finally demolished the remains of the building and used it to quarry stone for their war memorials in Berlin, the eagle from the Court of Honor was shipped back to the Red Army's museum in Moscow.

Martin Bormann's diary from the early days of February 1945 provides a compelling insight into the surreal nature of the death agonies of the Nazi state. Pounded by American and British bombers mounting daylight raids, much of Berlin was without power or water while Marshal Ivan Konev maneuvered the Red Army for its crossing of the Oder in readiness for its final attack on the city. "The Reich chancellery garden is an amazing sight," wrote Bormann. "Deep craters, fallen trees and rubble everywhere. Only fragments remain of the winter garden. Voss strasse is pocked with enormous craters."

This was the precise moment that Hitler's adjutant contacted Hermann Giesler, the architect who had toured Paris with the Führer in 1940. Giesler, who remained a devout Nazi even after the war, was summoned to Berlin to discuss his plans for remodeling Linz, Hitler's birthplace.

Giesler negotiated the rubble in Voss Strasse to reach the Chancellery on February 9, bringing with him a new set of plans. Hitler was determined to rebuild Linz to challenge Prague and Budapest as the Danube's most beautiful city. The architect brought with him a large model of his project, which involved not just a series of new buildings but also a new industrial suburb to provide the infrastructure to support Hitler's vision for the city.

Giesler's architecture had a lighter touch than Speer's. However, his vision of Linz shared the fundamentals of Germania, with an oppressive scale and an axis from railway station to the city center. Along the corridor were ranged a 35,000-seat concert hall and other cultural buildings, including a museum to house the art that Hitler had looted from across Europe. Overlooking the river was a 500-foot-high bell tower, with Hitler's parents entombed in a crypt at the base and a carillon playing Bruckner at regular intervals. Hitler's own burial place was to have been a mausoleum with a design based on the Pantheon.

Hitler was utterly absorbed by what he saw, and he spent hours with Giesler discussing his timetable to start work on building the project. Later the next day, an SS general named Ernst Kaltenbrunner, also born in Linz, came to the bunker to warn of the imminent collapse of civilian morale in Berlin. Hitler stopped him and took him to see the model. "Kaltenbrunner, do you imagine I could talk about my plans for the future if I didn't believe deep down that we are really going to win this war in the end." Even Hitler's madness and self-delusion had a tactical aspect too.

There is less of Hitler's Germany left than he would have wanted. There are some autobahns, bridges, and Volkswagens. In Berlin what is now called the Strasse des 17 Juni is wider than it would have been if Hitler had never existed and the victory column is a few meters away from its pre-Nazi location, but all that still marks the idea of Germania are a few lumps of concrete here and there. Munich has the museum that Paul Troost built for Hitler, rescued from destruction when the Americans vetoed plans to dynamite it, though the shrine to the handful of Nazis killed in Hitler's putsch was destroyed. In Nuremberg, there are the unfinished party Neue Kongresshalle, and the network of reviewing stands, established for the Nazi rallies. Ludwig Ruff and his son, Franz, began work in 1935 on the hall; it was designed to accommodate 60,000 seated spectators in a complex of buildings modeled on the Colosseum, and built by forced labor. When Hitler laid the foundation stone, echoing Speer, he claimed that "even if the voice of National Socialism were ever to be silenced, these masonry witnesses will still arouse astonishment." He was dismayingly correct.

It was tough enough to survive the war and decades of denazification. Total erasure would be to conceal the past. But the plans made by the Nuremberg city council to turn the complex into an innocuous sports center would have been even more sinister in the postwar years. Finally it was agreed to open a "documentation center" dedicated to providing a reminder of what had once happened on the site. The architect for the new museum, the Austrian Günther Domenig, deliberately set out to confront the architecture of the past. Domenig's additions to the original building read unmistakably as a stake nailed into its heart.

The Germany of today is a pacific state that is the least likely aggressor in Europe, and yet these places still have the power to chill the blood. The fragments that Hitler built are stripped of their power to intimidate and threaten. Yet they are still not neutral; they are both the material and the symbolic expression of Hitler's view of the world. They represent Hitler's objections to the bourgeois individualism of the modern city and his determination to replace it with a communal identity through the shaping effect of National Socialist architecture.

CHAPTER 3

LANDSCAPES OF POWER

ATTEMPTING TO DIGNIFY INDULGING THEIR TASTE FOR MONU-
mental marble by suggesting that the stone represented some deeper
purpose, in the form of a cultural ideology, is a vanity that all the totalitarians have shared. To suggest that there is such a thing as Nazi architecture, or socialist realist architecture, in the same way that there was a
Greek architecture or a gothic architecture is to inflate their status far
beyond what the confused reality can justify. For all the rhetoric of
Hitler and Stalin's paid ideologues trumpeting the principled nature of
the architecture of fascism or socialism, the substance of those styles
amounted to a pathological obsession with size, symmetry, and a blatantly
literal iconography. Five-pointed stars, hammers, sickles, and wheat
sheaves for Stalin; swastikas and eagles for Hitler; bundles of sticks and
axes for Mussolini, were the raw material for ground plans, façades, or
decorative detail as required. Architecture of real cultural significance
needs to work on less superficial levels. But for Hitler and Stalin, sheer
size was more important than the way in which the detail of a building
or its spatial hierarchy could be understood as representing a state.

We recognize a church as a church, because we have seen one before;
it has a steeple or a cross. Within the subset of Christian churches, we

can recognize an Orthodox church; it has a dome, and has done so for a thousand years. We recognize a minaret as the sign of a mosque, which is also very likely to have a dome. These archetypes are so familiar that those who design churches or mosques enjoy a wide latitude in interpreting their form, while still being understood.

Not all building types are so clearly established. We recognize an office building—it stacks up repetitive floors one on top of another. Telling a hotel from a hospital is not so clear-cut. Both have a porte cochere, though one is for taxis, the other for ambulances—a difference that can provide a useful clue.

The question of what makes us understand a building as fascist, democratic, or Stalinist is more difficult to address. The hammer and sickle as an architectural motif removes any doubt, but it is hardly subtle or capable of expressing many nuances. And so the qualities of subtlety and nuance have, perhaps by default, been adopted as the signs of democratic architecture. They imply a plurality of expression rather than a society dominated by a single voice.

A democratic building does not intimidate through its size, although there is no reason for it to be small. It embodies the sense of a public place to be used and enjoyed by a community of equals. In theory that means a building that can be experienced in many different ways by different people. It might therefore be designed to have many entrances, rather than just one. A long processional route to the leader's office is a totalitarian form. In contrast, a genuinely public space, such as a forum with many routes through it, is a democratic space.

A genuinely democratic building cannot have been built, one would think, by slaves. But what about buildings built by societies that either owned slaves or profited from the slave trade? By that definition we would have to rule out such otherwise apparently impeccably democratic institutions as the eighteenth-century town hall of Liverpool, a city that depended on Britain's participation in the slave trade with the Americas. Even Periclean Athens was a slave-owning society, though its architecture has come to be understood as the very embodiment of democratic ideals. That architecture was the monumental product of a society that— for its native-born citizens, at least—was a participatory democracy. And from the time of the American Revolution, Athenian architectural forms were put to work by many newly established states attempting to demonstrate a break with colonial or monarchic systems.

Despite the implausibility of defining the nature of a Nazi or a socialist architecture, from the point of view of a dictator any building that he manages to erect is an indisputable fact in support of his cause. Stalin, Hitler, and Mussolini all built as much as they could, in the interests of prestige, to demonstrate their energy and to provide a threatening reminder of their appetite for terror, as in the case of Stalin's transformation of a Moscow insurance company's offices into the headquarters of the NKVD.

Democracies are usually too self-conscious or squeamish for their leaders to be seen intervening in quite such a personal way as the totalitarians in architectural issues, yet notable exceptions exist. François Mitterrand's order for the roads around La Défense to be closed one sweltering August weekend to allow the biggest crane in France to winch a mock-up of the Grande Arche into place is oddly reminiscent of Stalin pacing the Moscow River bank in 1931 deciding where to put the Palace of the Soviets. The president wanted to see for himself the impact it would have on the view of Paris from the gardens of the Elysée Palace. The dictator was regularly driven around the streets of Moscow late at night so that he could inspect building work in private, fussing over the precise grade of marble to be used on the Moscow underground.

Stalin wanted to build the Palace of the Soviets, a structure that would have been taller than the Empire State Building and topped by a colossal representation of Lenin bigger than the Statue of Liberty, to demonstrate his triumph over both the old Bolsheviks and capitalism. Boris Iofan, architect of the ill-fated project, described Stalin's instructions on the form his design should take as "comments of genius." On one occasion Stalin was observed casually picking up a representation of the onion-domed St. Basil's Cathedral from a model of the Kremlin, to see how the city would look without it.

The Grande Arche at La Défense was, according to Mitterrand, a way of integrating the working-class suburbs beyond it with the wealthy central city. But the result was certainly a glorification of his presidency. And if French political circumstances had been different, Mitterand's architectural instincts suggest that he would have made a capable totalitarian.

Totalitarians use architecture as part of their strategy to present themselves as in control of events, and to demonstrate that the application of their will alone is enough to reshape the world. All three of the great dictators of the first half of the twentieth century took a minutely detailed interest in the monumental aspects of the buildings that marked their regimes. They were forever poring over architectural models, choosing between shades of marble and granite, and being photographed striking dynamic and decisive poses over city plans and architectural models. Just as they had learned from Louis XIV, Napoleon, Catherine the Great, and Kaiser Wilhelm I, they themselves were to influence another generation of tyrants. In China, Mao followed in Stalin's footsteps, while Saddam Hussein, for better or worse, learned from both of them. In Romania, Nicolae Ceauşescu's last years were marked by the destruction of large swaths of Bucharest to make way for a crude evocation of Haussmann's Paris, meant to suggest that Romania had finally escaped from the Balkans. But the transformation, a futile and absurdly old-fashioned exercise, belonged to the 1860s, not the 1980s. In Spain, Francisco Franco's Valley of the Fallen, outside Madrid, presents another version of the same bleak vision of monomania. In every case, there was a reference back to the glory of the distant past, as well as to the example of the more recent buildings of other tyrants. Franco, astute enough to keep out of the Second World War, was still ready to learn architectural techniques to glorify his regime from the example of Hitler's Germany, as well as from the Castilian kings.

Of all the dictators, it was Josef Stalin who has left the most conspicuous and most widespread legacy. Even as Stalin's criminal policies of forced collectivization, deportation, deliberately induced starvation, and mass murder of the peasants killed millions of Soviet citizens, he was busy painting a picture of abundance and success with his plans to rebuild Moscow.

Stalin killed the loyal as well as the disloyal, the honest and the dishonest. It was not simple fear that made his regime so devastating in its effect on its subjects. In building a regime that institutionalized chaotic random savagery, Stalin overwhelmed and brutalized Russia for three generations. He succeeded in destroying any lingering belief in the redeeming possibilities of reason and justice. Sincere old Bolsheviks were shot in cellars with or without the benefit of a show trial, almost always after a forced confession. Afterward, their children were expected to feel honored to be chosen to present Stalin with bouquets of roses for his birthday. Those Soviet prisoners of war who survived German prison camps and were repatriated were promptly rearrested and sent to the gulag. Some of Stalin's closest allies died the most appalling of deaths, hanging from the rafters of their jails and impaled through the neck on meat hooks. Meanwhile Stalin's newspapers were full of images of plans for bold new ministries, meeting halls, radio stations, libraries, hotels, and, of course, the *metro*. For the outside world at least, these images became the reality of his regime. The useful idiots from the West came to marvel at them and went home to broadcast the blessings of the cult of personality to the world.

The process of building was as important for Stalin's purposes as the finished product. Moscow's shop windows in the 1930s and 1940s could offer little in the way of food, let alone consumer goods. But they were filled with images that depicted the city's planned new buildings in that distinctive dreamlike style favored during the Stalin years. The dictator had himself portrayed as the fount of all this magnificence, as its creative genius, infantalizing the Soviet Union in the process. Hypnotic images showed the dear leader—decisive, stern, and, inspired by the light of genius, pencil in hand—indicating to the rapt members of the Politburo the future shape of the great capital of socialist struggle. Such images were only slightly less ubiquitous than the avuncular Stalin embracing golden-haired Russian children or, depending on the Soviet republic in question, doe-eyed Kazakh infants.

One painting shows him in the Kremlin poised over a plan of central Moscow, which is spread over a carefully modest table overflowing with books and papers. Stalin is Jesus at the Last Supper, occupying the center point of the perspective to emphasize his omniscience. Behind his shoulder, a photograph of John the Baptist, in the incarnation of Lenin, hangs on the wall, looking down on the scene to bestow his blessing on his rightful heir. The anointed one is surrounded by his disciples, their heads bowed. Vyacheslav Molotov sits at the table on one side of Stalin; Lavrenty Beria, his enforcer, is on the other. Lost in wonder at the dazzling insights offered by Stalin, they do not speak as they strain to catch every detail of what is clearly a moment of divine revelation. Even Nikita Khrushchev, his eventual successor, looks on with no sign of the doubts that he was later to voice.

The dazzling future that Stalin promised his people had the same tinge of traditional imagery. Stalin's skyscrapers borrowed from church spires and the imperial palaces that he clearly admired.

RUSSIA'S MONUMENTS HAVE ALWAYS BETRAYED A CERTAIN PROVIsional quality. Their details, which are easier to manipulate than their broader outlines, tell us the most about who they belong to and what they are celebrating.

The Winter Palace in St. Petersburg, built as an assertion of imperial status, has reflected the course of political life in Russia for more than three hundred years. One of its many halls was originally designed for the display of a sequence of portraits of generals from the czar's army. They were taken down after the revolution of 1917 and dispersed, signaling the triumph of a new order. In the new new Russia, or perhaps the new old Russia, the portraits are gradually being returned and rehung by a regime that manages to combine the double-headed imperial eagle with Soviet stars in its iconography. In the same spirit, Vladimir Putin has reinstated the tune of the old Soviet national anthem, albeit with new post-Communist lyrics. The thrones in the audience room of the Winter Palace were removed after the revolution and replaced by a diamond-and-ruby-studded map of the Soviet Union, an image that has itself recently been superseded by a feeble replica of the czar's throne, which is apparently upholstered in cotton wool.

Moscow still projects something of the absolutist quality of an Asian metropolis, a Beijing or a Tokyo, with the heart of power as its empty center. The Kremlin, like the Forbidden City or the Imperial Palace, is a void in the middle of the urban fabric. By the Kremlin wall, the Stalin-era Hotel Moskva spent months wrapped in a huge plastic temporary fence as it suffered its death throes while demolition men swarmed over it. A new hotel will be built inside a replica of the original skin, complete with its curious lopsided façade, one half with large windows and the other half with small ones. The mismatch is said to be the result of the architect Alexei Shchusev—also responsible for Lenin's Tomb—presenting a single drawing to Stalin that showed two alternatives for the windows. Stalin approved the blueprint without understanding that he was being asked to choose between them, and nobody had the courage to go back for a more specific decision.

Lenin's Tomb in Red Square is a reminder that the Soviet Union used to be interested in cultural innovation. Its open top, suggestive of a warrior's grave laid to rest under the open skies of the steppes, has a pathos that is far more impressive than Mao's Mausoleum in Beijing, even though it is a much smaller structure. For a few dollars, you can get your photograph taken outside with a surprisingly convincing-looking Lenin or, according to taste, with Czar Nicholas II. Both of them come equipped with the appropriate facial hair and head gear.

Facing the tomb across Red Square is GUM, the showcase of socialist abundance that was once the pride of the Soviet Union—now it's full of La Perla lingerie and Hugo Boss suits, like an airport duty-free shop. Walk farther down the slope of the square, past St. Basil's, and you get a glimpse of yet another monument that tells you Moscow still has its own, very particular way of doing things. Rising high over the river is the black bronze mast of a monument officially dedicated to Peter the Great's establishment of the Russian navy. It was unveiled in 1998 by Moscow mayor Yuri Luzhkov and occupies most of a small island near the Krymsky Bridge.

This gigantic object is the work of the feverishly overheated sculptor Zurab Tsereteli. The centerpiece is a giant Peter in period costume. He stands on the deck of a warship with its sails furled like washing drying on the line. The most disturbing thing about it is the absurdly incongruous scale. Peter's head comes up to the level of the crow's nest, more like a cartoon version of Captain Hook on a gigantically inflated toy yacht than a national hero, even if he has been rendered in millions of dollars' worth of bronze at the scale of a twelve-story apartment building. Stalin did these things better. At the Kremlin wall, a refined equestrian statue of Marshal Georgi Zhukov elegantly tramples a dead German eagle under foot.

Emerging from Moscow's Kropotkinskaya *metro* station, you pass the loafers drinking beer at the café tables and girls in dresses that stop a yard above the knee strolling in the sun. Across the street is a triple-parked black Audi sedan with tinted windows. A man with no neck emerges from it to move with surprising speed across the pavement to the nearest doorway under the watchful eyes of a younger, leaner man wearing blue and gray camouflage fatigues and boots, a machine pistol hanging purposefully from his shoulder. You turn and are confronted by a vision so dazzling that you can hardly see anything else. The five golden domes of the Basilica of the Holy Savior hurt the eyes, gleaming in the Russian sun with a patina that seems to turn a particularly vivid shade of turquoise. Across the Moscow River, mocking the red stars on the Kremlin's domes, a chrome and Perspex Mercedes star rotates slowly on top of the apartment block that Boris Iofan built for the party elite in 1929. During the purges, ill-fated residents were marched away by the NKVD most nights. The survivors would ask the doormen for the names of the disappeared. Beyond the Mercedes star, a selection of the seven skyscrapers that Stalin's slaves built in the 1950s call to one another over the heads of the city, waiting for the tower of the Palace of the Soviets that never came to redeem its promise to lead them to socialist nirvana.

The basilica is a sacred part of Russia's history. It was built in celebration of national deliverance from Napoleon's armies in the war of 1812–1814, paid for by *kopeks* dropped into collection boxes by peasants. A taper lit at one of its altars was believed to bring good fortune, if you could get it home without it blowing out. Easter services attracted thousands of worshippers to the vast white marble structure. A bronze relief frieze of figures runs around the exterior, charting Russian history. Warriors clutch their spears, and bearded priests brandish the word of God, held aloft on metal tablets, like digital cameras raised by supplicant tourists.

The basilica is protected by a gray metal fence and ringed by elaborately swagged cast-iron lampposts, lathe-turned stone balustrades, and endless sequences of steps. It sits on a band of slimy putty-colored polished granite, with a funereal gray rusticated stone base. Get closer, and you discover that the surface structure conceals a subterranean complex of ramps, roads, and underground parking lots, all of which betray the whole gleaming confection as a faithful hallucination. The original church was dynamited to make way for the Palace of the Soviets in December 1931. The new one was built in the 1990s. The elaboration of the bronze doors, the sculpture and the inscriptions and the gaudy flower beds, the evocations of the nineteenth-century lampposts, the carved stone are all the work of late-twentieth-century craftsmen, the kind of thing the people who make hyperreal effigies for Jeff Koons would do if left to themselves.

The new church, like the monstrous Peter the Great statue across the river, is the product of Mayor Luzhkov and Zurab Tsereteli, who was responsible for decorating the interior. Boris Yeltsin himself laid the foundation stone. And the gold leaf, applied by the bucketful to the domes, was paid for by some of the oligarchs who, with indecent speed, made themselves enormously wealthy during the dissolution of the Soviet Union.

The building of the original nineteenth-century basilica marked one important assertion of Russia's identity, its destruction was an attempt to radically redefine that identity, and its rebuilding is yet a third watershed in the power struggles shaping modern Russia.

In 1817 the czar commissioned Aleksandr Vitberg to design a cathedral of a scale and grandeur to reflect Russia's rank as a mighty and expansive state. With a dome more than 750 feet high erupting from a classical base, the basilica would have been twice the size of St. Peter's in Rome. But there were doubts about its feasibility. Then Vitberg was accused of embezzlement and exiled to Siberia. The project was handed over to another architect, Konstantin Ton, who redesigned it in a more traditional Russian style and on a smaller scale. Nevertheless, at 360 feet to the top of the cross on its biggest dome, it was still as tall as London's St. Paul's Cathedral when it was finally completed in 1883.

The basilica was one of the first of Russia's great monuments to be destroyed by Stalin in a spasm of iconoclasm that saw even the vast St. Isaac's Cathedral in St. Petersburg converted into a museum of atheism. Stalin set about erasing the landmarks of the past in an attempt to make his transformation of Imperial Russia into the Soviet Union irreversible. Red Square was turned into a giant parade ground. Its gates, built in 1680, were demolished to enable tanks and missiles to maneuver in and out on ceremonial occasions. The Sukharev tower, the tallest structure in Moscow, also built in the seventeenth century, in use as the city museum, was flattened. So were two miles of the medieval Kitai Gorod Wall, with its sequence of towers and gates, along with the Church of the Iberian Virgin in the Kremlin and the Kazan Cathedral, built in 1625 by Prince Pozharsky to celebrate Russia's triumph over Poland.

The destruction of the basilica was supervised by the secret police, who made sure that the gangs of workmen stripping the gold from the domes handed over the spoils to the state (the yield was almost half a ton of bullion). Those still brave enough to challenge Stalin's determination to destroy every trace of the old order protested angrily. Several priests who tried to salvage religious relics were summarily shot. Two technicians who refused to take part in dynamiting the remains of the hulk were sent to the gulags. Some of the marble and the granite from the exterior was salvaged for reuse in the building of the Lenin Library. The icons from the altar were sold to Eleanor Roosevelt. But much of the statuary and the commemorative stained glass were deliberately destroyed. Remembering the sacrifices of the Russian people in defeating an invader from Western Europe was off the agenda, until Hitler tried to follow in Napoleon's footsteps.

Taking the place of the basilica, the Palace of the Soviets was intended to be the supreme monument of the new order: a complex combining meeting halls for the Communist party and museums of world revolution, grand enough to demonstrate the final triumph of the proletariat. The process of selecting the design took place against the background of Stalin's consolidation of his grip on power after the death of Lenin. It reflected the Soviet Union's transition from a brief moment of cultural pluralism into a despotism, just as the murder of Sergei Kirov in December 1934, with Stalin's possible connivance, marked the start of the Great Terror and the end of political life.

In 1931, under the supervision of Stalin's close political ally Vyacheslav Molotov, a competition was organized to find a designer for this highly charged project. The mandate was to produce "a monumental structure outstanding in its architectural formulation." Molotov's men searched the world for suitable candidates. Walter Gropius and Hans Poelzig, competitors for the chance to build Hitler's Reichsbank just two years later, took part, alongside Erich Mendelsohn, Auguste Perret, Le Corbusier, and three Soviet architectural teams.

Le Corbusier's design would have been one of the greatest buildings of his career, a pair of fan-shaped auditoriums facing each other across a sequence of enclosed public spaces that would have been a forum for the whole socialist world, signaled by a soaring catenary arch. It did not make the short list of three, much to Le Corbusier's fury. His allies in the architectural world made a futile attempt to lobby Stalin to change his mind. Not only was it much too late, but they had fundamentally misunderstood the nature of the project. The Soviet Union had moved beyond the idea of presenting itself as the visionary center of world revolution, and was now more interested in consolidating its power over its own people.

Boris Iofan's winning design expressed the two main halls of the palace as abstract volumes, as Le Corbuser had done. However, Iofan placed a monumental tower between them, poised between modernity and tradition. The design somehow managed to suggest both the inventiveness of revolutionary Russian constructivism of Tatlin's tower and a Babylonian ziggurat as his sources. He topped it with a heroic sculpture of a worker that clearly attracted the attention of the Politburo, even though it was on a relatively modest scale.

Not yet forty, Iofan was a well-connected architect from the Ukraine who had already constructed a series of landmarks that served to define the new Moscow and, perhaps unwittingly, the schizophrenic nature of the regime. After studying in Odessa, he had trained as an architect in Rome, where he had clearly picked up some of the more feverish aspects of the futurists. He redesigned the Soviet embassy in Rome, then went back to Moscow. He built a hospital next to the Lenin Library for the exclusive use of the party hierarchy, as well as the 500-apartment complex on the banks of the Moscow River where they lived in communal luxury, while the proletariat they claimed to serve froze for lack of winter fuel.

At this transitional stage, Iofan's design could still be seen as belonging to the radical strand of Soviet architecture. The Soviet Union had initially seemed ready to embrace the architectural avant-garde as the appropriate dress for a revolutionary state. In Lenin's time, the Bolsheviks were ready to work with the cultural radicals who during the last decades of the Romanovs had taken part in the transformation of Moscow with art nouveau architecture, while St. Petersburg was a base for radical poets and artists. In the immediate aftermath of the revolution Russia became an important center of contemporary architecture.

Traces of that moment in Moscow's history still survive today even in the midst of the brashest expressions of Russia's kleptocratic post-Soviet economy. In the business district, Lukoil, a company that grew colossally rich taking over state-owned oil reserves, built offices, which it outgrew even before they were finished. On the opposite side of Miasnitskaya Ulitsa is a complex of offices, apartments, and meeting halls. Le Corbusier designed it as the headquarters for Centrosoyuz, Russia's cooperative movement, in 1928, and it now houses the State Bureau of Statistics. It comes swimming into focus in the summer haze like a ghost from the distant past. Its red basalt stone looks as if it has been scorched and sandblasted by centuries of use. A cantilevered theater juts out over the entrance, supported by a cluster of fluted Doric columns that seem unlikely to have been built exactly as designed by Le Corbusier. They are protected from traffic by precast concrete flower beds. From the outside, the basic dignity of Le Corbusier's conception remains intact. But inside the door, a militiaman in a bulletproof vest sits behind a crude wooden counter in a ramshackle coat room, like a squatter in this ravaged but still heroic space. Twin ramps snake back and forth over his head in a manner that is unmistakably Le Corbusier's. The vision of Le Corbusier's extraordinary drawings has faded into an inhabited Pompeian ruin. The marble floor slabs are cracked and broken, tipped up at a 45-degree angle. In some places, all there is to stop you disappearing into Moscow's pungent marshy soil oozing up from below are patches of rotting hardboard. A random forest of columns holds up the roof. Its inelegant complexity suggests that an engineer was asked for a second opinion about the stability of the structure after completion.

Moscow has a concentration of buildings from the same period that could have made the city a showcase of modernity. Why did Stalin turn away from that promise? The comforting answer would be to say that the avant-garde was too independent-minded for the controlling nature of the totalitarian state Stalin was building. Stalin understood that Iofan would be prepared to obey his detailed architectural instructions, and Le Corbusier would not.

There is also the possibility that the suicide of his wife tipped the balance of his reason. Certainly Stalin had started looking inward and backward in the 1930s. The past was where his literary tastes lay, with Gorky and Pushkin, rather than with Russia's twentieth-century avant-garde. There is an undoubtedly nationalist tinge to the choice of Iofan to design the Palace of the Soviets. The idea that the competitors could range from Le Corbusier to Boris Iofan seems scarcely credible. They were two architects who hardly seemed to inhabit the same universe (however, Iofan did later intercede on Le Corbusier's behalf to get the fees for his work on building the Centrosoyuz headquarters, outstanding for more than six years, paid in full).

One architect was exploring new ideas about space, unfamiliar ways of supporting structures, and a new architectural language. The other ended up manipulating traditional architectural signs of power in the crudest, most bullying way. And yet Molotov, the Politburo member supposedly in charge of the Palace of the Soviets selection process, was prepared to look at both.

That divergence between the social utopianism of Le Corbusier and the bombast of Iofan's design only widened as the competition's later stages unfolded. Stalin asked the finalists to incorporate "the best of the past, with modern technology" and, if Iofan's account is to be believed, to make the whole project bigger and more ideologically charged with the imagery of Stalinism. Iofan teamed up with the officially approved designers Vladimir Shchuko and Vladimir Gelfreikh and abandoned what avant-garde aspects his first scheme had shown to produce a truly megalomaniac art deco tower. This was the original Stalinist wedding cake. Even though it was never completed, its progeny were one day to appear as an unwelcome eruption on skylines everywhere from Warsaw to Shanghai.

Iofan's tower—or perhaps it should be called Stalin's tower—had seven tiers rising out of a rectangular base and would have been approached across a vast open space stretching all the way to the walls of the Kremlin. Reaching the conference hall would have involved ascending an endless cascade of steps up to an entrance hall fronted by a giant crescent colonnade.

In justifying the destruction of the basilica, Iofan coolly claimed the old church was "huge and cumbersome; looking like a cake, or a samovar, it overwhelmed the surrounding houses and the people in them with its official, cold, lifeless architecture, a reflection of the talentless Russian autocracy and the highly placed builders who had created this temple for landowners and merchants. The proletarian revolution is boldly raising its hand against this cumbersome edifice which symbolizes the power and the taste of the lords of old Moscow."

Having destroyed it, the lords of new Moscow started on building its replacement in 1935. Clearing the whole site would have involved jacking up the Pushkin Museum, mounting it on huge rollers, and moving it bodily out of the way, which the Politburo were fully prepared to do.

Aided by Stalin's genius, Iofan's design eventually reached 1400 feet, and the symbolic worker exploded into an effigy of Lenin 333 feet high. The outstretched right arm, pointing Kremlinward, would have been a major challenge to the laws of gravity, requiring a massive steel cantilever to support it. The tips of his fingers, 20 feet long, would have been lost in cloud much of the year.

Stalin continued to back the project until his death, almost twenty years later. During the German attack on Russia, Iofan was evacuated to the Urals with his studio and his models of the palace, and continued to work on the design, taking full account of Stalin's comments: "Why is the podium raised so little above the hall. It must be higher. There must be no chandeliers, the illumination must come from indirect light. . . ." The main hall was increased to a capacity of 21,000 seats, under a 330-foot-high dome. It was ringed by six smaller halls, each thematically expressing a section of the six-part oath Stalin took when he succeeded Lenin, including the Stalin Constitution Hall, and the Hall of the Building of Socialism, as well as a Museum of World Revolution. In the main auditorium, speakers would have addressed the masses from a huge tribune, topped by a cluster of triumphant proletarians carved in marble.

The tower was designed in classical fashion in three related parts. The base was to represent the precursors of socialism; the shaft of the tower, Marx and Engels; the whole was crowned, of course, by the vision of Lenin. From one point of view at least, the Palace of the Soviets was designed very differently from the monuments of Speer's Berlin. Rather than having an eye to its quality as a ruin as Speer always did, in the Soviet Union Stalin's sycophants claimed that "the centuries will not leave their mark on it; we shall build it so that it stands without aging eternally."

The Soviet Union, however, did not have the skill to build the structure. Accounts of the troubled construction of the original basilica, which had been plagued by flooding caused by a high water table and pressure from the river, were ignored by Stalin's cowed experts. Things seemed to go well at first. The foundations for the palace had been dug by the end of 1938, and work started on the steel structure. By 1939, the road closures necessary to prepare for moving the Pushkin Museum out of the way had been announced. But the site was getting waterlogged, and nothing that Iofan tried would solve the problem. The retaining walls were tanked with tar, and lined with tombstones, but neither stopped the water rising for long.

Many far more powerful men were executed as saboteurs for much less conspicuously embarrassing failures, but Iofan evidently had a special rapport with Stalin that saved him from the gulag. He was left to build the Soviet pavilion at the New York World's Fair in 1939, unhindered. It was a less aggressive version of his national pavilion for the 1937 Paris Expo, and was treated to admiring coverage in the pages of *Architecture of the USSR*, a magazine that mixed cover portraits of Stalin and Molotov with news of recent projects.

The May 1940 issue devoted twelve pages to Iofan, printing his picture next to the latest version of the Palace of the Soviets, with pages reproduced from his sketchbook showing watercolors of the Pantheon and the Roman amphitheater at Syracuse. He was described as a master of Soviet architecture, and the piece documented the transformation of the conference hall from its original 1932 design to its final incarnation. In the first version, three concentric drums surround the dome of the hall. Then they sprouted classical wings in the shape of two crescents equipped with an endless procession of giant Corinthian columns flanking the entrance. After that came the tower, and the ever more colossal statue of Lenin. Almost every subsequent issue of the magazine is haunted by the shadowy presence of the Palace of the Soviets in one form or another. It's there in the background of the artist's impressions of every new scheme designed for central Moscow, a huge rocket blocking out the light, all seeing and inescapable.

In the end, the German invasion of 1941 stopped work even on Stalin's most favored Moscow projects, and the palace's structural steel, by this time reaching as high as the eleventh floor, was dismantled for war use. But the project drifted on, finally abandoned only when Khrushchev came to power and the excavations were turned into an open-air swimming pool.

If Le Corbusier's version of the palace had been commissioned, it would certainly have been easier to build than the ludicrously overblown Iofan project. And such a striking demonstration of Stalin's commitment to modern architecture would have sent a very different signal about his regime. But it didn't win, and in retrospect it's clear that the choice of Iofan was of a piece with the seven towers positioned at strategic points across the city that Stalin authorized in the postwar years. One accommodated the university, another the Foreign Ministry, a third was the Ukraina Hotel, and others were full of apartments for the *nomenklatura.* They were, it was claimed, national in form and socialist in content. But it was their dispersal through the city center, rather than aligning them on a single axis in the manner of Speer's Berlin, that made them different from anything that the Nazis considered building.

Stalin's towers aside, and despite their supposed ideological differences, Nazi Germany and the USSR (and its postwar satellites) came to resemble each other more and more in their propaganda campaigns against the modern movement, which were expressed in strikingly similar terms. The essential nature of the Nazi and Soviet building programs was all but indistinguishable, as in the famous architectural confrontation between the two regimes at the Paris world's fair of 1937. Speer's pavilion and Iofan's counterpart faced each other. Only the gigantic rendering of two workers wielding a hammer and sickle on the Soviet side and the eagle and swastika that topped Speer's stone pylon made it immediately clear which was which. Huge buildings, as well as the use of vast quantities of stone deployed in ways that were designed to intimidate pedestrians, characterized all of the totalitarian regimes—Marxist, fascist, or nationalist.

In the Soviet Union, the hardening of the political climate against experimentation—as well as Stalin's manifest preference for a Soviet version of the classicism of St. Petersburg—prompted some of the avant-garde to shift toward the tastes of the regime. Rather than not build at all, they were ready to build what the state wanted. For Stalin's followers, "the Bauhaus architects were déclassé outsiders, dissatisfied with the existing order because of lack of commissions from the bourgeoisie," Karl Liebknecht's nephew, one of the German Democratic Republic's leading architects, declared. It's a prejudice that must have been confirmed in 1948, when General Lucius Clay invited Walter Gropius to act as an official architectural adviser in the American zone of Berlin. Meanwhile, in the Russian zone, inevitably the GDR turned against the Bauhaus and functionalism, arguing for progressive tendencies of national architecture in the manner of Karl Friedrich Schinkel, the great Prussian classicist.

"We are against the Bauhaus; it represents cosmopolitanism and decadence," said Liebknecht after the war—words that could have been used by the Nazis.

The rest of the Warsaw Pact was of course of the same mind. In 1948, Josef Revai, the newly appointed minister of education in the People's Republic of Hungary, asserted that "architecture is an ideological and therefore a political question." He did not have to look far for his answer: "Any architectural opinion contrary to Soviet architectural opinion is nothing but reaction. Modernist architecture is the only hostile cultural tendency still to be observed in our country."

To deal with this reactionary tendency, the first national congress of the architects of Hungary declared in 1951 that "the influence of the architecture and the architectural theory of the imperialist bourgeoisie is hostile both to art and to people, and must be radically liquidated in Hungary." Asked to indicate a suitably proletarian model for architecture, the minister pointed to the Moscow *metro*: "With its architecture adorned by statues, with, dare I say it, its luxury, it creates a holiday mood for the workers on the way to their jobs."

Like the condescending propaganda of socialist realist paintings, Stalin's seven Moscow towers were not hard to understand. Their designers claimed to have liberated Corinthian columns from the bankers and returned them to the people. Under the leadership of Moscow's city architect, they borrowed the battlements from the Kremlin wall, the spires on the Admiralty in St. Petersburg, and the zigzag motifs of Russia's Orthodox churches and applied them to skyscrapers. They spoke to the masses of a glorious, powerful, respected, glittering Russia, looking back and forward simultaneously.

Stalin and Hitler embarked on a competitive building campaign against each other. Speer with characteristic immodesty suggests that after the Hitler-Stalin pact he was invited to Moscow to offer the Soviets advice on city planning. He reports that he had to reassure Hitler that the Great Hall in Berlin was not going to be overwhelmed by the Palace of the Soviets.

Because he managed to hang on to power rather longer than his contemporaries, Stalin succeeded in rebuilding Moscow on a scale that eclipsed Mussolini's plans for Rome and Hitler's version of Berlin. But all three of them were embarked on what was fundamentally the same course of action. They tried to signal their prestige, and their close connections with historical precedent, in the marks that they made on their capital cities in brick and stone.

Hitler, like Stalin, was trying to make his transformations irreversible. However, even Hitler's most devoted sycophants never proposed memorializing his effigy on the scale of the Palace of the Soviets. But Stalin's Moscow is rather more sophisticated in its planning concepts, if not its architecture, than Hitler's ideas for Berlin. The pattern of Moscow, with its radial boulevards and its dispersed regional centers, is not so dissimilar from Sir Patrick Abercrombie's slightly later plan for the postwar restructuring of London, suggesting that the Soviet Union remained closer to the mainstream than Nazi Germany.

The most difficult question to address is whether a profusion of state-sponsored construction is actually the rational response of a ruler attempting to impose a system of government, or a symptom of the monomania that eventually turns all dictators into paranoid delusional sociopaths, betraying nothing but vainglory and self-aggrandizing desperation. In fact, is architecture a tool or a toy? Grand building programs could simply be a technique, or may rather be a reflection of the state of mind of those who aspire to dictate to a whole country how it should live. Most such regimes, in fact, seem to exhibit both pragmatism and megalomania at varying stages in their development.

All of the first generation of twentieth-century dictators sought to present themselves, despite the cult of personality that accompanied their rule, as governing on the basis of a systematic and fundamentally rational view of the world. They had the vanity to believe that they were presenting a philosophy—a scientific set of beliefs codified, where possible, in a manifesto—rather than acknowledging that they depended on brute force and that they ruled by fear. Whether by design or self-delusion, they attempted to develop policies for every aspect of cultural life, including that of architecture. Lately Saddam Hussein had the crutch of Baathism to lean on, just as North Korea's Kim Il Sung used Juche thought. But neither philosophy offers much in the way of an insight into architecture. Saddam's strategy was simply to present himself as the reincarnation of national heroes from the past and to rebuild the landmarks of their days. Kim Il Sung seemed to favor the Soviet-style modernity of the Sputnik years.

In the new Russia of the twenty-first century, oligarchs and semicriminal businessmen help to fund the reconstruction of pre-revolutionary landmarks. Meanwhile, they roam Moscow demolishing the architectural relics of the Stalin period that are just beginning to attract the concern of conservationists. Ironically, it is the conservationists who now understand these relics free from their political content and appreciate them both as the vanishing expression of a particularly tortured historical moment and as buildings with their own qualities. The meanings of architectural expression are, it seems, always subject to change.

STALIN'S EMBALMED CORPSE HAS BEEN BANISHED FROM RED Square for decades, but postcards of those images of Stalin the architect and Stalin the solicitous father of the nation are on sale everywhere in the Kremlin's souvenir stands. It becomes harder with the passing years to remember that they were ever taken at face value. Did millions really sacrifice themselves for the motherland on the basis of their love for a squalid and brutal dictator who was ready to murder and kill without mercy or reason and chose to have himself represented in the style of the illustrations from an Edwardian children's book? Did they follow without question a man who was so feared by his courtiers that he lay stricken by the brain hemorrhage that finally killed him, slumped on the floor, kept away from his doctors for hours?

The brutal reality behind the honeyed light of the propaganda images is revealed in the photographs that show the people of Budapest risking their lives in 1956 to tear down the massive statue of Stalin that still dominated the center of their city three years after the dictator's death. Stalin's graven images had an idolatrous power, and destroying them appeared to exorcise his lingering presence. Bringing down his statue in Budapest was a daunting task that involved considerable firepower, intense street fighting, ropes and ladders, oxyacetylene torches, and many hours of hard physical labor. For days, a fragment of the dictator's head—that fat sinister smile and the moustache—was battered and gouged, kicked and defecated on, as it lay on the ground.

Saddam Hussein was modeling himself both on Nebuchadnezzar and on Stalin. His borrowings from Stalin's cult of personality can be seen in the huge number of his own images that he erected all over Baghdad, and in the range of their subject matter, depicting him as everything from warrior to father figure to sportsman. At the start of the 1980s, when Hussein really began to get into his stride as a builder, he embarked on his own version of the Palace of the Soviets. The State

Mosque, with room for 30,000 worshippers, was meant to be the biggest place of worship in the Islamic world. Seven architectural celebrities, including Robert Venturi, the father of postmodernism, were invited to take part in a competition to design it. The jury's decision was never made public, although we do know that they did give Saddam Hussein their verdict. Rather than accept it, Hussein convened an international symposium of three hundred experts on mosque architecture to look at all the competitors again.

Evidently Hussein, like Stalin, was more interested in having his own way with the design than allowing an architect the chance to use it as a means of self-expression. Equally evidently, he did not learn many lessons about the eventual fate of dictators from Budapest or Prague, where all that is left of Czechoslovakia's gigantic Stalin monument is a plinth. But by the time of the second Gulf War, America certainly had. It is obvious that George W. Bush's advisers spent a lot of time looking in great detail at those grainy black-and-white newsreel images of Stalin being dragged down in effigy. They did everything that they could to restage them, frame by frame in Baghdad, for what they hoped would be a grand finale for their invasion of Iraq. Crowds were gathered, a noose was fixed around Saddam's effigy, as it had been around Stalin's. Slowly the statue toppled, and the hated features of the tyrant were subjected to the ridicule of the mob.

There is, however, still a difference between those images and the real meaning of what happened that day. Hungary's rebels needed no outside help to deal with Stalin's statue, although they might have appreciated NATO intervention to save them from being crushed by the Red Army. In Baghdad the American army's psychological warfare specialists provided the muscle to bring down Saddam Hussein's bronze effigy rather than a spontaneous act of Iraqi iconoclasm. Architecture too cannot be taken at face value. In spite of the ambitions of those who design and build it, it has meanings that change over time.

CHAPTER 4

THE WORD IN STONE

BY THE STANDARDS OF HITLER AND STALIN, BENITO MUSSOLINI presided over a relatively benign dictatorship, even if it was one that was still capable of genocidal colonial wars and a brutal contempt for domestic civil liberties. What is not clear is whether it was nothing more than his comparative restraint that saved Mussolini's architects from the same degree of hostility that faced Speer or Iofan, as well as the quality of their work, after the end of World War II. Is it that such dedicated Fascists as Marcello Piacentini, or Giuseppe Terragni, or Giuseppe Pagano, who rebuilt Italy for Mussolini, were better architects, or was it that they worked for a marginally less wicked regime?

Certainly architecture was as much on Mussolini's mind as it was on Hitler's or Stalin's. I have a photograph that shows a group of overweight figures in black-and-white uniforms looming over a model sitting on the floor. In his immaculate double-breasted white suit, finished off with a somewhat unlikely peaked yachting cap, Mussolini is flanked by a group of courtiers. I hadn't realized that the standard Blackshirt uniform involved white trousers, never a good look for the paunchy. The men stand enthralled by Piacentini, Mussolini's personal architect, eloquently enthusing about his master plan for Rome's new city, E 42, the culmination of the Fascist onslaught on Rome's historic fabric.

Piacentini is poised over the model in that very special moment of animation that every architect knows. He has the clients' full attention for a brief second and knows that this is his only chance to convince them that everything they have been dreaming about over months of work should go ahead at last. The facts that the new Rome had already displaced thousands of families from the working-class slums in the historic center and had a profoundly damaging impact on the monuments of Augustus were issues of which, of course, Piacentini was aware. But at that moment, we can see, they count for nothing. For an architect, in the instant that he has the undivided attention of a patron with the power to realize his designs, literally nothing else matters: not a fire alarm, not even an earthquake; there is simply nothing else to talk about but architecture.

Piacentini himself had no doubt about the political purpose of architecture. The most prominent sites in Rome were, he said, to be reserved "exclusively for the great temples of Religion and of the State, to celebrate the virtues of our race, to inflame and move, to glorify and acclaim." Yet his architecture, but for some of the inscriptions and the iconography of the sculpture, looks nothing like what we conventionally describe as totalitarian. Certainly his work is big and intimidating. It is meant to impress, to make the individual feel small and insignificant. But it doesn't project the perverse, claustrophobic sense of wickedness that we can read into the sinister cottage style of some of Hitler's buildings, or his monstrous plans for rebuilding Berlin. Perhaps it's what we know of the transient nature of Italian fascism that makes them seem less threatening, or maybe it's that Piacentini retained his own architectural voice in a way that Speer did not.

Mussolini, Stalin, and Hitler all treated architecture as an indispensable instrument of political propaganda, one that they took an enthusiastic and obvious pleasure in using to maintain their grip on the apparatus of state power. The extraordinarily personal nature of their involvement with construction was a demonstration of their munificence and their omniscience. For the benefit of the newsreel cameras, Mussolini "let the pick axe speak," as he swung it up over his head to initiate the destruction of the medieval structures that crowded around the classical monuments along the Tiber. The image was created not just to suggest his own vigor and potency but to claim that he was the equal of Caesar Augustus and the other emperors who built Rome.

Benito Mussolini had two decades to rebuild Italy, and he seized his opportunity with as much enthusiasm as Hitler. Hardly a city in Italy has been left unmarked by the Fascist years. Mussolini's architects built the country's modern infrastructure: its new railway stations and its post offices, its law courts and universities, its factories and sanatoriums. In doing so, they did their best to identify fascism with progress. Disquietingly for those who doubt that a brutal political system is capable of generating great architecture, Giuseppe Terragni, a long-standing Fascist dedicated enough to Mussolini's cause to volunteer to fight on the Russian front, produced one of the great buildings of the twentieth century. His Casa del Fascio in Como, a stone-faced hollow cube, is ostensibly just as ideological in its intentions as anything designed by Speer or Iofan. And yet it is based on a subtle and richly imaginative exploration of space, used to glorify the Blackshirt movement, without having to fall back on the obvious visual triggers of size, intimidation, or explicit iconography.

Like Troost's Nazi shrine in Munich, the Casa del Fascio was dedicated to a cause. Terragni put the propaganda behind glass, rather than in a classical temple. The building had a row of doors that were electrically operated to open simultaneously, allowing a Blackshirt column to pour out in force and overwhelm the square outside. The building has a hollowed-out center, dignifying the various party organizations disposed around it with an impressive entrance. The absence of extended bureaucratic corridors is intended to signal the comradeship of Fascist volunteers rather than a professional hierarchy in its planning. It's not easy to call the Casa del Fascio a humane building, but it does not obviously oppress, even if those who built it did.

Fascism was once described as a house of glass, words that contemporary architects would do well to remember before making facile attempts to suggest that transparency and, by implication, glass are inherently democratic. The Casa del Fascio is certainly transparent. But while it doesn't look hostile or out of place under the mountains in the beautiful town of Como, across the way from the neoclassical opera house and the cathedral, it certainly speaks of the faith that a generation of Italy's architects had in the Fascist revolution. Terragni used architecture to create the sense of a building with a character that put it beyond the boundaries of everyday experience. He gave fascism the prestige his political patrons wanted with a building that was based on a mystical exploration of proportions. That quality has survived, even in the present incarnation of the building as the district headquarters of the Italian customs police.

Terragni was far from alone among Italian architects in eagerly participating in the Fascist regime's building program. His colleagues designed Mussolini's new towns and built his colonial settlements in Libya, Somalia, and Ethiopia. They designed the party headquarters buildings in every Italian city. They designed the propaganda exhibitions that glamorized fascism for the masses. They took part in the competitions for Mussolini's palace in Rome.

In fact no prominent architects fled Italy to Britain or America, as they did from Germany. And few careers were cut short by resistance to the regime. Giuseppe Pagano, a former Fascist who bravely joined the partisans and died in a concentration camp, and Gianluca Banfi, another leading architect who met the same fate, were notable exceptions.

The most complex aspect of Mussolini's view of architecture was in his relationship with Rome. He was simultaneously presenting himself as the inheritor of the empire of the Caesars—a new Augustus—and as a modernizer. That meant demolishing swaths of the city, supposedly with the objective of creating an appropriate setting for such monuments as the Mausoleum of Augustus. The mausoleum was preserved, isolated in the middle of a new square, designed in grandiloquent Fascist style by Vittorio Ballio Morporgo. The Ara Pacis, the altar built by Augustus to commemorate his victories, was rehoused in a glass and steel box overlooking the Tiber. Sixty years later a left-wing mayor demolished the box and invited Richard Meier to design a new pavilion to accommodate the altar. Meier promptly fell afoul of Silvio Berlusconi's junior minister for culture, Vittorio Sgarbi, who attempted to kill the project as much for political as for aesthetic reasons.

Mussolini's interventions in the Forum, the Colosseum, and the Capitoline did enough damage to Rome's archaeological heritage, but it could have been even worse. He toyed with the idea of creating a palace for his own use, the Palazzo de Littorio, to act as the Fascist party's headquarters, directly opposite the Colosseum. He staged a competition for a design, attracting what in contrast to Hitler's Chancellery are clearly modern schemes. But the language of architectural abstraction was just as capable of creating a sense of intimidation, and of the subjugation of the individual to the will of the leader, as were Speer's endless classical extrusions.

Mussolini eventually changed his mind and created the Foro Mussolini, to the north of the city. It's a more archaeological-looking version of Fascist urbanism. The forum is surrounded by a complex of new buildings modeled on the circuses of ancient Rome. It's balanced by EUR, another architectural showcase on the south side of the city. Mussolini's new extension to Rome, known as the Esposizione Universale di Roma, or EUR, as E 42 was renamed, was built for an expo planned for 1942 to mark the twentieth anniversary of his seizure of power. The original intention was to construct a series of buildings that would be used during the fair as exhibition and event spaces, before being turned over as the nucleus of a large-scale expansion of the city southward toward Ostia and the sea. The war intervened and the expo was abandoned, but enough of the site was developed to leave a powerful taste of what an authoritarian city that used a modernist vocabulary would look like.

The plan was a compromise between Italian architectural modernizers and traditionalists, with the balance of power shifting toward the traditionalists as time went on. It became the focus of conflict between sharply different visions of what the new Rome should be, provoking what was to be the final and fatal break between the regime and Giuseppe Pagano. The loyal Fascist who had been involved with the early stages of the planning of EUR denounced Piacentini, who took charge with a brief to create a more formal, classical character for the plan. The break did not affect Pagano's devotion to the Fascist cause, until he went to fight in Mussolini's army in Albania.

Despite Pagano's doubts, EUR is considerably more sophisticated as a piece of urbanism than Speer's Berlin would have been. The ever competitive Hitler declared the plan "a meaningless copy without any import." Piacentini had indeed seen Speer's drawings for Berlin before he set about regularizing those aspects of EUR judged to be too freely expressive or, as the Fascists put it, "Hebrew." However, EUR is planned on a grid rather than a single monumental axis. A number of landmark structures establish the area in the landscape, the most prominent of which is the Palace of Italian Civilization, the so-called Square Colosseum. The structure is visible all the way from the Villa Borghese in the center of the city. With its six layers of Roman arches stacked one above the other, it sits on top of the hill at the southern edge of EUR. There are 150 steps, untroubled by any sign of a handrail, leading to the entrance. It looks like a travertine mountain and feels as daunting to climb as if you were ascending a stepped pyramid in Mexico.

At the summit, these days you will discover that the Palace of Italian Civilization is closed for repairs. Carved in stone across the top of the cube, back and front, is the legend "A people of poets and artists, of heroes and saints, of thinkers, scientists, navigators and migrants." An inner stone cube with floor-to-ceiling arched windows is wrapped in an outer stone skin, pierced by matching arched openings. The forms could not be simpler. This is as much a stage set as it is architecture, and yet the tension between solid and void gives it a real presence.

The Square Colosseum forms the end of one of the grid of avenues running north–south; at the other is Adalberto Libera's Congress Hall, less obviously classical in its inspiration, with its flattened dome rising over a white stone box. Its entrance is marked by a colonnade of fourteen gray granite columns set in a dazzling snow-white marble screen. The blank front wall has a mysterious floating triangular wedge, designed to carry Francesco Messa's sculpture of a four-horsed chariot, a contemporary version of the quadriga on top of the Brandenburg Gate. The sculpture was never finished or installed. As finally completed, the building was shorn of the elaborate iconographical imagery that would have attempted to root the hall in the Roman tradition. Libera also designed a giant elliptical arch, left unbuilt, that would have been EUR's most visible landmark. It later inspired Eero Saarinen's St. Louis arch of 1948 (he seems not to have been troubled by the Fascist associations of the form).

The gridded plan of EUR avoids the monomaniacal quality of Speer's Berlin. It has a suburban, dispersed quality, more like Milton Keynes or Orange County. Libera's building and the Square Colosseum conduct a civilized dialogue with each other. The two most prominent buildings of EUR avoid the central axis, which is marked by an obelisk looted from Egypt. They are designed as part of a composition with a third major element that appears on the skyline, the domed church on the southern edge of the complex.

Most of the center of EUR is made up of monumental blocks of offices, incorporating colonnades at ground level, designed to accommodate shops and cafés, and arranged around landscaped squares. In most places that have as little pedestrian traffic as EUR, it's a gesture that would have resulted in nothing more than abandoned storefronts, revealing the unbridgeable gap between architectural aspirations and commercial realities. But Italy's embrace of street life has breathed some life into the area. Even so, in many parts of EUR, the ground floors are all but abandoned, with activity concentrated on the *piano nobile* above, almost as if this were Venice. Piacentini's plan subjugated individual buildings to the demands of the overall urban composition. The block next to Libera's Congress Hall has four sides, each with a different character. On one side it forms part of a square; on the next, the block becomes an arcade, while the third side is a sweeping crescent. It's an arrangement that leaves all of them vulnerable to the problems of conflicting geometry at the points where the different elements meet.

There is the stench of stale urine in the air as you shelter from the rain in the sweeping colonnades, cut out of the base of the building blocks. The squalor is poignantly framed by the most exquisite materials that Mussolini's architects could find: turned granite columns, carefully laid cobblestones, pale pink plastered vaults, lit by generously proportioned glass-globe lamps. White marble frames the doors and the windows. Evidence of tramps sleeping out, sheltering from the weather, haunts some corners. Loudspeakers dangle from cables in the vaults, as if in memory of a long-ago harangue from the Duce.

Peering in through the De Chirico–like windows and the dust, you see glimpses of abandoned spaces, rooms that have not been used in sixty years, bricked-up openings, and runs of pipe in front of unusable doors. The buildings are embellished with low relief carvings of allegorical classical themes. On the ground floor of what is now an outpost of the Italian Social Security Ministry, Icarus floats overhead. Through the door you glimpse a cleaner's trolley with a running shoe stuck over the brushes. Around the corner, flanking the entrance to the museums in the center of EUR, five-story-high mosaic murals depict the glories of Italy's craftsmen and tradesmen. Open the museum's ground-floor door, and you find yourself confronted by a wall of sixty steps, a daunting climb to reach the exhibits for even the most determined.

Some of the early buildings are marked by outcrops of rough masonry blocks scattered in a seemingly random fashion. They erupt from the smooth dressed-stone walls as if to suggest the patina of age and imply that this is architecture that has been built, like the center of Rome, on ancient foundations, rather than an instant city. The banality of the later additions from the 1960s that radiate outward from the edges of EUR has the curious effect of making the original buildings look simultaneously both ancient and much more modern than they really are, as if reinforcing Mussolini's original intentions.

The Museum of Roman Civilization is organized as a series of symmetrically planned pavilions on both sides of a central axis, bridged at intervals by giant porticos, so tall that they don't keep the rain off your head. It has a massive blank exterior that makes it look more Egyptian than Roman. The walls are penetrated only by a deep narrow cut that forms the entrance, marked on either side by a giant order of granite columns. There is a play between rough and smooth stone, between tufa and travertine, between open and closed.

On a quiet Saturday morning, EUR has an ordinariness that seems to deny its sinister origins. It was meant to glorify fascism; as it turned out, however, the area has become a dignified if neglected suburb with an unusually urbane character. EUR has effortlessly outlasted the comic-opera regime that gave birth to it and shrugged off its ideological purpose. To live and work here poses no obvious threat to the health of present-day Italian democracy.

AT LEAST TWO OF ITALY'S LEADING ARCHITECTS IN THE 1930s whose work brought them into close contact with Mussolini, and who were themselves convinced Fascists, died with particular poignancy in the concentration camp at Mauthausen—the camp originally established as part of the SS's attempt to profit from the supply of building materials for Speer's monumental architecture. Gianluca Banfi was a partner in the Milanese firm BBPR. Among other projects for Mussolini,

Banfi worked on several of the exhibitions celebrating the triumph of the Fascist revolution. Pagano, the other architect to suffer this fate, had been far more deeply committed to fascism. His career would reflect the tortured relationship of architecture with power. Born Giuseppe Pogatschnig in Parenzo in 1896, he had changed his name to Pagano when he joined the Italian army to fight in the Austrian campaign in the First World War. In 1919, he took part in Gabriele D'Annunzio's seizure of Fiume, and he joined the Fascist party the next year. Pagano was a true believer, dedicated to the cause of Mussolini's revolution, rather than an opportunist. He became a senior member of the Fascist sect established by Mussolini's nephew. Its members described themselves as missionaries devoted to spreading the Duce's word and warriors pledged to defend the revolution to the end. The group was a center for the manufacture of party ideology. Pagano was responsible for developing a Fascist philosophy for the visual arts, as well as a member of the editorial board of *Doctrine*, the sect's quarterly publication.

Unlike most party zealots, Pagano did not allow his commitment to Mussolini and Fascist politics to compromise the quality of his architectural work. He was a gifted designer and, despite his connections with the regime, an independent-minded polemicist. In Milan he was responsible for the sensitive and entirely modern design of the Bocconi University, a private institution that is Italy's version of the London School of Economics. Pagano was also one of the architects responsible for Milano Verde, a radical master plan to modernize Milan free of the grandiloquence and rhetoric of what is generally described as Fascist architecture. He also worked with Gio Ponti on designing Italy's pioneering new electric trains.

Pagano moved to Milan in 1933, where he edited the magazine *Casabella*, which was as interested in Italian modernism as it was in fascism. While remaining a committed party member, he became increasingly critical as Mussolini's plans for rebuilding Rome developed. But that did not stop him from working closely with the Duce's official architect, Piacentini.

In 1941, when Mussolini joined Hitler's invasion of Yugoslavia, Pagano volunteered for military service in the Balkans even though he was well into middle age. A year later, however, he had lost his faith in fascism and left the party to join the partisans. He was arrested and jailed in Brescia, where he organized a mass breakout in which 260 political prisoners escaped. A pen-and-ink self-portrait in beard and glasses survives from his prison days. He was recaptured in September 1944 and died in Mauthausen in the last days of the war, a casualty of totalitarianism whose death was a lesson in the nature of courage to all of us, not least Albert Speer.

Pagano gives us a different perspective on Speer's career. Speer helped make totalitarianism possible, by making it visible. An architect can conjure a dream of what fascism or Stalinism or Saddamism might be, even before it exists. He can make an ugly possibility into a terrible reality. An architect can choose to help make architecture an instrument of repression. Certainly that is how the Poles understood Stalin's building of the Palace of Culture in the middle of Warsaw, which explains Poland's determination to re-create the city's historic center exactly as it had been before the Nazis erased it. Less clear is how we should react to the physical legacy of vanished authoritarian regimes. Italy to this day is full of rotting buildings, many of real quality, that were put up by the Fascists to house their party organizations. They were confiscated by the postwar government, and nobody knows what to do with them. To demolish them all both would be profligate and would represent a historical whitewash, and yet to restore them could suggest a rehabilitation of the regime that built them. Fifty years later, the country is still unable to make up its mind about most of them.

PHILIP JOHNSON'S CAREER PROVIDES ANOTHER EXTRAORDINARY example, so different in its outcome from that of Giuseppe Pagano, of the relationship between architecture and power. Johnson was sympathetic to fascism, but never worked for a tyrant. Pagano was a fascist who built for Mussolini. In his architecture, however, as in his life, he achieved an integrity that Johnson never could.

Johnson was born in 1906, just a year after Albert Speer, and, like him, came from a prosperous provincial middle-class background. Speer's father and grandfather were architects; Johnson's father was a lawyer.

If, as I did, you feel you really must read Philip Johnson's mail, the first step is to book an appointment in the special collections section of the Getty Center's research library in Los Angeles. That way you don't have to reserve a place in the parking lot, or wait in line for the tram to take you up to the top of the hill that the Getty library shares with the better-known museum of the same name. The four-minute journey delivers you to the Getty plaza, carpeted with travertine and carefully tended gardens, a democratic cousin of the Square Colosseum. A tidal flow of respectful visitors look mildly awed at the scale of this gigantic bubble of artificial pedestrian life in the the land of the freeway. You can see the cars far below, as they push their way through the Santa Monica Mountains, but you can't hear them. And the air up here is fresh enough to keep the smog at bay.

The research library, away to the right of the museum, is a stone doughnut the color of sour milk. It is the least convincing piece of Richard Meier's monumental complex of galleries and research institutes housed in a collection of cubes and cylinders scattered across the landscape like toys on a nursery floor. But for all that, the library is still suffused with Pacific light and that lush sense of space that is the very particular product of the deep pockets of American cultural philanthropy. Visiting scholars, as well as the occasional tourist straying off the circuit of the Getty's old masters, postcard stands, and cafés, find themselves in a gilded world of deference and custom-made furniture.

To reach the special collections you must first produce a driver's license or a passport, then have yourself digitally photographed and complete a registration form. Only after all that are you ushered toward

Meier's staircase, spiraling down into the bowels of the library. The door to the special collection is locked, and when you buzz for attention the librarian presses a button to release it. Bags are confiscated, and you are issued a yellow-lined foolscap pad and a pencil, sharpened to the finest of points. Of course there is no charge. Finally, you reach the archive, a series of outsize envelopes, numbered, cataloged, and chronologically sorted. All this feels like an elaborate piece of glossy packaging, deliberately calculated to banish any doubt about the significance of the yellowing documents that are about to pass through your hands.

Johnson's papers provide an insight into the last era in which prominent architects chose to play a direct and leading political role. Some attempted to use their architectural work in the pursuit of a political cause; others, such as Philip Johnson, decided to abandon the built world for a time in pursuit of direct political power. The Johnson archive doesn't take up that much shelf space. It would have fit into a couple of suitcases in his attic, if only his Glass House in New Canaan had one. You will find just a glimpse through a keyhole in this careful selection of Johnson's personal papers. Johnson's involvement with the art world and the Museum of Modern Art, the professional correspondence, and the architectural drawings are all documented elsewhere—a fact that is, needless to say, scrupulously made clear in the catalog.

The selection includes such sentimental souvenirs as a stack of Johnson's canceled passports from the 1950s and 1960s, collections of photographs, magazine cuttings, brochures, and notes for speeches. There is the honorable discharge that Private Johnson, an intelligence observer in the U.S. Army, collected in December 1944, twenty months after he had finally succeeded in joining America's armed forces. In 1941 his application for a commission as a lieutenant in the naval reserve, also here, had been turned down without any explanation. The file that the FBI had opened the previous year on Johnson and his connections with at least one known German agent may have had something to do with his rejection, though that file isn't in the archive. In 1942, he tried the navy again but failed his physical examination. Although he at last succeeded in signing up for the army, he never served overseas.

And then there is the file that contains a sequence of Johnson's letters to his mother. Only one is addressed to both of his parents, suggesting a certain lack of sympathy for his father. Johnson typed them on his portable, two fingered and closely spaced. They date back to 1926, when he was studying Aristotle and Plato at Harvard, and run through to the end of 1931. By that time he was working for the Museum of Modern Art (MoMA), and the archive includes the letters he wrote on the stationery that he had specially printed with his Berlin address: Achenbachstrasse 22 IV.

The letters are funny, clever, and disturbing. They reveal a young man dividing his time between philosophy tutorials with fellow students he despised—"they disgust me"—and the Harvard Glee Club. He describes his comic dismay when its performances were accused of "lacking virility" by *The New York Times*. He writes of spending his allowance on pianos and freesias, and reveals his twin obsessions with architecture and fast cars. In fact, Johnson sometimes devoted almost as much space to writing about the cars in his life—Packards and Cords mostly—as he did to the buildings he saw. These dual obsessions are encapsulated in one of the Getty's envelopes, which contains a postcard that Johnson sent his mother from Dessau in 1929. On one side is a photograph of Gropius's Bauhaus. On the other is Johnson's message: "This is one of the most beautiful buildings in the world; you must see it some day." In the same envelope is a cutting from a German newspaper, showing a photograph of a new Cord roadster unveiled at the Paris Motor Show that week. "How would you like me to call on you in this?" asks a roguish Johnson. "It's the best car I have seen yet." Later, he goes on to describe a near-fatal collision with a cyclist in Czechoslovakia.

Johnson was always ready to lapse into purple when writing for effect. In one letter, he describes going to a concert: "Sokoloff did a wonderful job on a new Bax symphony that some might call cacophony, but I was put out of commission with the gorgeous polyphonic harmonies. It was a gory thing and I saw red blood in my eyes most of the way through. But all the mist and blood of killing was in it, until I had thoroughly convinced myself that I had slaughtered the whole world and that God and I were rejoicing in it. A horrible imagination no doubt but I think it was impossible not to feel that way with it."

These are the words of a young man in his early twenties, trying out alternative identities for size, just as he would one day switch his allegiance year by year from Mies van der Rohe to Ledoux to deconstruction. But Johnson was no longer a young man when a dozen years later he wrote an account of the German invasion of Poland in which he described the burning of Warsaw as "a stirring sight."

Given that Johnson did indeed suffer a nervous collapse not long after, it is almost as disturbing to read a letter in which he suggests, "I think I'll have a convenient nervous breakdown next month, and come to Pinehurst [the family home] where at least the emphasis would not be on trying to think, or trying not to either."

Also of interest in the archive is a file of newspaper cuttings documenting Johnson's career as a special correspondent for *Social Justice*. Johnson contributed to the hate-filled propaganda sheet for more than two years. To *Social Justice*, the Ku Klux Klan were natural allies, while Roosevelt was the hired hand of the rich, and America was threatened by one Communist plot after another. The magazine was published by Father Charles Coughlin, the rabidly anti-Semitic Catholic priest whose radio broadcasts in the 1930s attracted huge audiences. Although not everything that Johnson wrote for the paper is in the Getty archive, there is enough to get the flavor. Here is Johnson writing from the Polish frontier with Germany just a couple of days before the outbreak of the Second World War: "The Poles are so excited and so worried about the crisis which they feel is at hand that they arrested me at the border, merely for taking pictures. They should have let me go after seeing my American passport, and my American car but the Polish police are in no mood to believe anyone. After eight hours of grilling they let me go."

Before Johnson was allowed to go back across the frontier to Germany, the Polish police chief took him to see the whole town, young and old, digging trenches. He said to the American, "Tell the Germans what you saw, we shall fight them until we die." Johnson later "told some Germans about the trenches, they roared with laughter, and pointed to their tanks."

This was the same trip on which the respected *New York Times* correspondent William Shirer was forced to share a hotel room with Johnson by the German Ministry of Propaganda. Shirer later described him as "an American fascist, and a suspected Nazi agent," a suspicion that was evidently shared by the FBI.

Certainly Johnson could have been counted "an agent of influence" by Germany, as the Soviet Union described its informal allies within the British establishment in the 1930s and 1940s. Such "agents" might not have been ready to cross the line to become active spies, but they were certainly prepared to play their part in the propaganda war. Johnson's journalism is neither neutral reporting nor simple personal prejudice. It reads like part of a sustained campaign first to suggest that neither Czechoslovakia nor Poland was a legitimate state, and thus fair game for Germany, and then to stop America from entering the war. His intention was to assist Hitler's victory. Johnson, and Hitler's other American apologists, represented the German attack on Poland as no more Britain's business than any of the countless minor colonial wars that Britain had fought in India were Germany's. When that failed to convince, Britain was accused of sacrificing the Poles, who in any case weren't worth fighting for. And by the way, Germany's overwhelming strength meant that it had already won the war, so that any effort to stop Hitler was leaving it all much too late.

Johnson's dispatch from Munich in October 1939, a month after the war started, is in the archive: "Germany talks peace. It only fails of its object in the British Empire and her crown colony, the US of A. English talk affects us deeply, but leaves all other neutrals cold. Italy goes as far as to answer, 'what do you mean when you say Europe is at war, you are not fighting our battle Great Britain, we want peace, and so do Spain, Hungary, Jugoslavia, Holland, Belgium, Denmark, Sweden, Norway and Finland.'"

For some reason Johnson's report from Paris the previous year, in which he wrote as a fact that "only Jews had a right to free speech in France," is missing. In it Johnson quoted at length, and with apparent sympathy, "a true born Frenchwoman," as he described her, lamenting the influx of Austrian, Polish, and German Jews, and the way those she calls their local cousins were running the country on their behalf. Also absent is the essay that he wrote in *Today's Challenge* in 1939, for the American Fellowship Forum, claiming that "the USA is committing race suicide."

A picture of a troubled and not very likable man emerges from his writings. Johnson's anti-Semitism and racism went well beyond the level of casual American country-club prejudice of the time. Writing in *Social Justice*, Johnson describes his trip to Poland: "I thought I must be in the region of some awful plague. The fields were nothing but stone. There were no trees, mere paths instead of roads. In the towns, no shops, no automobiles. There were not even any Poles to be seen in the streets. Only Jews. I visited Lodz, with 680,000 people; it's called the Chicago of Poland. I found it a slum without a city attached to it. The Jews form 35 per cent, dressed in their black robes, their black skull caps, they seem more like 85 per cent."

He disliked Czechs, or at least the non-German-speaking section of the country's population, whom he appeared to consider his racial inferiors. Writing to his mother, he describes a visit to the opera in Prague: "We heard *Don Giovanni* last night sung in Tschek or Cesk or whatever the damn language is. Just so much spitting as far as we were concerned. At least when you were here everything was in German. And the stupid people with their too broad mouths and blank expressions." To judge by his article in *Social Justice* describing the nonchalance with which everyday Germans regarded the outbreak of war, Johnson was prepared to condone prejudice against American blacks too, even if one of his first lovers was black. "This war can't be worse than our negro occupation after the last one," he quotes an anonymous German as telling him.

Why would Johnson want to put even a limited selection of these papers into the public domain? Was it an attempt at making a frank disclosure? Johnson's relationship with his own past, which has always been ambiguous, would suggest that the answer is no. He made a regular series of apologies for his bigotry, including a visit to the Anti-Defamation League in New York in the late 1940s. Johnson's otherwise sympathetic biographer, Franz Schulze, questions the sincerity of this gesture, suggesting that it came only after Edgar Kaufman, his rival at MoMA, commissioned a private detective to probe Johnson's political past and was aimed more at damage limitation than at contrition.

Johnson had long and close relationships with many American Jews. He designed Israel's first nuclear reactor and built a synagogue in New Canaan free of charge. But in 1993, when he was in Berlin, he made a speech in which he claimed to "loathe Hitler, but love Friedrich Wilhelm." He called them "bad client, good client," summarizing in a way his worldview, in both his weakness for the never entirely apposite one-liner and in the essentially frivolous sentiments that it represents. Much as he would like to have been, Johnson was no Oscar Wilde. He went on to say, "I spent almost three years in Germany at the end of Weimar. The sex life was new and thrilling. The beer was good and the friendship was better. In my intoxication with Berlin's modern life, I completely missed the underlying political difficulties. I knew no outspoken Communists or Nazis." This is scarcely a credible claim from a man who had been seduced by the messianic sight of Hitler in full flow at a Nazi rally in 1931. Johnson was well enough informed of Hitler's interests to write a perceptive commentary on architecture in the Third Reich for an

American literary magazine in 1933. He identified three distinct camps, from Christian Schultze-Naumburg's kitsch, to Paul Schmitthenner's vernacular style, to the Miesian rigor that he hoped would be adopted by the National Socialist modernizers.

Unlike most other architects, Johnson devoted six years of his life to a political project that included establishing a right-wing political party, Youth and Nation, for which he devised a flying wedge symbol, and which sometimes called itself the Gray Shirts. He had decided to leave the Museum of Modern Art in 1934 and to devote himself to politics. The most informative of the few traces in the archive of this period are a couple of newspaper cuttings. In one of them Charles T. Luccy, the *Toledo News Bee*'s evidently star-struck reporter, describes Johnson the political activist as possessed of "a kind of priestly fire." Johnson's political program was the usual proto-fascist populist brew of the 1930s: "We oppose Communists, but we admire them for their smartness. Reactionaries are our enemies, the ones who have enough, and want to keep it that way." Johnson promised "an American solution for American problems. A central bank, a strong air force . . . more emotionalism, less intellectualism." Decades later Johnson telescoped all this into a rather less contentious précis: "I started a radio campaign for higher prices for milk farmers."

Despite his willingness to explore every form of architectural expression, from ziggurats to art deco, and to make each of them the starting point of one of his buildings, Johnson preserved an absolute silence on the subject of Speer and his architecture. He was less squeamish about the work of Stalin's architects. In 1994, Peter Noever, the director of Vienna's MAK museum, invited Johnson to open an exhibition on Soviet architecture in the Stalin years. Except for its title, "The Tyranny of Beauty," the show would have delighted Stalin, with its respectful tone and its glamorous view of authoritarian architecture, depicting a kind of Manhattan on the Moskva. According to Johnson's address at the opening, "Stalin is today counted as one of history's greatest villains. No doubt he was. This evening however we are asked to look at one small facet of this interesting tyrant, the beautification of Russia, and the glorification of himself." However, not even such a determined puncturer of conventional liberal preconceptions as Johnson could afford to take the same narrow-focus view of Hitler for fear of reopening old questions about his own past. Not even an architect who is ready to describe all architects, himself included, as whores.

As a politician Johnson was hardly convincing. His isolationist, pro-Nazi campaign to keep America from intervening in World War II would have been unsuccessful, even without the attack on Pearl Harbor. The various unsavory right-wingers that Johnson backed financially to run against FDR got nowhere. His own party failed to attract mass support. Johnson's appeal to the American extreme right was his money—derived from a block of Alcoa shares his father gave him, which made him a millionaire—and his status as a public figure, thanks to his early career at MoMA. Even if circumstances had been different, Johnson would never have had the organizing energy to be useful to a Führer in the way that Speer was. But he was able instead to establish himself as a power broker within the world of architecture, and for Johnson that in the end seems to have been enough.

Despite the enthusiasm with which the Nazis and Italy's Fascists were eagerly exploring architecture as a political tool, and his own political activism, Johnson never made a connection between architecture and politics in the 1930s. Quite the reverse: the two always appeared to occupy different compartments of his life. In his political self, Johnson had nothing to say about architecture. He did his best to present architecture as apolitical, perhaps because he found his enthusiasm for Mies van der Rohe to be in conflict with official architectural taste in Hitler's Germany, a society that he otherwise sympathized with. Johnson tried to portray his hero as a German patriot, reflecting Prussian values in the austerity of his work. He tried to paint Mies as the victim of left-wing prejudice, presumably in the hope that this might endear Mies to the right. "The Mies home is admittedly luxurious; for this reason Mies is disliked by many architects and critics, especially the Communists," he wrote in his critique of the Berlin building exhibition in 1931 for *The New York Times*. But his separation of politics from architecture does not mean Johnson kept his political prejudices out of his cultural life entirely. He never took to Erich Mendelsohn, one of many of Germany's Jewish architects forced to flee the Nazis. "Mendelsohn thinks he is God Almighty, and won't give us the photographs. We feel like being nasty and making out his architecture as even worse than it is, in retaliation," Johnson wrote to his mother while in Berlin collecting material for MoMA's International Style show. He described Hannes Meyer, Walter Gropius's left-wing successor as director of the Bauhaus, as "a stupid man," and claimed that since Meyer's arrival in Dessau, "what one learns there is not comparable to what can be got elsewhere."

While his political campaigns got him nowhere, Johnson's adventures in the politics of architecture itself were much more effective. America was introduced to modern architecture in the 1930s by Johnson and Henry-Russell Hitchcock. And by and large the country took to it, perhaps because Johnson presented it as a style shorn of any sense of a social program. Of course, he succeeded even more effectively in constructing a position for himself at the center of American architecture, thanks to the perception he created of his proprietary hold on a successful new movement. Johnson, who failed to build a personal relationship with Le Corbusier, bet heavily on Mies as the greatest of European architects, and was rewarded by Mies's success in America. Johnson's judgment has continued to cast a long shadow on the Museum of Modern Art, an institution that has staged no less than eight exhibitions on Mies in its history. Much later on, after Johnson had fallen out with Mies in a late-night bourbon-fueled argument about the finer points of the design of Johnson's own house, he missed no opportunity to paint Mies as a self-serving and amoral architect ready to do anything to build. Indeed, Johnson's subsequent career after his break with Mies can be seen as the attempted patricide of a long-admired father figure by a spurned young disciple. All that Mies had believed about timelessness, consistency, and rigor, Johnson systematically set out to caricature with an architecture of indulgence and caprice, with a whirl of designs that lurched through every period in history with bewildering speed.

"Nazis, schmatzis, Mies would have built for anyone," the architectural historian Elaine Hochman reports Johnson's telling her. It is a remark that can certainly be seen as a case of Johnson projecting his own attitudes onto others. It is hard to think of Mies—who was so cool with Jacqueline Kennedy about designing JFK's presidential library that she assumed he didn't want the job—cultivating Donald Trump with the unseemly eagerness adopted by Johnson in the hope of securing a commission to erect a wall of high-rise apartments for the most lumpen of New York's property developers. Johnson's flattery persuaded Trump to see him as a useful marketing tool, for just long enough to call him "the greatest architect in the world," but the relationship left Johnson diminished by its transparent opportunism.

The donation of his archive to the Getty, rather than representing an appetite for frankness, might have had more to do with Johnson's lifelong search for attention. It was a strategy of titillating disclosure aimed perhaps at diverting closer scrutiny, rather than representing genuine candor. Johnson was the first architect of the twentieth century to understand exactly how much a successful architectural career depends on a mastery of the techniques of publicity. On one level, this was not such a new departure. From Vitruvius to Palladio, to Robert Adam and Le Corbusier, publishing handsomely illustrated editions of complete works has been a vital step in successfully establishing a long-lasting architectural reputation. Johnson, however, saw that getting himself on the cover of *Time* magazine was a more useful career move than publishing an architectural monograph that would be seen only by other architects, and he decided to do both. He understood the art of the sound bite, and he was always careful to remain close to the levers of power through the exercise of patronage. Above all, he was entirely at home with the culture of celebrity.

DURING THE COURSE OF AN INTERVIEW WITH ALBERT SPEER SHORTLY before he died, the art critic Robert Hughes claims to have asked him to suggest a contemporary architect to serve a hypothetical new Führer. "I hope Philip Johnson will not mind if I mention his name. Johnson understands what the small man thinks of as grandeur. The fine materials, the size of the space."

Hughes wrote that Speer went on to ask him to deliver a copy of a book of his own architecture to Johnson in New York. "Speer carefully opened the book, to the title page, uncapped his heavy gold fountain pen with the floppy nib, and wrote in blue ink in his peculiarly crabby, vertically squished-up hand. 'For Philip Johnson, a fellow architect. With sincere admiration of his most recent designs. Best Regards Albert Speer.'"

Hughes says he subsequently met Johnson for lunch at the Four Seasons in New York to hand over the gift.

"You haven't shown this to anyone?" Johnson asked.

No, Hughes lied, he hadn't.

"Thank heavens for small mercies," Johnson muttered.

JOHNSON ALWAYS COURTED PUBLICITY, BOTH IN HIS OVERTLY POLITical years and as an architect. He had an unwavering determination to be at the center of things. *Vanity Fair*, with its tooth-rotting but irresistible diet of celebrity, middle-class murders, and Hollywood politics, celebrated Philip Johnson's ninety-fifth birthday in almost exactly the same way that it had celebrated his ninetieth. The magazine commissioned the fashion photographer Timothy Greenfield-Sanders to take a picture of American architecture's oldest grand old man, seated in the thick of a dense cloud of his acolytes in the lobby bar of the Four Seasons, the restaurant that he designed at the foot of the Seagram Building. It is inconceivable that any other architect would have received the same treatment—not even Frank Gehry, who, with Brad Pitt in and out of his office, is certainly no stranger to stardom.

The *Vanity Fair* photograph is not so much a tribute to the significance of Johnson's contribution to the history of architecture as a reminder of his importance to the cult of fame. Frank Gehry sits on one side of Johnson, alongside Peter Eisenman. Arata Isozaki has flown in from Tokyo, Rem Koolhaas from Rotterdam, and Zaha Hadid from London. Their presence seems to suggest not just a tribute to Johnson, but a sense of an acceptance of the old man's benediction, a laying on of hands that has certainly helped their careers over the years. Johnson looks exactly the same as he did at ninety, while the selection of guests in the *Vanity Fair* photograph gets steadily younger to demonstrate his continuing grip over architectural life.

Johnson's decision to make his papers part of an academic archive while he was still actively pursuing a professional career could be seen as an especially calculated form of self-advertisement. Even Frank Lloyd Wright's correspondence didn't get this kind of treatment when he was still alive.

It is hard to point to a single building that Johnson designed during his long career that served to change the course of American architecture, let alone architecture anywhere else. Even Johnson's so-called Chippendale skyscraper on Madison Avenue, the granite-sheathed tower that began life as the AT&T Building and now accommodates Sony—presented on the cover of *Time* as ushering in a new age of corporate pomp in the 1980s—was actually a case of jumping onto a bandwagon that was already rolling, set in motion by Michael Graves and his Portland, Oregon, government building.

To treat Johnson's correspondence with this much respect is clearly trying to tell us something more elevated about him and his historical significance. Thanks to his endlessly energetic efforts to put himself on show, he acquired the status of a national institution. The archive is a two-way transaction, one that shores up Johnson and at the same time adds to the reputation of the Getty, which in itself is one of the most re-markable expressions of the determination of an individual to perpetu-ate his own legacy. J. Paul Getty paid minimal attention to the design of his museum's first building, other than to decide that it should take the form of a Pompeian villa rather than replicate Sutton Place, the tudor mansion that was his English home for years. And he was dead long be-fore the Meier campus opened. He never looked inside many of the packing cases containing the art that his agents acquired in his name be-fore they were shipped off to California. Yet he ensured that his memory would far outlast his financial empire by investing in building a collec-tion of art from all over the world.

Through Johnson's seventy-five-year association with the Museum of Modern Art and its department of architecture and design, he con-trolled one of the more conspicuous platforms on which architectural reputations have been made in America. He was around in 1932 to champion the international style, and in 1957 to help Phyllis Lambert, heiress to the Seagram distillery fortune, persuade her father that the family firm needed a real architect for its new Manhattan building. He suggested Mies, a move that did far more for Johnson's reputation than trying to design it himself would have done. His reward was to be named associated architect for the tower, a necessary arrangement since Mies did not have a license to practice in New York.

Twenty years later, Johnson was ready and waiting at the moment that corporate America finally decided it was bored with working in buildings shaped by well-bred architectural restraint and wanted to in-ject a little imperial splendor into its surroundings. Johnson's answer was postmodernism, offering stone façades and classical columns to soothe the fevered corporate brow—a style that he adopted ready-made from Graves. He used the same trick a decade later when he abandoned the sinking ship of postmodernism in favor of the very next thing, architectural deconstructivism, putting his stamp on an exhibition on the subject at MoMA. The transition was no mean feat of intellectual agility for a man of any age, let alone an octogenarian.

Johnson had the worldliness to understand that architecture is not a hermetic discipline, no matter how much some of its practitioners persist in behaving as if it were. His architecture has itself been designed for the maximum generation of publicity. He was the Harley Earl of architecture, and like Detroit's greatest stylist, he was constantly looking for taller tail fins and more chrome each season to make buildings that attract attention. It's a hunger for effect that has produced designs for quite a few works that thankfully have never seen the light of day. One of his most grotesque proposals was to build an office development for the Kuwaiti Investment Office on the Thames, opposite the Tower of London, in the guise of a replica of the Houses of Parliament

London's planning authorities and a weak property market torpedoed the Westminster replica, but in Dallas, Johnson built an office and condominium development in the form of a giant French château, and in Pittsburgh there is an outsize mirror-glass version of the Tower of London. In Houston, Johnson designed an architecture school in the form of a previously unrealized Ledoux design for a temple. In the ever wilder fluctuations of his enthusiasms, and Johnson's own laboriously public protestations of cynicism, he seemed to be deliberately bent on undermining the very idea of architecture as anything but a personal caprice, stripping it of any other kind of meaning than a craven attempt to pander to jaded tastes. It is as if he were trying deliberately to undermine his more gifted colleagues—and perhaps to satirize the clients that he flattered to their faces, then abused behind their backs.

While Johnson continually presented architecture as an end in itself, rather than the political tool so many authoritarians have tried to make it, he never offered any real sense of knowing what that end might be. He had every opportunity to build, but did surprisingly little that is memorable with those opportunities. He had no lasting beliefs, except his determination to go on being relevant. Johnson's career survived his involvement with fascism unscathed, but in the end he became a revolving door, running through architectural history, in an apparently random but ever faster order, to find the source material for his next project.

Of the many architects who worked, or who wanted to work, for the dictators, few were any more coherent about their motivations than Johnson. Some certainly sincerely believed that it was their duty to put their skills at the service of a political cause. Hannes Meyer, the second director of the Bauhaus, who attracted Johnson's contempt, was one of these. For him the architect had a part to play in constructing socialism to help build a society in which the masses were housed in civilized conditions. He wanted decent workplaces, schools, homes, and hospitals for the proletariat.

For Meyer and others who thought like him, architects had an essential responsibility to be as economical as possible with materials to make scarce resources stretch as far as possible. This could even take on a symbolic as well as a functional aspect. Certain materials were designated as bourgeois. Other materials were regarded as honest, simple, or robust.

It's clear that Le Corbusier understood his work in a political context: Architecture or Revolution, he once promised (or was it a threat?). But he was prepared to ally himself with almost any political regime in the search for work. In France in the 1930s he flirted with right-wing nationalist politics. In Vichy France he joined the collaborationist regime, and he did the same in Algiers. He declined the invitation of the French Communists to join the party even when Picasso had accepted. Whether he had joined or not, Le Corbusier was the subject of a violent campaign that claimed his work in itself was politically subversive. A pamphlet published in 1928 described him as "the trojan horse of Bolshevism," and it was translated in the 1930s and reprinted in German.

But Le Corbusier was as ready to work for Stalin as for Mussolini, just as Mies van der Rohe worked for Hitler and for the Spartacists. Working for both fascists and socialists to design what are essentially political projects, as so many architects have done, leaves them open to the charge of hypocrisy. Given the readiness of architects to suggest that their work is somehow the embodiment of an inner "truth," it is not surprising that when they are taken at their word, they do not come out well.

The architectural issue is how much their work is tainted by the association with the more unsavory of patrons, or whether, like the legal profession, architects are in a position to carve out the space for themselves to operate with apparent integrity independently of the merits, or lack of them, of their clients.

Certainly in the case of Giuseppe Pagano, or Giuseppe Terragni, it was possible both to be a gifted, even a great, architect and at the same time to work for Mussolini, with personal integrity intact. Philip Johnson was also a fascist, at least for a time. But, although he never worked for a figure as notorious as Mussolini, he also never managed to match the talent of Terragni or Pagano, or the courage of either.

CHAPTER 5

THE ARCHITECT WHO
SWEPT THE FLOOR

YUNG HO CHANG'S STUDIO IN BEIJING LOOKS MUCH LIKE ANY other aspiring architect's office anywhere. The walls are white, the floor is bare concrete, and rows of twenty-somethings are plugged into computers listening to Dr. Dre on their headphones. There are cardboard and foam models everywhere, and an avalanche of magazines in the corner. The difference, as California-educated Yung Ho Chang points out, is that the Beijing of the first years of the twenty-first century isn't like anywhere else.

The studio used to be part of the dormitory for the gardeners who tended the grounds of the Dowager Empress's summer palace. Western soldiers considered destroying the Forbidden City during the Boxer Rebellion, but decided that would be going too far. They confined themselves to burning her palace, as a reprisal for her role in the uprising against foreigners and Christians. They torched it again after she had it rebuilt, but spared Yung Ho Chang's modest gray-brick terrace next door.

Cruise round Beijing's first ring road, the site of the city's medieval walls, laboriously destroyed brick by brick between 1950 and 1962, and you pass the chrome-trimmed glass and granite façade of the Grand

Hyatt Hotel. In its forecourt the circle of red flags is a fleeting vision of what latter-day capitalist pomp on the Washington Beltway might be reduced to after the revolution. On Chang An Boulevard, Beijing's version of the Las Vegas strip, one block thick, where each grandiloquent institution is protected by its own private garage and gated forecourt, you pass high-rise banks topped with pagoda roofs and golden footballs. They are the confused attempts of a culture emerging from half a century of violent ambivalence about both banks and the very idea of tradition to lay claim to some kind of roots in place and time and perhaps to atone for the senseless demolition of Beijing's gates and walls. A brief campaign in the 1990s to create a conspicuously Chinese version of contemporary architecture has left a rash of superfluous tiled roofs and upswept eaves, tacked on to generic functional designs, an uncomfortable tendency typified by the city's bus station.

Every so often you find little encampments of olive drab army tents pitched along sidewalks as temporary homes for building workers. Construction sites spill out of every gash in the old gray walls that used to define the city. You drive and drive and see no end to the cranes and the clusters of new apartment buildings, interspersed with fields of brick fragments—the remains of recently demolished suburbs. Throughout its history Beijing has, like so many capital cities, been an urban landscape designed to reflect the authority of the regime that controlled the city; one imperial dynasty after another has made Beijing its own. Mao Zedong did the same, and now his ideology-free successors are following in his footsteps.

Chairman Mao's war against the Four Olds—Old Thought, Old Culture, Old Customs, and Old Habits—which drove the Red Guards in their brutal and bloody campaign of book burning and persecution of the intellectuals, has been applied to city planning. The rebuilding of Beijing is certainly a cultural revolution of a kind. At pavement level, the city's most ubiquitous new building type is the residential marketing suite: stainless-steel boxes and glass blobs, decked with balloons to tempt in customers, who are being sold a concept that reached China only at the very end of the twentieth century, the domestic mortgage. They offer the chance to buy unbuilt apartments from a floor plan, in a gamble that they will double in price before the builders have finished.

Yung Ho works on what are, by Beijing standards, tiny projects. He has done a few houses, a couple of art galleries, a bookshop, and some offices for a publishing company. In a city in which the basic unit of architectural scale has become the skyscraper, erected a dozen at a time, Yung Ho's buildings are so modest that they threaten to disappear from view altogether. He struggles to make architecture that offers a degree of continuity, as a respite from the relentless pace of change; to maintain something of Beijing's character before it vanishes forever; and at the same time to work as an architect in the western way. He doesn't say so, but you feel an overwhelming sense of his powerlessness in the face of the turmoil all around him.

Yung Ho designed the Today Gallery as a temporary conversion of an industrial building, spared briefly from the demolition all around. To reach it you must negotiate streets clogged by the traffic of a city that has reached gridlock with just 2 million cars for its 14 million people. It used to be the Beijing Beer Factory's boiler house, a utilitarian brick and concrete structure from the 1960s caught in a sweeping bend of the electrified tracks leading into the city's central railway station. But like almost everything else in Beijing, the Today Gallery's future was provisional from the moment it was finished; it is slated for demolition along with the tens of thousands of traditional courtyard houses, shops, power stations, and factories that are being pulled down all over the city.

The main space is a four-story-high void, a miniature version of the Tate Modern's turbine hall. It was inaugurated with a group show by a dozen Chinese artists and an opening that was nothing like a private view at the Tate, if only because half the guests looked ready to spend the night on the floor. Beijing, despite the influx of Australian chefs, cigar bars, and Big Macs, is still very far removed from a western city.

Just look at the kitchen hands chopping trays of slippery gray poultry entrails on tables set up on the pavement outside the restaurant across the street. Once you negotiated the students guarding Yung Ho's striking steel-mesh entrance ramp (they were dressed in fancy dress camouflage uniforms and plastic helmets), you were confronted by a screen showing a continuous loop of mute film, celebrating the women of the People's Liberation Army, storming trenches, marching through the countryside, and repelling the imperialist paper tiger. It was a counterpoint to the evening's main event, a performance by four women artists dressed as nightclub dancers in color-coordinated satin and sequin outfits. Upstairs on the mezzanine level, a twice-life-size fiberglass representation of Chairman Mao is sleeping peacefully under a floral print quilt.

"Is this irony?" I ask Zhang Xin, a young property developer.

She invited a dozen Asian architects—Yung Ho Chang among them—to each build a villa for a residential development aimed at China's new rich, on a privileged site next to the Great Wall, shortly before trying to get her company listed on the New York Stock Exchange. She called it the Great Wall Commune and dressed the staff in fitted black Mao suits with red stars on their breast pockets.

"You know, the Mao years have left a mark on everything," Zhang answers ambiguously.

Edging past the sleeping Mao, you open a door and are instantly hit by the acrid tang of cheap confectionery. Eating the City, an installation by an artist named Song Dong, is a megalopolis made of cakes and biscuits, organized on two huge tables, lit like a billiard hall. There are wobbly towers of wafer fingers and swiss rolls, plazas of licorice and chocolate. Song Dong's cakes could be the closest thing that you will find to a coherent vision of what kind of place Beijing will be in the next decade.

At the point of the most rapid change in its history, nobody is entirely clear where the balance of power between the conflicting forces shaping the city rests. The municipal planning commission attempts to use regulations drawn up half a century ago by fraternal party experts based on Eastern Europe's height limits and sunlight angles to direct the growth of the city. Overlaying their efforts is the system of connections and corruption that mysteriously transforms consents for ten-story towers into twenty-story buildings, and randomly dispossesses leaseholders. But there are enough Chinese developers with no preconceptions about how to build to ensure that there is nowhere else in the world where architectural theory can leap into practice with so little time lag.

Within this rapidly mutating city and its apparently chaotic turbulence, there are nevertheless attempts to construct fixed points that will serve to define the focus of power within it, just as there were in Mao's time, and in the dynastic city before that. In the struggle for the power to shape the city's future, the mayor's office and the central government can be regarded only as contenders. They must take their place alongside the hard-faced young men hurrying to make as much money as possible before moving to Switzerland. Together, they have built a model of tooth-and-claw laissez-faire urbanism that makes Houston look like a social democratic utopia.

Land is nominally owned by the state, but scores of bankrupt nationalized enterprises that used to control much of the city are frantically engaged in capitalizing on the development value represented by their obsolete buildings. They sell seventy-year leases that are sometimes parceled up and resold several times before a development actually takes shape. What happens when those leases expire is still far from clear, but the uncertainty encourages developers to take their profits quickly and move on. The city insists on residential developers finding the space and the money to build schools; otherwise, just about anything is possible. There is some financial compensation for the dispossessed former occupants of these sites written into most contracts, enough to see them moved out to distant new settlements. But there is no redress for those who do not want to go. Every so often, China's newspapers devote a brief paragraph to an account of a desperate victim of this process setting fire to himself in Tiananmen Square.

YUNG HO CHANG KNOWS ABOUT THE EXERCISE OF POWER AND ITS connections with architecture in China at first hand. His father, Zhang Kaiji, was also an architect. Zhang Kaiji built some of Mao's villas, as well as the State Guest House in Beijing, inflating its scale at the urging of the party, eager to overawe a visiting Khrushchev who was skeptical about the achievements of modern China. Mao had recently returned from Moscow's celebration of the fortieth anniversary of the Bolshevik revolution, where his hosts built him a special bathroom in the Kremlin, and he was determined not to give the Russians the chance to patronize him again about China's expertise with plumbing. Khrushchev's bathroom was certainly impressive, but he cannot have been reassured to see the architectural embodiment of Stalinism, which he had just begun to denounce at home, apparently still flourishing in China.

Zhang Kaiji was also responsible for designing the twin museums of the Chinese Revolution and Chinese History in 1958. But his personal relationship with Mao did not save him from a decade spent working as a janitor during the Cultural Revolution. With the Great Hall of the People, the museums form a pair of massive Sino-Stalinist landmarks that serve to define the long sides of Tiananmen Square. They have their contemporary counterparts in two new landmarks that will represent the new China, Rem Koolhaas's headquarters for Central China Television, and Jacques Herzog and Pierre de Meuron's Olympic Stadium, both due to be completed by 2008.

Ten years in the making, Tiananmen Square is still China's most highly charged and symbolically important urban landscape. It was a very deliberate creation by Mao, initiated for his ceremonial proclamation of the People's Republic of China in October 1949. Tiananmen was both the physical embodiment and a metaphorical representation of a new political order, a theatrical setting for the regime to celebrate its triumphs, to threaten its enemies with its parades of tanks and missiles, to define itself, and to help secure its grip on a vast country. The square was used to mark the shift in power from the Nationalists to the Communists and to lay claim to the legitimacy of history, as well as to demonstrate the Communists' place in the global order. Mao's Tiananmen was the most ubiquitous image of China, the icon by which the country was recognized all over the world. Not surprisingly, such a charged arena has also been used by those who have challenged the repression with which the Communists have maintained their hold on power. It has become the most contested of spaces, a representation of the authority of Mao and his successors, but also a reminder of the tragic massacre of 1989 and the events leading up to it. And it is now being supplanted as the new urban iconography of Beijing is manufactured with astonishing speed.

Before the Boxer Rebellion, the area in front of Tiananmen was the administrative center of the imperial city. The emperor's more distant kin lived in this buffer zone between the palace and the merchant city beyond, fringed by shops and narrow lanes, muddy underfoot, dotted with little groves of trees, and still enclosed by walls. Rather like London's Whitehall, another seat of administrative power with its origins in a royal palace, or the Louvre in Paris (from which the French Finance Ministry finally moved only in the 1980s), it became a bureaucratic complex by accident. The imperial ministries were concentrated around a courtyard directly facing Tiananmen, among them the Office of Embroidered Robes, as the imperial secret service was known. Foreign legations congregated here after the Opium Wars, determined to extract trading and political concessions from an enfeebled emperor. They became a target during the Boxer Rebellion, and the international struggle to crush it, which caused such serious destruction in Beijing. Tiananmen wasn't yet a formal urban space in its own right, but served as a gateway to the palace. It was the place that supplicants gathered on their way to an audience at court, and where proclamations were posted. China's students rallied here in 1919 to protest at the national humiliation represented by the terms of the Treaty of Versailles. Beijing fell into warlord hands, until they were expelled by Chiang Kai-shek's Nationalists in 1927 and the official capital was moved to Nanjing. The invading Japanese filled the vacuum ten years later and proclaimed their hegemony over Asia from Tiananmen.

In the aftermath of the People's Liberation Army's military victory in the civil war with the Nationalists, the Communists simultaneously wanted to control the existing symbols of power, but also to wipe out every trace of them. They briefly considered establishing a new capital in the industrialized city of Lanzhou, but in the end opted for Beijing and the legitimacy that assuming the traditions of an ancient capital city would bring with it. To make Beijing their capital and, through it, China into their state, the Communists knew they had to make an unmistakable mark on the urban landscape. This would have to go further than replacing the huge image of Chiang Kai-shek painted on flattened oil cans that used to hang from the Gate of Heavenly Peace, first with twin photographs of Mao and his most successful general, and later with a row of four portraits of Stalin, Lenin, Marx, and Mao. In fact Stalin's image remained on show well into the 1980s, perhaps to suggest that China and not the Soviet Union was the true heir of the first Communist revolution or, more likely, because of the inability of the party to make up its mind on the correct line to take about its past.

When his victorious army rode into Beijing on its American-built trucks and jeeps, Mao shifted the emphasis away from the private world of the palace inside the gate and focused instead on the more public space in front of it. The trees were cut down and the legations expelled in preparation for his proclamation of the new Chinese state, and the simultaneous adoption of the Christian calendar and a new national flag. When Mao declared from a platform on top of the Gate of Heavenly Peace that the Chinese people had stood up, neither Chang An, Beijing's primary east–west boulevard, nor the square itself yet existed.

Mao spent his first night in Beijing in a pavilion among the lakes and parks of Kublai Khan's pleasure palace, Zhongnanhai, next to the Forbidden City. There he slept in a room that his imperial predecessors would have recognized. He chose a selection of Confucian texts for his bedside reading, rather than Lenin or Marx. It is not surprising then that the iconography of the ancient city was so important to Mao's imposition of his authority on Beijing. He wanted to show that he was in command, but also to draw on the legacy of the past to underscore his own position. As if to act out his personal hold on the city, he led a delegation of the party hierarchy precisely 850 feet south along the central axis of the Tiananmen Gate, in a ritual to cut the sod for the Memorial to the People's Heroes, his first permanent addition to the city.

For some it was a crudely blasphemous intrusion into the ordered symmetries of Beijing's historic city plan, with its complex layers of overlapping symbolism. The blasphemy culminated in the opening of Mao's Mausoleum, a huge lumpish structure in the center of the square, completed in 1977, which conspicuously blocks the axis that runs right through the city. It was a gesture that François Mitterrand echoed when he commissioned I. M. Pei to build a pyramid in the courtyard of the Louvre aligned on the axis that runs all the way up the Champs-Elysées and on to La Défense.

Tiananmen's walls and existing buildings were steadily demolished over a decade to create what has become a sixty-acre open square. It's big enough to lose both Moscow's Red Square and St. Peter's in Rome, vast enough to absorb one million people. Only Hitler and the Shah of Iran considered creating a public space to match it in size. Big though the buildings around Tiananmen are, they hardly register on the vast emptiness of the square. This would not be a place to linger and feel comfortable sitting on a park bench, even if there were any. The distances are so large that traversing the square on foot becomes an ordeal for even the mildly agoraphobic. Tramping across it in a punishing summer heat, the horizon seems hardly to change as you move from end to end. In winter the dust storms can make Tiananmen positively hostile. At this scale, it is hardly an urban space in the way that it would be understood in a conventional city. It's so big that any coherent idea of space is negated. With no sense of scale or incident, bigness in the end becomes merely an endless blank flatness. Mao wasn't interested in the idea of townscape or the beautification of the capital. He didn't want a democratic space, or a place that would welcome people and allow them to take possession of it. Tiananmen was intended to be the exact opposite, a vast parade ground, its character hinting at what Hitler and Speer would have done to Berlin. This was where thirty years ago the pioneers, children in uniform, pledged allegiance to the party and to liberate humanity from its chains. They were the children who belong to a generation that is now presiding over the most rapid transformation of a society that the world has ever seen.

The regimented ranks of the crowds, uniformly dressed in olive green, bused in for party and national festivals, the red banners, the trucks rolling through the square with their painted and polished missiles, the faces of the party inner circle on the reviewing stand, these were the architectural elements that defined the square as much as the decorative architectural detail on the façades of the Great Hall of the People. Even in today's China, where Tiananmen is a place in which you can find children flying kites and fairground tableaux depicting the scenic highlights of the Chinese landscape in Styrofoam, it is only the underpasses opening into the square from Chang An that seem genuinely to belong to Beijing's people. Here they can linger out of the rain, sipping fluorescent orange soft drinks and dodging the hawkers handing out flyers advertising unofficial bus services. The square itself belongs unequivocally to the state, and not to its people.

Stalin, a leader who never hesitated to rewrite the past, pulled down Moscow's Red Gates and the seventeenth-century Sukharev tower. He flattened the great Basilica of the Holy Savior to make way for the never completed Palace of the Soviets. And he pushed his satellites to mutilate their capital cities in the same way. The gesture did more to demonstrate their allegiance to Moscow than to impose national party authority on their own countries. Stalin's architects were called on to build a series of "gifts" from the blood-soaked dictator to his vassal states to underscore the message. Beijing got a Red Babylonian Palace of Exhibitions, just as Warsaw had its Palace of Culture. With technical help and ideological direction from his Soviet allies, Mao was attempting to turn Beijing into the center of a modern China for the pre-television age, to create an arena in which the nation's fate was to be acted out—in the same way that the priesthood of a Mayan city-state would demonstrate its supernatural powers in the ball courts and plazas of Chichén Itzá. Tiananmen was a puppet theater, and every performance followed the party's carefully choreographed triumphalist script to the letter. The buildings around the square had their own part to play in that script.

The tenth anniversary of the proclamation of the People's Republic was the trigger for a wholesale remodeling and expansion of Tiananmen. It was the most conspicuous of the ten construction projects Mao initiated to mark the occasion and impress both his own people and his increasingly disenchanted allies in the Soviet Union. It was both a celebration and a maneuver against his rivals in the party and the army.

Just at the time that China's peasants began to starve to death in their millions from the famine that was the result of the economic disruption that Mao had deliberately wrought on the countryside, the People's Republic was devoting its energies and scarce resources to glorifying state, party, and leader.

Paving the enlarged square, and the construction of two vast new buildings on its edges, was completed in just ten months, from November 1958 to September 1959, by a workforce 12,000 strong. They were described as volunteers, working in three shifts for up to sixteen hours a day, for the standard daily pay. They lived, ate, and slept on the site, so eager were they, claimed Mao, to complete this monument to the revolution. Work went on throughout the night under floodlights. At the end of 1958, Mao's Soviet advisers had warned him that it would be impossible to finish the project on time. The following June they had said it might be done. In September they said, "China has made a great leap forward," giving Mao a slogan to make his own. The architecture of Tiananmen—indeed, the whole concept on which the square was based—slavishly followed the example of Moscow.

Mao was ready to follow Stalin's lead, even after his Soviet counterpart's death, to the extent of asking his architects for an aesthetic approach reflecting Stalin's own taste for monumental forms on a vast scale. Soviet architects held seminars in Moscow to brief fraternal visitors on the most appropriately national form of classicism for a socialist state to use. That China proposed to celebrate its revolution in such a fossilized architectural language at precisely the moment that Mies van der Rohe was completing the Seagram Building in New York, a time when even Khrushchev was turning to prefabrication, suggested both the cultural isolation of the Chinese Communist system and its determination to build a society that looked different from its western foes, capitalist or Communist. By the time that Tiananmen was complete, Khrushchev had already made his secret speech denouncing Stalin. One of the major issues that he focused on was his predecessor's compulsive expenditure on monumental architecture. His visit to China troublingly confronted him with Stalin's eastern echo.

China in 1949 had not been like Russia in 1919, which with its almost 250-year experience of western architecture had created its own indigenous architectural avant-garde. Under the Nationalist government, China had only just begun to devise an architectural education system. It required the wholesale importation of a profession that hardly existed in China and was led by individuals who had been trained in America and Europe. China's own architectural culture was still based on the principles so powerfully demonstrated by the Forbidden City. Western architecture, of the kind visible in Shanghai or Hong Kong, represented an unwelcome intrusion, a reminder of China's powerlessness in the face of foreigners. It was the last thing that Mao wanted to build. In any case, China simply didn't have the expertise or the resources to build a glass curtain wall, to work with structural steel except in the simplest way, or to build a skyscraper, any more than it could build submarines or private cars.

For Mao's architects, dissent was dangerous. Those few who did criticize the Soviet-inspired remodeling of the city were forced to recant. Architects who remained active had limited room to maneuver in what they designed. But some looked to introduce a more nuanced interpretation of what Chinese architecture might be than others, and the break with Moscow seemed to offer them an opening.

The Great Hall of the People was designed in 1958 by Zhang Kaiji's contemporary and long-standing rival, Zhang Bo. The two architects were both in their forties when they took on leading roles in the Beijing Institute of Architectural Design and Research. The institute was one of the series of state monopolies, still in existence today, that the party established throughout the country to reorganize the architectural profession on socialist lines. Zhang Bo, the son of the last governor of Guangdong and Guangxi provinces in the days of the Qing dynasty, and Zhang Kaiji, a schoolteacher's son, were both graduates of the National Central University in Nanjing, where architecture was taught on the Beaux-Arts model.

With its massive Stalinist colonnade and its intimidating bulk, Zhang Bo's Great Hall of the People—an endless and repetitive sequence of assembly halls, one for every province, each decorated with appropriate iconography rendered in the manner of a wall poster—is clearly a descendant of that classically inspired tradition of symmetry and axial compositions where each room leads into the next. There is an auditorium for ten thousand people, the scene of successions of assemblies with no power other than to respectfully applaud their leaders, and a banqueting hall big enough for five thousand, where Nixon and Mao toasted each other. In its sheer square footage, the spaces of the Great

Hall exceed those of all the palaces of the Forbidden City combined—an attribute that is anything but accidental. Zhang Bo gave the hall the character of an imperial palace rather than a parliament with its monolithic exterior and generous use of golden yellow, a color traditionally reserved for royal buildings in China. Zhang Kaiji's Museum of the Chinese Revolution and the neighboring Museum of Chinese History, planned around twin courtyards, stand directly opposite the Great Hall of the People and respond to it by establishing a deliberate sense of contrast.

The dominant architectural motif of the two museums is the loggia, which defines the edge of the square but also welcomes visitors. Just as Mao was ready to embrace the techniques of emperors in ruling the vast Chinese population, so Yung Ho's father, Zhang Kaiji, tried discreetly to incorporate elements of the architectural language of China's heritage into his buildings. He commissioned painters from the Central Academy of Fine Arts to create murals based on themes from Chinese mythology for a central hall that pays tribute to Marx, Engels, Lenin, Stalin, and Mao. Beyond these unassailable party heroes, the faction fights of the Cultural Revolution proved too much for curators, struggling to keep up with the twists and turns of who was in and who was out. The Museum of the Chinese Revolution remained closed for long periods as they tried to catch up with the party line. It now shows waxworks of Mao and Lenin alongside Bill Gates and Marilyn Monroe.

Even when it was first finished, the loggia was a more inviting gesture than the intimidating wall of giant columns across the square. Over time, the museums have sprouted an accretion of cafés and shops spilling out from the podium level that have begun transforming it into an inhabited monument, in the same way that Diocletian's palace in Split shelters fifteenth-century houses and eighteenth-century shops in its massive masonry structure.

These are such vastly scaled buildings that they intimidate pedestrians into insignificance, even as they attempt to suggest a grandeur that reflects the aspirations of the state. They appear to float in the endless wide open spaces of Tiananmen, detached from their setting, like ships at sea. The Communist monuments were larger and physically more imposing than those of the emperors. But Tiananmen Square was aligned on the Forbidden City, and Beijing's fundamental structure remained unchanged. The risk for Mao in the face of a culture as old and as sophisticated as China's was that the crudeness and the wooden massing of his intrusions in the imperial iconography of the city would be seen as exactly that. By measuring himself against China's traditions, as Saddam Hussein would later co-opt the architecture of ancient Iraq, he could be seen to be failing to live up to them by the country's intellectuals.

Mao's ideologues never took a consistent view as to whether the regime should seek to surpass the past, or else try to wipe it out entirely, as the most decisive statement of power possible. Mao was capable of collecting ancient Chinese calligraphy privately, while at the same time encouraging its destruction in open-air book burnings. Some saw the building of Tiananmen Square as an onslaught against one of the greatest creations of Chinese civilization, but other leaders wanted to go much further than destroying just the city's walls and its gates, which had been built not so much for defensive purposes as a representation of the Chinese view of the universe. During the Cultural Revolution detailed proposals were drawn up to demolish the Forbidden City altogether, extending Tiananmen Square directly into it, and to create a supposedly more proletarian new government quarter on its ruins. Designs were prepared for new buildings for the Foreign Ministry, offices for the party's Central Committee, a 5000-seat cinema, a twenty-story department store, and a skyscraper hotel. Indeed, tall buildings on this kind of scale would be the only way to make sense of Tiananmen's sixty empty acres.

The Forbidden City survived intact to celebrate the 850th anniversary of Beijing's foundation as an imperial city. For the first 800 years of its existence, it retained essentially the same character: the walled palace city at its center, organized on a strict north–south axis; concentric rings of walls and gates containing a sea of courtyard houses and narrow lanes; and not much in the way of water-borne sanitation. Tiananmen was a huge hole torn in that fabric, but not yet a fatal wound. Despite the rhetoric of revolutionary change, Mao could see practical advantages in Beijing's traditional layout in controlling a restive urban population.

What appealed about Beijing's ancient structure to an authoritarian regime attempting to consolidate its hold on power was that the city had no democratic urban tradition in the western sense. Life was lived in the neighborhoods, while the center was reserved for the governing class. The party took the traditional Beijing courtyard and used it as the model for the division of the city into self-contained compounds. There was one for each big industrial complex, and others for the universities, the army, the hospitals, and the embassies. The regime ensured that there was minimal communication between them and that such potential trouble-makers as the university students were isolated by the two-hour walk to the city center from their newly relocated campuses.

A big factory compound could house ten thousand people, offering them somewhere to sleep, canteens for them to eat in, and schools to educate their children, ensuring that they would spend most of their lives within the perimeter wall under the constant surveillance of the party faithful. The masses were dispersed, coming into the center only for events in Tiananmen that were under the watchful control of the regime. A city like this presents less of a challenge to a ruling autocracy than one in which public space belongs to the people. There was no free, public space in Mao's Beijing; no commercial area, no restaurants or cafés for the disaffected to gather in. After 9:00 P.M. the city seemed to shut down altogether, reduced as late as the 1990s to medieval darkness.

Beijing no longer goes dark. There are neon lights along most of Chang An now. The city is evolving in ways that its rulers cannot fully control. Private money has, for example, allowed a group of artists to turn a bankrupt engineering factory built by the East Germans near the airport into an enclave of galleries, studios, and cafés that coexist with the survivors of the old workforce, bringing a sense of the euphoric cultural freedom of the early days of the collapse of communism in Eastern Europe—temporary paradise syndrome, it might be called. When the SARS epidemic closed the city's cinemas and theaters in 2003, informal bars sprang up in the streets. Such liberalizing tendencies have had to contend with equally strong currents pushing in the opposite direction. Immediately west of Tiananmen Square, hundreds of courtyard houses were flattened to build the National Opera House, a megalomaniac glass egg designed by Paul Andreu, a French architect specializing in airports. His contribution to Beijing's wide-open urban prairie is to put the opera house in the middle of an artificial lake. It's the perfect contemporary face for a regime that believes in the use of tanks as a modern instrument of crowd control.

Zhang Bo's and Zhang Kaiji's work in Tiananmen is the core of a handful of untouchable monuments in a city in which nothing is immune from the threat of destruction. And even Zhang Bo's museums are being reorganized—they are now being turned into a single National Museum of China. Tiananmen is so central to the foundation of the present state that it could not be any other way. But almost everything else is potentially subject to demolition. And the regime itself is looking to create a new identity for the city that could yet leave Tiananmen marginalized.

Beijing has embarked on the largest building campaign that the world has ever seen. It is the capital of the world's fastest-growing economy, provoking a titanic struggle between a totalitarian political system and the liberalization that is the presumed product of its economic transformation. Half the world's annual production of concrete and one-third of its steel output is being consumed by China's construction boom, according to one estimate. The second ring road that marked the city limits until the 1980s has been followed by the construction of a third, fourth, and fifth ring. The sixth is under construction. Cars move sclerotically around disconnected clumps of newly completed towers that threaten to leave the center as marginalized as Detroit's. The city map looks like a dartboard, with the void of the Forbidden City as its empty bull's-eye. And with the abruptness of a randomly aimed dart, entire new districts appear arbitrarily, as if from nowhere. A city that until 1990 had no central business district, and little need of one, now has a cluster of glass towers that look like rejects from Omaha or Singapore. Almost by accident, the area to the east of the city center has become the focus of a random sprouting of high-rise towers. They are here because this is where the embassies were built when the Communists moved the diplomatic district away from the city center into what were fields. When China's opening to the outside world came, it was the obvious place for hotels to be built, and the commercial towers followed. The government tried to create a counterbalancing financial center on the western side of the city, demolishing thousands of courtyards to build the Bank of China, but found that it was already too late to challenge the dominance of the east side.

What was the China No. 1 Engineering Enterprise, the largest factory in China and the setting for vain efforts by the Gang of Four to rally support from the proletariat, has been wiped out by a flock of dazzling white skyscrapers designed by the Japanese architect Riken Yamamoto. Construction started in 2001. The 8-million-square-foot project was scheduled to be completed within four years. The first residents of the four thousand flats had moved in by the end of 2003. Taking me on a tour of the construction site, one of the developers, a young woman in her thirties, pointed out the fading slogan painted on one of the brick sheds that used to dominate the site: "Long Live the Party." The shed had already been scheduled for demolition.

Not far away, the twenty-five acres of the Beijing motorcycle factory, once so dear to loyal party hearts, have been leveled to allow Rem Koolhaas to build the new headquarters of Central China Television (CCTV). It will be a colossus that takes the form of two leaning towers, seventy floors high, that prop each other up with links at top and bottom to form a gigantic Möbius strip, containing everything from studios to offices. An adjacent hotel block takes the form of an open chest of drawers. This is not just another tower; it has ambitions every bit as explicit as the Great Hall of the People to represent China's place in the world, and its new-found might. In the years since Deng Xiaoping took the first steps toward unleashing China's economic potential, Beijing has built a vast number of new buildings, many of them designed by foreign architects with international reputations. But with the exception of the Fragrant Hills Hotel, I. M. Pei's fruitless attempt to show the land of his birth that modernity did not have to mean the destruction of Beijing's extraordinary urban fabric, few have yet shown any real architectural ambition. However, CCTV was looking for something more than simply another large building.

Koolhaas was invited to take part in a competition that was intended to produce something spectacular, but the competition was organized by people who had no idea what that something could be, even if they saw it. A building emerges from such a process the product of a whole series of small decisions and accidents, as well as political lobbying, and the manufacture of consensus. Not the least of those accidents was the choice of jurors. Among them was a close friend of Koolhaas's, Charles Jencks. According to Jencks, whose book on postmodernism was first translated into Mandarin in 1986, "The rhetorical part of the brief was describing the Guggenheim in Bilbao. Though height was not mentioned, they clearly wanted a landmark."

Jencks recalls his initial caution. "I was afraid of being duped, that whatever I said would be used to endorse what might turn out to be a different outcome from the jury's decision."

He was eager to depoliticize what some see as an essentially political process. "I am here for architecture independent of any other considerations," he announced at the jury's opening session, a meeting full of silence with a room full of people still reluctant to voice an opinion.

"We were taken to a resort outside Beijing with an artificial lake. It felt like a British country house in a Kansas wheat field. There were lots of fences and gates, and a very prestigious classical gleaming white marble hotel. We were being isolated in a cocoon. It was building the mentality of a team, in a way that some people might find sinister," says Jencks. Behind the jury sat a whole row of officials, taking notes. "There was the sense that if CCTV made the wrong decision, it would be tough on those who took that decision. It felt a bit like Mandarin times, when people spent a whole lifetime taking a single exam. How could you take a risk when everyone is taking notes?"

The competition had been interpreted by two of the American architects taking part, who between them had designed Shanghai's two tallest buildings, the Jin Mao Building, with its tapering supposedly Chinese geometry, and the knitting-needle-shaped Shanghai World Financial Center for the Mori Corporation, as an invitation to build another skyscraper in the same mold. Koolhaas won because he didn't. "Rem saw at once that in a central business district with 300 towers, building the 301st tower was not going to create a landmark," Jencks explains.

Koolhaas's design is not a tower, it's not a slab, it's not even a ziggurat. The design suggests an alien architectural species, an extraterrestrial life-form from another galaxy gasping to breathe through its fishy gills in the unfamiliar oxygen-rich atmosphere of Earth. Cecil Balmond, the engineer working on the design, makes a direct comparison with another high-rise icon: "Cut the loop, unfold the pieces, and you end up with the twin towers of the World Trade Center."

Rather than projecting smooth technocratic efficiency or nostalgia for the golden days of the Empire State and the Chrysler Buildings, the two poles of contemporary high-rise architecture, CCTV has a certain roughness—even a random accidental quality.

Aware that a competition jury's verdict is never enough on its own to secure a project, Jencks set about organizing consent, marshaling arguments in favor of Koolhaas's design that would make its outlandish form seem acceptable to the Chinese hierarchy. He described the design in terms of its evocation of Chinese tradition—issues that Koolhaas himself had never mentioned in his presentation. "It is a Chinese moon gate, a framed hole, or the heavy shape made in bronze and jade thousands of years ago in China as a symbol of exchange." But Jencks wanted to cover other positive aspects of the design too, to make sure that he could not be outflanked by those arguing that China at this stage in its development should be looking forward and not back. It would be not just a Chinese icon; it would be understood in any culture. "It's a pop image, it can be seen as suggesting the Arc de Triomphe, or the Grande Arche."

The jury struggled to push a state corporation into spending more money than it had planned to, on a project that would stretch China's engineering and construction capabilities to the limit. Building a leaning tower of this scale in an earthquake zone is without question taking a risk.

Koolhaas himself knew that he would have to fight for the project, which was clearly more expensive than both of the other two frontrunners, Ito's design and that of the Shanghai Architecture Institute. Koolhaas remade his model to make it easier for CCTV officials to understand, and it was sent off on a tour of the villas of hierarchy as part of a strenuous lobbying campaign.

How tense this process became is reflected in the more than three months that passed between the jury's decision and a public announcement. Even a year after that, the foundation stone still hadn't been laid. Skeptics suggested that the regime still wasn't convinced that it should go ahead with the Koolhaas design. There was more at stake than architecture in the CCTV project. China is still a country that imprisons journalists, that persecutes its dissidents, and that is ruled by an autocracy which refuses to loosen its grip on the state, despite its lack of interest in ideology. And Koolhaas's building is understood by some critics as playing a part in maintaining that hold.

"What should one make of famous architects competing to build a new HQ for Central China Television?" asked the writer Ian Buruma before the result of the competition had been announced. "Unless one takes the view that all business with China is evil, there is nothing reprehensible about building an opera house in Beijing, or indeed a hotel, a university, or a corporate headquarters. But state television is something else: CCTV is the voice of the party, the center of state propaganda, the organ which tells a billion people what to think." China's capitalism is the kind that comes with an absolute prohibition of independent trade unions. It is not a society that believes in consultation, or social welfare. Nor has it developed a legal system yet that will defend its citizens against either state or private enterprise. Buruma continued, "It's hard to imagine a cool European architect in the 1970s building a television station for Pinochet."

Koolhaas refused to take part in New York's Ground Zero design competitions. He said they were an attempt to create a monument to self-pity on a Stalinist scale. Yet at exactly the same moment, he strained every muscle to get his hands on the job of building Beijing's tallest towers, in the service of a state that can hardly be described as less authoritarian than America.

When questioned about the ethical implications, his first response was to suggest that China's system is changing so fast that, by the time his building is completed, CCTV will have been privatized, and China will have given up repression as a political tool. It is unlikely that Mies van der Rohe would have had a very sympathetic hearing if he had won the 1933 competition for the Reichsbank in Berlin and advanced a similar argument about the bright future promised by the imminent economic transformation of Hitler's Germany, although it's exactly what Philip Johnson was suggesting when he pushed Mies for the job.

When Koolhaas staged a retrospective of his own work in Berlin in the New National Gallery designed by Mies, he splashed the title of the show, "Content," dripping simulated spatters of yellow paint across its immaculate bronze-tinted glass walls, as if in reproach to the void at the heart of Mies's sublime building. If you ventured inside, you found an effigy of Koolhaas himself. It's a doll, made by the artist Tony Oursler, impaled on a steel rod emerging from the middle of a pile of discarded and broken models. Its miniature black shirt and its gray striped trousers, just like Koolhaas's, were clearly meant to suggest that they came from Prada. A digital projection of the architect's face played over the doll's blank white head. If you listened carefully you could catch snatches of him reading from one of his essays about "junk space." It could have been a lament for all the dead projects in the show. His abandoned plans for a new film studio for Universal in Hollywood, dropped when Vivendi aquired the company. The megalomaniac scheme to save the Los Angeles County Museum of Art's twenty-acre complex by demolishing it, the architectural version of General Westmoreland's strategy for Vietnam, scrapped when it failed to persuade L.A.'s voters to fund it. The Las Vegas Guggenheim, closed for lack of visitors a year after it opened. The scheme to extend the Whitney in New York with a banana-shaped tower bursting out of Marcel Breuer's sober ziggurat, aborted after three years' work at a cost that included the museum director's job.

It's a litany of disappointment that forced Koolhaas to look for work outside America. He couldn't help himself but find reasons beyond expediency to justify the switch in continents, represented at its sharpest by his fit of bad temper over the Ground Zero competition. Koolhaas's own autobiography was suddenly turned into the pretext for some sort of historical watershed. He paraded his belief that a vibrant Asia has culturally eclipsed a stagnant, intellectually bankrupt America, after accepting a commission from a glossy magazine publisher in New York to devise teenage magazines. Would he be quite so bitter if Eli Broad and Ian Schrager and the board of the Whitney had not all chosen to dispense with his services? And when Seattle finally opened Koolhaas's Public Library to a universally warm response, Koolhaas himself softened somewhat in his attitude to America.

According to Charles Jencks, Koolhaas was decisively influenced by

Andy Warhol's book *From A to B and Back Again*, but Warhol would never have allowed his personal feelings to become so transparent.

To some degree, Koolhaas's career can be seen as a process of dead-pan acting out in the blank Warholian manner. At various points he has modeled himself on Skidmore, Owings and Merrill, Le Corbusier, and Mies van der Rohe. When Koolhaas and his early mentor, Elia Zenghelis, established an architectural practice in London, they called it the Office of Metropolitan Architecture, an ironic attempt to pitch themselves at the midpoint between North American technocracy and Stalinist centralism, even as they worked from a kitchen table and struggled to pay their photocopying bills. Koolhaas and Zenghelis parted company, leaving Koolhaas in command of the OMA name. He went to Rotterdam, where he created a parody of a big corporate American architectural practice. It was housed in an appropriately bland office slab rather than the usual converted warehouse, but with a bargain-basement rent and a workforce looking like students just out of their teens rather than crew-cut types with bow ties.

But really it is Le Corbusier that obsesses Koolhaas. He has mirrored every stage of Le Corbusier's career in his own person. He shows some sympathy for Le Corbusier's self-flagellating paranoid belief that the world is against him, even as it presses new commissions on him. He also has Le Corbusier's prodigious appetite for words—no architect has published so many pages as Koolhaas. He has even, after an initial love affair for Manhattan, acquired something of Le Corbusier's contempt for America. And since he has been working in China, he appears to have caught up with Le Corbusier's authoritarian phase. Le Corbusier was associated with right-wing French politics in the 1920s, courted Mussolini in the 1930s, and then Marshal Pétain and Vichy France in the early 1940s. Koolhaas's most important client is the Chinese Communist party. And he seems to have embraced strong government in his apparent enthusiasm to find a patron for his designs. Today's China may not be Mussolini's Italy, but it's not a liberal democracy either.

"What attracts me about China is that there is still a state. There is something that can take initiative on a scale and of a nature that almost no other body that we know of today could ever afford or contemplate," he told one interviewer. "Everywhere else, and particularly in architecture, money is everything now. So that is blatantly not a good situation as it leads to compromises of quality. Money is a less fundamental tenet of their ideology."

Koolhaas has not always been so dismissive of the power of money. "I think it's very important to say that we live without complaint, fear or trust under the following regime that you see here: the major currencies of the world, the Yen, the Euro, and the Dollar," he wrote in *The Harvard Guide to Shopping*. "They describe a regime that sets our parameters, and those parameters are fairly immutable. But on the other hand, it is also a regime that gives us an almost unbelievable amount of freedom to establish our own trajectories within it." Of course, that was when he was attempting to find a way to demonstrate that it was possible to maintain a critical detachment when working for Prada and a Las Vegas casino, rather than the Chinese Communist party. Now he is doing both at the same time, searching the streets of Shanghai for a suitable place to build an outlet for Prada, and monumentalizing the new China.

Koolhaas has come to grow increasingly impatient with criticism: "Participation in China's modernization does not have a guaranteed outcome. The future of China is the most compelling conundrum. Its outcome affects all of us. A position of resistance seems somehow ornamental. On our own, we can at most have good intentions. But we cannot represent the public good, without the larger entity, such as the state. To make matters worse, the more radical, innovative and brotherly our sentiments, the more we architects need a strong sponsor."

It does not sound like the architect who managed the feat of building a museum in Las Vegas's simulacrum of the Doge's palace, and who spent $30 million building a clothes shop in what had once been the SoHo branch of the Guggenheim for Prada. For much the same combination of enthusiasm, image building, and self-indulgence, the company has poured almost as much money into contemporary architecture as it has put into building gigantic sailing boats for the America's Cup.

At least for Koolhaas, who clearly had no personal interest in accumulating wealth, if not for the rest of the stream of architects now being drawn to Beijing, the real attraction of China is the chance to be at the center of what is clearly the defining urban project of the twenty-first century. He claims that his 700-foot-tall structure is not a traditional tower but is rather a "continuous loop of horizontal and vertical sections that establish an urban site, rather than point to the sky." The project is a chance to establish himself as the inventor of a new form of high-rise building, and to provide the vindicating project of his entire career. "I want to kill the traditional idea of the skyscraper—it has run out of energy," he told the BBC when he won the Royal Gold Medal for Architecture.

While the CCTV design looks willful and counterintuitive as a structure, Koolhaas and Cecil Balmond, his engineer collaborator, claim that it has an underlying logic. The two main towers lean toward each other and are connected at the top with a ten-floor L-shaped wing that juts out into space; there is a similar balancing block at ground level. To the non-expert eye, it looks as if the unsupported section of structure spanning across the void is increasing the load on the two towers. In fact it allows them to stabilize each other, so reducing the quantity of reinforcing steel needed to build the scheme. Propping is one of the two basic principles on which the structural design is based. The other is what Balmond calls the skin. Externally the towers will have a mesh of diagonal bracing in a seemingly random pattern. Rather like the creases on human skin, the greatest concentrations of lines occur at points of maximum stress. "I knew that there would be some places where you want a lot of bracing, others where you don't," says Balmond. Together, the skin and the propping allow the interiors of both towers to be free of columns, except for a single row around the elevators, which acts as the backbone of the building. The original idea was to incline the elevators, at 6 degrees, parallel to the slope of the towers, like a particularly steep funicular railway. Every floor would have had the same plan, just shifted by a few meters. But it turned out to be too expensive and too complicated, so the elevators are vertical, skewering the sloping towers like kebabs. The skin belongs to the same family as the exposed diagonal bracing of Chicago's heroic tapering John Hancock Center. The steel-box beams of the CCTV towers will be just as muscular and impressive as Chicago's, wider than a man is tall, and almost as deep by the time they reach the ground.

This is an attempt to push the high-rise building into entirely new territory. To build it, Koolhaas is ready to risk everything. Designing a shop for Prada, or a hotel for Disney, or a Hollywood film studio, still allows him to maintain a nuanced distance from his clients. It is a nuance whose meaning has not escaped the old men of the Central Committee who will be paying for the CCTV project. They did not get there without aquiring a detailed understanding of the realities of power.

For Koolhaas, working in China brings with it the belief that he is moving from mere theory into the making of history. He needs China—but not as much, he believes, as China needs people like him. It is an illusion shared by many architects in their dealings with power. Yung Ho Chang's father had ten years to reflect on it, while sweeping the floor during the Cultural Revolution. Both father and son have confronted the essential dilemma of architecture. Their work has brought them into an intimate relationship with power, but they have remained powerless in the hands of those who wield it.

Architecture defines a regime, but it is never the architect who frames the meaning of the definition. Zhang Kaiji's Maoist patrons wanted to construct Beijing as a city that reflected and enforced their power. His son works within a system that has embraced the market, but in which the architect is even less in command.

For CCTV, building a vast skyscraper that looks like nothing else in the world is the architectural equivalent of the Chinese space program, or the Three Gorges Dam. Koolhaas is trying to move beyond the projection of sheer size as a signal of power. He is offering another message: that CCTV's prestige can be reinforced through cultural innovation rather than by using the more conventional architectural signals.

Koolhaas, at sixty, has never attempted to build anything even remotely approaching the size of this project. The fact that the Chinese agreed to hire him was based on the reputation of Arup, the engineering firm led by Cecil Balmond that he is working with. The successful completion of the building depends entirely on the warmth of Koolhaas's relationship with his engineers. Any cracks in it will open up the possibility of a repeat performance in Beijing of Jørn Utzon's inability to complete the Sydney Opera House. But for China, it offers the prospect of finally moving beyond an attempt to build a representation of a repressive ideology, and of instead constructing a new version of the country's national identity.

Switch on CCTV and, instead of the clunky propaganda that you might expect, you get MTV-style graphics and, in English at least, a tone that appears to be from the 1950s in its style, with respectful, measured coverage of the news, a far more convincing package for the party line than harping on about the Great Helmsman. In the same way a Koolhaas building is a visible demonstration that the Chinese state is no longer an out-of-touch, culturally backward dinosaur. It may be one of the last nominally Communist regimes left in the world, but China has no intention of going the way of North Korea's hermit kingdom.

The focus of demolition in Beijing is shifting from the center toward the Olympic area north of the city. Officially the site is called a park. But this was a busy residential area once, full of little gray-walled houses, workshops, and stores. A huge area has been cleared by bulldozers as effectively as the firestorms caused by American bombing raids gave Tokyo its postwar canvas. For months after the bulldozers had gone, traders brought their donkey carts to pick over the rubble, scavenging for bricks and roof timbers to salvage and sell, before the soil was covered in plastic sheeting, to keep down the dust that plagues Beijing and the site was hidden behind corrugated iron walls.

China is using the games to signal that it has moved beyond the sweatshop economy characterized by low-wage commodity production, bicycles, and social conformity. Stung by criticisms of its murky approach to the allocation of construction contracts, Beijing's municipal government has been proclaiming its determination to pursue design excellence and maintain a fairer tendering process. That is why the competition to design the Olympic Stadium had an unwieldy, thirteen-strong jury. Seven Chinese experts sat alongside Rem Koolhaas and two French architects, Jean Nouvel and Dominique Perrault, the last three representing the interests of the flying circus of the perpetually jet-lagged. Submissions came mainly from the usual collection of firms, known only by their initials, that have come to dominate international stadium design by turning out an interchangeable series of huge spectator machines that can process crowds quickly and efficiently yet entirely lack personality or charisma. In this context, the appointment of Jacques Herzog and Pierre de Meuron is certainly a sophisticated choice. It demonstrates that China has reached the stage where it does not need to do the obvious thing. But in an echo of the planning methods of the Mao era, a precise date and time was set to begin construction of the Olympic Stadium, even before the architects had been selected.

Their design is both radical and simple. It will be the most distinctive Olympic stadium since the building of Munich's Teflon-coated tents three decades ago. The architects call it a bird's nest. It is formed from an apparently random pattern of structural bands rising out of the ground to create the stadium bowl, like a gigantic piece of papier-mâché. The structure is composed of a network of threads of concrete woven together. "We wanted to get away from the usual technocratic stadiums, with their architecture dominated by structural spans and digital screens," said Herzog. "It is simple and almost archaically direct in its spatial impact. The architecture is the crowd, the proportions are intended to shift the spectators and the track and field events into the fore-ground." In this it will be a forum with a character that is almost exactly the opposite of Tiananmen Square, which was designed to reduce the crowd to passivity, with no sense of itself and its own presence. The stadium by contrast will celebrate the people's presence.

There is a certain symmetry in the presence of both Rem Koolhaas and Jacques Herzog in Beijing at the same time, working on such significant projects. They like to see themselves as the Picasso and Braque of contemporary architecture, towering over their peers in the same way that the two cubists once monopolized painting, "roped together like mountaineers for the final onslaught on the summit," as Braque put it.

Herzog and Koolhaas have indeed set out to collaborate with each other from time to time. There was talk of a joint project to design Tate Modern, before Herzog and de Meuron won the competition to build it on their own. Later they worked on a plan for a hotel in New York for Ian Schrager, but that was torpedoed by Koolhaas's way of breezily antagonizing his client. In their personalities, and in their architecture, Koolhaas, restless, gifted, and erratic, is everything that Herzog, subtle and calm, is not.

At various stages in his career, Koolhaas has expressed a lacerating contempt for his fellow professionals, a nihilistic despair at the possibility of making architecture in the contemporary world at all, and a complete lack of interest in the material qualities of building. Herzog and his partner, Pierre de Meuron, by contrast have realized a series of designs that brilliantly demonstrate that these qualities are indeed still profoundly at the root of architecture. Their two projects in Beijing demonstrate precisely this divide: Koolhaas's leaning towers are an ideological statement; Herzog's stadium is an architectural one that nevertheless embraces a humanistic view of the world. And in this sense they could be seen as reflecting precisely the divide between Zhang Bo and Zhang Kaiji on opposite sides of Tiananmen Square.

Both Koolhaas and Herzog have made more headway in Beijing than

Albert Speer, the son of Hitler's architect, who invested considerable energy in lobbying the city's authorities to take up his plan for a fifteen-mile-long north–south axis for the city, with the Olympic Stadium at one end and a huge new railway station at the other linked by a series of tree-lined freeways. Speer is an urbane, spry man approaching seventy. If it wasn't for his name, he would be the personification of postwar Germany, the worthy Bonn-based republic of serious newspapers and liberal politics, where ecology and competently managed car factories are taken for granted. I meet him in his sun-filled Frankfurt office with its blond wood floor and its atrium full of primary-colored art. Speer would rather be in Beijing, but in the spring of 2003, the SARS epidemic has made him cautious about traveling there. He is, however, still busy in Germany, where he worked on Leipzig's unsuccessful bid for the 2012 Olympics, surrealistically in partnership with Peter Eisenman, the architect of Berlin's Holocaust memorial, itself built on the site of his father's studio, where Hitler and the elder Speer spent hour upon hour with the model of Germania.

"What I always try to do is to find a politician who will take my plans, look at them, and say, this is my idea—then it works," says Speer. He is talking about how to turn his plan for the north–south axis into a reality in time for the Olympics. I feel an overwhelming urge to ask if this strategy is a lesson that he learned from his father. I want to snatch the gold chain, the only discordant note in his otherwise impeccably understated outfit of fine cashmere and tweed, from his trouser pocket, grab the watch dangling from it, to see if it is a legacy from his father and check it for incriminating inscriptions. A tiny, paranoid fraction of my mind half suspects that the words *"Auf Albert Nach Adolf"* will be engraved on the back in thick Gothic script.

The scale of his scheme eclipses even his father's work for Adolf Hitler and his axis for Berlin. But as an understanding of how the Chinese state works, Speer's strategy is rather less sophisticated than Koolhaas's. There is a certain bathos in Speer's belief in the power of architectural will to impose a sense of order in the chaos of contemporary Beijing. Koolhaas by contrast is a connoisseur of chaos.

China is a place where western architects come in search of work, or to gawk on the edge of the urban abyss of monstrous, uncontrollable growth in much the way that Friedrich Engels and William Morris used to visit nineteenth-century Manchester looking for the same frisson of confronting the unthinkable.

What nobody really understands yet is how the inscrutable set of rules that govern Beijing's startling transformations will work, which is what makes Speer with his neo-Haussmann approach seem so quaintly irrelevant. Lining up Beijing's museums in neat rows as Speer proposes is not going to do much to change the lives of the city's displaced victims of development. And still less can anyone foresee what will become of the city, with its six ring roads and its diminutive subway system, when it starts to approach western levels of car ownership. It is already difficult enough to negotiate with one car for every seven inhabitants.

Beijing is a city that is changing so fast that there is even a chance that it may manage to finesse its way out of the grip of a party organization that is no longer Communist but is still ruthless. If it acquires the street life and the public realm of an authentic city, then it could support a culture more independent of the regime. If that happens, then Koolhaas could be off the hook.

IN 1949, A WORKMAN PAINTED A STRIPE ACROSS THE COBBLEstones of the Potsdamer Platz to demarcate the line between the British and Russian sectors of Berlin, and so defined the fault line between two warring world orders. The Potsdamer Platz was as battered then as the center of Sarajevo is today. It was still dominated by the smokeblackened serpentine façade of Erich Mendelsohn's Columbushaus, a department store and office building from the 1930s that became a base for the Gestapo. The tangle of tramlines and the stone hulks of the buildings whose clifflike frontages once defined Central Europe's version of Times Square were still visible.

The workers' riots of the 1950s turned the Potsdamer Platz into a battlefield. Then the building of the Wall caused the entire area to revert to scrub, inhabited only by wild foxes. What had been the center of one of Europe's greatest cities turned into a wasteland at the edge of two provincial backwaters that no longer spoke to each other.

The stalemate came to an abrupt end with the reunification of the two Germanys. For Berlin the destruction of the Wall was the urban equivalent of the Big Bang. It was like two soap bubbles colliding and turning into one with a rush of air. The scrub briefly became some of the most sought-after development land in Europe. In the euphoria of reunification, definitions of the new shape of Berlin ranged from the utopian dreams of the city's Greens, who talked of turning the line of the old Wall into a nature reserve, to those who wanted a clump of skyscrapers to rival lower Manhattan.

The crucial sites, the ones that spanned the wall (the Potsdamer Platz and the Pariser Platz), were acquired within weeks of reunification by a consortium of developers. Despite the attempts of the city's planners to take charge, the building of the new Berlin has essentially been in the hands of a group of multinationals and developers, who staged a succession of architectural competitions to help give legitimacy to their schemes. Sony chose Helmut Jahn, a German-born architect who has worked in Chicago since the 1960s, to build their plaza. Renzo Piano designed Daimler Benz's site. An acrimonious row accompanied the city's own competition to choose a designer to draw up planning guidelines for the development of the site as whole, to which Piano's design was supposed to conform. The judges fell out, calling one another dilettantes, provincials, and philistines.

Unlike China, which has been under the control of a monolithic party regime for the six decades of its existence, Germany in the same period moved from the Third Reich to four-power occupation, to the division between the Federal Republic and the Democratic Republic, and then to reunification. And each regime has attempted to make its mark on Berlin's urban landscape to undo the legacy of its predecessors and impose its own identity and authority.

In 1945 the Soviets rushed to seize as many of the landmarks of power in the city center as they could. The ministries and the museums, the universities and the opera house were all occupied by the Red Army before the western allies could get to Berlin. Only the Reichstag was in western hands, and with the federal parliament transplanted to Bonn, it had no obvious role left.

In 1949 the Russian occupiers made the decision to demolish Hitler's damaged but substantially intact Chancellery, to erase the physical legacy of the old regime. And they used the salvaged stone to build Berlin's huge Soviet War Memorial.

The German Democratic Republic had other targets. Ignoring the protests of his own architects and art historians, East German leader Walter Ulbricht decided to demolish Berlin's royal palace, which was built over several centuries. The ostensible reason was that it was too badly damaged and too costly for the country to be able to afford to restore it. In fact it can only be seen as an attempt to erase the architectural history of the city in order to construct a new socialist order, following in the footsteps of Stalin's Moscow and prefiguring Mao's Tiananmen Square. Indeed, there was a proposal to bring Karl Marx's remains back from Highgate Cemetery in London and build a tomb at the heart of Marx-Engels-Platz, in a conscious echo of Lenin's mausoleum in Red Square.

Ulbricht was later to declare to a party congress, "The center of our capital, the Lustgarten and the site of the palace ruins, must become a great demonstration ground where the will of our people to fight and reconstruct can find expression."

The massive stone palace, with its baroque façades, its corner dome, its two inner courtyards, and its twelve hundred rooms, was dynamited in September 1950. "May it no longer remind us of an inglorious past," proclaimed a triumphalist party newspaper. It made no comment, however, when Göring's Air Ministry building was transformed into the GDR's House of Ministries by the simple addition of East Germany's hammer and compass insignia to the exterior.

Clearing the rubble from the site of the Hohenzollerns' palace to create what was named Marx-Engels-Platz took another four months. Ulbricht led the Politburo as they trooped onto a specially built tribune to take the salute at the May Day parade in 1951. The East German architect Edmund Collein worked on a classical high-rise building to take the place of the palace in approved Stalinist style, but it was never built. With Stalin's death, East German architecture went through a sea change.

Part of Khrushchev's denunciation of Stalin's excesses involved a new dispensation on architecture: "Soviet architecture must be characterized by simplicity, austerity of form, and economy of layout. Buildings must be given an attractive appearance, not through the use of contrived expensive decorative ornamentalism, but by an organic connection between the architectural form of the building and its purpose, between good proportions and a proper use of materials, structures and detailing, and through high quality workmanship." There is, Khrushchev said, "no need to transform a modern apartment block into a church or a museum." Over the next decades, Marx-Engels-Platz began to fill up with buildings that give a taste of how the Forbidden City in Beijing would have looked if the plan to demolish it had materialized.

The square was originally conceived as a piece of Stalinist urbanism, but its architectural language belonged to another moment. It is a simultaneous expression of two very different messages. The GDR was playing its part in the overthrow of Stalin's cult of personality, loyally following the path set for it by his successors in Moscow, on a site that was originally created as a mark of allegiance to Stalin. At the same time, the GDR was trying to build a convincing capital for a shrunken rump state. Michael Wise, in his account of the rebuilding of Berlin, quotes Joachin Nather, East Berlin's chief architect between 1964 and 1973, who describes these developments as driven by "a raging passion for power, and a raging passion for recognition." The rebuilding of the center of Berlin was shaped "by a desire to send a signal that we are here, we are not going away."

Immediately after the construction of the Berlin Wall (the Anti-Fascist Rampart, as the GDR called it), in itself the most telling architectural symbol of the regime, Ulbricht commissioned Roland Korn and Hans-Enze Bogatzky to build the Council of State Building on Marx-Engels-Platz. This was where he entertained all those visiting heads of state who were prepared to ignore the Bonn government's threats to break off diplomatic relations if they recognized the East.

Korn and Bogatzky's building uses granite, sandstone, and glass in a manner that would have suggested modernity in its context, and incorporates the only fragment salvaged from the Hohenzollern palace, the balcony from which Karl Liebknecht proclaimed the German Soviet in 1919 shortly before being murdered by a right-wing militia. The balcony forms part of a slice of the baroque building that goes from the ground to the cornice, projecting forward of the main façade. Its richly detailed moldings, pilasters, and cornices make the thin-lipped façade around it look mean and pinched.

The Council of State was followed by another piece of gratuitous destruction on the west side of Marx-Engels-Platz. Schinkel's pioneering Prussian state architecture school was demolished in 1961 to make way for the GDR's Foreign Ministry, a twelve-story slab faced in white aluminium that crashed through the traditional height limit that gave Berlin its character. The television mast on the Alexanderplatz was finished in 1969, with its height of 1200 feet and its position driven mainly by the determination to make its presence felt in every corner of West Berlin.

Proudly, Ulbricht's successor, Erich Honecker, tried to demonstrate that the German Democratic Republic was as capable of creating banal modern buildings as anybody else. He built the Palast der Republik, with the kind of brash orange mirror-glass façades newly, and briefly, fashionable in America at the time. Finished in 1976, it stands more or less on the site of the old palace courtyard. As a building, the Palast der Republik was an intriguing mixture of the formal and the informal. It housed a parliamentary chamber that, although it sat only occasionally, was the setting for post-Communist East Germany's free vote in favor of reunification with the West. But there was also a theater and concert hall, a bowling alley, and an array of restaurants that actually accepted East German marks, putting them within reach of ordinary East Berliners. The interior was a blizzard of tufted velvet banquettes, swirling op art patterns on the floor, and cascading crystal chandeliers that seemed to represent the triumph of disco over dialectical materialism. The main façade was adorned with a huge state seal, the same hammer and compass attached to the old Air Ministry, and a tribune for reviewing the May Day parade.

West Berlin's response was to create its own vision of a modern city, albeit one that precious few East Germans would see for another two decades. East Berlin's Stalin Allee was a reflection of Beaux-Arts planning. The Kulturforum, the epitome of modernist urbanism, of objects swimming in space, was the response of Berlin's western suburbs attempting to replace the cultural institutions lost to the east. Hans Scharoun built the Philharmonic Hall at exactly the same time that the East was building the Wall. He went on to design West Berlin's new library, while on the other side of the forum Mies van der Rohe built his last great work, completing the New National Gallery in 1968, shortly before he died. Its construction involved demolishing the remains of the German House of Tourism, the only section of Speer's north–south axis for Berlin to have actually been built.

In the West, even the most modest traces of the past were the subject of anxious argument. Should they be eradicated to protect us from a recurrence of the malevolence they represent, or should they be retained as a reminder of German guilt and a warning of the horrors that Nazism was capable of? A few even argued that Speer's surviving architectural work should be preserved because of its intrinsic aesthetic merit.

Alfred Kerndl, head of the municipal archaeological office in the reunified Berlin, argued in terms of historical significance rather than aesthetic quality when workmen digging close to the site of the Chancellery discovered the bunker used by the SS guard unit protecting Hitler in the closing days of World War II. He wanted to move the crude, racially offensive murals they found inside to the German Historical Museum. Christopher Stolzin, the museum's director, busy transforming the museum from a Prussian arsenal to a modern monument with the inevitable I. M. Pei addition, refused to take them. But Norman Foster did manage to persuade Chancellor Helmut Kohl to preserve the chalk and paint cyrillic graffiti left by victorious Russian soldiers on the pockmarked walls of the Reichstag behind glass within his remodeling of the building.

THE FIERCEST ARGUMENT ABOUT REBUILDING BERLIN HAS BEEN between those who, like Berlin's city building director Hans Stimman, wanted to restore the city's character of dense urban blocks, soberly designed, with regular window patterns, following as much as possible the old street lines, and to preserve the memory of the events that had shaped the city, and those who wanted to erase them to create an entirely new city.

The new Germany was less prepared to wipe out the traces of Hitler's Berlin than it was ready to eradicate the traces of the GDR. The Palast der Republik was abandoned when it was found to be riddled with dangerous asbestos. The East German Foreign Ministry was demolished with no regrets in 1996, triggering a campaign to reconstruct the Schinkel building that had stood on the site.

For almost a year in the mid-1990s, you could have seen a ghostly glimpse of an icon of the lost Berlin, the Prussian city. A businessman from Hamburg called Wilhelm von Boddien paid for a team of art students to paint a trompe l'oeil image of the old Hohenzollern royal palace demolished at Walter Ulbricht's command in 1950, as part of his campaign for its reconstruction. Just as the destruction of the palace had been used to symbolize the triumph of the Communist system, so its reconstruction would demonstrate the system's final extinction. Working from old photographs and drawings, they created the illusion of the palace's baroque façades on a strip of canvas, following its original outline as closely as they could. But if the project ever comes to fruition, this would not be the re-creation of the city that the Prussian monarchs built. The center of the new Berlin is the product of a group of developers funded by Sony and Mercedes stumbling to fill the vacuum left by fifty years of uncertainty.

The Federal Republic's Foreign Ministry, meanwhile, was in the process of moving from Bonn into a relic of the Nazi period: the Reichsbank. Originally built to a design selected personally by Hitler, the building was deftly converted for its new role by Hans Kolhoff. And the old Air Ministry commissioned by Göring has been restored a second time, purged of the East German hammer and compass, its Nazi iconography tactfully kept out of sight. A layer of white paint, Eames chairs, and spotlights was considered inoculation enough against the potential danger of contagion from both incarnations of its past. But despite the widespread protests in the East against the loss of the Palast der Republick, the Bundestag voted to demolish the building and, when funds become available, to authorize the reconstruction of the façades of the old royal palace—at a cost of at least 400 million euros. In the meantime, the deadly asbestos had been painstakingly extracted and the marble and the lights and the swirling op art stripped out, giving the interior a new, sparse modernity as it awaits its fate.

The price of the Federal Republic's decency seemed to be an absolute prohibition on monumental architecture. In 1949, in the same year that Mao claimed his capital, the Federal Republic of Germany was also establishing itself a new capital in Bonn. It was in many ways the mirror opposite of Beijing—its first parliament building was a former teacher training college. It's a theme that permeated German postwar thinking on design and architecture. For example, the distinguished graphic designer Otl Aicher, a founder of the Ulm school of design, the originator of Lufthansa's modern corporate identity and the man who devised the rotis typeface, was prepared to follow Adolf Loos and argue that the very use of the capital letters meant that German typography had contributed toward making an authoritarian culture possible. And when the British architect and D-day veteran James Stirling won the competition to design a new building for Stuttgart's Neue Staatsgalerie, a building with a monumental classical plan, he was accused by at least one leading German architect of returning to the forbidden territory of the recent past and producing a Nazi building. Architecture had been such an essential part of the presentation of the Reich that the postwar period went to the opposite extreme.

What had been one of Europe's leading architectural cultures in the 1920s and 1930s, the home of the Bauhaus and the avante-garde Ring group, has turned into a backwater. So much so that Austria, with 9 million inhabitants, has produced far more architecture of interest than pre-unification Germany, with 70 million people.

CHAPTER 6

INVENTING A NATION

WELL BEFORE THE START OF THE GENOCIDAL WARS OF SUCCESSION that tore much of the former country of Yugoslavia into blood-soaked shreds, its two most independent-minded components, Slovenia and Croatia, had already begun to think about the aesthetics as well as the mechanics of making a nation. While they were still part of Yugoslavia's federal government, manufacturing the iconography of their own nationhood was as significant for their leaderships as was planning military action to escape the clutches of Slobodan Milosevic. The one was inextricably linked with the other.

Creating the imagery of a state and successfully applying it to as large a territory as is plausible can be seen as warfare by other means. And sometimes by the same means. When states or potential states attempt to destroy one another's shrines, parliaments, and palaces, extreme acts of violence are involved.

How the Slovenes and the Croats were going to assert their sense of themselves in a visible form was an issue that preoccupied both states in the winter of 1990. Persuading their own people to risk their lives for an ideal of independence was one thing. Patriotic or tribal sensibilities run deep in this part of the world. Getting oil shippers and arms suppliers and European air-traffic-control authorities and the International Monetary Fund to acknowledge their independent statehood was another issue altogether. What would make Slovenian and Croatian banknotes accepted as worth more than the paper that they were printed on? What would make western governments recognize the ambassador of an alleged state with no flag or national anthem, let alone an embassy? What would persuade Heathrow or Frankfurt to provide airliners with landing rights, when the airline had no name and no logo?

Most of the answers to these questions, despite the sinister fantasies of the more gullible of nationalists, turned out to be technical rather than instinctive. What was needed was the development of what might be called the architecture of the state: the official insignias of power and authority that help define countries to both internal and external audiences. They are of course artificially created and depend for their success on the confidence—even the sleight of hand—with which they are applied. Some countries are better at this than others, even the most cohesive of them. But to suggest that there are pragmatic or manipulative ways of creating a sense of national identity is to puncture the great myth of nationalism: that it is somehow innate and as inevitable as mother's milk.

State architecture is successful to the extent that it can rapidly take on the quality of inevitability. Architecture has been important to nation builders since even before the time of the Romans and their determination to use the same town plan for every settlement, from their frontier forts guarding against the Picts in the north to Libya in the south. In a faint echo of the same strategy, the British left their municipal architecture and their red cast-iron postboxes everywhere they went. Look at the remaining fragments of British Shanghai, the surviving residential compounds of New Delhi, or the post offices of New South Wales, and there is no doubt what the architecture is vainly trying to tell you: that this territory is part of a cohesive whole, and even its remotest fringes belong to the center.

JUST AS IMPORTANT A NATIONALIST SIGNAL IN MANY CULTURES AS government and official buildings are religious structures. Religion and national identity have a way of going hand in hand. In the lead-up to the conflict in Yugoslavia, the Croats and the Serbs engaged in a bout of competitive church building in order to lay claim to disputed areas. It was immediately visible which side was which. The Roman Catholic Croats built demonstratively modern churches, in concrete and glass. The Orthodox Serbs built equally demonstrative Byzantine-domed "traditional" structures in stone and tile. The message was not just about which community an area belonged to. The Croat churches seemed to be suggesting that they belonged to a state looking west rather than east. Of course this might not have been a deliberate message. Perhaps the image of what constituted a church was simply different in the two communities. Or again, it could be that Croatia in 1990 provided a more sympathetic climate for contemporary architecture than Serbia. That openness to the new might also be understood as part of a program to use culture in a deliberate effort to create a distinctive identity. Such a use of architectural style can be described as a kind of cultural nationalism, a tactic with which the Croats and the Serbs were both familiar. All the Marxist states were inculcated in the political uses of culture.

Once the Balkan Wars had started, the obverse side of this policy was the deliberate targeting for destruction of the architectural landmarks of the peoples that the Serb extremists were trying to destroy. Later, the other warring parties in the former Yugoslavia joined in too; the Croats and Bosnian Muslims and Kosovars engaged in a round of mutual destruction. Minarets in Bosnia were blown up. Mostar's sixteenth-century bridge was destroyed by Croats. The national library in Sarajevo, with its collection of precious books going back centuries, was obliterated by Bosnian Serbs. Fortunately, the damage inflicted on the ancient city of Dubrovnik by Serb shelling was, by the standards of this grisly war, relatively minor. But in Kosovo scores of historic Orthodox monasteries and churches were burnt out by ethnic Albanian separatists; frescoes were defaced and altars smashed.

Architecture in its role of nation building can be understood as a species of military uniform, a powerful way of signaling allegiances and aspirations, of rallying your own side, and intimidating the perceived enemy. Uniforms, like buildings, are ostensibly shaped by practical, functional considerations, but are actually designed to convey a message, to make soldiers look intimidating and organized. In the eighteenth century, British redcoats wore shiny black shakos, or bearskin hats, to make them look taller. Big buildings look more impressive than small ones. But for small countries to invest in overblown government buildings is simply to reveal their insecurities rather than to demonstrate self-confidence. Talking softly and carrying as big a stick as they can manage is a more convincing policy.

British prime ministers ran a worldwide empire from 10 Downing Street, a nondescript Georgian town house no different from all the rest of Downing Street. In their eyes, only insecure dictators built anything as vulgar as the Berchtesgaden, Hitler's Alpine retreat, or needed the reassurance of the Sala di Mappa di Mondo, the vast Renaissance hall in the Palazzo Venezia that Mussolini used as his office in Rome. And yet those sensible British ministers in their no-nonsense worsted wool suits, found themselves hypnotized by the stage set that Paul Troost designed for Hitler in Munich.

With architecture as with military insignia, a sense of reflected glory can come from adopting the style of a conspicuously victorious power, synonymous with efficiency, valor, and success. In the early part of the nineteenth century, the United States and Japan dressed their armies to look like the French troops who had been such models of victorious élan until 1870, when they were crushed by the Prussian occupation of Paris. Many armies established or reorganized after that modeled themselves on the Prussians. Chile and Bolivia still have dress uniforms that make them all but indistinguishable from those of the officers of the Kaiser's army.

The Yugoslav army, the last federal institution left before the collapse of the country, wore olive uniforms and forage caps with red stars that made them look exactly like the Soviet Red Army, despite Tito's quarrel with Stalin. The Slovenes and the Croats were already working on uniforms to make their troops look as much as possible as if they already belonged to NATO. They could see how the television pictures would play even before hostilities started. If one side looked like part of the evil empire and the other looked like a western ally, it didn't take a Clausewitz to see which side was going to get a better press in the United States.

The banknotes both countries ordered well before either had a national bank also reflected national aspirations. The old dinar notes of Yugoslavia were dignified with representations of heroic workers and apple-cheeked peasants. They brandished sickles and gazed over power stations and tractors. They tended blast furnaces and molded ingots, symbolizing the triumph of the working classes. Naturally the new Balkan states went for images of baroque composers and Renaissance astronomers rather than of an idealized proletariat. These images signaled a new and more optimistic future, paradoxically by looking backward. The Croats designed their paper money, the kuna, to look as indistinguishable from the deutschmark as possible—much to the concern of the Bundesbank when the kuna started being passed off as the real thing. The Slovenes were less influenced by Germany and had their much more graphically sophisticated tolars printed in Britain. Given that the creation of a Croatian puppet state had been part of Hitler's strategy for neutralizing Yugoslavia in World War II, even the banknotes of the two countries were a stark reflection of two rather different political legacies.

Architecture has long been a means used by small or new countries to project their presence on a world stage. From the time of Antonio Gaudí and his Finnish counterpart Eliel Saarinen, the Catalans and the Finns both used radical architecture to express a sense of themselves, to define as well as to reflect an identity.

Kemal Atatürk set out to signal his ambitions to build a modern new state by importing the architecture of the West to build his capital in Ankara. Pakistan engaged Louis Kahn to build a parliament in Dacca, and India brought Le Corbusier from Paris to design Chandigarh as the new capital of the Punjab after its partition with Pakistan.

The question is always one of degree: How much is a nationalist architectural identity a self-conscious, "artificial" creation, and how much is it an authentic reflection of specific national traits, of climate, materials, and customs?

The greatest difficulty in creating a convincing sense of national identity through architectural means is that the process is essentially artificial in its attempts at mimicking the supposedly organic characteristics of a country.

Design languages grow out of climate and locally occurring raw materials. In countries with a lot of rain, houses tend to have steep pitched roofs. In forested areas, they will have wooden tiles. Elsewhere they will have slates or clay pan tiles, depending on the soil. In hot dry countries, flat roofs are more likely. These styles become, in time, a reflection of a national identity. But the impact of technological change and a global market for building materials make slate, clay, or timber available anywhere; as a result, style is no longer a reflection of a living architectural tradition, but a question of symbolism. Muslim minarets or Swiss chalets can be manufactured from fiberglass or concrete to project the right message, even when the practical reasons for choosing the original material have gone.

Some new states look to the past for their architectural language; others see prestige in the embrace of modernity and a rupture with tradition. Slovenia belongs to the latter camp. It was the most determinedly modern of the former Yugoslav states, and the one with enough confidence to allow it to take the most creative risks with its visual identity. It was prepared to countenance very young architects designing major official buildings. Their work was a signal of the distance that the emerging Republic of Slovenia was putting between itself and the old regime. Slovenia wanted to move toward the West, culturally as well as politically. It also had the most striking banknotes, including one that featured an image of Jože Plečnik, an architect who did much to define modern Slovenia with his highly original buildings.

Plečnik was born in the nineteenth century, when Slovenia was still part of the Austro-Hungarian Empire, and studied in Vienna. He worked as an assistant to Otto Wagner, the architect whose bold use of such modern materials as aluminum and ceramic tiles gave turn-of-the-century Vienna a sleek new look. Wagner designed the subway system and the city's striking Postal Savings Bank with its aluminum sculpture and its glass-vaulted banking hall. Because he was not a native-born Austrian, Plečnik was passed over for Wagner's chair at the Academy of Fine Arts. Just before World War I, he moved to Prague, where he played an important part in transforming what had once been a provincial city in the Austro-Hungarian Empire into the capital of the independent state of Czechoslovakia. He was responsible for remodeling Prague Castle, working with President Tomáš Masaryk to turn that monument to the power of the absolutist Hapsburgs into what he called a democratic castle. Plečnik went back to Slovenia in 1920, by then part of the kingdom of Yugoslavia. In the years of the monarchy, Plečnik was responsible for the sensitive development of Slovenia's capital, Ljubljana, knitting carefully scaled modern building into its traditional fabric and looking for new ways in which to interpret the traditional signals of the country's vernacular tradition as an assertion of national identity, much in the same way that a Czech composer, like Antonín Dvořák, say, made Slavonic folk music the starting point for his symphonic work. Plečnik survived the Second World War and continued to work discreetly on proposals for what could be the landmarks of an independent Slovenia—a new parliament, for example—long into the Tito period, proof of the resistance of postwar Yugoslavia to the monomania of Stalin's architectural tastes.

Just as Plečnik's was one of the faces that Slovenia chose to use on its banknotes, suggesting a link with the past but presenting its traditions in a strikingly contemporary way, so the new state designed its passports to suggest a sense of modernity, but also to remind us of its roots in a very specific landscape. In place of the usual florid engraver's abstractions that serve as security marks, Slovenian passports use a collage of fragments of the contour map of the country's highest mountain, and national symbol, Triglav.

On the twenty-tolar bill, Plečnik was portrayed in an outsize fedora that casts shadows in curious places on his face, his profile rendered in the manner of an architectural diagram. This mix of the naturalistic and the abstract reappeared in the drawing of the national library Plečnik designed for Ljubljana, which appeared on the other side of the note.

Architects feature with surprising frequency on banknotes. The Swiss still show the angular features of Le Corbusier on their ten-franc note, despite the fact that he was a French citizen for the greater part of his life. The Finns put Alvar Aalto on their fifty-finmark note, until they adopted the euro. Charles Rennie Mackintosh, who did just as much as Aalto for Finland or Gaudí for Catalonia to create a sense of a modern distinctive Scotland, never made it onto a British banknote. Mackintosh's equally talented architectural predecessor from Glasgow, Alexander Thomson, was however featured on a twenty-pound note.

STRIKINGLY INDIVIDUALISTIC BANKNOTES, PASSPORTS, AND, OF course, architecture are all the kind of apparently artificial signals that small anxious nations use to demonstrate who and what they are. But big confident ones do it too, or something very similar. Like every successful nation, the United States is a carefully constructed artifact. It is the product of a farsighted set of founding fathers and their vision of what the country should be. Architectural landmarks play an essential role in shaping national identity, all the way from Pierre Charles L'Enfant's master plan for Washington, D.C., and the skyscrapers of Manhattan, in the United States, to Britain's Victorian gothic Houses of Parliament.

Of the countless photographs of Winston Churchill in the role of Britain's war leader, none is more poignant than the image of him picking his way through the rubble of a half-destroyed Westminster on a May morning in 1941. Behind him is the shattered gothic tracery of the west porch of St. Stephen's, from which fragments of glass still cling in jagged clumps. Churchill's hunched bulk, in homburg and dark overcoat, his face caught in a burst of spring sunshine, is balanced by the equestrian statue of Richard the Lionhearted still in the saddle in his chain mail, despite the direct hit scored by a German pilot with an incendiary bomb on the House of Commons the previous night. The crusader king's sword, swung high over his head ready to smite his enemies, is bent and twisted from the heat of the fire that swept through Parliament.

There could be no clearer image of the crisis facing Britain at the most critical moment of the Second World War, and of its continuing defiance, if it had been deliberately constructed—which indeed this photograph was.

By 1941, the Palace of Westminster, even though most of it was less than a century old, embodied the identity of the United Kingdom, an identity rooted in the language of architectural tradition. Westminster was designed in the gothic manner at the insistence of Parliament, as the style best capable of expressing a specifically British identity. Classicism was regarded as a decadent alien import by the more militant of the Victorian enthusiasts for the gothic revival. Pointed arches, they believed, both were a reminder of a glorious past and represented a home-grown architectural style. Germany destroyed this of all possible targets to communicate with unmistakable finality that Britain was finished. Churchill came out of his Whitehall bunker the morning after the bombing to demonstrate for the benefit of the cameras both defiance and reassuring continuity in the face of the destruction.

In fact, Britain at war functioned perfectly well—some would say better than it had ever done before. The substance of its democracy survived even without its symbolic home. The House of Commons moved initially into the Lords and then Church House, seat of the Church of England synod, just down the road.

When the crisis passed, the Commons debated how to reconstruct Westminster. Those few eccentrics who argued for a modern chamber for the House of Commons within the burnt-out gothic shell were no match for Churchill's rhetoric. "We shape our buildings, and afterwards, our buildings shape us," he famously told Parliament. "We have learned not to alter improvidently the physical structures which have enabled so remarkable an organism to carry on its work of banning dictatorships within this island, and pursuing and beating into ruin all dictators who have molested us from outside."

Churchill outlined what he saw as the two most crucial physical characteristics of the House of Commons: "The party system is much favored by the oblong form of chamber. It is easy for an individual to move through those insensible graduations from left to right, but the act of crossing the Floor is one which requires serious consideration. The second characteristic of a chamber formed on the lines of the House of Commons is that it should not be big enough to contain all its members at once. If the House is big enough to contain all its members at once, nine-tenths of its debates will be conducted in the depressing atmosphere of an almost empty chamber."

Here was Churchill as the consummate actor-manager, well aware of both the symbolic aspects of government and the practical stagecraft of state needed to present it.

This was not the first time that the British legislature had burnt. Parliament was almost totally destroyed when a careless builder overloaded the furnace in the old House of Lords in 1834 and the resulting blaze got out of hand. But the rambling Palace of Westminster, the product of centuries of building and rebuilding since William Rufus established it as the court of the Norman kings, had never been a self-conscious landmark. It was a ramshackle collection of buildings, constantly extended and altered, much like the terraced house at 10 Downing Street that is the prime minister's official residence, rather than a deliberately created national symbol. Would Westminster still have been targeted by Germany in 1941 if it had survived the nineteenth-century fire intact but remained as an anonymous clutter, rather than being rebuilt as the best-known landmark in Britain?

Certainly Germany had no equivalent—least of all the Reichstag, which was a symbol of neither unity nor national identity. It had been built in the closing years of the nineteenth century by the Kaiser to accommodate a tame parliament that never had real power. Its baroque façade, closely modeled on Vanbrugh's Blenheim Palace, achieved authentic symbolic resonance only twice. The first time was right after the Nazi seizure of power in 1933, when a mentally disturbed Dutch Marxist was accused of having torched it, and a billowing smoke cloud erupted from its dome, blotting out the inscription on its pediment. The second was on the day in 1945 when the Red Army was so taken with the heroic figure it cut storming its way up the Reichstag's steps and then fighting hand to hand through its corridors that it restaged the onslaught for the benefit of its newsreel unit. Christo's wrapping of the structure before Norman Foster started work on transforming it into the federal parliament of a reunited Germany was on some level a kind of exorcism of those previous images.

How many other parliaments have the same international instant recognition as Westminster? After Washington, the list runs out quickly. How many non-Spaniards would recognize Madrid's parliament instantly, or non-Belgians that of Belgium? But Westminster is another matter. It is a logotype for Britain. And it sets a precedent that has threatened to overshadow every subsequent attempt to design a parliament.

Architects who seek to create buildings that project an identity as highly charged as that demanded by a parliament must negotiate a path between reflecting the past, expressing a convincing sense of national roots, and demonstrating an interest in the future. They must avoid the appearance of seeming too manipulative, and give the impression that their work has authenticity, rather than betray its essentially artificial nature.

Architecture in such circumstances is neither simply a functional nor an aesthetic issue. It has a directly political quality too. It is intended to make states look important and to help to manage the political process. There can, however, be a wide gap between the objectives of the politicians who commission architects to design buildings to serve their purposes and the ambitions of those architects.

A BUILDING CAN SET OUT TO BE MEMORABLE ENOUGH TO MAKE IT a landmark recognized around the world. It can try to look important or significant enough to invest the activities it accommodates with an aura of equivalent importance. It can be designed to represent, in a metaphorical way, the aspirations of the state or its leaders. A modern building can be used, for example, to suggest that the state that built it is also forward-looking and progressive. The use of traditional architectural languages, by contrast, may be an attempt to suggest pedigree and roots, or a specifically national style.

Such national styles are often rooted in building materials that are the product of the specifics of time and place, and the search for economical building techniques. In Amsterdam, the canal houses started off with much the same kind of basic ingredients as contemporary Georgian domestic architecture in England: brick, sash windows, and a classical language for the door frame. But it doesn't take an expert eye to see that the Dutch version is distinctively different. The bricks are narrower and have different proportions, reflecting the techniques adopted for pragmatic reasons at Dutch brickworks. The windows occupy a larger percentage of the walls to bring more light into narrow-fronted but deep plans, in response to the specifics of place. And because Amsterdam's canals crowded people together, those houses have more floors, and steeper staircases than their London equivalents. They also need hoists projecting from their distinctive gables to lift furniture and supplies in and out.

These were all originally technical issues, but they metamorphosed into an emotional expression of national identity that could be turned into an instantly recognizable style. Once the Dutch had established their outposts in Indonesia, questions other than the use of conveniently available raw materials and a response to climate came into play in the construction of the capital that they called Batavia, now known as Jakarta. Thousands of miles from home, colonists reminded themselves of who they were by the shape of the houses that they built. The same was true in other Dutch settlements. Walk some of the streets of Cape Town, and you can see another re-creation of Holland, built originally to reassure fearful, homesick colonists that, even here, civilized life was possible. In Greenmarket Square, Cape Town's Old Town House, once the seat of its local government, dates back to 1755. It reflects Dutch authority, with a clock, a cupola, and a balcony that make it look as if it belongs on the other side of the world. A century and a half later, and 110 years after the colony had come under British administration, the Old Town House was superseded by the building of a new City Hall made from yellow Bath stone (allegedly shipped all the way from England) in a florid Palladian style that made it look as if it were in Bristol, Liverpool, or Glasgow.

The old Cape Colony became part of a larger South African state in 1910, following the defeat of the Boers by the British. But after the First World War, as the balance of power shifted back toward the Afrikaners, Dutch traditions started to reassert themselves. Afrikaner companies in Cape Town signaled their newfound confidence in the 1920s with structures such as the Old Mutual Insurance offices, designed in a heavy deco style suggesting the Amsterdam of the time. The history of the province was carved into the Cape granite frieze on its façade, with its polished bronze doors, its Transvaal granite lobby, and its gold-leaf decorations.

Two decades later the Voortrekker Monument in Pretoria was the most overwrought manifestation of this version of Afrikanerdom. It was the work of Gerard Moerdijk, a Dutch architect who had moved to South Africa in 1935. Only completed in 1949, it is designed to allow the sun to shine through a hole in the vaulted roof, casting a ray of light to illuminate the sarcophagus asserting the birth of a new Boer republic through sacrifice.

In a colonial society, the manufacture of a new independent identity can rely as much on architecture as on the evolution of distinct speech patterns and an accent. Herbert Baker was an architect who worked in two very different colonial contexts. He arrived as a young man in South Africa when he was just thirty and developed a close friendship with the arch-imperialist Cecil Rhodes. In its personal closeness, its quasi-erotic intensity, and its political consequences, the relationship prefigures that of Albert Speer with Adolf Hitler. Rhodes first encountered Baker at a dinner party shortly after the younger man arrived in Cape Town. He was so taken with "the silent young man," as he called Baker, that he asked him to remodel his newly acquired house, Groote Schuur. Baker developed a style based on blending the Cape Dutch vernacular with the arts and crafts movement fashionable in England at the time, as if self-consciously trying to reconcile the two white settler groups in the colony.

Baker went on to build the landmarks of English-speaking white Cape Town, designing the City and Civil Service Club on Queen Victoria Street, the Anglican St. George's Cathedral, and the lepers' church on Robben Island. Eventually, when the city became the seat of the legislature for the Union of South Africa, he designed a wing for the Houses of Parliament.

Rhodes, who had an abiding interest in monument making, financed his protégé's tour of the classical sites of Europe, from Sicily to Greece, as a preparation for designing a memorial to the dead of the Kimberley campaign, one of his many empire-building skirmishes with the Boers. Baker proposed a white marble bath, open to the skies and surrounded by Ionic columns, a project that was stopped only when Rhodes's partners at De Beers took fright at the cost, and refused to sign the checks.

When Rhodes died in 1902, Rudyard Kipling and Baker between them chose a site for his memorial on Devil's Peak overlooking the sea above Cape Town. Baker's design was based on the Temple of Segesta in Sicily, featuring colonnades and flights of steps set off with a series of lion sphinxes. Inside stands a bust of Rhodes with Kipling's words carved from locally quarried stone: "The immense and brooding spirit still shall order and control. Living he was the land, and dead his soul shall be her soul." If things had been different in South Africa, it would have been part of the foundation myth of a white, Anglo-Saxon state.

Baker returned to the United Kingdom ten years after Rhodes's death, but his colonial building campaign was not over. He went home to work with Edwin Lutyens on the design of India's new capital in Delhi. In the summer of 1912, after King George V laid the foundation stone of his imperial capital, his viceroy unilaterally decided to build it on the other side of the existing Indian city of Delhi. This act of lèse-majesté went by almost unnoticed in Britain, where the question of how the city should look was much more of an issue than exactly where to put it.

The foundation of New Delhi, on the edge of a city that had seen empires come and go, was almost the last act of Britain's three-hundred-year imperial history in India. It was the result of a decision to move the seat of power away from Calcutta, out of the reach of the violent campaign waged there by increasingly determined Bengali nationalists, and start again in a less troubled province. But it was also an attempt to transform the nature of the British presence in the country. The East India Company had arrived in India as traders and built Calcutta as a European port city in the image of Britain. New Delhi was to be something far more ambitious. The plan for the new city was attempting to draw on the traditional roots of power in India, to situate British India in a millennia-old history, and so, in some sense, to legitimize it. If the strategy was to work, it depended on the absorption of the colonizers by the colonized. But in fact New Delhi was shaped by civic officials from London and Liverpool working by remote control, and based on plans brought over on steamships.

THE IMPERIAL CITY'S CHIEF ARCHITECT WAS THE QUINTESSEN-tially English figure of Edwin Lutyens, a brilliantly gifted designer who was deeply condescending about India. His late father-in-law, Lord Lytton, had been the viceroy, a connection that didn't hurt when Lutyens was angling to design New Delhi. While he was affable enough with his Indian servants, he was shockingly racist about the country to which he owed so much. "The very low intellect of the natives spoils much," he wrote in one of his letters home. "I do not think it possible for Indians and whites to mix freely; mixed marriage is filthy and beastly and they ought to get the sanitary office to interfere."

But the British had not run an empire for three centuries without acquiring a certain sophistication about the need occasionally to see things from the point of view of their subjects. And so for several months, a heated debate raged between those who, like the editors of *The Builder* magazine, understood the issue of New Delhi's architecture as a crystal-clear case of imperial branding, and those such as George Bernard Shaw and Thomas Hardy, who argued for an Indian design, and an Indian designer. *The Builder* would have none of it. For them, New Delhi should be made to look as British as possible: "An empire can nurse no finer ideal than the cohesion of its dominions in cities erected in one style of architecture recognized throughout the world as the expression of its own imperial ideals. The encouragement of such an empire pervading style throughout the colonies, dependencies and protectorates will tend to annihilate distance and conduces to an imperial liberty, equality, and fraternity."

Baker, an old friend of Lutyens who had recently joined the New Delhi team, wrote to *The Times* a week after *The Builder*'s outburst about the capital that he and Lutyens were planning: "First and foremost, it is the spirit of British sovereignty which must be imprisoned in its stone and bronze. To realize this ideal, the architecture of the Roman Empire—as embodying the more elemental and universal form—should be used as the basis of the style, while eastern features must be woven into the fabric as a concession to Indian sentiment." Just how little of a concession Baker was prepared to make is made brutally clear from the inscriptions that he incorporated in his design for the Council House, the circular building that now serves as India's parliament: "Liberty will not descend to a people; a people must raise themselves to liberty, it is a blessing which must be earned before it can be enjoyed."

This was a far from isolated view. Lord Curzon, speaking of the Victoria Memorial in Calcutta, the relic that he left behind as a reminder of his own viceregal period as much as a monument to the first and last Queen Empress, stated, "In Calcutta, a city of European origin, and construction—where all the main buildings had been erected in a quasi classical or Palladian style, and which possessed no indigenous architectural type of its own—it was impossible to erect a building in any native style. A mogul building, however appropriate for the mosques and tombs of the Moslem kings, or even for the modern palace of an Indian prince in his own state, would have been quite unsuited for the memorial of a British sovereign. A Hindu fabric would have been profoundly ill-adapted for the purpose of an exhibition. It was evident that a structure in some variety of the classical or renaissance style was essential, and that a European architect must be employed."

William Emerson, president of the Royal Institute of British Architects at the time, got the job of designing the monument. Curzon's only concession to local tastes was to insist on the use of marble from the same quarry that supplied the Taj Mahal. Curzon left India in 1905, and the project was not finished until 1921. Even with its revolving sixteen-foot-high angel of victory on top of a huge dome, which covers a vast chamber that is occupied only by a bust of Victoria as a young girl, it had already been eclipsed by the new capital rapidly taking shape in Delhi, where work had started nine years earlier.

Charles Hardinge, Curzon's successor as viceroy, was busy trying to damp down the unrest bequeathed him and suggested to Lutyens that his design should "harmonize externally with the monuments of old Delhi and the traditions of Indian Art." Sir Swinton Jacob, an expert on the subject, was brought in to advise Lutyens on the details. The design would be "western with an oriental motif." Lutyens responded by using an Indianized version of classical architecture, based on what he called the Delhi order, with columns topped by a graft of Greek acanthus leaves and Indian bells.

The plan, aligned so that its major avenues point toward the mosques, temples, and palaces that form the focal points of the old city, made a clear claim to the control of the past. New Delhi's design was both the symbol and the instrument of a society that embodied not only the hierarchical nature of the colonial world, but also India's own caste system. British India was organized according to the infinite shades of status conveyed by an official document known as the Warrant of Precedence. As the historian Philip Davies points out in *The Splendours of the Raj*, his account of British architecture in India, "the Civilian Superintendent of Clothing Factories, 44th grade of the warrant, ranked a cut above Deputy Director General of the Indian medical services but beneath the Director General of Public Information, all three inferior to the Financial Advisor, Post and Telegraphs."

Within the grid of New Delhi's suburbs as defined by the master plan, five were allocated according to race, occupational rank, and social status. According to Davies, one was designated for senior military officers, another for European clerks, a third for indigenous clerks, a fourth for Indian princes and nobility. The princes each received a plot of land between 4 and 8 acres, generals were allocated rather less, from 2 to 3.5

acres, while members of the legislature qualified for only 0.25 acre. The senior ranks lived in houses facing onto the major avenues, while their subordinates had the minor roads. So it wasn't just the size of the house but the address that designated an individual's status.

New Delhi was designed to demonstrate its position as a British possession, and emphasize the power of the viceroy, whose domed residence occupied the highest part of the city. Flag Staff House, the residence of the commander in chief of India's armed forces, deferred to the Viceroy's House, a careful reminder that power was exercised through civil rather than military authority. The Council House, the seat of an elected assembly, a first concession to Indian democracy, was added to the plan only in 1919.

Despite the abundance of imperial symbolism that defines New Delhi, just fifteen years after the completion of the city, it became the seat of government of a newly independent India, a reminder that the iconography of power is not the same as its substance.

KEMAL ATATÜRK, THE SOLDIER TURNED STATESMAN WHO CREATED the modern state of Turkey, was a much more successful nation builder than Lutyens had been. Architecture and urbanism were key parts of his campaign to rescue Turks from the ruins of the Ottoman Empire. His strategy worked well enough to set an example followed by a whole range of authoritarian nationalists, including the Shah of Iran, Saddam Hussein, and the Marcoses in the Philippines, all of whom faced a similar range of challenges, as well as more benign figures such as Juscelino Kubitschek, who built Brasília.

What differentiates Atatürk and Kubitschek from the others is that they resisted the temptations of the incipient megalomania that hovers over any national building campaign and remained focused on an objective wider than personal vanity.

Atatürk made the decision to set up a new capital in Ankara to replace the Ottoman seat of government in Constantinople partly from military necessity. The old capital on the extreme western edge of the country was still the seat of the Ottoman court until Atatürk finally deposed the last sultan by establishing the Turkish republic in 1923. Constantinople—or Istanbul, as it was to become—had been occupied by the British and the French since the closing months of the First World War. Much of the Mediterranean coastline had been seized by the Greek army, with British prime minister David Lloyd George's tacit encouragement. Given these threats to the survival of a state still struggling to be born, Atatürk chose Ankara as a secure base, far inland on the Anatolian plain, as he fought to save the country from dismemberment in the wake of the collapse of its empire.

His decision reflected his view of what modern Turkey should be: a country based on Turkish nationalism, in which Turks would be the dominant ethnic group, as they had not in the Ottoman Empire. Istanbul's largest structures had been Christian cathedrals before they became mosques. The city had a polyglot diversity of ethnic groups and was hard to define as specifically Turkish. Ankara was a chance for the Turks to create a new capital in their own image.

For centuries the Ottomans had been locked in an ambiguous embrace with the Arabs, adopting the Islamic religion and many aspects of their culture, including their alphabet, even as they attempted to subjugate them. Over the course of a thousand years, the Turkish empire had spread across North Africa, into Europe, and eastward into Asia. It subjects included Christians and Jews, as well as Arab and non-Arab Muslims. The Ottoman state extended a considerable degree of tolerance to its minorities.

Despite its modernizing mission, the new Turkey was less sympathetic to those who did not accept its ethnic basis. Atatürk's conception of a new state involved a renewed idea of the Turkish national identity and reflected a search for the historical roots of Turkish culture with which to form the basis of a secular state. This search had ominous implications for the country's Greeks, Kurds, and Armenians.

Ankara, an ancient city whose origins may go back to Hittite times, offered a chance to root the new nation in an ancient and glorious past. But at the same time, Atatürk, who had himself been born in what is now the Greek city of Salonika, wanted to make the new Turkey a significant presence in the European context. He wanted to embrace European modernity as well as the Turkish past. He imposed the Latin alphabet in just five months, banned the fez for Turkish citizens, and adopted western dress. He is still represented on Turkish banknotes in morning suit and white tie.

By the time that Atatürk first saw Ankara, it had withered into a small, dusty town of twenty thousand people, albeit one with an impressive ancient citadel. In the fifteen years between Atatürk's proclamation of his new capital and his death in 1938, he took rapid steps to transform the city and its infrastructure into a convincing reflection of his idea of what Turkey should be, a country clearly rooted in Turkish history and prehistory.

Turkey built its institutions bit by bit. Stylistically some of them looked back to the most distant past, in a bid to claim legitimacy. But the most significant architectural projects reflecting the new state were designed by the Austrian Clemens Holzmeister in a sober and contemporary style. Holzmeister's Turkish buildings were austere, symmetrical, and free of historical motifs, a kind of architectural Esperanto.

Holzmeister had initially been invited to go to Ankara in 1927 by the Turkish ambassador to Austria, to build a new war office. That project turned out to be the first of a dozen more commissions. He would eventually be responsible for the Presidential Palace, the National Assembly, the High Court, Central Bank, General Staff Building, and Ministry of the Interior. Atatürk quickly realized that Ankara needed more than the piecemeal construction of monumental institutions in order to become a real capital city. He commissioned a master plan to direct the increasingly rapid growth of the city. In an invited competition held in 1932, Hermann Jansen, an academic from Berlin, was chosen to design it. Jansen's plan took a practical strategic approach, very different from the unsubtle axial formality of Europe's authoritarians. But his informal layout, with extensive green areas close to the center, still gives privileged status to the landmarks of Atatürk's state, and Holzmeister designed almost all of them. Holzmeister's relationship with Turkey deepened over the years. Eventually he was named official state architect, and Atatürk personally selected him after an international competition to design the new Turkish parliament just before his death in 1938. The building was not in fact completed until 1960.

Holzmeister was educated at the Technical University in Vienna and, by the time he started to work in Turkey, was a professor at the Academy of Fine Arts there. Holzmeister, a political liberal, was stripped of his professorship by the Nazis after the absorption of Austria into the Reich. He moved to Turkey as a permanent resident and stayed until 1954. He was joined by a number of other refugees from Nazi Germany. They included Bruno Taut, Hans Poelzig, and Grette Schutte-Lihotsky, who helped to give a progressive tinge to the cultural development of the new state. But the relationship between Turkey, Nazi Germany, and Fascist Italy was a complex one. Atatürk had both democratic and authoritarian tendencies. Among his supporters were groups who came close to fascism with their own racial policies. And there were aspects of Hitler's architecture that were directly applicable to Ankara. Among the Germans in Turkey was Paul Bonatz, who had designed some of the most conspicuous buildings for Speer's Berlin. And Holzmeister himself brought Josef Thorak, Hitler's favored sculptor, to work on his Turkish projects. Adalberto Libera and a number of other Italian Fascists took part in the competition to design Atatürk's mausoleum. Even the winning design, by Emin Onat, bore an uncomfortably close resemblance to Paul Troost's martyrs' memorial in Munich.

At the same time as left and right battled for influence, Atatürk was determined to curb clerical influence in the new state. Ankara can be seen as the physical embodiment of the ideological struggle for the direction that Turkey would take. Its major monuments represent Atatürk himself, and his view of the nature of a secular republic. Its forms were western, tempered with the memory of Turkey's ancient past in their decorative detail. Atatürk imported a number of European artists to work on a series of monumental works of representational sculpture that had been taboo for centuries in the Muslim world and scandalized the more conservative Islamists.

Despite Atatürk's prestige, the country's Islamists have today begun to reassert themselves. One recent mayor of Ankara threatened to permit the construction of buildings that would have the effect of screening Atatürk's monuments out of sight. But to a remarkable extent, Atatürk's national iconography succeeded in its purpose. The secular state that he built survives intact. He had explored the pre-Islamic history of the Turks and their forerunners as far back as the Iron Age to find decorative motifs that could be revived to shape a new national architectural language. He had sponsored archaeological research to produce the necessary historical evidence as legitimization for his view of Turkey. And he had attempted to bypass the authority of the entrenched Islamic clergy by using the memories of pre-Islamic national glories to construct an alternative patriotic tradition.

AS A HUGELY VISIBLE INTERNATIONAL FIGURE WHO HAD TAKEN on the western powers and come off best, it was not surprising that Atatürk would form a model for other rulers facing comparable challenges. Among the first was Reza Khan, the Shah of Iran, who with his son would attempt exactly the same strategy in Tehran. Reza Khan was deposed by the British in 1941 when he started to become too close to Hitler's Germany, and started trying to play the Allies off against the

Axis powers. But his son, Mohammad Reza Pahlavi, installed with CIA help after his father abdicated, turned out to be even more interested in building.

Atatürk wanted to replace Ottoman Turkey with a westernized, republican system that in theory would embrace democratic government, but this was not an idea that appealed to either of the shahs. Nevertheless, they adopted Atatürk's methods to build a secular state, and in particular his cultural strategy to outflank dissenting Islamists, which depended in equal measure on archaeology and architecture. In this they were far less successful than Atatürk had been, in large part because their efforts came to be seen as aimed at personal aggrandizement rather than national renewal.

Before Mohammad Reza Pahlavi finally took the controls of his personal Boeing 707 in 1979 and flew off to exile and a premature death in Egypt, he had embarked on a building campaign that was even more ambitious than either his father's or Atatürk's. And as the country's oil reserves accumulated, he had the money to indulge his passion. The Shah claimed that he wanted to turn Tehran into the capital of a modern, technocratic nation that would reflect his vision of Iran as one of the world's leading industrial economies. It was a conception he had inherited from his father, Reza Khan. And it was a project undertaken in the hope that those of his subjects who were not grateful for being transformed from rural peasants living a subsistence existence into prosperous citizens of the modern world would at least be dazzled into silence by the glittering new state taking shape all around them. The speed with which the Ayatollah Khomeini took power in an orgy of revolutionary violence and religious intolerance demonstrated that the Shah's project was manifestly unsuccessful. In retrospect his passion for building looks less like the nation making of Atatürk, and more like self-obsessed narcissism, which became more and more detached from reality as the Pahlavi family's grip on power weakened.

The Pahlavi dynasty (if it can be called that, with only two crowned monarchs to its credit, both of them deposed) occupied the peacock throne that they had appropriated for just over fifty years. The Pahlavis were eager patrons of architecture from the moment the first Shah, a former cavalry officer, seized power. His strategy for building a strong state was to adopt the style of an imperial despotism; relying on the iconography of past glories was an essential part of his attempt to silence opposition. He looked for ways to purify the state culturally of Arab and other non-Iranian influences. And he rapidly set about acquiring the requisite trappings: the thrones, the crowns, and the uniforms.

In theory, the Turkish and Iranian strategies were essentially the same, even if the historical references were different. Nearby Iraq wasn't far behind on a similar path. Perhaps as a not unintended side effect, the strategy involved re-creating ancient enmities too, which eventually helped fuel Hussein's appallingly bloody war against Iran.

For Atatürk it was the Hittites who had the most appeal, in terms of past glories. The Shah looked back to Cyrus the Great, and Saddam Hussein, when he wasn't presenting himself as the new Stalin, suggested not so subliminally that he was the reincarnation of King Nebuchadnezzar. Which is why Saddam Hussein rebuilt the walls of Babylon, and why you can find groups of strange horned beasts on the traffic circles along Ankara's Atatürk Boulevard, enlarged versions of the bronze figures unearthed by archaeologists from the Hittite tombs. It's also the reason that the central bank in Tehran, built in the time of the first Shah, has an exterior that suggests it belongs to the Persian empire of the Achaemenians of 558–330 B.C., even though it shelters a conventional modern interior.

Unlike Atatürk, the two shahs did not construct a new capital city. Tehran was originally established in the tenth century and by the fifteenth century had become a substantial walled city, guarded by four gates and 114 towers. Reza Khan demolished Tehran's walls and drove a grid of tree-lined boulevards through the ancient structure of the city— and beyond, to set the framework for its future growth. In the late 1970s this exercise in strategic traffic management would turn out to be more help to the demonstrators calling for his son's overthrow than it was to the soldiers trying to intimidate them into silence.

The elder Shah's urban strategy extended beyond Tehran. Every town and city throughout Iran had to conform to a standard template. A public space, ringed with imperial statues and named either Nation Square or Pahlavi Square, was mandatory.

In 1968 his son commissioned Victor Gruen, the inventor of the modern shopping mall, to devise a strategy for Tehran's future growth. Gruen identified an area of vacant land to the north of the city as the site for a new government center. Lord Richard Llewelyn-Davies won the commission to plan this vast tract of empty land, after an invited competition in 1975. The submissions were presented to the Shah while he was on a skiing holiday, and he was said to have come down from a morning on the slopes to see all the competing models, laid out side by side for his inspection. Llewelyn-Davies's vision of a two-mile-wide slice of Manhattan transplanted to Tehran caught his eye.

Llewelyn-Davies, who was apparently somewhat unprepared to take on the design of the largest new capital city in the world, hurriedly assembled a team of American architects and planners to boost the intellectual firepower he could bring to bear on the job. He went to the well-regarded American planner Jaquelin Robertson, who recruited a group of architects and planners, many of whom had been involved with Mayor John Lindsay's plans for New York. It included a young Princeton graduate who left the project to marry King Hussein of Jordan, and Thierry Despont, who later became a decorator—his most celebrated commission has been Bill Gates's house.

In the mid-1970s, daily life in Tehran was a dangerously unstable mix of the medieval and the twentieth century. The Shah's wife invited Peter Brook to stage avant-garde theater in the city, the National Gallery of Modern Art was buying up western art, including a remarkably sexually explicit Francis Bacon triptych. But many women were veiled, re-

flecting a society in which a conservative form of Islam was asserting itself. While the Shah was investing in a modern mass transit system, regular visitors to Tehran were keen to avoid making the drive into town
from the airport after dark. Packs of wild dogs roaming the highway
shoulders could be a problem if you had a breakdown. Streets were
named for the Shah's allies. There was a de Gaulle Expressway, an Eisenhower Boulevard, and an Elizabeth II Boulevard. None of these new
roads penetrated the bazaar, apparently untouched for five hundred
years. Parts of the city were home to an elite that had become hugely
wealthy with remarkable speed, thanks to booming oil revenues, while
other sections still lacked clean drinking water. And the population was
growing explosively, rising from 700,000 in 1939 to 4.6 million by 1975.
It is now home to 12 million people.

Whether he was aware of it or not, the strategy for the new government center Llewelyn-Davies was working on closely reflected the underlying realities of Iranian politics. The country was divided not on
class grounds, but between the secular and the religious. And the biggest
threat to the Shah was not the Iranian Communist party, agitating on
behalf of Moscow, but the Islamic priesthood, whose power base in
Tehran was to the south of the city, in and around the bazaar.

The plan accentuated the divide between a westernized, affluent
northern city and an ancient city of narrow lanes, courtyard houses,
mosques, and bazaars that was slipping out of the state's control. The relationship between the two took on the nature of an occupation by a
colonial power. There was a division between North and South Tehran,
as sharp as that between the European and Algerian section of Algiers.
Regular boulevards and glass and concrete buildings collided with twisting lanes and alleys.

Llewelyn-Davies's team thought it was devising a plan that could
provide what it called a tangible image of the city for the future, one
with which the population could identify. In fact they were formalizing

the division of Tehran into two warring camps. In his submission to the Shah, Llewelyn-Davies ringingly declared, "A worldwide image must be created where Tehran is known as the finest city of the middle east."

The architect conceded, "We have given as much emphasis to developing an aesthetic and symbolic base for Shahestan Pahlavi, as we have to setting land uses and housing densities." The core of Llewelyn-Davies's plan was the creation of Shah and Nation Square, a gigantic urban square. This landmark would have given Tehran a public space that would eclipse anything in Europe, and would be matched in size only by Tiananmen Square in Beijing. The planners called it a national center for the twentieth century and compared its proportions and the arcades that lined it to Isfahan's great sixteenth-century central square from the country's last golden age.

The key institutions of a modern Iran would be ranged around the square. The prime minister's office would go on the western side. Kenzo Tange won a competition to build City Hall on the northern side, next to the Ministry for Foreign Affairs, a hotel, and a theater. Facing them would be the National Museum, the Handicrafts Museum, the Carpet Museum, and the Pahlavi Library. Robertson and Llewelyn-Davies believed that this government quarter would give Tehran an alternative center to the bazaar, miles to the south, creating a two-center city, like London, divided between its original square mile and the Westminster precinct, or New York, with Wall Street and Midtown.

Tehran's mayor set about implementing the plan. Contracts to build the infrastructure were let. A French company started tunneling for the *metro* system. And each of the planned institutions was designed in detail.

One of the biggest architectural competitions of the 1970s was launched to find a design for the library. The ethics of entering were a hotly debated issue among liberal-minded architects. By this time the streets of western capitals were constantly full of demonstrations by Iranian exiles and dissidents, protesting against what they described as the fascist regime of the Shah and his sinister secret police, the Savak. But political repression did not deter more than seven hundred submissions. Participants could see only the obvious enthusiasm for contemporary design of the Shah's wife, who had had two years of a Parisian architectural education before she married. She had already commissioned Hans Hollein and James Stirling—in those days, two of architecture's most radical talents—to work in Tehran.

The result of the master planning team's work was boiled down to a privately published two-volume book. Copies are numbered, and came in a maroon slipcase. It was written primarily by Jaquelin Robertson, who was to go on to help design Disney's attempt at themed living, the company's planned community of Celebration, Florida. The title page proclaims that "this master plan for Shahestan Pahlavi has drawn inspiration from the country, customs and people of Iran, and most particularly from its great building tradition. It is dedicated most respectfully to His Imperial Majesty, the Shahanshah, the guardian of that tradition." It's a theme that the book warms to. "No great city has been realized without the support of strong men." According to its designers, "this is not just another large capital city, it has an opportunity for greatness."

The pitch was aimed directly at the vanity of the man who was paying for it all. He is pictured on the title page, in a dapper needle-cord suit and silk tie from Yves St. Laurent, standing over a concrete tube onto which a block and tackle has been maneuvered. Helping the Shah bury the solid gold plaque marking the inauguration of construction on the site is Tehran's last Pahlavi mayor, G. R. Nikpay. He wears a long black robe, embroidered in gold braid around the collar and cuffs, and is decked in medals in the style of a Soviet hero.

Six months later, in the spring of 1976, the Shah was back for another ceremony. This time he was busy planting a grove of trees to mark the fiftieth anniversary of the Pahlavi dynasty at the highest point on the development site. But there was not much time left for the new capital, or the Pahlavis. By 1980 the Shah had fled and Nikpay was dead, executed during Khomeini's bloody settling of accounts.

Haussmann's Paris was the inspiration for the reconstruction of Tehran. Llewelyn-Davies himself claimed, with what in retrospect sounds like a stunningly blinkered understanding of the closing years of the Shah's reign, that "since Iran is in a period of national resurgence, it is only natural that the capital should become such a monumental expression of national pride. A similar spirit of ascendancy as in the time of Napoleon III."

He later suggested that "so long as the Shah still ruled, tight central control over the final form was expected and feasible. Baron Haussmann was luckier than we were, Napoleon III survived just long enough to see his city built, but the Shah did not."

In the event, of course, the Shah packed his bags for exile, leaving his airports, his armed forces, and his infrastructure to the ayatollahs. Even before the Islamic Republic of Iran closed the Shah's art galleries and abandoned the plan for the library, the mob had swarmed over the site of the square, ransacking the pavilion in which a huge model of the new city had been on show. It had been brought from London in 1977 on a special Iranian air force flight. Tehran's dispossessed destroyed it in moments and went on to try to dig up the gold foundation stone that the Shah had laid four years earlier. Not long after, the ayatollahs gleefully dynamited Reza Khan Pahlavi's tomb. After the hiatus of the revolutionary years, Chinese contractors were brought in to finish the *metro* system. But the square, the library, and the new city disappeared, swallowed up in the explosive growth of Tehran.

DURING THE KLEPTOCRATIC RULE OF HER HUSBAND, FERDINAND Marcos, the president of the Philippines, Imelda Romualdez Marcos was as self-absorbed in her attempts at monumentality as the Pahlavis. She collected buildings with almost as much enthusiasm as she brought to her better-known passion for shoes. From the moment in 1966 when her husband came to power, until her flight from the presidential palace just ahead of the Manila mob, Imelda Marcos did her best to make her mark as the first lady by building landmarks that she claimed represented a national resurgence. Almost all of them were designed by a single architect, Leandro V. Locsin, who was ideal for her purposes. She declared him one of the Marcoses' "national artists." Locsin produced a stream of buildings with the swaggering self-confidence of corporate American modernism, but with just enough of a local twist.

Locsin was an authentic product of the Philippines, a graduate of San Tomas University whose only experience of the United States was a brief study tour. He met both Eero Saarinen and Paul Rudolph, the two architects he most admired.

Locsin was one of a group of architects in the Third World who found themselves called on to design the offices and ministries, hotels and theaters, that ambitious leaders needed to convince themselves that they were in command of dynamic modern states, while also serving as the guardians of national pride. Locsin's formula was to blend a sullen monumentalism, which seems to have been borrowed from Gordon Bunshaft at Skidmore, Owings and Merrill, with a strategic dash of national color, manifested by picturesque roofs and open courtyards. It's a formula he applied over and over again, for the Manila Cultural Center's Theater of Performing Arts, the International Convention Center, the Folk Arts Theater, the National Arts Center, the Center for International Trade and Exhibitions, the Philippines Plaza Hotel, and in other buildings scattered like giant pieces of sculpture across Manila. With their blank façades, they looked at their best and most striking floodlit at night and seen through the lens of a camera. Locsin used great expanses of water and grass like moats to keep chaotic Greater Manila at bay.

"They were planned to foster national pride," Locsin said of his buildings. He claimed that in the view of the Marcos administration, the arts were "the soul of the nation," and as a result, "both the creative arts and the performing arts are therefore actively encouraged by government policy to help develop in Filipinos a sense of national consciousness, too long dormant under centuries of foreign domination. The edifices commissioned for social civic and scientific projects with which the first lady is equally concerned also reveal the unmistakable features of what is Filipino."

But the symbolism was stultifyingly predictable. For Expo 70, in Osaka, Locsin's Philippine pavilion had one of those overexcitable roofs, sweeping up from the ground, that was intended to express the "soaring prospects and future orientated outlook of the Philippine people," but it could just as well have said the same thing about Bulgaria or Canada.

The beginning of the end of the Marcos period was marked by the collapse of scaffolding on the Manila film theater, one of Imelda Marcos's pet projects, as it was being rushed for completion. Several construction workers were killed, crushed by falling steel. The very buildings being presented as the icons of a bold new republic suddenly seemed to embody the corruption and incompetence of the regime. Locsin's patrons fled the country, but he managed to find an even wealthier client in the shape of the Sultan of Brunei, who has managed to remain in power rather longer than the Marcos family.

THERE HAVE BEEN MORE SUCCESSFUL ATTEMPTS AT CREATING A sense of national identity through architecture. And they have not always depended on the reworking of tradition. Brazil's particular circumstances—a huge country with a racially mixed population, seeking to free itself from the burden of a colonial past—made it particularly susceptible to the tabula rasa approach. In city planning it took a stance even more radical than Atatürk's Ankara, building a brand-new capital.

At the far end of the grassy mall that forms the spine at the heart of Brasília, from the presidential palace to the twin slabs of the Parliament

Building, is a curious structure that apparently floats on a reflecting pool. In the context of the dazzling white concrete shells of the legislative assembly, the swooping glass colonnades of the ministries that form the centerpiece of the city, or the huge sculptural monuments that signal the Defense Ministry and the cathedral, it's discreet to the point of being invisible. A slender male figure, extending his arm in the direction of the Plaza of the Three Powers, stands on a pencil-slim concrete mast, embraced by a dramatic concrete ribbon. The object marks the entrance to the JK Foundation. The initials stand for Juscelino Kubitschek.

In fact, this is a museum to Kubitschek, the Brazilian-born son of Slovak migrants, who was to Brazil what John F. Kennedy was to America. Glamorous, dashing, Kubitschek was the subject of a wild popularity cult, and his initials are still instantly recognizable to Brazilians even after the JFK magic has faded. He was the president who, in an apparently throwaway remark during the 1955 election campaign, committed himself to implementing a long-ignored provision in the Brazilian constitution. He would move the national capital out of the colonial port city of Rio de Janeiro and build a new seat of government in the empty heart of the country. It was a deliberate attempt to create a new identity for Brazil, reversing centuries of political and cultural subservience to Europe. And it was one of the few examples of a national identity built on an architecture entirely free of historical memories.

You enter the museum, designed by Oscar Niemeyer, architect of most of the city's monuments and a lifelong friend of Kubitschek, by descending a monumental flight of steps that sinks beneath the surface of an artificial lake. Then you find yourself in a re-creation of Kubitschek's study—his books, his pictures, his mementos, and his Eames chair are all here. In the next room is his life, recorded in photographs and documents. They show his childhood home in the remote state of Minas Gerais, his diplomas, doctorates, and medals. And then there are the theodolites and other surveyor's instruments that were used to set out the city that is Kubitschek's most lasting contribution to his country. You realize that this is no ordinary museum when you find the light level sinking, and you emerge into a darkened space in which you become gradually aware of a polished stainless-steel object, floating above a purple-neon-lit plinth. It is Kubitschek's tomb, a catafalque irresistibly suggestive of an ancient burial site. (No wonder that hawkers distribute leaflets in the city that claim Brasília was planned by ancient Egyptian astronauts.) After a few moments of contemplation, you emerge to find yourself in the sunshine, face-to-face with a 1975 Cadillac encased in a glass cube. This was the car in which Kubitschek died after a crash on the road to São Paulo from Rio.

The tomb is the embodiment of the architectural representation of power, an essential part of the foundation myth of a city whose very existence is a potent demonstration of the political uses of architecture. In the context of a city without history, it provides an injection of memory and a sense of the supernatural. Even in the most apparently rational, coldly logical, and man-made of cities, the magic of architectural myth-making is still apparently an essential ingredient in the creation of a sense of national identity. For strong leaders, like Kubitschek in Brasília and Atatürk in Ankara, embarked on a building program from strategic calculation, there is always the risk of toppling over the edge into the kind of vanity and narcissism that drove the Pahlavis and the Marcoses.

CHAPTER 7

IDENTITY IN THE
AGE OF UNCERTAINTY

OF ALL THE MODERN BUILDING TYPES, THE AIRPORT, EVEN MORE than the skyscraper, has become the focus for national and civic rivalry, a sign of status in the competition between one city and another. While air travel itself has become ever more squalid, terminal designs fluctuate between the search for economy and prestige.

They are a powerful demonstration of the fact that modern democracies are as interested in the uses of monumental architecture as the authoritarians and the dictators. Paris's Charles de Gaulle Airport at Roissy dates back to the era of its namesake, so it does not qualify as one of the *"grands projets"* initiated by François Mitterrand. But it might just as well have been: it is a project rooted firmly in the French monumental tradition of doing things not just on a big and intimidatingly impressive scale but in a manner deliberately different from anybody else.

Competition from London's Heathrow helped France to make the costly decision to build a brand-new airport at Roissy in 1964. First Le Bourget and then Orly had reached the limits of their capacities, and a new airport was a necessity. To compete in the European context, the French government decided that it had to start again. A decade in the making, Charles de Gaulle opened in 1974. In the autocratic French way, traffic was switched from Orly by decree to make the new airport into the country's main international gateway overnight. When the first terminal was full, plans were drawn up for a fivefold expansion, around a second terminal, built in a completely different style. And with the same clear-sighted, unsentimental ruthlessness that has typified the French way of doing things, the government went ahead and built it, without wasting time on consulting the public or the airlines.

Neither of the terminals at Charles de Gaulle is like any other major airport in the world. The first looks like a beehive. Designed by Paul Andreu, and apparently inspired by a set from Fritz Lang's *Metropolis* (a vision of the future that was intended to have a threatening edge), it was embraced by France in its determination to become the personification of modernity. The second, built gradually in five sections, was planned to allow passengers to be dropped off by car as close as possible to the aircraft door. It requires them to know exactly which section of the terminal their flight is departing from, and it uses up a great deal of land. But it allowed France to bask in the sleek modernity of the airport's soaring concrete roofs, the great oval windows cut out of them, and the dramatic glass air-bridges reaching out to the planes. Or at least it did, until part of the concrete roof collapsed in the spring of 2004, less than a year after Terminal 2E had been completed. The collapse marked a temporary setback for Paris's ambitious plans to build Europe's preeminent airport.

The Paris airport is the largest single example of French state architectural patronage, and it reveals a lot about the country's taste for a particularly imperial version of modern architecture. It shows France as a country with a tradition of politicians with strong views about building. In recent times there has been Mitterrand, with his pharaonic schemes for Paris, and Jacques Chirac, who, on becoming mayor of Paris, killed off the development of a new shopping complex at Les Halles initiated by then-President Valéry Giscard d'Estaing and imposed his own solution, announcing, *"L'architect en chef, c'est moi."* Despite Chirac's democratic mandate, he sounded more like an Atatürk or a Pahlavi than a Western European mayor.

It's certainly not the kind of remark that any British prime minister of modern times could conceivably have uttered. But when Tony Blair decided to go ahead with the building of London's Millennium Dome, three months after his overwhelming election victory in 1997, he came close. The Dome was nothing less than a deliberate attempt to create a landmark that would serve as the opening salvo in his campaign for election to a second term. In building it, Blair was adopting the style of a French autocrat, even if he did not have the brio to carry it off.

Britain is a country that has had a historic aversion to spending money on large-scale cultural projects. The National Gallery's principal façade, the one overlooking Trafalgar Square, was built using recycled Corinthian columns salvaged from a demolition site. The British Museum was funded through a lottery. Until the late 1990s, monument making had not by and large been an activity that had found much sympathy with the British political elite. Quite the contrary: it seemed to go hand in hand with vulgar display and even carried with it a hint of the corruption that had seen T. Dan Smith, the American-style city boss of Newcastle, jailed for accepting kickbacks during his campaign to rebuild the city in the 1960s. The commitment of public money to the Dome cut right across that puritanical streak.

The assumption of power by the Blair government, so often described as presidential in its swagger, was accompanied by what was, by British standards, an unparalleled burst of political interest in the imagery of architecture and design. Suddenly new architecture was no longer an affront, the way that it had been when the Prince of Wales had taken up such a passionate interest in the subject fifteen years earlier. A crop of eccentrically shaped buildings was sprouting all over the country. A plethora of nebulously conceived cultural projects, which were high on pious hope and mostly low on common sense and longevity, began in quick succession. Many of them did not survive.

In Spain, Barcelona had used high-profile architecture to awake from the malign neglect of the Franco years. London, still struggling to remake itself in the collapse of its old industrial and port economy, began to think that it might be able to do the same. But the idea of government patronage in architecture was fundamentally alien to British politicians, who schooled themselves in the mantras of consensus, partnership, and inclusiveness. The idea of a single vision, which is what a building of intellectual challenge and aesthetic quality must be, simply didn't fit with this worldview.

Blair's government deliberately set out to portray the British state in terms of modernity. Their strategy coincided with the abandonment of the assumption that it is the duty of British governments to preside over at least the façade of continuity. There was in this rupture a clear echo of the self-conscious youthfulness of the no longer derided Labour administration of Harold Wilson in 1964, with its embrace of new technology and popular culture. Tony Blair wasn't after all the first prime minister to bask in the reflected glory of rock stars. At Wilson's behest, the Queen had awarded the Beatles membership in the Order of the British Empire. In his early days in power, Blair invited Oasis, the self-proclaimed successors to the Beatles, to Downing Street, as well as a room full of architects. But Blair was the first to have surreptitiously rechristened his party.

Labour had become New Labour when the electorate wasn't looking. Where once the British valued the marks of tradition above all else, a series of financial disasters, from a Lloyd's of London insurance underwriting fiasco, which bankrupted scores of middle-class families, to the collapse of the stuffy centuries-old Barings Bank, brought down by a single delinquent (and working-class) trader, suddenly created exactly the opposite assumption. The outward signs of tradition seemed to signal disaster. Elderly retainers, doormen in frock coats, and offices lined with ancient wooden paneling had once suggested probity and solid decency. The mess at Lloyd's and then at Barings suddenly reversed the signals.

The survival of ancient tradition became synonymous with an institution in terminal decline.

The new political class that took power when Tony Blair was elected in 1997 convinced themselves that they could move beyond a threadbare, time-expired vision of Britishness rooted in pageantry, the royal family, and cricket. They thought that they had learned the lessons of François Mitterrand's Paris and Pasqual Maragall's Barcelona, about the importance of constructing a state based on the idea of modernity. Carefully briefed by the Labour peer Richard Rogers, Britain's politically best-connected architect for half a century, Labour leaders, including Blair's deputy, John Prescott, made the pilgrimage to Spain to see what impressive new buildings could do for a government. They returned from Barcelona determined to impress their own electorate with a similar crop of landmarks. Some of them had even understood what they were looking at. And as a result, they embarked on a campaign "to rebrand Britain," as they put it—a campaign that claimed to be about both symbolism and, in theory at least, substance.

No single building embodied this preoccupation as clearly as the government's plans to commemorate the millennium with a massive structure on the Greenwich peninsula. As a result, the 300-acre site of what had been toxic Victorian dereliction is now occupied by what was for a while the most highly charged piece of political architecture England had yet seen, and what has turned into a painful piece of scar tissue for the government. The Millennium Dome, although initiated by the fading Conservative government of John Major, was eagerly adopted by Tony Blair to represent the apotheosis of New Labour, a propaganda tool to signal a new political dispensation. As revealing as the official rhetoric crowding around the structure were the unintentional meanings it unwittingly highlighted with even greater force.

It was meant to be a yearlong exhibition to celebrate the millennium, which would not only charm the British public but also reflect well on the government.

In the end it became a huge embarrassment. The government poured £1 billion into the Greenwich peninsula in the belief that it was embracing modernity. In fact, the usually sure-footed grasp of political iconography of the prime minister's inner circle deserted it. The Dome turned out not to be about the future at all. It was actually a fundamentally nostalgic and even inept return to the 1950s, a reprise of the Festival of Britain, the event that celebrated the country's emergence from the Second World War. The Dome recycled the two most enduring images of that 1951 fair, the Dome of Discovery and the Skylon, a needle-shaped landmark supported on steel cables. Both were evoked in the shape of Richard Rogers's Teflon-coated tent, with its vivid yellow crown of thorns. However, a world-weary, seen-it-all-before Britain was in no mood to listen to portentous collective statements about the future. Or even less to be force-fed pious homilies, condescendingly sugarcoated with the dubious presentational skills of public service advertising.

Although the Dome became the very embodiment of New Labour aspirations, the Conservatives initiated the National Lottery that was to end up paying for it. They came up with the idea of celebrating the millennium by allotting one-fifth of the yield from the lottery to the Millennium Commission, which would then build a series of monumental projects across Britain.

Such interparty promiscuity was new for Britain. The Festival of Britain was instigated by the reforming Labour government of Clement Attlee and begrudgingly opened by its Conservative successor, which went on to tear down all its physical legacies, save for Royal Festival Hall, as soon as it decently could. Blair's embrace of the Dome was all the more surprising in that the scheme could have been canceled without the slightest political risk. Blair chose to take it on against the firm opposition of Chancellor of the Exchequer Gordon Brown. Indeed, it might have been precisely because Brown, his great party rival, was against the scheme that Blair backed it.

The government charged the millennium commissioners, a group of the great and the good, with selecting where to spend the lottery money. As they toured the country in 1994, dispensing largesse to such unlikely projects as a plan to garnish Portsmouth harbor with a giant fountain, while refusing to fund Zaha Hadid's design for an opera house in Cardiff, they came up with the germ of the idea that would lead to the Dome. Two commissioners in particular, the Conservative politician Michael Heseltine and the journalist Simon Jenkins, believed that they should create a single national focus for the millennium celebration.

The Dome went through a roller coaster of different and often conflicting objectives and goals. It began as an attempt to harness the market at the tail end of Thatcherism, as a private enterprise project, and turned into an almost entirely publicly funded scheme. It was conceived of as an attempt to provide a vision of the future, and yet the Dome's creative director, Stephen Bayley, said even before he quit that it was fundamentally a "quaint" idea of an exposition in the nineteenth-century mold.

The Dome was obviously a project that could only be delivered by public sector money. But the Millennium Commission was committed by the government to embrace the idea of market forces. In pursuit of the mirage that private investors would take on the risk, the commission went as far as begging British Airways to take it on.

The commission also asked Lord Rogers to come up with an architectural strategy for accommodating the exhibition, once the Greenwich site was selected, and his proposal was accepted in 1996. The plan was a solution born of necessity, its elements dictated by lack of time and lack of certainty about content. Rather than wrestle with designing a series of individual pavilions to deal with all this, the Rogers team proposed the so-called Dome—actually, it was a cable-supported tent. Not only did it look striking, it offered enough flexibility under its capacious shelter for the organizers not to worry about the lack of clarity on what to put inside. Instead, construction could safely start and detailed consideration of its use could be left until later.

At the very least, this highly practical approach to creating a structure meant that the Dome could open in December 1999. As a result, English Partnerships, the government's urban renewal arm, bought the site in February 1997 for £20 million, finally committing taxpayers' money to the project. Three months later, a general election swept the Conservatives out of power. But even before that, Michael Heseltine had been making representations to Tony Blair about a future Labour administration's adopting the Dome. That would be, he implied, the most obvious means of celebrating the achievements of a modernizing new government, and this was a new government that was determined to celebrate its achievements.

Which is how the Millennium Dome, the greatest empty gesture of British cultural life, happened.

Tony Blair may be as much of an autocrat as François Mitterrand, but he lacks Mitterrand's instinctive confidence in his own judgment in architectural issues. Blair needs to be told what to like, or rather what to say that he likes. And there was nobody close enough to Blair on whom he could rely for decisive guidance.

The question of what to put inside the Dome was equally difficult. The intention was to be popular, inspiring, and thoughtful, while also commercially attractive to sponsors. And the Dome needed to meet an enormously ambitious target of 10 million visitors. It was an impossible combination.

The detailed design of the Dome's contents involved some architects of striking ability, including Zaha Hadid. But their political patrons had no way of distinguishing them from the hack designers who specialized in launching new trucks in flurries of lasers and dry ice, who had been brought in to devise large chunks of the Dome's exhibits.

Even before the Dome opened, it became the focus of enormous popular hostility. Not only was it regarded as a huge waste of money, but sharp questions had begun to be asked about the precise nature of the message that it would be putting across.

Preparations had focused on how to get the structure finished in time, with no agreement on what should go inside the Dome. And as the opening neared, the confusion increased. One after another, the individuals nominally in charge of devising the content resigned in frustration or were moved on.

The prime minister was forced into mounting a vigorous defense of the project. But with the Dome's designers still not clear on the exact nature of the contents twelve months before it opened, he had to rely on carefully crafted bombast rather than specifics:

> Picture the scene. The clock strikes midnight on 31 December 1999. The eyes of the world turn to the spot where the new millennium begins—the Meridian Line at Greenwich. This is Britain's opportunity to greet the world with a celebration that is so bold, so beautiful, so inspiring that it embodies at once the spirit of confidence and adventure in Britain and the spirit of the future in the world. This is the reason for the Millennium Experience. Not a product of the imagination run wild, but a huge opportunity for Britain. So let us seize the moment and put on something of which we and the world will be proud. Then we will say to ourselves with pride this is our Dome, Britain's Dome, and believe me, it will be the envy of the world. We are leading the world in creativity, so why not put it on display? Why not shout about it? The Dome will be a celebration of the Best of Britain. The Dome's content will contain a rich texture of feelings: spiritual, emotional, fun. It will combine the best of other attractions in a unique experience. Exhilarating like Disney World—yet different. Educational and interactive, like the Science Museum—yet different. Emotional and uplifting like a West End musical—yet different. It will be shaped by the people. Visitors from all around the world will have the time of their lives.

Blair put on a remarkable performance, but in the end he was attempting to justify the unjustifiable: the building, at enormous public expense, of a theme park, a government-run one that would close after just a single year. What on earth made him believe that his government was in any way equipped to deliver such a thing, any more than it could deliver soccer champions or chart-topping musicians?

And when the Dome opened, its content—the Millennium Experience, as it called itself—was predictably disappointing. The Faith Zone, which attempted to portray a suitably ecumenical view of religion that would offend nobody, rubbed shoulders with displays on banking, ecology, and time, along with musical performances closely related to *Starlight Express*.

This was a not very exciting version of a world's fair. And in the light of the condescending, ill-conceived, and vastly over-budget nature of the majority of the Dome's content, for anybody who actually went, Blair's words are impossible to read now without cringing.

To WALK TO THE NEW WORLD OF THE DOME FROM FAMILIAR, scruffy nineteenth-century London, you must first negotiate the grimy Victorian streets of Greenwich. They peter out with disconcerting suddenness as you make the transition to the twenty-first century through what feels like an asteroid belt dotted with a few gigantic objects: anonymous sheds, elevated motorways, and an empty landscape of reclaimed heaps of construction debris and industrial waste. (Everyday normality vanishes into the howling urban void that constitutes the margins of most contemporary big cities.) In this setting, the Dome has become an anchor in a wilderness. But it is unclear whether it is teetering back into the oblivion of dereliction that the waste dumps that once stood on the site represented, or pointing the way to a more optimistic future.

On a summer lunchtime, four humiliating years after the Dome finally closed its doors without finding a new use, the yellow masts towering over the Thames have faded a little, and the huge white Teflon tent looks as if it has begun to sag. The whole place has taken on that desolate, sour sense of emptiness that is the aftertaste, or perhaps the lingering hangover, of most attempts at official grandiloquence, like the rotting glimpses of the future that are still a pungent reminder of the two New York world's fairs in Queens or the unfulfilled promises of the 1992 Seville Expo.

The weeds are determinedly trying to force their way through the blue mesh fences that ring the Dome's site in untidy clumps. The red concrete surface of the piazza in front of the entrance plaza and the paving of the concourse linking the Dome to the North Greenwich tube station have been set in undulating motion as the mud tries to heave its way back into view, surging up from where it has been banished.

Dandelions are sprouting through the cracked paving slabs. There are fences within fences, and security men in their high-visibility vests reminding you of the vivid shades of yellow of the Dome's masts as they were before the paint started to fade. The ticket booths, which were never busy during the Millennium Experience's sparsely attended run, are shuttered and empty. Strange, unidentifiable pieces of electrical equipment sit stacked upside down inside them. The vegetation around the perimeter is dead, the once carefully tended planting boxes have gone to seed, and their luxuriant green leaves have faded to brown. Security patrols still drive around the perimeter aimlessly, dodging the tumbleweed in the scores of deserted parking lots. Only the one nearest the Underground station is still in use, filled with commuters from Kent who leave their SUVs and dive down into the tube as quickly as they can to take the subway into town.

When the Dome's contents had been emptied out, the government's urban renewal agency, desperate to attract businesses and home owners into the area, moved in. The bright showrooms it set up to bring the brittle promise of regeneration to the area—offering businessmen incentives to build factories and open offices—are locked and empty now.

Through the windows you glimpse the cheap purple sofas of the new tomorrow. They have chairs tipped upside down sitting on top of them. The specially built bus station—designed by Norman Foster in the form of a stealth bomber—above the specially built subway line is a ghostly shadow of its former self. Though the station is big enough to handle huge crowds all day long, the flow of commuters has been reduced to a rush-hour trickle. As they emerge from the tunnels, they have a chance to look back at the towers of Canary Wharf from the east, a reminder of just how far the Dome still is from the seat of power in London.

The official budget, £758 million, was big enough—a sum so huge in fact that nobody questioned its accuracy. The true cost was a long way beyond £1 billion. Of that original budget, £466 million was allocated to building costs, and the remainder to operations, marketing, and contingencies. All of it was to be financed by £150 million in sponsorship, £209 million in revenue (and the eventual sale of materials after the Dome closed), and £449 million in cash from the Millennium Commission. Laughably, the Millennium Experience's business plan contained a notion that some of that commercial revenue would be paid back to the government. This sum did not, however, include the cost of site acquisition or decontamination. When these costs are taken into account, the actual price tag is £905 million, with millions more in interest payments and security costs. Both the sponsorship and the ticket receipts fell far short of what was promised, while four years after the millennium, the government had still failed to find a new user and continued to pay the maintenance and security bills. Its first attempt to auction the site collapsed. Finally it managed to unload it onto an American sports entrepreneur.

EXPO 2000 IN HANOVER, WHICH OPENED A FEW MONTHS AFTER the Dome, was Germany's attempt to celebrate the millennium with a world's fair. It's what the Dome could have been if the Millennium Commission hadn't insisted on reclaiming the toxic waste dumps of Greenwich, and had instead chosen a proposal to celebrate the dawn of the year 2000 at the National Exhibition Center in Birmingham. On a site in the middle of nowhere, Hanover opted for a makeover of a collection of glum concrete sheds (normally used to show off machine tools and construction equipment) plus an assortment of specially constructed new pavilions of variable quality, rather than a brand-new project. At a declared cost of £1 billion, it was at least as expensive as the Dome, and by predicting visits of 40 million people in six months, it had a target that the Millennium Commission never dreamed of, even in its most optimistic moments. But because it stuck to the traditional formula of the world's fair—acres of brilliantly crafted junk, with the occasional flash of genius—it was less of a disappointment.

Despite all the morally improving rhetoric about sustainability and new technology, Hanover featured a series of pavilions of such baroque kitschness that it was impossible not to warm to them. They at least had the courage of their convictions in a way that very little at the Dome did. You could find a fortress straight out of *Beau Geste* built by the United Arab Emirates, complete with cannon at the main gate and an Airbus load of authentic desert sand. It was sandwiched between the ski lift swinging across the site and the Ferris wheel. There was a traditional village from Bhutan embellished with eight hundred specially commissioned carvings. Croatia's sky-blue box allowed you to walk over a glass-covered beach strewn with archaeological fragments. Monaco constructed a pavilion in praise of tax exile, a dazzling white apartment block with a millionaire's yacht floating in its own tank of water. The Poles couldn't make up their mind whether to go for cutting-edge architectural modernity, like their Baltic neighbors, or opt for the ethnic end of the market, exploring the same territory as the UAE. They tried to have it both ways, building a plate-glass box into which they inserted a collection of thatched cottages, an effect much like putting a ship in a bottle. But alongside all this was a beautifully chaste pavilion designed by Alvaro Siza for Portugal, as moving a piece of architecture in its way as any of his permanent buildings. The Japanese pavilion was built by Shigeru Ban using only paper.

The German pavilions, while none of them were particularly distinguished pieces of architecture, did manage to be genuinely engaging. One pavilion the size of a football stadium featured nothing but a flock of seventy-two self-propelled robots as big as elephants silently circling the giant, darkened interior. Another contained Bach's piano, the first car ever built by Benz, a slice of the Berlin Wall, and the actual peace treaty the Federal Republic of Germany had signed with France in 1956 to settle the future of Alsace. Rather than build a pavilion, as even the Hungarians and the Yemenis managed, Britain rented a ready-made industrial shed from the organizers, customizing it with red, white, and blue stickers on the exterior. It purported to celebrate the quality of Britain's architects and designers. However, the government hadn't employed any of them to design it, selecting instead HP: ICM, a previously obscure firm that can hardly be said to have covered itself in glory when it worked at the Dome. Inside, you could find a curious hymn to Blairism subtitled "Diversity, It's in Our Nature." The sum of Britain's contemporary achievements in design was represented by ashtrays from assorted Conran restaurants, alongside a Dyson vacuum cleaner, a wind-up radio, and the somewhat presumptuous suggestion that, based on the birthplace of its designer, the iBook for Apple is in some mysterious way an example of British design.

The British exhibit sat in the shadow of the Dutch pavilion, designed by MVRDV architects, which was everything that Britain's was not. In the flat and featureless landscape of Hanover, it stood out with the force of a skyscraper in the prairie. Taking the form of a layer cake that symbolized the Dutch landscape, it contained no exhibits as such, but the architecture was integrated with content. One floor was a greenhouse growing a meadow of daisies under artificial sunlight. Piled on top of that was a forest of oak trees. From the ground, you could look up and see the surreal spectacle of the trees sitting on the neon-strip-lit ceiling. The top slice of the cake was a clutch of wind-powered generators and an artificial turf mound.

The whole thing established a jangling tension between the natural and the man-made, which is what Holland is all about. It will go down as one of the few truly great pieces of world's fair architecture, alongside Mies van der Rohe's Barcelona pavilion and Moshe Safdie's Habitat flats at Montreal's Expo 67.

We remember successful world's fairs for the innovation of their architecture and engineering, none more so than the first, the Great Exhibition in London of 1851, and Joseph Paxton's huge prefabricated structure, the Crystal Palace. But the reality of the Crystal Palace was that it was filled with replicas of the Venus de Milo carved in butter. And the same Universal Exhibition in 1889 in Paris that built the Eiffel Tower also boasted a replica of the Bastille, stormed every hour on the hour by a troupe of actors dressed as sansculottes. The Dome was neither one thing nor another, not bad enough, but not good enough either. It was too polite to follow in the full-blooded tradition of the great expositions, and its exhibits were too bland to have the redeeming confidence of the Crystal Palace.

SCOTLAND HAS, FOR A COUNTRY OF JUST FIVE MILLION PEOPLE, a remarkably high level of what might be called brand recognition, and not just at the level of caricature. A Scot in rural China, Russia's Far East, or Brazil has a far better chance of successfully explaining where he is from than, say, a Norwegian, a Quebecker, or even an Austrian or a Belgian.

Scotland has a distinctive accent, or rather accents. It has the clan tartans (actually, a nineteenth-century invention) and the bagpipes that it shares with several other Celtic nations. It has whisky and shortbread. It has a national poet, its own banknotes and legal system, a national church, and an educational system all its own. In the hands of a young generation of writers, it has bred an energetic and distinctive literary voice.

Scotland and England have shared a head of state for four hundred years, since James VI was seduced by the prospect of acquiring the crown of a country so much more prosperous than Scotland into moving down to London to become James I of England as well. What followed was no conquest, but a gradual merger in which both parties retained their individual identities, formalized in the Act of Union in 1707.

And now, after almost three hundred years, it has its own parliament again, with a new building in Edinburgh. Designed by Enric Miralles and Benedetta Tagliabue before Miralles's tragically early death, it is a project that demonstrates the engagement of architecture with political life on a variety of levels. Every step of the process has been charged with resonances that go far beyond pragmatic construction issues, from the site eventually selected to the materials used and the nationality of the architects.

Even before the design was addressed, choosing the location provoked endless, mainly politically rooted arguments. Should the parliament meet in the Scottish capital at all? If it did, should it be on the edge of the city, where the land was cheaper, or in the middle? Should this parliament take over the former Edinburgh High School, the classical landmark earmarked for an earlier, failed attempt at setting up a devolved parliament? The latter was rejected ostensibly on grounds of practicalities, but many assumed that it was not considered suitable by Labour politicians because it had become so closely associated with the politics of the Scottish Nationalists, who were looking for full independence from London rather than a devolved government. Eventually a former brewery building just off the Royal Mile, adjacent to the Palace of Holyroodhouse was chosen, a spot that could be seen as locating the new institution within a traditional context, but one free from excess baggage.

The choice of a Catalan architect after a drawn-out selection process and the personal involvement of Donald Dewar, Scotland's first minister, were clearly anything but accidental. The Catalans are the leading role models for ambitious small European nations attempting to assert their own distinctive identities, shorn of any of the darker overtones of nationalism. Scotland, it would seem, wants to be seen in this way, asserting its national identity but offering an inclusive kind of nationalism, not a narrowly chauvinistic one.

Nobody asked Miralles to use a national style in Edinburgh. And his design is clearly a highly personal one that springs from his own deeply felt architectural sensibility. His original submission touchingly showed as his point of departure a photograph from a student trip to Britain of two upturned turf-covered rowing boats he had found on a beach that may or may not have been in Scotland. He was suggesting that he wanted to build a parliament that felt like a natural part of the site, rather than an imposition on it. Despite this poetic vision, he had to work with the political ambitions of the Scottish system.

The civil servants leading the project were asked to deliver a building that would accommodate a system of government based on collaboration and consensus, one in which committee rooms would be the focus of activity as much as the debating chamber. Above all, those planning the project believed that it should not look anything like the Westminster parliamentary model. If it did, it would risk being understood as a deferential offshoot. Scotland—or at least the tiny political and administrative elite that claimed to speak for the country—wanted to show that it had left the bad old days of Westminster politics behind. Westminster, so they told themselves, represented the politics of confrontation and obstruction. The very form of its debating chamber—a rectangle lined by opposed ranks of benches set two sword lengths apart—was, they claimed, calculated to bring out the worst in its members. Actually, however, the arrangement is an accident of history: England's Parliament had begun to meet in the thirteenth century in the choir stalls of the chapel of St. Stephen at the Palace of Westminster, and simply took over the existing furniture.

Scotland wanted a supposedly gentler, more constructive layout. The circular model common on mainland Europe, which first saw the light of day in modern times in Dublin, in the Irish House of Commons (now the Bank of Ireland), was a possibility.

After a protracted argument, a couple of redesigns, and countless fact-finding missions by the politicians, Miralles ended up giving Edinburgh a gently curved crescent-shaped debating chamber. It takes rather more than an adjustment to the seating arrangements to instill a collaborative spirit into a fractious legislative assembly, as the members of the Scottish parliament have amply demonstrated in their many bad-tempered exchanges in their temporary, circular chamber.

THE OLD MAPS OF EDINBURGH MAKE THE CITY'S MEDIEVAL MAIN street, the Royal Mile, running along the ridge on which the city grew over the centuries, look like an elongated fish spine. The castle, sitting on its rock at the top, is its tail. Holyroodhouse, the official residence of the kings of Scotland, next to the ruins of the abbey at the bottom of the slope, is its head. In between, a procession of spiky curved bones mark the wynds and closes of urban Scottish domestic life that open off it on both sides. These narrow lanes and tight courtyards were surrounded by tenements six and eight stories high. The well-to-do lived on the lower floors, and the poor took the attics. Halfway down the spine, behind its cool, elegant early nineteenth-century façade, stands Scotland's old parliament house. It was built as a hurried job-creation scheme funded by the city council in the 1630s. Charles I made it clear that the price of a continued legislative presence in Edinburgh—with all the attendant implications for the ongoing employment prospects of fencing masters, wig makers, tavern keepers, courtesans, and claret importers—was the construction, like some sort of seventeenth-century Bilbao Guggenheim, of an impressive new Scottish parliament. The place was shut down after the Act of Union, finding a new role as Scotland's high court, but not before the distribution of copious quantities of English gold to persuade wavering members to disband themselves.

The new Scots parliament, which began life in a temporary home in 1999 as the guest of the assembly of the Church of Scotland toward the top end of the Royal Mile, is now in Enric Miralles's building, a lyrical and complex composition of oak, granite, and steel, half buried into a meadow and wrapped carefully into Edinburgh's medieval fabric, that looks the palace straight in the eye. Much, so it is said, to the distaste of the Prince of Wales.

There is always room for a gap to open up between architectural intentions and the message that a building actually transmits. That is certainly the case here. On one level, Miralles's parliament is a delicately wrought, romantic poem to the expressive qualities of architecture, and the tactile qualities of wood and stone. On another, and especially in the eyes of Scotland's newspapers, it is a shocking, even scandalous case of the gross mismanagement of public money. A project first budgeted at £50 million ended up costing £431 million. Those first figures didn't include the cost of the land, any professional fees, or tax, but the actual total still reflects a huge increase, and an embarrassment that has at times threatened to overwhelm the parliament, as well as the message it was intended to convey. The officials who were charged with getting the project off the ground made educated guesses about costs that were deliberately minimized so that they wouldn't look too frightening. The parliament building is double the size that was originally planned. In addition, Queensberry House, a seventeenth-century mansion at the center of the site, was rescued from ruin and incorporated into the parliament, and the whole site rendered truck-bombproof. But those extras aren't much compensation for the scale of the cost overrun. Miralles died just after work had started on the building, shortly before the death of Donald Dewar, the new parliament's political sponsor. Their deaths came in 2000, just at the beginning of a series of crises that afflicted the financial aspects of the project.

The cost overrun is so extreme that it makes it hard to discuss the architectural qualities of the parliament. If you talk only about the architecture without mentioning the money, you end up sounding like a feeble-minded design victim. Lord Fraser of Carmylle, who was appointed by Scotland's first minister to conduct a yearlong public inquiry into the cost overrun, had an easier time of it. He promised, in a way that makes it sound like a perfectly reasonable proposition, to avoid any consideration of aesthetics in his judgments. But it simply isn't possible to divorce what the parliament looks like (and feels like as it's used) from what it has cost. It would be as pointless as writing a Michelin guide that evaluated only the cost of a meal's ingredients and overlooked how they taste.

The figures certainly look bad. If you had set out to build a kitchen for $40,000, and it ended up costing you $400,000, you would need a special kind of stoicism to take much pleasure in the exquisite workmanship of the oak cabinets and the Portuguese limestone floor. But a parliament is not a kitchen extension, and the quality of the architecture will last much longer than the burden of the cost.

However, to say that the building is worth the nightmarish cost escalation is not a view that is very popular in Scotland. The embarrassments of the Holyrood building program have been an all-consuming obsession for the country for so long that it's going to take time for the parliament to be understood as anything other than a monstrous waste of money.

Lord Fraser, the thickset former Scottish lord advocate who had presided over the Lockerbie bombing trial, turned himself into a public spectacle on the strength of Holyrood. He set up his own Web site, hired a spin doctor, and commissioned a purple logo for the inquiry. And he took to posing for the cameras in front of the cranes at Holyrood, multiple chins prominent, promising with startling originality to leave no stone unturned. Clearly delighted with his own performance, Fraser conducted the public inquiry with the colossal self-regard of a man who believes that he is presiding over a Watergate hearing combined with the South African Truth and Reconciliation Commission. "This inquiry should be part of the cleansing process," he intoned, suggesting that he felt Scotland's pain about spending all that money. "We have already brought into the public domain much which was unknown, unexplained, or inexplicable. And for that, I can compliment the subtle brilliance of my team."

From the tone of his pronouncements immediately after he was appointed, Fraser appeared to have already made up his mind that he was going to be digging up serious evidence of wrongdoing. He opened a hotline for anonymous whistle-blowers, which by all accounts never even got so much as tepid. And, presumably in an effort to encourage candor in his witnesses, he promised no testimony would be used in criminal proceedings.

"If anyone, or any organization attempts to stop me, I will have no hesitation in naming and shaming them," he said. "I am determined that this inquiry will provide the people of Scotland with answers. The people of Scotland expect the truth, they deserve the truth, and I am determined that they will get the truth."

To give him his due, Fraser's showmanship managed to extract far more courtroom drama from the finer points of building prices, contract law, and project management than anybody could have imagined. He discovered that Miralles's Barcelona office and his Edinburgh collaborators, RMJM, had all but stopped talking to each other. He may or may not have found that Miralles had no up-to-date professional indemnity cover when he won the competition. He can't be sure because the official who scrutinized a photocopy of a Spanish insurance certificate testified that he had only just enough Spanish to order a beer.

Fraser managed to skewer a couple of Scottish executive officials hopelessly out of their depth and flushed some of the more self-indulgent of the many grotesques who infest the edges of Scottish political life. Margo MacDonald, an erratic former Scottish Nationalist who left the party to become an independent MP, claims that the parliament at Holyrood is the greatest catastrophe in Scottish building history. Given that Scotland gave the world the Tay Bridge disaster, when a railway viaduct a mile long blew away in a storm while a train was crossing, that was certainly not an understatement. But all politicians tend to talk that way. Fraser also listened politely to the evidence of David Black, who has bafflingly attempted to portray Donald Dewar as a Richard Nixon figure. He wrote a confused book about the project, titled *All the First Minister's Men.* Yet Black can't make up his mind whom to blame. Sometimes it's the Glaswegians, who rigged the competition jury in order to embarrass Edinburgh. Sometimes it's London, which apparently deliberately used the parliament to demonstrate how incapable the Scots were of governing themselves, or else to make the institution invisible by fobbing it off with the wrong site.

The Fraser inquiry scrutinized the tens of thousands of decisions big and small that shape any complex building. In the process two different worlds—architecture and the law—collided but somehow failed entirely to engage with each other.

Early in the hearings Fraser produced Richard Armstrong, a civil servant who had left the project in angry circumstances, of whom he clearly had high hopes. Armstrong, who had been the parliament's project manager, produced a memo to his superiors at the Scottish Executive written at the time of the competition: "I am sorry to say that my overall impression is one of disappointment. I find it hard to believe that such an allegedly massive architectural talent cannot produce one approach which is convincing, or acceptable."

Armstrong said that, if the decision had been his, he would not have short-listed Miralles. "With Miralles's other commitments, devoting twenty-one hours a week to this project was totally inadequate. I scored him in forty-fourth place out of seventy. I would instantly have moved him to seventieth if I had known then that he had no insurance cover."

Armstrong's reputation for consistency was undermined somewhat by another memo in which he claimed that of all the short-listed designers, Miralles was one of only two who could seriously be considered. John Campbell, Fraser's counsel, probed witnesses with questions that seemed to suggest that he believed Miralles had been placed on the short list improperly because of the Catalan's alleged friendship with one of the jury, and that he wasn't up to the job, presumably with a view to establishing that this was the root cause of the cost overrun.

Andy McMillan, onetime head of the Mackintosh School of Architecture in Glasgow, was the most forceful architectural member of the competition jury. Disarmingly, he responded to the interrogation with his recollection of Miralles's talking to Dewar: "To illustrate his scheme, he produced some leaves and stems which he laid on a plan to show us how the building would sit in the Canongate site, but also sit in what he described as the land of Scotland."

That gesture apparently won Miralles the commission. He was an architect who was much too smart for the obvious metaphors. In particular, he steered well away from that feeble idea about the literal representation of democracy through the transparency of glass. Instead Miralles created a landscape as much as a building.

"The parliament should be able to reflect the land which it represents," wrote Miralles. "The land itself will be a material, a physical building material. From the outset we have worked with the intuition that individual identification with land carries collective consciousness and sentiments." And he maintained the analogy, from that first image of the leaves and the stalk that he showed Donald Dewar, all the way through to his idea of a parliamentary chamber that he conceived of as "an amphitheater carved out of the rock for gatherings of people sitting on the landscape and identifying with their country."

These are not concepts that are easily expressed in the charged atmosphere of a judicial inquiry. And John Campbell skirted past McMillan's enthusiasm to ask him if he had ever stayed at Miralles's house in Berlin.

"I didn't know that he had one," was the reply. McMillan then went back to architecture. "Miralles had a poetic idea that there would be a bank of earth which people would sit on, a bit like Speaker's Corner, and discuss things."

In the transcript of the cross-examination, McMillan pauses, then addresses Campbell directly: "You may smile; you know what I mean. It is a charming idea. I think he had a passion which came across. One should not really say it, but it is a bit like football matches. We thought we had picked five people, all of whom were capable of giving us a world class building. But on the day of the final presentation, Miralles was clearly better."

On that day, I am sure that is exactly what Miralles was. Better than Richard Meier, better than Rafael Viñoly. Better than Michael Wilford and all the other competitors.

Walk around the foot of the Royal Mile, past the gates of Holyroodhouse Palace, and up toward Salisbury Crags, the volcanic cliff that looms over Edinburgh's Georgian terraces. It's a site of quite exceptional beauty and there, unwinding in front of you, is Miralles's parliament. It suggests an elusive sense of settled ease. It belongs to its surroundings.

Miralles's design breaks down the parliament's bulk into modest individual pieces that merge with the landscape. They open up to the sky to bring sunlight and the landscape into the lobbies and committee rooms, and even the debating chamber. The design uses concrete as a polished sculptural material, with a rich palette. Everywhere you see traces of Miralles's drawings: in the strips that are woven over the windows of the members' offices, in the gashes and gouges in the vaulted ceilings.

The parliament is a cluster of buildings. The easiest to grasp is the block that accommodates the members' offices, not that it could conceivably be described as an office block. There is room in it for 129 members and their staff. It is made from concrete, oak, and steel. There is granite, some of it from Scottish quarries in deference to the idea of national pride, and more of it from South Africa in the interests of economy.

Miralles was never prepared to tolerate the bland or the anonymous. For him work was not simply sitting at a desk. It meant thinking, contemplation, noticing that there is a soft rain falling on the slate roofs outside your window, and allowing yourself to be distracted from your computer screen. So the members' offices have vaulted concrete ceilings that make them feel like monastic cells. They have window seats, thus allowing members to climb up into a rounded wooden perch, away from the stresses of daily political battles, and read or think. Who knows whether they will actually do this, or what those offices will look like covered in the detritus of political life, with their electric kettles and their posters and their trophies. But the members and their staff have been offered individual spaces with character, where you feel that somebody has actually taken the trouble to make a space that is personal and individual, not the product of a random accident between floor, walls, and ceiling.

The west façade is a rock face, marked by a series of irregular protuberances that reflect the shape of the window seat inside the thickness of the wall. It sits at right angles to Queensberry House, originally built in 1667 and mutilated over the years by successive occupiers to the point of being unrecognizable. With nothing left of the interiors, Miralles's strategy in bringing it back into use was to create entirely new spaces within the surviving shell. It's here that the parliament's presiding officer and his team are based, and it's where Donald Dewar's library has been installed. At ground level, Queensberry House is linked, by way of a foyer, to the members of parliament's offices and the debating chamber. The foyer has a dramatic timber roof structure, supporting a series of petal-shaped roof lights.

If Miralles couldn't make members be nice to one another, he could at least give them a ravishingly beautiful space to meet in. His concept of the chamber as a sunlit room with glimpses out to the surrounding landscape survived the attempts of the media consultants to black it out to provide better TV pictures. Miralles took the theme of the hammer-beam roofs of the old parliament building up the hill and used it as an inspiration for an extraordinarily intricate timber roof in the chamber that takes the form of a series of bow-shaped segments.

Miralles's subtlest move was to create a sense of ambiguity about the debating chamber. It is the heart of the building, but it does not instantly reveal itself as such. It takes a careful look to understand where it is, for it is only one among a whole series of sculptural elements that make up the building.

The business of this parliament takes place just as much in the six committee rooms, built in a cluster of towers at the back of the debating chamber, or in the television studios in the press tower that sits over the Royal Mile, or in the corridors that link the chamber with the members' offices and with the administration's offices in Queensberry House.

But this is a parliament that was born in the twentieth century, a moment in history overburdened with the mission to explain, so there is also a sense in which the building has been designed to represent itself. It has been built to house members of parliament and their debating chamber. But it has also been designed as a place for the public to visit. Sweeping planes of concrete and stone erupt from the green meadows of the landscape to define the public entrance. The public can come for a lesson in Scotland's democracy, and visitors can wander through exhibition spaces, classrooms, cafés, and a foyer that has become the public face of the parliament.

When he was alive, Enric Miralles never really seemed to lay all his cards on the table. He hinted and finessed and imagined rather than directly described what he was intending to do with the parliament. His evocative drawings and collages were hard to read; they seemed to show an eruption of organic forms from the landscape that didn't quite add up to a building. Only now is it possible to see what he had in mind—and the reality is a powerful confirmation of his talent.

Miralles was an architect of what might be called an old-fashioned kind; his work was full of symbolic and representational qualities. He had a romantic vision that, had he lived, might have encouraged others to follow his search for a richer architectural vocabulary. When he died, his career cut cruelly short at just forty-five, he was on the verge of becoming a major figure, but without having yet completed the Edinburgh parliament that would demonstrate he offered much more than promise.

This is haute couture architecture—every door, every handle, every window, every light fitting has been designed as if it were a one-off—and it was almost as difficult to build as a Gaudí cathedral. Miralles designed spaces that surprise you as you move from one to another, and where you can suddenly find yourself looking up at the sky, or across another part of the parliament complex to see the landscape beyond.

If Holyrood is to be judged as a success, it is how it will work in twenty-five years or in a century that really counts, not the immediate response. The parliament will have proved itself architecturally if it can do something to persuade the fractious, the tired and emotional, the exhibitionists, opportunists, and zealots who make up the mainstream of political life—as well as the idealists and the self-sacrificing—to think a little bit more about the country that they represent, and to behave in a slightly more measured way. Could it have been built for less? Certainly. Is it value for money? No. But how do you place a value on the view of the green slopes of the hillside outside or the sense of continuity that comes from installing Donald Dewar's library in the shell of the aristocratic house in which the Act of Union was hidden from a Edinburgh mob?

In the end, the saga of the Edinburgh parliament building tells us that there is no such thing as historical inevitability. Dewar was in many ways the least likely of politicians to indulge in a taste for monumentalism. He was an ascetic—and for a politician, curiously unworldly—lawyer by training. Such people are preternaturally skeptical of aesthetic self-indulgence and of architects. And yet once he had engaged with the issue, he rapidly understood the parameters of the architectural world, and how to use them to achieve the building that he needed for his political purposes and his nation-defining objectives.

A parliament, or any other kind of democratic assembly, demands a complex combination of uses that even an opera house or a museum does not have. There is the debating chamber itself, as well as the backstairs aspects—the briefing rooms, the lobbies, the corridors, and the committee rooms—that all play their part in creating a political theater that can make real the ambitions of those who use it. Such chambers are not necessarily the embodiment of elevated ideals. Politics in the raw is about as interesting as a reading from the telephone directory, with endless procedural discussions and nit-picking points of order. For most of the day members sit in rooms, shuffle paper, talk on the phone, and check their e-mails. The struggle to make something out of this deeply unpromising material is the real story of the design of Miralles's parliament. This is also the story, although one with a very different outcome, of another political building, London's new City Hall. The seat of power of Mayor Ken Livingstone is one of the most conspicuous new buildings in London and represents British municipal politics translated for the television age.

The London Assembly's twenty-six members and the staff of five hundred could easily have been accommodated in an anonymous office building with no public recognition or iconographic significance. Doing so would have been presented as the financially responsible option. But it would also have left London's government invisible and lacking any sense of authority in its premises.

On the outside the building looks like a giant motorcycle helmet. On the inside it has been scooped out, to make way for a spiraling ramp of baroque complexity rising along its entire height. The carpet is purple, and the walls are yellow so that they look good on television. The ramp is there to celebrate the symbolic heart of the building, the debating chamber. But of course all this architectural drama is almost comically overblown. London's political representatives meet here just once a month. The rest of the time the chamber sits glorious but unused, unless the city rents it out for weddings and dance performances.

The real business is carried out in the offices. The mayor is up on the top, naturally. Livingstone, who has a finely pitched ear for the meaningless but telling symbolic gesture, asked for an office smaller than the one that he was originally allocated. The elected members are downstairs. They get individual offices with doors, clustered in the middle of the building—which allows the secretarial staff the windows.

The spiral starts beneath the chamber, wraps around it, and then soars up to the roof. It makes an impressive alternative to taking the stairs or the elevator. But the ramp is really there to raise the architectural temperature much more than to get from one floor to another.

Fundamentally, City Hall looks the way it does because it is trying to tell us something about itself. It's meant to look special.

THE DOME AND SCOTLAND'S PARLIAMENT WERE BOTH ATTEMPTS to celebrate democratic institutions. As Australia marked a century of nationhood in 2001, Prime Minister John Howard opened the new National Museum in Canberra. It's a project that is less a celebration of national identity than a critique of it. The architects have used what was intended to be a celebration of Australianness to ask difficult questions about the origins of Australia as a modern state and the nature of its culture. While you can find sporting hero Donald Bradman's cricket bat inside, along with the van that ferried Australia's first mobile television film unit around the outback, the museum is anything but a mindless celebration of the lucky country. It does not shrink from addressing the brutal history of its treatment of the Aborigines, both in its content and in its very fabric. You can see the pistols and metal clubs that colonists used to murder women and children when Tasmania's first Australians were exterminated. All of this, in the name of a celebration of Australia, was paid for by a conservative government.

But nothing on display is more controversial than the architecture itself. The architects, Ashton Raggatt McDougall from Melbourne, put those sections of the museum devoted to the Aborigines into a replica of Daniel Libeskind's Jewish Museum in Berlin. The scale is slightly reduced and the materials are different. Walls are made from black concrete, puckered to look like rubber, rather than the zinc sheet that Libeskind used. But the plan is an exact copy of the lightning-flash zigzag that Libeskind created by breaking a five-pointed Star of David, except that Howard Raggatt prefers to call it a quotation. Libeskind claimed to be angry at the use of his design, calling it "shocking, banal and plagiarism." For Raggatt, however, it is a legitimate strategy, put to work to make a comparison between the plight of the Aborigines, whose world was all but destroyed by the settlers' weapons, diseases, and alcohol, and the horror of the Holocaust. The message about white Australia's treatment of the Aborigines could not be clearer. The comparison made Ashton Raggatt McDougall far more unpopular with some of the more conservative members of the Australian government than they are with Libeskind. After all, John Howard is the prime minister who has refused to apologize on behalf of white Australia to the Aborigines for their maltreatment.

At another level, the design could be seen as a reflection of a particularly subtle way of white Australia's asserting its moral superiority by appearing to be so sophisticatedly critical of its history.

The museum certainly manages to press a lot of buttons in a way that suggests a rare ability to make architecture matter. It's not how the building looks that counts, but what it is saying. With a remarkable site in the heart of Canberra, overlooking Lake Burley Griffin, and aligned directly on the giant flagpole that crowns Parliament House, the museum forms a long ribbon, strung out along the waterfront and turning back on itself in a wide arc to create at its heart a sheltered garden of what the architects call Australian dreams. It's filled with a fragmented map of Australia pockmarked with the names of massacre sites and battlegrounds.

It's not just Libeskind's Jewish Museum that provides the architectural source material. The building is made up of a series of fragments, seamlessly and surreally joined one with another with the smoothness of a computer simulacrum. There are enough design quotations threaded together here to suggest that Australia has built a national museum of architecture rather than one dedicated to its social history. One part of the complex is a reworking of Le Corbusier's landmark of modernism, the Villa Savoie outside Paris, but the smooth, white skin of the original has turned fuzzy black and it has inverted the original façade as a mirror image. In conversation Raggatt reveals that this is a reference to the sense of cultural inferiority that Australia took so long to shake off. It's a reflection in the architectural sphere of Australia's colonial incarnation as a country in which all culture was imported from a long way off, and which had a habit of getting it slightly, but embarrassingly, wrong. When photographs of the Villa Savoie were first published in an Australian magazine, they were reproduced back to front but, according to Raggatt, nobody noticed. Australians took their cue for what they should be building from the other side of the world, and were too provincial even to be able to get their borrowings the right way around.

Elsewhere on the site a vivid red, flattened cutout of the façade of the Australian parliament is used to provide a suitably important-looking home for the Institute for Aboriginal Studies. It looks across a sweep of grass toward the Australian version of Libeskind's museum in Berlin, which in turn morphs into a central entrance hall in which Raggatt has painstakingly re-created fragments of the brown glass and the window mullions used in the Sydney Opera House. Again this is a two-edged sampling of an Australian architectural icon. It is a reminder of the crude and unsympathetic glazing that was the work of the Australian architectural team appointed to finish the opera house, after its European designer, Jørn Utzon, was driven out of the country by what have come to be stigmatized as antipodean philistines. Also incorporated into the museum are little souvenirs of James Stirling's Stuttgart Staatsgalerie and an Aldo Rossi building.

The museum could have turned out as a would-be high-culture version of Las Vegas, but it isn't. Raggatt has created a building that amounts to a book, even if it is written in a language that most people will have trouble reading. Ashton Raggatt McDougall don't content themselves with using buildings as metaphorical words—they have also covered their building with literal words, to provide another, all-but-incomprehensible layer of meaning. The aluminum skin is pitted with regular patterns of dimples, giant Braille characters used as a form of decoration. It's a language that very few sighted people can make sense of, and which is out of reach of the fingers of those blind visitors who might be able to read it. Raggatt, however, is happy to translate as he leads you around. "Who are my neighbors?" he asks, pointing at one strip of aluminum on the sculpted skin. "She'll be right, mate," he interprets, pointing to another fragment of everyday Australian speech. The symbolism of the building doesn't stop there. The colors tell their own story. Fragments of the exterior are painted black and red to reflect the Aboriginal flag. Another slice is buff and blue, the colors of the uniforms worn by the convicts in the early Australian penal colonies.

Coming to grips with this museum on its architect's terms isn't easy, even if it is possible to experience it simply as a physical sensation devoid of the intellectual content.

There is no Rosetta stone to unravel all the meanings, just a few broad and not so broad hints. The building is the expression of an architecture of intelligence and anger, with an ambition to redefine not just Australia's sense of itself, but the role of architecture too. It's an attempt to free it from the demands of function, and to allow architecture the room to comment on the society that has created it. And it is perhaps just a bit too angry to be tolerated by the state as an example of its cultural sophistication. Official Australia intended the museum to become part of the country's national iconography, but Ashton Raggatt McDougall's design makes it almost impossible to co-opt. So awkward is the relationship of the museum with the state that the federal government tried to find a way to replace the landscaped courtyard with a more conventional, or rather less challenging, view of what an Australian garden should be.

The Dome was a failed attempt to portray contemporary Britain in a favorable light, to celebrate its achievements, and to make its people feel good about themselves and look warmly on their government, in the conventional manner of authoritarian monuments. Scotland's parliament almost failed in its attempts to celebrate newly devolved democratic government because of its grotesque cost overruns. Australia's museum demonstrates that architecture is a language that is capable on occasion of being used to say much more than governments who pay for it feel comfortable with. Buildings can do more than intimidate or impress. They can sometimes be used to ask questions too.

CHAPTER 8

THE USES OF MARBLE

FOR A WHILE AMERICA—OR AT LEAST THOSE READERS OF *TIME* who still accepted the infallible authority of its judgments about who did, and who did not, get their picture on its covers—believed that Wallace Harrison was one of the greatest architects of the twentieth century. But what really distinguished his career was his closeness to the most pharaonic Rockefeller of them all, Nelson, who—like so many businessmen—took an extraordinary pleasure in the process of building. Partly the appeal lay in the way that building could demonstrate his lasting grip on power. But in Rockefeller's case it had as much to do with the sheer satisfaction of shaping marble and concrete to his will.

For forty years Harrison faithfully served Nelson Rockefeller and his obsessive determination to build. He made possible Rockefeller's own architectural ambitions. Harrison outmaneuvered Le Corbusier in the protracted struggle to get his name in the biggest type on the credits for the design of the United Nations headquarters building, a project that briefly looked like the most significant piece of architecture of the century. But it was Rockefeller who was really to overshadow Harrison's career.

That victory over Le Corbusier may have been due more to Harrison's capacity for stony silence and pragmatic introspection than to his talent as a designer, but it was impressive all the same. And he certainly had every chance to show off his genuine architectural skills on a series of large-scale, highly visible buildings with generous budgets. Harrison helped to shape the New York's World's Fair of 1939. At just the moment that Stalin's architects were borrowing New York's skyscraper vernacular, wrapping it in the iconography of socialist realism, Harrison was drawing on the spatial gymnastics of Russia's revolutionary constructivists to bring a little of their weightless radical glamour to the fair's celebration of the triumph of capitalism.

Harrison's landmark in the form of a huge globe for Flushing Meadow had a clear debt to the most successful member of the Russian avant-garde, Konstantin Melnikov, and his drawings from twenty years before. Harrison built New York's first modern airport terminal at La Guardia. He devised the early version of the plans for Battery Park City on landfill on the banks of the lower Hudson River. He also designed such crucial American landmarks as the CIA's headquarters in Langley, Virginia.

But even more significantly, for almost the whole of his working life Wallace Harrison was court architect to the house of Rockefeller and those bafflingly interchangeable generations of sons, brothers, and cousins who all seemed to be called almost the same thing. He was on the team building Rockefeller Center for John D. Rockefeller Jr. in the 1930s. Twenty-five years later, he coordinated the fractious group of architects who designed Lincoln Center for John D. Rockefeller III. They added up to two of the three key projects that have served to define the grain of contemporary New York. And the third, the World Trade Center, owed a lot to the Rockefellers and Harrison too. He rebuilt the Bronx Zoo for Laurance Rockefeller. David Rockefeller called him a friend. But most of all, he was Nelson Rockefeller's architect, a relationship that Victoria Newhouse explores in her biography *Wallace K. Harrison, Architect,* to which this account is indebted.

Harrison began his working relationship with Rockefeller by designing an apartment for him on Fifth Avenue in 1934—complete with a specially commissioned mural by Fernand Léger. And thirty years later he was still working for Rockefeller, by this time the governor of New York state, on the design of the Albany Mall, the most ambitious government complex ever attempted in America outside Washington, D.C. The Albany government complex was a stab at building Brasília on the Hudson, or even, given its artificial hilltop site and its plaza ringed by pyramid-shaped office towers, a kind of modern-day Mayan city-state, transplanted from the jungles of Yucatán, displacing an entire neighborhood.

It was the most conspicuous American example of a phenomenon common to so many politicians: their pursuit of solace and consolation in the process of building.

To Harrison, who was particularly good at cultivating useful friendships, even before he met the Rockefellers, Nelson was someone who could provide, as he said, "opportunities to work with great people and do beautiful buildings." He made many other useful friends. On the strength of lunch with Harrison, one such friend, an executive at RCA, signed up as an anchor tenant for Rockefeller Center. Robert Moses, New York's fatally flawed answer to Paris's Baron Georges Eugène Haussmann, was another friend. Moses involved Harrison in planning both of New York's world's fairs. William Zeckendorf, Donald Trump's rather more engaging predecessor as the most flamboyant developer in New York, also developed a close relationship with Harrison before I. M. Pei became his in-house architect.

But above all there was Nelson Rockefeller. Fresh from college, Rockefeller walked into the marketing suite at Rockefeller Center one morning and questioned Harrison about every detail of the project his father had initiated, fascinated by the process of building as much as by its financial engineering aspects. Despite his patrician style, Harrison had left school to work as an office boy in a local contractor's office. But military service in the navy and a spell at the Ecole des Beaux-Arts in

Paris gave him the air of confident polish that appealed to Rockefeller. Harrison found Rockefeller easy to talk to, and they fell into a routine of friendship, meeting regularly to discuss buildings, art, and ideas. Then came the Rockefeller commissions. "For an architect, it was like being handed a meringue glacée—it was almost too easy," Harrison said later.

When Rockefeller started to behave like America's viceroy in Venezuela, where he had acquired huge landholdings, Harrison went with him to build the country's first modern hotel. When Rockefeller went to Washington to run the Office of the Coordinator of Inter-American Affairs, Harrison went too, as head of the organization's cultural program, abandoning his practice for several years. Harrison had the use of a Rockefeller-owned apartment in Manhattan. The family made him a present of enough land to build himself a house in the Rockefeller holiday compound in Maine. For a while his ailing daughter was cared for by a Rockefeller trust fund. Harrison became a trustee of at least three of the Rockefeller's cultural fiefdoms: the Museum of Modern Art, Colonial Williamsburg, and the Museum of Primitive Art.

Harrison's great moment came when the newly established United Nations began to look for a site for its permanent headquarters. The search committee considered San Francisco on the West Coast as well as a range of sites in the east. For New York's masters the chance to make their city the capital of the world was too tempting to miss. Harrison was the essential link between the three men who did the most to secure this prize for New York. They had a range of motives. Robert Moses wanted the U.N. building on the site of his world's fair at Flushing Meadow, to tidy up the project he had initiated two decades earlier. When it became clear that the organization wasn't going to accept a suburban site, Rockefeller and William Zeckendorf, undoubtedly driven by enlightened self-interest, became involved with putting forward an alternative in Manhattan. As well as all its intangible benefits for civic pride, bringing the United Nations to the city was certainly going to boost the value of their property holdings.

Harrison had been working with Zeckendorf on speculative plans for a massive residential and commercial development to replace the old slaughterhouses on the East River, and it was immediately clear that the site was a possible location for the United Nations. Harrison acted as the go-between to make the deal when Nelson Rockefeller persuaded his father to put up the $8.5 million to buy the land from Zeckendorf, and then donate it to the United Nations.

With that much political and financial clout, there could be little question that when it came to designing the Secretariat, and the General Assembly, Harrison was going to get his way sooner or later. But faced with a room full of bad-tempered architects from all over the world appointed to plan the project by the U.N. Secretary General Trygve Lie (among them, Oscar Niemeyer and Gordon Bunshaft), the process wasn't easy for Harrison. On one occasion, Le Corbusier, who clearly believed that the job should be his alone, was moved to such furious frustration that, under the shocked gaze of his collaborators, he started tearing down every drawing except his own from the walls of the studio that the design team shared. But with Rockefeller's gift in the background, Harrison was in a position to sit out the tantrums, presenting himself as responsibly responding to the technical and budgetary demands of the United Nations.

As Harrison grew older, and Nelson Rockefeller became ever more imperious, the nature of the relationship between them shifted. Harrison, like Speer and Iofan before him, found himself in the position of primarily interpreting the ideas of his patron. Max Abramowitz, Harrison's partner, later said, "The wonderful thing about Wallace was that he could say no to Nelson. But that changed toward the end. Wallace did what Nelson wanted."

In the days when Harrison was in a position to bring major tenants to Rockefeller Center or to secure Zeckendorf's landholdings for the U.N. project, he had an authority that few architects have ever had—usually they must rely on their force of personality and their gift for drama in the battle to have their own way. Harrison's connections with the rich and powerful gave him more room to shape buildings. But at Albany, Rockefeller, with a tame government machine in his hands, had not the slightest intention of being diverted from his campaign to preside over the transformation of a dim little city on the Hudson into what he unblushingly called at the foundation-laying ceremony "the most beautiful, the most efficient and electrifying capital in the world." Nothing would stop him—not the electorate, and least of all not his notional architect.

Nelson Rockefeller might have been an architect himself if his family had let him. When Rockefeller took Harrison up to the family compound in Maine to show him the site for a new country house, according to Victoria Newhouse, Rockefeller sank two wooden posts into the ground with his bare hands to mark out exactly where he wanted a picture window to go.

During his years as governor, Rockefeller insisted that New York state become a serious patron of architecture, a policy that extended as far as giving Richard Meier his first civic commission, the Bronx Developmental Center.

But to judge by Albany, Rockefeller would not have made a particularly skillful architect. Harrison was still in control of the architecture of the Rockefeller house. Albany, in unflattering contrast, is as much a product of Nelson Rockefeller's urge to make his mark as it is of Harrison's gifts for design.

Rockefeller conceived of the idea of a monumental new government center for Albany in 1959, halfway through the first year of his first of four terms as governor. The scheme carried with it an uncomfortable echo of those of other authoritarians with overweeningly ambitious plans for their capital cities—except in this case with no ideology, bar a slight tinge of Republicanism's liberal wing. Realizing the project involved rooms full of big models, extensive demolitions, a lingering relish in the taking of the decisions and the making of plans, and a complete lack of interest in the fate of those who would be displaced by them. Rockefeller's brother David was to follow precisely the same pattern when he encouraged the construction of the World Trade Center at the cost of the destruction of the lively neighborhood of small specialist shops and businesses of Radio Row. In this he was aided by Nelson, who as governor was able to guarantee the viability of the development by leasing space for a thousand state employees in the Twin Towers.

When Nelson Rockefeller started out on the rebuilding of Albany, he was still intent on becoming president of the United States, and he had good reason to believe he would succeed. Building Albany was an obsession for Rockefeller, a process he pursued neurotically—down to the selection of every plant pot, light switch, and door handle and the approval of every drawing. Eighteen years and $1 billion later, when the Albany Mall was at last finished, Rockefeller's political career was long over. His imperial capital, initiated as an attempt to establish him as a national figure, had turned into what looked like bereavement therapy for his lost presidential ambitions. Albany was compensation of a kind for the political power he had aspired to but never managed to achieve. When Nelson Rockefeller left the state capital to serve as vice president in the lame-duck administration of Gerald Ford, in the wake of the Nixon fiasco, he said good-bye to his own ambitions. He didn't even make the ticket for Ford's failed attempt at reelection.

To assemble the critical mass to make the Albany complex look big enough and impressive enough for his purposes, Rockefeller insisted on rounding up every available state agency, organization, and official body that he could bully, intimidate, or bribe into moving to the mall. The government compound ended up including an unlikely mix of scientific laboratories, an art gallery, a convention center, and an auditorium, as well as endless acres of offices.

So determined was Rockefeller to build his monument that he insisted on construction work starting on all the major elements of the project at the same time, to make it impossible for any future occupant of the governor's mansion to stop it. As many as twenty-five hundred workers at a time swarmed over the hundred-acre site, creating chaotic conditions and, in the resulting confusion, causing serious cost overruns.

Rockefeller claimed it was all being done in the name of civic improvement. According to Rockefeller, Albany's center was in danger of being overwhelmed by a threatening wave of slums that supposedly lapped at the gates of the governor's mansion. He offered the conventional planner's remedy of the time, wholesale clearances. In fact six thousand people lost their perfectly adequate homes, demolished to make way for the mall, destroying a stable middle-class community, and if anything worsening the plight of the city's fragile downtown. Rockefeller promised that the redevelopment would include nine hundred affordable new homes to replace those that had been torn down, as well as an old people's housing complex.

When Harrison's model was unveiled at the end of 1962, the scheme did indeed include a number of low-rise blocks of housing for the elderly, positioned directly south of the mall. The governor was not impressed by the intrusion. He thought that they would get in the way of the views of his buildings. "These buildings are too big, don't you think so, Wally," he announced, disturbed that the purity of his conception of an Olympian government center was being compromised by its mundane neighbors. According to one eyewitness, Rockefeller was so irritated that he grabbed one of the blocks and tried to slip it off the model before the press were allowed in to see the scheme.

Although the project was funded by the taxpayer, the citizens of neither New York state nor Albany itself had any say in the development. If the state had tried to raise the money for the mall, Rockefeller would have needed to put the scheme to a ballot. He didn't, and it was funded instead by a city bond issue (municipal officials did not have to seek voter approval for such a measure). Albany's mayor then engaged the state to act as its agent in the building process and handed over primary control of the money to Rockefeller. From then on, Rockefeller treated the reconstruction of the city as if he were an eighteenth-century English landowner adding a wing to his country seat and supervising the construction of a series of pavilions in the grounds. Rockefeller insisted on the creation of a huge man-made platform, spanning across the shallow valley that ran through this part of Albany, like a continuous wall. He instructed Harrison put the mall on top of it. The inspiration, bizarrely enough, seems to have been the Dalai Lama's palace in Lhasa. According to Harrison, Rockefeller showed him how "he wanted to stop the valley with a great wall going north and south. He had seen something like it on a trip to Tibet. He wanted the feeling of separating the mall into a localized community, up on top of the hill so that he could not only get the vista of the wall, but of the whole Capitol adjunct at the top. And that was one of the main things that he kept asking for as the project developed."

As a symbol of democratic government, creating an upper city, reserved for bureaucrats, towering over a humble lower city saddled with the burden of supporting them, could hardly be less appropriate. But it seemed to reflect the insecurity of an official America during the riots of the 1960s and 1970s. Unrest created the sense that authority was under siege everywhere: in the courts, in the universities, and in the legislature. As governor in September 1971, Rockefeller ordered state troopers into the jail at Attica in western New York to put down a prison riot in the most brutal way, killing ten hostages and twenty-nine prisoners. In this context, with its walled ramparts, and its insulation from contamination by the poor and the dispossessed, the mall looked as if it could readily be defended against any future insurrection.

Harrison made a reflecting pool, a not so subliminal reference to the mall in Washington perhaps, the centerpiece of the Albany Mall. Ranged along one side is a forty-story office tower—far taller than anything else in the capital—and the auditorium. On the other side of the water is a row of four shorter but still extremely imposing towers. Their distinctive wedge shapes were another Rockefeller idea.

Rockefeller insisted that only marble would be good enough for Albany. Against Harrison's advice, he demanded the use of two particularly unsympathetic shades of white stone for the skin of the buildings: Vermont pearl white and Georgia Cherokee. They look more like plastic than marble, giving the buildings the appearance of objects inflated to the scale of buildings, rather than of genuine architecture. The auditorium—known for reasons that are all too obvious as the egg—is an oval shape hoisted up on stubby legs, with the entrance most inelegantly threaded between them. It was the result of another direct intervention by the governor. At lunch one day with Harrison, Rockefeller picked up a grapefruit, balanced it on a piece of silverware, and demanded, "Make it something like this."

The governor was interested in the overall composition as well as the details. Looking at the model of the mall one day, Rockefeller decided that it needed something extra, a bold and abstract geometrical element to balance the neighboring Capitol, a building in the ornate French Renaissance style. He suggested a "freedom arch." Harrison came up with a flattened ellipse on the same lines as the arch originally proposed for Mussolini's EUR and built by Eero Saarinen in St. Louis. In the event, as cost overruns escalated, it was never realized.

Harrison was already aging as the project was built and seemed to be uncomfortable with anything but the bold simple shapes of his youth. This inability to look forward, coupled with the long, drawn-out building process, gave the design a dated feel well before it was completed. What might have been impressive in the 1950s seemed like a fossil when it was finished in the 1970s. Compared with Brasília, Albany has a parade-ground stiffness and an awkward formalism that fails to come alive as an urban composition. As a social experiment, it looks even more out of time. The cynical, traumatized 1960s, when America's cities were at their lowest ebb, were no time to try to repeat the success of Rockefeller Center, a development with the innocent optimistic faith in the future. By the time it was finished, Rockefeller's mall had turned into a kind of historical freak, a throwback that spelled out its self-obsessed origins only too clearly, under the skimpiest veneer of contemporary

styling. All the effort felt like a vain attempt to face-lift a turboprop air-
liner struggling to compete in the jet age. Rockefeller's Albany Mall
seems hardly to belong to the real world, let alone a modern city, suggesting instead nothing so much as adolescent fantasy from a science fic-
tion magazine.

It's hard to believe that in dreaming of his city, Rockefeller had not
been looking at Oscar Niemeyer's designs for the Chamber of Deputies
and the Senate in his Parliament Building in Brasília, unveiled two years
before the planning for Albany got started. Niemeyer's plan also involved a gigantic platform, like Albany's. It linked two bowl-shaped debating chambers, one turned upside down, and was attached to twin
office towers—a layout with echoes of the United Nations complex in
New York, on which Niemeyer had also worked. With a constitution
that limited him to just one five-year term in office, Juscelino Kubitschek
was even more interested in making a bold start on building than
Rockefeller.

In the end the effort to turn Albany into what looked like a genuine
center of power was futile. Although it was the seat of the state government, it could never hope to compete with New York City. Brasília faced
a similar problem in its attempts to emerge from the shadow of Rio de
Janeiro. As far back as 1891, Brazil's first republican constitution had
specified moving the seat of government out of Rio. Despite the reluc-
tance of Brazil's legislators actually to live in their new capital, despite
the massive expenditure, and the eruption of shantytowns out of sight
of the city's monumental center, Brasília was widely understood by
the country at large as a piece of nation building on a heroic scale.
Kubitschek was seen to be motivated by patriotism, rather than ego.
Moving the capital promised to elevate Brazil to the brink of the first
world from its postcolonial torpor, by breaking with the past, and building a symbol of modernity and self-reliance. And it did, creating an
enormous impact in Brazil, and beyond.

But as far as the impact of Rockefeller's monuments on Albany's future was concerned, in fewer than twenty-five years Harrison's convention center began looking so sadly outmoded that the city embarked on building a replacement on another site to compete with more up-to-date rivals across the country.

Albany was a melancholy finale for Harrison's career, and even more poignant an outcome for Rockefeller himself, a cultured man who had wanted so badly to become an American president. A man who did all that he could to be remembered as a master builder and a statesman will forever be known as the man whose first contribution to the cultural history of the twentieth century was to order the painter Diego Rivera off his ladder at Rockefeller Center for including Lenin in the mural that he had commissioned, and whose last was his death of a heart attack while in the arms of his young mistress.

Harrison outlasted Rockefeller, and lived long enough to attempt to serve an autocrat even more unabashed in his enthusiasm for architecture as a political tool than Nelson Rockefeller. The Shah of Iran was a ruler who did not pay even lip service to the notion of democratic government, and who in the end was still more unsuccessful than Rockefeller in his attempts to hang on to power. The last project that Harrison worked on in a sustained way was a competition submission for the Pahlavi Library, intended as much as a huge monument to the Shah as to the secular state that he was trying to build.

THE LINE DIVIDING THE SWEEPING VISION OF A KUBITSCHEK FROM the vanity of a Rockefeller is easily crossed, as the story of the egotistical French civil servant Jacques Attali demonstrates. Left to himself, Attali would certainly have wanted to build his fledgling European Bank for Reconstruction and Development (EBRD) from the ground up. He might have opted for something on the lines of Marcel Breuer's UNESCO building in Paris—on a site near Les Invalides, with its Noguchi garden, a specially commissioned Calder, and a Picasso mural, but bigger and with an even better view. Or, at a pinch, a building with the sculptural quality of the headquarters of the French Communist party, designed by Oscar Niemeyer, though its location in a working-class Parisian suburb would have counted against it.

Attali would have looked for the most prominent possible site, something like that of the French Ministry of Finance, which has the presumption actually to dip its feet into the Seine. He certainly wanted the most famous architect he could get: Jean Nouvel, or Dominique Perrault, although the latter might have been seen as an act of lèse-majesté. Perrault was still busy on France's new Bibliothèque Nationale for Attali's patron, François Mitterrand, who was stubbornly refusing to yield in his pursuit of Cartesian geometry and all glass walls, even in the interests of safeguarding some of the most precious books in Europe.

In part, Attali's boundless ambition is a reflection of the relentless sense of entitlement of an *énarque,* a member of the French political elite educated at the Ecole Supérieure des Mines, and the Ecole Nationale d'Adminstration. Attali, born of a European settler family in Algiers that moved to France from North Africa, still had a great deal to prove. He was moving, or so he hoped, from the political boiler room to the center of events to establish the EBRD, and he wanted his new office to signal that shift.

But the search for a high-visibility building for the bank was also the product of Attali's calculation that a new international institution would have to establish itself as rapidly as possible if it was to be taken seriously. And to do that, it has to construct an image of the kind of organization that it aspires to be, long before it has any chance of that aspiration becoming substance.

If you are a Jacques Attali, you believe that if you build the palace, the kingdom will follow. In his pitch with Celebrity Speakers International, a lecture agency, to sell his services on the conference and after-dinner circuit, Attali unblushingly describes himself as "a man of action and of reflection." Supposedly an economist, he was better known in the

1980s as Mitterrand's resident intellectual, and was later accused of involvement with some of his less savory financial transactions (the accusations were dropped). But prolonged exposure to his patron's obsession with building gave him a fascination for the architectural trappings of power. Mitterrand had a taste for a peculiarly French architectural language, of perfect cubes, spheres, and pyramids, one that connects the new Louvre to the world of the Sun King, by way of Ledoux and Boullée and their gargantuan schemes for monuments to Newton. It's an iconography of ruthlessness that comes naturally to the country that invented the year zero when it introduced the revolutionary calendar after 1789 and tried to replace Christianity with a synthetic state religion.

France takes it for granted that the architectural landscape is shaped in the most direct way possible by its presidents and mayors and their advisers, with minimal involvement by the taxpayers whose money actually pays for all these monuments. It is a country in which, following the president's example in Paris, every ambitious provincial mayor from Nîmes to Lille has built himself either an art gallery, in which all the walls and probably the floors too are glass; or a new high-speed rail station, with a roof like the skeleton of a whale; or a conference center wrapped in pink corrugated plastic, betraying France's childlike enthusiasm for novelty. To manage the process of building all these political landmarks, Mitterrand's Socialist party established a special consultancy that allowed it to harvest millions of francs from construction companies eager to secure contracts from Socialist local authorities, money that it then used, illegally, to finance its election campaigns.

Attali was part of Mitterrand's personal entourage for almost twenty years and watched from close quarters as the president poured $2.5 billion into eight prestige projects calculated to change the face of Paris— nominally in celebration of the bicentenary of the French revolution, actually from a mix of political calculation and vanity. And, on top of all that, Mitterrand wanted to live forever.

Mitterrand, just like Napoleon III—and Napoleon and Louis XIV before him—wanted to create the institutions to match his imperial ambitions. The Louvre was determined to eclipse the British Museum as the most visited museum in the world, just as Charles de Gaulle Airport was challenging Heathrow and Frankfurt in an attempt to become Europe's busiest air transport hub. In the days before the rise of Al Qaeda, the Institut du Monde Arabe, Jean Nouvel's bladelike structure with a glorious view of Notre Dame, was intended to make Paris the Muslim world's window into Europe and Europe's view of Islam. The Science Center at La Villette was a vast high-tech complex that tried to redefine the nature of the contemporary museum.

When Mitterrand moved into the Elysée Palace in 1981, Attali had the office next door to the president and, so he claimed, the use of a desk that had once belonged to Napoleon. His brother, Bernard, was appointed to run Air France at the same time, confirming the sense of belonging to the charmed circle around this self-styled socialist with the demeanor of a prince. Jacques Attali was the gatekeeper for Mitterrand, learning at close quarters from his imperial style.

Mitterrand set the tone for his presidency by commissioning Philippe Starck to design the furniture for his private office. The desk was based on the president's initial, its tubular steel legs taking the form of a winged M. It looked fashionable enough to mask the underlying vanity of the gesture. In those days, Starck was a bright young iconoclast, so the desk could be presented as an act of state patronage aimed at showing official France's commitment to the brightest new talents. But it was also a move that seemed to suggest that the president was too grand to work at anybody else's desk, and thus had to have one designed specifically for his own use. Stripped of the traditional signs of status and ostentatious wealth, the desk looked modern. But it was at the same time still an unmistakable signal of Mitterrand's taste for power, which from the point of view of a French autocrat trying to make his mark was the perfect combination of authority with cultural ambition.

Attali contributed a few ideas of his own to Mitterrand's building plans. He claims to have had the idea for a new national library to be packed with high-tech equipment rather than books, a notion that eventually became the four glass towers of Mitterrand's library in the Paris suburb of Tolbiac.

Attali would have loved to go through the ritual of a full-scale architectural competition, to find a design for a suitably magnificent home for his empire at the EBRD when he was appointed in 1991. He would no doubt have learned from the fiasco of the Opera House at La Bastille, where Mitterrand's judges picked a design they confidently assumed to be by the well-regarded American architect Richard Meier, only to discover, when they opened the envelopes to identify the anonymous drawings they had chosen, that it was the work of a previously unknown Uruguayan, Carlos Ott. His design, built on the most sacred site of revolutionary history in France, not only was an inelegant overdevelopment, but failed on a technical level. It was meant to revolutionize scenery changes, but the computerized hydraulic stage machinery failed to work as advertised, and the structure suffered for years from falling cladding tiles.

Undoubtedly Attali was involved in Mitterrand's personal intervention in reshaping the plans for the Musée d'Orsay and the Louvre. Several hundred million francs were wasted on abortive design work at the former before, on a whim, the president handed over the architecture of the museum spaces to the Italian architect Gae Aulenti. She obliged by creating an interior within the old railway terminus that felt like a tomb. Attali would have seen at first hand the negotiations with the British publisher Robert Maxwell, who was revealed soon after as a fraudster on an epic scale, over his investment in the pointless gesture of the Grande Arche at La Défense, in the hope of who knows what quid pro quo from the French state.

But even for the president of France, the exercise of power is still a matter of checks and balances. Mitterrand could persuade the rest of the

Group of Seven governments to provide the money needed to set up the European Bank for Reconstruction and Development, even though it was essentially conceived of as a means to extend the French sphere of influence over Eastern Europe. He could even get his bespectacled protégé the job of president of the EBRD. The price, however, was that its headquarters would not be in Paris, but in London, a city that wasn't yet ready for the monumental aspirations of the French political class.

The job of setting up the EBRD gave Attali the chance to pursue his ambitions, if not yet on a scale that matched those of his patron. For Attali this was not going to be just any bank; it was deliberately designed to be a political center of power and hence a personal stepping-stone. The bank's constitution bound it to deal only with countries committed to democratic government—a definition that has become increasingly flexible over the years. Ostensibly the intention was to bring the rigor and the freedom of the market to societies emerging from decades of life under a planned economy. Given France's own predilection for dirigiste central planning, and the recent nationalization of large sections of its industries, Mitterrand's inner circle was an unlikely source of expert advice on the subject of privatization.

The headquarters building was originally intended to have been at the heart of a network of branch offices—"embassies" would have been a better word for what Attali had in mind—spreading across Central Europe to Central Asia to fill the vacuum left by the collapse of the Soviet empire. But the British treasury, which was reluctantly footing the bill for the offices at the personal insistence of Margaret Thatcher, who had agreed to the project against her better judgment, wouldn't allow Attali the option of a new building, or let him get away with the idea of the viceregal outposts. For once Attali had to accept defeat. By way of a compromise, he briefly explored the idea of taking over an existing building in London with sufficient grandeur to make it a suitable home for what he called "a central tool in shaping a new political and economic world order." The classical splendor of Somerset House on the Thames might do, or a couple of the more splendidly baroque wings of Greenwich Palace. The fact that Mrs. Thatcher's civil servants refused to come up with anything he considered suitable provoked a prolonged sulk from Attali, one that was to resurface later, when he left London.

He did, however, end up signing the lease for a building in the Broadgate development on the edge of the City of London's financial district. It was a speculatively built office block known as One Exchange Place, designed by Skidmore, Owings and Merrill in a curious neo-Chicago style, a throwback to the early days of skyscrapers, with pinnacles, giant bay windows, and turrets that made it look like a Belle Epoque jukebox. It was brand-new, ready to move into, and lavishly equipped, and it contained some of the most expensive office space in the world. But Attali didn't want a ready-to-wear office, no matter how costly. He wanted a building that would be a faithful reflection of the status of the organization that he was trying to establish, and hence of his own importance.

In Attali's mind, generic office buildings clearly equated with bloodless, neutral administrators. How can you persuade the world to take you seriously when you are working from behind a desk in what might as well be the offices of an insurance company? Attali had his court decorators, Jean Louis Berthet and Yves Pochy, brought in to transform Exchange Place's twelve floors into a stage set for his pet project. That meant going a whole lot further than choosing the color of the wallpaper for the boardroom.

There were limits on what Berthet and Pochy could do. The landlords wouldn't let Attali touch the exterior. And the lease specified that whatever he did to the inside would have to be put back the way it was at the end of the term of the tenancy in 2016. But that didn't stop him from knocking huge holes out of the floors and walls. Attali's first priority was to make the building imposing enough both to impress the bank's own staff and to convince its visitors that they were dealing with an authentic seat of power.

Impressive buildings need impressive entrance halls. Attali was con-

vinced that Exchange Place simply couldn't do the job. As far as he was
concerned, it wasn't nearly big enough. It could be made to look a bit
better by demolishing a couple of the side walls and putting mirrors on
the ceiling. Better, but still really nothing like enough for Attali's regal
pretensions. So he decided to sacrifice the whole of the first floor and
make that into a suitably imposing reception area instead, leaving the
original entrance on the level below as a kind of throat-clearing prelude.
Of course, if visitors were allowed to use the elevators on the ground
floor, they would go shooting past the grand entrance space and miss the
effect Attali had planned, so a bank of escalators was installed to bring
visitors up once they had gotten past the six-foot-diameter polished steel
globe, supposedly a symbol of a world without frontiers. That way, they
had no choice but to appreciate the full impact of EBRD's magnificence.
To drive home the message that this was no ordinary city office block, a
team of Russian artists spent months painting a 200-meter-long mural
beside the escalator, in the manner of Raphael, to celebrate the achievements of European culture.

Given that this is space that costs £52 per square foot annually, sacrificing most of one floor is certainly a profligate way to spend £200,000 a
year. But the conspicuous use of space is a very traditional, and highly effective, way to delineate status, just like wasting water on golf courses in
the desert in Las Vegas. Attali installed his private theater, a 300-seater
set behind the tricksy kind of glass that goes opaque at the touch of a
switch, complete with a raked floor, which required major structural
work to accommodate. It sits next to the bank's own art gallery, where
Attali planned to show off the collection that the EBRD had started as-
sembling even before it got to see its first customer.

Impressing visitors, which is the primary purpose of a reception
area, requires the right mix of deference and sustained anticipation.
Banks with political aspirations are run, after all, by busy people who
need to keep their less important visitors waiting a little to make them
understand just how privileged they are to be there at all. And for the

important visitors, the building needs to be arranged in such a way as to make sure that they can't miss the power and the glory of the organization whose corridors they are being ushered through.

Attali also commissioned a special room just past the reception in which guests are invited to wait once they have been issued with their visitor badges. It boasts a view across the garden at the foot of the atrium. The visitors aren't put on show, but they do get to see the scale of the bank while they are waiting. And there are other such spaces scattered throughout the building as holding areas for the more significant director's offices. A waiting room is a clear signal of the importance of the office that it serves. But for visitors to be shown into one, despite the apparent deference of the maneuver, is a signal that they aren't as important as all that. The real elite are met at the front door by the president.

The theater is not the only ceremonial space injected into the banal structure of Exchange Place. Up on the tenth floor, a large circular hole was cut into the floor slab to allow for the construction of what was officially called the boardroom. It's a double-height space, big enough for 150 people, with a spectacular view of St. Paul's. Occupants sit in a circle, a format that betrays Jacques Attali's vision of this as more of a parliamentary debating chamber than a boardroom, in the sense that a commercial organization would understand it.

Why he thought he needed a debating chamber, as well as the theater downstairs, has never been made clear, but he obviously had a complex series of rituals in mind for the running of the organization, some of which involved addressing an audience in the manner of a schoolmaster from the front, and others in a setting to suggest a gathering of equals sitting in a circle.

The specially designed boardroom chairs are in white leather and solid sycamore, and Attali commissioned the previously unknown artist Isidore Gooderis to make a sculpture for the chamber. Using recycled bricks that are set into patinated steel shelves, the piece is a calculated evocation of the ancient crumbling volumes of an Asian monastery library.

But for all the effort that went into the boardroom, the real center of power is elsewhere in the building. The president's own office—located on the top floor, of course, and positioned immediately next to the press department and his spin doctors—represents the building in microcosm. It replicates the hierarchical layout of waiting areas and offices. It uses space to signal status, and even has its own debating chamber.

"Office," of course, is not a word that does all this space justice. It features a casual seating area large enough for eight people to lounge around on sofas, a coffee table stacked with books, a specially made leather and sycamore desk, an assistant's office, and a second private office. This opens into a dressing room, a shower room, and a private sitting room. It's big enough and expensive enough for Attali to be able to gently patronize visiting heads of state. Imagine the Bulgarian president, say, coming here cap in hand looking for the money to decommission an elderly and incontinent nuclear reactor. Attali—like those two overmighty French and English ministers Nicolas Fouquet and Cardinal Wolsey, and every other royal favorite to have faced the wrath of a patron piqued by attempts at grandeur that rivaled their own—certainly must have imagined exactly that.

Well-connected decorators Berthet and Pochy were close to the French Socialist party. Perhaps as a result of pandering to their most loyal clients, their work comes wrapped up in a great deal of vacuous political rhetoric about creativity and accessibility. "As we were planning the building, we had a very strong visual impression in mind, a gigantic tree with a trunk [the eight elevators], branches [the passages], and leaves [the offices]." And of course they make much of their claims about the openness and transparency of the building. "Only the meeting rooms are equipped with blinds to provide confidentiality," they claim, somehow managing to ignore all the protective screens around the president's own office.

In the elevator lobbies, Berthet had another idea. "For this new institution, we wanted to express the idea of human creativity, without necessarily using detachable pieces of art. We wanted to work on the marble itself, to demonstrate its transformation from a rough material to smooth, from rough hewn to bush hammered to polished."

All the original travertine was stripped out, and Berthet went looking for the whitest, costliest Carrara marble that Tuscany had to offer instead. Finding it was apparently not an easy task. The ideal material had, or so say the designers, to be simple and pure. "We wanted the marble to keep its original aspect, its colors, its mineral oxides, the marks made by wind and rain," claimed Berthet. "It had to be cut in several pieces, with lasers, following the structure of each block; then the pieces were fitted together, like a puzzle on the walls of the bank." The marble ended up costing the bank £800,000, but the polished mirror ceilings make it look as if there is twice as much, presumably as a gesture toward achieving value for money.

Not content with the banks of elevators, and the existing staircases, Berthet insisted on installing four more purely decorative sets of stairs, throwing away yet more costly square feet of office space. All of them use different materials and configurations, for the benefit of those who want to save a couple of minutes walking from the third to the fifth floor, or from the fourth to the seventh, without using the lifts or the escape stairs. One is a solid sycamore spiral. Another is cone shaped and made from wood and glass. A third is in poured concrete with timber inlay treads.

Then there is the bank's art program. Along with the faux Raphael in the entrance, there is a cartoon Vermeer in the elevator lobby, and two sculptures that are supposedly tributes to Leonardo (a winged horse) and to Copernicus (a mobile demonstrating the movement of the solar system). To reinforce the sense of a Europe-wide perspective, the meeting rooms are all named for major rivers, from the Danube to the Volga. Even the carpets, crockery, glassware, rugs, and secretaries' desks have been specially designed and made for the bank.

This is a building that was self-consciously designed to shape the destinies of an entire continent. The questions Attali never answered were: Did the continent really want itself to be shaped by this particular organization? And if it did, why did it need to be housed in the lavishly brash style of a Riviera nightclub?

Perhaps it is not entirely surprising to find that Berthet and Pochy numbered Saddam Hussein among their clients. Just before the Iraqi dictator attacked Iran in 1984, he presided over the opening of Baghdad's new Saddam Hussein International Airport. Scott, Brownrigg and Turner, the architects who built it, were British, and it bore, on the outside at least, an uncanny resemblance to Heathrow's Terminal 4, which they also designed. But the interior was all Berthet and Pochy. The baggage halls were graced by renderings of the gates of Babylon and the spiral ziggurat of Samarra in metal relief fifteen feet high. The departure hall featured supposedly Islamic vaults decorated with thousands of twinkling spot lamps, while Hussein's personal terminal, positioned outside the main building for instant access to the runways, had marble floors and mirrored ceilings just like the EBRD.

In London, for all Berthet's rhetoric about openness and democracy, the EBRD's offices are a precise representation of an entirely predictable hierarchy. The staff are in open-plan offices on the lower floors. The directors, who are herded together on floors ten and eleven, get to decorate their 1000-square-foot private offices as they please, and have the use of the private dining rooms, with their starched linen tablecloths and haute cuisine, something of a contrast to the café for the other ranks on the reception floor.

In all, fitting out the bank cost £60 million, more than enough in fact to build a completely new office building. But Attali wasn't there to enjoy it for long. A skeptical British press, led by the *Financial Times*, started looking beyond the propaganda coming out of the bank about its heartwarming altruism and discovered that in its first two years, the EBRD had budgeted to spend £1 million on hiring private jets to shuttle Attali back and forth between London and his apartment in Paris. "I am sorry, but I can't do without them," said an unrepentant Attali when confronted with the figure. The whole project was driven by personal vanity, of course, an assertion of status by a man determined to build an institution that didn't exist, one that Attali wanted to bring into being through sheer willpower.

Attali's project crumbled when his critics began to focus on the absurdity of the gap between the imperial trappings of his court and the poverty of Eastern Europe that he was supposedly attempting to help. Even more absurd was the mismatch between the £116 million in loans that Attali had authorized in the first two years of the bank's existence and the £208 million he had spent in the same period on staff, furniture, and the rebuilding of its premises. He was pried, slowly and painfully, out of office, kicking and screaming at the philistine Anglo-Saxons, a process eased by a £160,000 payoff.

Without the protection of his patron, François Mitterrand, Attali has had a difficult time of things since leaving the bank. First, he was accused of forty-three individual counts of plagiarism in his book *Verbatim*, a record of life with Mitterrand. Then, when France's special investigating magistrates began exploring the seamier aspects of Mitterrand's son's relationships with unsavory arms dealers, Attali was accused of receiving questionable payments from a French middleman allegedly involved in selling Soviet weapons to Angola—although those charges were later dropped. Attali was last heard of trying to conduct the Grenoble Philharmonic Orchestra, to the disgust of its musicians, who threatened to strike in protest at his musical incompetence.

The bank survived Attali, but only just. There have been three presidents since his time, and by 2003 the bank was negotiating with its landlords to leave the building to find somewhere smaller. It chose to stay when it became clear just how much the bank would have to spend to restore Exchange Place to its original condition when it finally does leave.

The whole saga is a reflection of the different approaches to the trappings of power between the Anglo-Saxon and the French world. In the French context, Attali had done nothing less than what was expected of him. He had learned the lessons of Mitterrand, who had in turn learned them from Louis XIV and Versailles.

Neither Rockefeller nor Attali achieved his ostensible objectives. The Albany Mall will never be a Brasília, never mind a credible metropolis. And the EBRD will never live up to the ambition of Attali's headquarters. The feeble quality of the architectural outcome of their ambitions is far less interesting and less telling than the state of mind that drove both of them to such extreme lengths. For them, as it is for so many other individuals with the chance to do as they did, building, for all their claims to the contrary, was the end, not the means.

CHAPTER 9

EGO UNCHAINED

ON A DECEMBER MORNING AT THE VERY END OF 1995, FRANÇOIS Mitterrand, the president of France, was near death. He rose from his sick bed. His veins were flooded with morphine to dull the excruciating pain of the pancreatic cancer that would finally kill him three weeks later, and he was dressed, slowly, in a suit that had become too big for him. After his puffy face was powdered for the television cameras, he was driven to Tolbiac, in working-class eastern Paris, to preside over the opening of the Bibliothèque Nationale. Never mind that it was the opening of a library with no books—of the 10 million volumes that the 24 miles of shelves had been designed to handle, just 180,000 were in place. Never mind that it would be another two years before all the staff moved in. This was a building that Mitterrand himself had conceived, and he imposed it on the country in the teeth of the bitter hostility of France's scholars.

Death had been much on his mind in the last years of his presidency. The philosophers he used to invite to dinner at the Elysée would find themselves drawn into long meditations with the president on the meaning of mortality. Books, readers, or librarians were not the issue. For Mitterrand, seeing his personal monument finished was all that counted.

He himself had chosen the untested Dominique Perrault as the architect. And in the knowledge that he was nearing the end, he found the $500 million needed to force construction to move at breakneck speed expressly so that he could experience a glimpse of immortality in the glassy splendor of the world's most modern library—a library that would bear his name.

The pyramid at the Louvre and the open cube at La Défense were both products of Mitterrand's personal preferences. Now he had the library with its four, wildly impractical eighteen-story towers looming over the Seine, marking the corners of a huge sunken garden. Short of installing his tomb here, the comparison with Napoleon's last resting place at Les Invalides could not be clearer. The architect's original idea of putting the books in the towers and the readers in the base had to be inverted to ensure that precious first editions did not fry inside the glass towers, even though the inversion put the works at risk of being washed by the Seine if it burst its banks. Perrault's design no longer made sense as anything other than a mausoleum. But there was no time for him to change the library's shape if the president's timetable was to be met. Mitterrand insisted that it be, even at the expense of his architect's reputation.

This is a universe in which, however reluctantly, all of us, even the most powerful, must continue to face the unremitting possibility that at any moment we might cease to exist. Not because of the wrath of an angry god, which would at least suggest, flatteringly, that humanity was worthy of his attention, if only briefly. Even a deliberate suicidal act of nuclear self-destruction would imply the possibility of shaping our destiny. But oblivion could be the product of something as meaningless as the random, arbitrary, emotionless intervention of a wandering asteroid, a volcanic eruption, or even the emergence of a previously unknown bacillus or species-jumping virus. Against this dismaying background, architecture offers the possibility of a brief interlude of lucidity. Through it, the logical, the ordered, and the meaningful are acknowledged as options, even as the future of the world itself lies in the hands of the random, the arbitrary, and the meaningless, which could wipe out even the cockroaches.

Architecture is a device that allows us the chance to forget the precariousness of our position for a moment, and to create at least the illusion of meaning when we measure it against its own internal logic and find some sense of correspondence and predictability. It cannot, of course, impose order on an orderless universe. But architecture can provide a reference point against which we can measure our place in the world. It cannot make us live forever, but architecture can be used to confront our fear of death, and to offer the hope of some kind of permanence.

Most of the very earliest efforts of humans to make a lasting mark on their surroundings were essentially architectural, and they clearly show the traces of the impulse to find a way to connect the transience of flesh and blood with the apparent eternity of the stars. They involved creating platforms of flat earth imposed on an undulating landscape and aligned with the heavens, as if demonstrating the connections between human intelligence and the world beyond its understanding. There could be no clearer sign of a human presence, and the exercise of its intellect, than to show the contrast between order and disorder.

To draw a straight line on the landscape, and make it into a permanent form, a human society needs to have developed skills of measurement and observation. And placing that straight line in a natural landscape immediately suggests the presence of intelligent life. But can we really be sure that it is the straight line and the flat plane that represent order and logic, and not the possibly more complex order of the natural world?

Making a mark is an impulse that can quickly seem to take on the aspect of a religious experience. Those early platforms were the starting points for the creation or, depending on your degree of engagement, the celebration of sacred sites connected with the supernatural. They produced an architectural language that provided the basis for the monuments and the mausoleums of so many different cultures, from the

Egyptian pyramids to the Meso-American cities and the classical Greek sites. Platforms were approached by steps and superimposed on other platforms.

Architecture like this is an attempt to engage and interact with natural phenomena, with the landscape, and with what man can observe of the behavior of the stars and the seasons. Stonehenge makes the sun and the moon appear as if they are aligned in certain ways, on particular days of the year. It's like buttonholing God in the street and demanding his attention, as if to make our insignificant activities worthy of notice, or part of some purpose more elevated than the fitful cycles of our own existence. If there were no monument, and no architecture, then there would be no phenomena to observe. But when the priesthood is able accurately to predict such phenomena, it can use its knowledge to demonstrate its power to the uninitiated. Even more impressive a demonstration of the priesthood's power is its ability to persuade the uninitiated to build the object that will enforce their subjugation.

Before Gianni Agnelli, Fiat's supremely elegant and charismatic patriarch, was finally interred in the family vault, his body lay in state at the heart of the company's empire in Turin. Thousands of car workers and their families, as well as politicians, bankers, and industrialists, filed past the coffin to pay their last respects as if he were a medieval king. This was not in some marble-lined chapel or in the classical *palazzo* that you might have expected for the uncrowned prince of Italy. Just a few weeks before his death, Agnelli had presided over the unveiling of his parting gift to his country, a gallery designed by Renzo Piano to house Agnelli's personal collection of western culture's greatest hits, a selection of trophy pieces chosen from the last thousand years. They were acquired during the course of his life and were now presented to the nation as a keepsake. Piano's gallery took the form of a steel and aluminum pod, perched as tentatively as a helicopter on the rooftop test track of the Lingotto, the cathedral of car factories built by Agnelli's grandfather and converted after production stopped in the 1980s into a glistening postindustrial honey trap of galleries and concert halls. The Lingotto *pinacoteca* was never officially described as a mausoleum, but it was there that Agnelli's body was brought before burial.

Agnelli's wish was a poignant reminder of the use of architecture as a means of defying mortality, of shaping memory, and as a reflection of the psychopathology of power. The apparently fundamental human impulse to leave behind some kind of mark after death and the unbreakable connection between architecture and the exercise of power were briefly obscured by the sunnier preoccupations of the 1960s. The counterculture persuaded Piano and others who thought like him that even architecture could be liberated from the weight of tradition and custom. Piano himself looked for alternatives to the conventional ways of doing things, not just in materials or in style but in the relationship between the architect and the real users of his work.

Monumentalism, seen as an excuse for architects to indulge in futile attempts at large-scale sculpture, had gotten a bad name. Piano's generation tried to reinvent architecture by embracing the everyday world, rather than pandering only to affluent patrons of the kind typified by Gianni Agnelli. Piano was interested in architecture as a matter of problem solving, rather than representation, in technological solutions as much as in formal issues. As he saw it, architecture should have a light touch; it could be temporary and provisional rather than burdened with the illusory search for permanence. He also believed that architecture should serve the poor and the disadvantaged rather than the state or the rich or the church.

But for all Piano's fascination with the technological possibilities for social change offered by the modern world, for all his enthusiasm for the participatory politics of the 1960s and the 1970s, it is the traditional definition of architecture that has characterized his career as much as it did that of Alberti or Palladio. Delicately wrought steel and apparently gravity-defying glass can carry the same messages as heavy marble or bronze; they serve equally well to define the institutions that society regards as the most important or the most significant. Piano's own work, in the end, has been shaped not by the activists from the inner cities, but by his relationship with bankers and insurance tycoons. He has built their monuments, galleries, and memorials, and he has had to answer to them for it. He has managed the relationship with consummate skill. From Eli Broad, the L.A. billionaire, to the publishers of *The New York Times* and the followers of the recently canonized Padre Pio, they have made the pilgrimage to one or other of his studios. Perhaps to Paris, where much of the design work is done now, or to the "research base" that he maintains under UNESCO auspices on a wild cliff overlooking the coastline west of Genoa. Chauffeurs drop their passengers off there at the shoreline, leaving them to ascend the rocky slope on a makeshift glass cable car that arrives at the architect's retreat, with its imperial views over the sea. One grilled fish lunch there, served by Piano's crisply uniformed housekeeper, and they know they have chosen an architect to live up to their aspirations. Even Irvine Sellars, the fashion retailer turned property developer who dressed swinging London in the 1960s in unfeasibly wide trousers, succumbed to Piano's charm and commissioned him to design Europe's tallest building, an office tower above London Bridge Station.

Renzo Piano was involved with Agnelli for a quarter of a century. At the beginning there was no clue that the nature of their relationship would shift so much that it would eventually come to include the design of what amounted to a tomb. Agnelli's first commission for Piano and his long-term collaborator, the brilliantly gifted engineer Peter Rice, could not have been more different. They were asked to design a car for Fiat. Agnelli wanted an open-ended, speculative exploration of new production and assembly methods rather than a styling exercise. Between that commission and the gallery-cum-mausoleum came the long, drawn-out transformation of the Lingotto itself, once it had outlived its usefulness as a car factory. For Turin, where Fiat was the biggest employer, the old plant had represented the largest intrusion on the city's landscape since the cathedral was built. It was an enormously important project, both in practical terms and as a symbolic reminder of Fiat's sense of obligation to the city. And it was a two-way transaction. Because Fiat is so closely identified with Turin, its own prestige is diminished if the city is seen to be in trouble and its fabric is allowed to atrophy.

Piano is not interested in creating an immediately recognizable architectural signature, and that is perhaps what made his work appeal to Agnelli, a man who was interested in being known for acquiring the best rather than the obvious. To ask Piano to design a building for you is to do so in the knowledge that it will not necessarily look like anything that he has ever done before. For some patrons, less sure of their own taste, this would be a handicap. For Agnelli, it was clearly anything but.

It's not hard to see that Piano's genuine fascination with elegant mechanisms and high-performance materials represents a passion that would have aroused a sympathetic response in a tycoon who was equally passionate about speed in the form of fast boats and even faster cars. But however the buildings look, and whatever they are made of, as it has turned out, Piano has all along been designing structures that are in fact the embodiment of the most traditional of all architectural impulses. They speak of power, continuity, and memory.

IN WHAT MUST BE ONE OF THE MOST UNLIKELY PIECES OF SELF-promotion for an architectural practice in the history of public relations, Anthony Browne has posted a dozen images of Hamilton Palace on his Web site, showing the project under construction. He calls it the largest country house built in England since the time of Blenheim but concludes, somewhat out of date, by suggesting that "unfortunately, the house may never be finished as . . . the Client was convicted of manslaughter . . . and was sentenced to 10 years in prison."

Mohammed Raja, a prosperous, slightly sinister businessman with a reputation as a slum landlord, opened the door of his comfortable suburban house on the southern fringes of London one hot July day in 1999 to what looked like a couple of gardeners, dressed in coveralls, and with floppy brimmed hats that partly hid their faces. His two grandchildren, Rizwan and Waheed, were upstairs when he went to the door. They heard raised voices and shouting, then the sound of a shotgun blast hitting the ceiling. The boys ran downstairs to find their grandfather holding his chest, a spreading patch of wet blood on his shirt. He had been stabbed in the chest five times, but the bullet fired at him had missed. Rizwan and Waheed could see two men on the porch; one had a sawed-off shotgun over his knee. Rizwan saw him break it in an attempt to reload.

Rizwan shouted to his brother to call the police. As he did so, he could see the gunman in the hallway take aim. He heard his grandfather crying out in pain. He saw that his grandfather had a knife in his hand. The man in the hat pulled the trigger and shot Raja in the face at point-blank range. Both attackers then walked back to the road and escaped in a white van that was later found nearby, burnt-out and abandoned.

Three years later, Robert Knapp and David Croke stood trial at the Old Bailey for Raja's murder. The jury was told that neighbors had seen two men acting suspiciously that day, and had noticed a white van with the words "Thunderbirds Two" inscribed on a spoiler above the cab. According to the police, it had been sold three weeks earlier to a man who had given a false address.

The case was relatively straightforward. Blood found on Raja's front door was matched to a sample of saliva taken from Croke after he was arrested. According to the prosecution, DNA testing proved that the chances of it not being Croke's blood were "one in a billion." They were found guilty.

The trial of the third man in the dock, Nicholas van Hoogstraten, a millionaire property developer and an ex-partner of Raja, was more problematic. At the time of the murder, van Hoogstraten was driving to Gatwick Airport to catch a flight to Nice. The prosecution's case was that Croke and Knapp had carried out the killing on his behalf.

Although not present, van Hoogstraten was a party to the murder because it was carried out by the two men at his instigation, for his purposes (because of the problems and difficulties that had originated between him and Raja), David Waters, the prosecuting counsel, told the jury. Van Hoogstraten was eventually convicted of manslaughter and sentenced to ten years in prison. He was released after just one year, when the appeals court overturned the conviction. At a subsequent retrial, the judge decided that van Hoogstraten had no case to answer.

With his leather greatcoats and his bouffant hair, van Hoogstraten has the look of a minor rock star from the 1960s. He has a taste for sharp black suits, worn with a black tie and a black shirt, occasionally set off with an ankle-length white mink coat. Van Hoogstraten is not a man to cross, vengeful in pursuit of debts, delighting in a crudely vulgarized Nietzschean contempt for the polite conventions of bourgeois life. Van Hoogstraten built a property empire based on buying a chain of cheap flats and houses across the southeast of England, and made a fortune in the process. He is not, by all accounts, a solicitous landlord.

Van Hoogstraten is clearly aware of the figure that he cuts, reveling in the sense of dark menace that surrounds him. Twenty years before the Raja trial, he was convicted of setting ablaze the home of a rabbi in the English seaside town of Brighton. The judge at the earlier trial described him as "a sort of self-imagined devil, who thinks he is an emissary of Beelzebub." In the crudest terms, he insults members of the public who attempt to exercise their right to access the footpaths that cross his land near Uckfield in Sussex, defying those who have attempted to enforce the law.

What really makes van Hoogstraten stand out from the run-of-the-mill criminal, with a taste for inflicting measured doses of sharp pain on his enemies, is his taste for building. No two men could be more different than Agnelli and van Hoogstraten: one is a criminal who has spent years in jail, the other was regarded as a kind of national hero in Italy. But they have this one thing in common. Architecture is as much a part of van Hoogstraten's self-dramatization as his wardrobe and his permanent air of barely concealed aggression. Van Hoogstraten, who seems to have spent at least as much time as Agnelli thinking about death, has gone as far as to commission an actual tomb for himself. He has been building it for almost twenty years, interrupted by his two jail terms, and then by the freezing of his assets by the British courts.

Three generations of wealth made Agnelli look and sound like a patrician, one who at the end of his life was regarded as a statesman by his country, despite the dissipated postwar years that he had spent in the pursuit of pleasure, mostly in the form of women and fast cars. Van Hoogstraten left school at sixteen; made his fortune by the time he was twenty-five, albeit not on the scale of an Agnelli; and has been building Hamilton Palace, the house that he says will be his tomb, since 1980. It is a project that is poised uncomfortably on that strange dividing line between the kind of self-belief that can be impressive, despite its transparent vanity, and the semicomic vulgarity of a criminal with artistic pretensions.

Hamilton Palace—named after the capital of Bermuda, where the young van Hoogstraten took the first steps to making his fortune—is a sprawling neoclassical house tinged with a postmodernism that reveals the era in which it was conceived with pitiless precision. Six hundred feet long, it sits incomplete and partly roofless in a glorious stretch of the Sussex countryside. Van Hoogstraten claims its walls have been designed to last as long as the pyramids, which seems unlikely given that he also says they are only three feet thick. The gallery that forms the most substantial part of the house is intended as a permanent home for what van Hoogstraten says is a major collection of classical European art. The house is like a merciless parody of the aspirations of the period in which it was conceived, an exaggeration of the tastes and fantasies of the generation of supposedly respectable self-made men of the Thatcher and Reagan years. Van Hoogstraten's house could almost have been conceived of as a subversive act of satire, embodying the collision of two worlds: the respectable and the criminal. Neither side comes out well.

The wonder is that van Hoogstraten didn't take the whole project to its logical conclusion and commission his architect to build a pyramid for him. But in his idea of making the house into his mausoleum, van Hoogstraten has touched on something disturbingly visceral and compelling about the nature of an architectural monument.

Anthony Browne was still an architecture student at Brighton Polytechnic when he first met van Hoogstraten. Browne, who is no Renzo Piano, says that he also had the murdered Raja for a client. He works as a kind of glorified set builder for those who hire him, creating evocations of the worlds that they ask for, rather than offering his own architectural narratives. But his design for Hamilton Palace is far from unsophisticated. It is effectively sited, with a picturesque but dignified silhouette. By the standards of the run-of-the-mill rows of rich men's houses that line the streets of every affluent suburb from Moscow to Bridgehampton—with their fiberglass pediments and porticos, their carriage drives and their endlessly bifurcating grand staircases and chandeliers, their vast garages, and their relentless quest for size—it is positively chaste.

The house is certainly big; Browne claims it sprawls over a scarcely credible 70,000 square feet, and had a £35 million budget. It is really just one endless façade, with a central dome, and twin wings terminating in pavilions at each end. Browne says the inspiration is Blenheim, the grand baroque house built by the Duke of Marlborough, "and it's not a lot smaller." Actually, unlike Blenheim, it is more neoclassical than baroque in style, with paired columns and broken pediments.

Browne's portfolio includes a commission from the late Marquis of Bristol, disgraced heir to a vast and authentic Palladian house, although it's hard to understand how an English copy of an Italian original designed two centuries earlier can be considered authentic. The marquis, who squandered his fortune on cocaine, asked Browne to design two bathrooms for him: one in baroque style, the other in the Egyptian manner. By these standards, Browne's work for van Hoogstraten is a surprisingly accomplished design. Set off by a boathouse built on the edge of the lake at the center of the site, it shows his command of an impressive range of effects, from the grand manner to a more lighthearted capriccio. But it was Agnelli who felt secure enough to commission Piano to design a conspicuously contemporary design, while, for all his bravado and aggression, van Hoogstraten has hijacked the most saccharine sweet image of the traditional English country house that he could find to serve as the model for his lair.

Why does Browne think that van Hoogstraten asked him to build Hamilton Palace? "It's just showing off really, isn't it?" says Browne. "These sorts of houses make a statement. It's the desire to create a monument, one of those primary artistic urges. Quite often in people's minds, creating something amazing is confused with creating something big, and big means expensive."

Even before van Hoogstraten went to jail, the unfinished palace was suffering from the problems that often accompany the building of a house for, to put it mildly, a strong-willed client. The general contractor had walked off the site over a dispute about an unpaid invoice for £407,000. And the architect claims that he had also resigned. "These projects start off being tremendous fun," Browne says. "But then you get on site and have to deal with the builders. Then the client changes his mind. It's somebody else's dream, but it becomes the architect's nightmare."

During the course of the Raja trial another side of the story emerged. Mark Hylton, described in court as van Hoogstraten's current architect, was asked to describe what had happened when his client discovered that there were major structural problems with the pillars and the floors in the boathouse. "His response was quite unforgettable really. He went ballistic, very angry, and with very good reason. He said, 'Whose fault is this, why has this happened?'"

If Browne were to return to Uckfield, it's a fair guess that he would be treated with even less sympathy than the architect Sir John Vanbrugh, who was forbidden from entering the grounds of Blenheim by his client, angered by escalating costs. Years later Vanbrugh was turned away when he appeared at the gates of the completed house, hoping for another glimpse of the masterpiece from which he had been excluded for so long.

During the course of the trial, evidence was heard to suggest that van Hoogstraten had planned to move one of the murderers into the boathouse. Van Hoogstraten denied it, but he agreed that the man's mother did indeed have the use of a cottage on his estate.

Van Hoogstraten was finally forced to stop work on the house when his funds were frozen by a lawsuit brought by Raja's family, who wanted control of assets worth £5 million that had been the subject of his dispute with his former partner.

It's hard to understand what van Hoogstraten imagines he will be doing in his palace, if he ever gets it finished, in the interlude before it becomes his tomb. His children, born to an assortment of mothers in various countries, are scattered across the world. His friend Robert Mugabe—whose army drove thousands of squatters off van Hoogstraten's estate in Zimbabwe after they slaughtered a herd of his cattle—would be unlikely to be allowed into Britain, so there is not much chance of his entertaining a head of state there.

To use the traditional form of the country house is to suggest that you are the natural successor to the system that it represented, and to try to cloak yourself in its authority, to project a sense of how you would wish to be seen. Living up to that way of life is a harder trick to perfect than it might look. For all van Hoogstraten's studied contempt for the social norms, the feat demands at least the tacit acknowledgment of a wider community, if for no other reason than to provide an audience to fill up all those grand rooms.

And for van Hoogstraten, that was exactly the purpose of the palace. It offers him the chance to differentiate himself from the rest of the world, to demonstrate that while most of humanity amounts to nothing more than a faceless ant heap, he, Nicholas van Hoogstraten, through the sheer force of his will, has made himself visible on the historic scale of events. He and he alone will be remembered and, as a result, his existence will be given some sort of meaning. From van Hoogstraten's point of view, the project has signally failed in its objective. What he needed was a Renzo Piano to work for him, or a Thierry Despont, the architect turned decorator whom Bill Gates hired to work on the interiors of his gigantic house outside Seattle. Gates ended up relying on Despont to teach him how to spend his money, how to buy wine, and how to look at pictures.

IT IS NOT JUST WEALTHY BUSINESSMEN WHO BUILD THEMSELVES mausoleums. They have been the tribute exacted from their subjects by the dictators of the twentieth century, from Lenin to Mao, and perhaps more surprisingly, they have an echo in contemporary America, in the shape of the presidential libraries. Since their beginnings with Franklin Delano Roosevelt, these buildings have had less and less to do with books and are more concerned with safeguarding the memory of a former president. In several cases they have actually taken on the role of a mausoleum.

No American president with an instinct for self-preservation would willingly submit to a direct comparison with Thomas Jefferson unless he had a compelling reason to. Nonetheless, George Bush the Elder commandeered the University of Virginia's rotunda, designed by his distant predecessor, for use in his own presidential library. But Jefferson's rotunda is one of the great landmarks of American architecture, and Bush's version is not.

Jefferson was a gifted architect and a discriminating critic. Bush allowed the design of his library to fall into the hands of an architectural plan factory best known for churning out a stream of baseball stadiums, each new one indistinguishable from the last. Jefferson's university at Charlottesville was one of the defining institutions of the growing American republic. Bush's building at College Station—spread over the carefully watered acres of Texas A&M University—narcissistically limits itself to portraying his own career. It sets out to place America's first ambassador to Communist China, the former director of the CIA, and Ronald Reagan's vice president in the heroic tradition. In much the same way, the eighteenth century portrayed even its least competent leaders as classical heroes, equipped with breastplate and helmet, laurel leaves and toga.

Despite the Bush library's aspirations to grandeur, and an all but complete absence of Dan Quayle, it is a masterpiece of unintentional architectural frankness. It offers an eloquent insight into the emptiness at the heart of Bush's presidency. The rotunda, a form synonymous with civic monuments since at least the time of the Caesars, is deployed in front of the library, like the floodlit sphinx on the Las Vegas strip that sits outside the Luxor casino, distracting the traffic. Bush's rotunda is there as a signpost, camouflaging a warehouse filled with racks and racks of gray file boxes, each marked with the single black dot that identifies it as containing the president's papers. They are tended by National Archives and Records Administration staff, who work like H. G. Wells's Morlocks from *The Time Machine*, in troglodytic conditions untroubled by sunshine or by more than a handful of visiting scholars in the course of a day.

What the 100,000 or so paying visitors each year come to 1000 George Bush Drive West to see is not the warehouse or its files. They come for a slick and highly partisan account of Bush's life, full of flaps to lift, levers to pull, buttons to press, and fluffy toy dogs for children to pet. The exhibition display was devised by Alexander Cranstoun. He is a designer who, apart from working on Nixon's library and applying a cosmetic face-lift to Lyndon Johnson's museum in Austin, is responsible for the trademark Nickelodeon geyser at the Universal Studios theme park in Florida. It's a vat of bubbling, squirting, green slime constantly boiling away inside a giant test tube, thirty feet tall.

Eight masts, each flying the Stars and Stripes, stand in a circle in front of the library's rotunda. They form one side of the pastel-colored plaza that is at the middle of the George Bush School of Government and Public Service. On the other side is an excessively ample parking lot. At the center of the plaza, five horses cast in bronze gallop over an all too literal replica of a smashed segment of the Berlin Wall, also rendered in bronze. This sculpture is by an artist named—improbably but somehow unsurprisingly—Veryl Goodnight. She calls it *The Day the Wall Came Down* and proclaims it to be a monument to freedom.

Like so much else about the library, the intended message of Goodnight's work has to be spelled out in words because its symbolic language, noisy though it may be, is too vague to say anything definite. Goodnight calls herself a western artist. She says she chose to avoid the art schools of the 1960s, which she saw as dominated by abstraction, and learned bookkeeping instead before being apprenticed to a master in what has become her craft. Now she raises buffalo on the ranch where she built her studio, and keeps up a steady output of art based on western themes. When a second casting of *The Day the Wall Came Down* was installed in Berlin, Goodnight was awarded the CIA's Medal of Freedom, perhaps the least well-known, and certainly the most two-edged, honor that the world of culture can offer.

To judge by her horses, executed in a manner that might owe something to the animators of the *Lord of the Rings* trilogy, Goodnight is backing into territory occupied by the rather better-known artist Jeff Koons. Her work is no doubt every bit as sincere, even if it is less famous and less knowing than that of the man who put a giant topiary puppy outside the Guggenheim in Bilbao. But her attempt to capture the spirit of a divided country, liberated from the Stasi yoke, in the form of a pack of horses— roaming through Berlin, pawing at the ground in front of the Brandenburg Gate, and getting in the way of the traffic on the Ku'damm—is just maladroit. Casual observers might conclude that Goodnight's sculpture has been attacked by a gang of anarchic Texan troublemakers wielding spray cans. In fact the graffiti on the rubble beneath the horses is officially sanctioned. It has been carefully transcribed by the artist from the originals in Berlin, as Goodnight's commentary reassuringly points out. "At President Bush's request, the names of people killed at the Berlin Wall are written on the dove of peace. These names represent over 900 people who were killed trying to escape to the west."

The source of the figure is not revealed, but it does not match the 82 names recorded as having been killed at the Berlin Wall itself during its twenty-eight years of existence. The sheer scale and effort needed to realize the work are presented with more conviction than its content: "The life-size horses weigh seven tons between them and took three and a half years to complete," she explains, as if to demonstrate that the achievements of the Bush administration are to be measured quantitatively rather than qualitatively. According to the helpful gloss, there for the benefit of those of us too literal-minded to fully understand the equine allegory, "President Bush's diplomatic skills enabled the hole in the wall to become so large that all of Eastern Europe was set free from Communist rule; the Cold War had ended."

Rival claims are made by the Ronald Reagan Library in California. Both men have fragments of the authentic Berlin Wall on show to bolster their claims that they personally won the Cold War. Over at the Reagan Library visitors are invited in semibiblical language to "touch a piece of the Berlin wall He sent crashing down, relive the history He made, and look with Him into the limitless future He dared to dream for us."

For all its celebration of the triumph of America over the evil empire, the Bush Library is set in a landscape glittering with paranoia. Highway billboards proclaim the gospel of permanent vigilance in terms Orwell's hero Winston Smith would have recognized from *1984*, albeit translated to the Internet: "Be Afraid or Be Ready; www.ready.gov." The university Web site provides continual updates on America's terror alert status, and cautions students planning to travel abroad against wearing bright clothes or white socks, or allowing their shirttails out of their jeans. Except, of course, in the countries where only Americans tuck them in, where they should be equally careful to do no such thing.

If taken seriously, the strategy would start modifying behavior to the point that the most obviously American thing to do would be not to look obviously American. Only an American wouldn't go to McDonald's in Athens. To reinforce the paranoid atmosphere, a necklace of concrete barriers of the kind originally devised to deter truck bombers in Beirut guards the entrance to the rotunda. There is a metal detector at the door.

It's not hard to understand why Bush the Elder might want to suggest that he had things in common with one of the most talented presidents, the scholar philosopher who managed to buy Louisiana from Napoleon at a bargain price. But Bush, or his handlers, also wanted to make the point that even though his was a presidency shaped by America's traditional virtues, the twentieth century did not entirely escape his attention. So despite its classical form, there are no columns on the exterior of the rotunda, and those on the inside have been stripped of acanthus leaves, volutes, and entablature, and all the other carefully graded secret signs of the Freemasonry of authentic classical architecture. The second half of the 1990s was not the moment for an ex-president to attempt an exact archaeological reconstruction of a Jeffersonian original or a creative reinterpretation of one. In contemporary America, even a member of Skull and Bones must reflect the values of popular culture. An overtly classical presidential building would simply have carried too much baggage for Bush to have gone to Robert A. M. Stern, Allan Greenberg, or any of the handful of other architects still interested in and capable of working with this kind of material in a literate way. Doing so would have suggested an unwholesome level of erudition, and no president or even ex-president can afford to be seen as a pointy-headed intellectual. A literal classical building would be equated with the unnecessarily conspicuous display of learning. Instead, the design is simplified to suggest that it is a modern building, but the library is close enough to a classical model to demonstrate an intimate acquaintance with traditional values, especially if you half close your eyes.

Just as Bush himself, for all his down-home manner, always lets slip just enough details of his patrician education at Phillips Academy and Yale not to be taken for a real cowboy, so the façade of the library is studded with clues hinting at a patrician pedigree. It is decorated with alternating narrow and thick bands of stone to suggest that this is a descendant of the kind of rusticated wall built by the Romans. It sits on a contrasting colored stone base. There is a vestigial piece of cornice pinned like a lapel version of the Légion d'Honneur to the front of the porch. It succeeds in looking more like a trophy than a commitment to an architectural language. Above it the rotunda has a line of little square windows incised between more stone bands. Since the top of the drum is all glass, their only purpose is to demonstrate how luxuriously thick the wall is, rather than to let in the already abundant daylight.

Stone is the traditional way to signal that a structure is important. But an exposed steel I beam over the entrance is another badge, implying that this is a building with at least some contemporary aesthetic ambition. Caudill Rowlett Scott, the once proud Texan architectural practice that designed the building, was swallowed by HOK, a faceless conglomerate, before the library was finished. If you know where to look you can find clues to the bitter disappointments of the architectural firm inscribed into the fabric of the building. Cut into the veneer-thin stone of the neighboring George Bush School of Government, an inscription claims: "This final project is a visual tribute to the excellence in design and quality of leadership Caudill Rowlett Scott achieved, as practitioners and mentors to thousands of students of architecture." Yet it is not their names, but HOK's initials, that are carved into the sandstone of the library itself. Caudill Rowlett Scott still had the grace to understand that it is only good manners to provide a proper entrance to a circular drum. It is not quite such good manners to put up a porte cochere sheltering the roadway in front of the door with Bush's name on it, as if this were some kind of five-star hotel with a chip on its shoulder.

The semidetached porch that Hadrian designed for the Pantheon, projecting well forward of his rotunda and topped by a pediment, which Jefferson quoted so skillfully in Charlottesville, has been reduced to a simple box at College Station. The effect is less neoclassical than late postmodernism, influenced more by a Michael Graves's cartoon version of Jefferson than by Jefferson himself.

Hadrian's rotunda, under its sublime dome and its oculus, was the setting for altars to all the Roman gods. Later it became Raphael's tomb, and then the last resting place of the short-lived line of kings of Italy. Jefferson's University of Virginia was filled with classrooms and a library where each volume was carefully selected by the former president. Bush's rotunda is empty but for the donors' names, carved—in the same serif capital letters first used for Trajan's Column in Rome almost two thousand years ago—into a black and gray granite wall. With all the ingenious inventiveness that American corporate fund-raisers can muster, it spells out exactly how many dollars each benefactor has donated without being quite so vulgar as to lapse into actual numbers. There is one column of names of individuals and organizations, described as patrons, another of benefactors, followed by the founders. Then comes the president's cabinet and finally the president's circle, a group that turned up for the opening ceremony, parking their private jets at the nearby airstrip. This last cohort includes the Washington Times Foundation (nobody else's newspapers are used in any of the exhibits), the Sultanate of Oman, the citizens of Kuwait, and the people of the United Arab Emirates. The Halliburton Foundation, part of an enterprise that went on to cover itself with so much glory in the second Gulf War and that made Bush the Younger's vice president an extremely wealthy man, is there of course. So is the government of the People's Republic of China, listed as mere patrons. The list says as much about the life and times of Bush the Elder—and his son—as the sum of all the thousands of exhibits in his museum, and with considerably more candor. It was, of course, Harlan Crowe, the library's treasurer, whom *The New York Times* revealed as a major funder for the campaign smearing John Kerry's war record in the 2004 election.

There are other presidents who have equally unsavory names on their library walls. In Atlanta, Jimmy Carter includes the Playboy Foundation among his donors. At the Reagan Library, the name of Robert Maxwell, the disgraced British tycoon and alleged Mossad spy who fell, jumped, or was pushed over the side of his yacht into the Mediterranean just before news broke that he had stolen his employees' pensions, is still proudly on display. There are certainly more inept ways to design a donor wall. Caudill Rowlett Scott knew enough about architecture to avoid the most obvious mistakes.

The Richard Nixon Library and Birthplace in Yorba Linda, a suburb southeast of Los Angeles, was designed by Langdon Wilson, the architects who built the first Getty Museum in Malibu in the manner of a Pompeian villa. The donor wall here is flanked by twin entrances to the men's and women's restrooms, like a giant version of one of those rain-or-shine dollhouse weather forecasters.

Nixon's is not a federally recognized library, and there are in any case precious few signs of any books. As the sign in the entrance proclaims, "This is the only presidential library that doesn't cost the taxpayer a penny." That's because the Nixon archive, including the Watergate tapes, was taken over by the National Archives and Records Administration after his disgrace and is accommodated in a shed in Maryland (at the beginning of 2005, however, it was announced that it would be handed over to the Nixon Foundation).

In Texas, the architecture of the Bush Library rotunda, vestigial though it is, certainly has a more commanding presence than what lies beyond. The bulk of the museum is a tall industrial shed, in which the structural beams and the profiled metal-sheet cladding of the roof are pitilessly revealed, floating above a display fitted out with all the skill and slickness of a casino floor. It takes visitors on an emotionally manipulative roller-coaster ride through the Bush years. Any sense of architectural space disappears in the face of a zigzag layout designed with the ruthlessness of a Disney attraction, and an equally hazy interest in authenticity.

Once past the foyer, visitors turn right and are ambushed with the sudden revelation of an Avenger torpedo bomber hanging suspended from the roof, frozen in the steep banking turn that is now considered obligatory when displaying military aircraft indoors. This is the type of warplane in which Bush took off from the deck of the aircraft carrier *San Jacinto* on the day in September 1944 that he was shot down over the Pacific, after bombing a Japanese radio station. This is not the actual plane, of course. Nor is the parachute hanging in a glass case on the wall the one that saved his life, but one from the same production run. Bush spent hours in his life jacket alone in the ocean, drifting inexorably to the island he had just attacked. He was snatched from sharks and Japanese patrols by a submarine, the USS *Finborough*, a rescue symbolized in the exhibition by a bit of business involving a submarine hatch. "I had faced death, and God spared me," Bush recalls in his commentary.

Around another sharp bend comes the next carefully orchestrated incident, a Wurlitzer from the late 1940s. It plays a tape loop that features "Boogie Woogie Bugle Boy" and stands next to a '47 Studebaker of "exactly the same type" that Bush drove across the country on his way to a new life in Texas after Yale.

Alexander Cranstoun, the exhibition designer, unlike the architects, was smart enough not to do the obvious thing. Bush alone among the more recent presidents has avoided the replica Oval Office that has been obligatory since Lyndon Johnson's wife, Lady Bird, forced one on a reluctant Gordon Bunshaft in Austin. Bush serves up the Laurel Office at Camp David instead. Bunshaft, who thought that a replica in the LBJ Library would be tasteless, declined to include it until the library was so well advanced that it was supposedly too late to find the space to make a full-size office. But Mrs. Johnson just kept bringing it up. Under pressure

Bunshaft did manage to shoehorn in a seven-eighths-scale version, providing fake Washington windows with a view of genuine Texas sunshine. It's curiously detached from the rest of the museum display; the glass, incidentally, is bulletproof, a precaution specified after a tragic campus sniper incident in Austin during the Johnson administration.

What all the Oval Office simulations have in common is the hushed respect they demand from visitors. They are shrines, preserved behind glass, or at least behind thick, red tasseled ropes, to protect them from any act of lèse-majesté. Nobody is going to get to sneak behind the replica presidential desk for a quick photograph. Nobody is going to carve their initials here. The partial exception is in the Kennedy Library, which alongside JFK's Oval Office has an evocation of Bobby Kennedy's office at the Justice Department. You can walk around the back of his desk to get a closer look at his children's crayon drawings taped to the walls and at the dented white steel helmet worn by one of the three hundred federal marshals sent into Oxford, Mississippi. There is a moving letter from James Meredith, the black student those marshals protected, celebrating his graduation. These, for once, are *the* helmet and *the* letter.

Oval Offices come and go, as each administration decorates and redecorates. But the president's desk, which puts his back to the window and faces the fireplace at the far end of the oval, is the fixed point. The replicas provide a compelling insight into the political uses of furniture. Carter had a pair of sofas positioned back to back across the middle of the room, each flanked by a pair of armchairs. One sofa faces the desk. The other is trained directly at the fireplace. This arrangement allows visitors to get carefully graded privileges depending on their status. The basic visit begins with the dignitary/supplicant entering. The president rises, shakes hands, arm-squeezes, body-hugs, kisses on the cheek (if considered culturally appropriate), and waves the dignitary into the sofa. Both visitor and president have an aide join them in the designated flanking chair. The encounter proceeds to its conclusion. The less privileged visitors then leave. In stage two, useful for bringing troublesome discussions to a positive conclusion or indicating a particular degree of warmth, all rise, and move to the second sofa in front of the fire. The president comes from behind his desk to join the visitors and sit side by side with them, in steps as hallowed by custom as a rainmaking dance. This is no doubt exactly what happened when, as Carter puts it, "Deng Xiaoping came to Washington to visit with me." What does it matter if nobody remembers a word of what was said, what does it matter if you have inadvertently left the impression that America would sit on its hands in the event of a Chinese invasion of Taiwan, when you have gone through a ceremony like that?

In Reagan's day, the layout was more static and offered less in the way of ritual. A pair of three-seater sofas were positioned in the middle of the room on the long axis, allowing the president a direct view of the fireplace from his desk and of visitors who included Mother Teresa, Mikhail Gorbachev, Margaret Thatcher, and a selection of Beirut hostages.

Lyndon Johnson clearly wasn't keen on working at his desk: the coffee table with its speakerphone on a pull-out flap, close to the rocking chair with the footstool on the sludge green carpet, was the seat of power in his day. Kennedy's Oval Office, on the other hand, with its ship models and yachting mementos, had a wider role when it became a soothing TV studio for the duration of the Cuban missile crisis. What his audience would not have seen was the daybook of his secretary, Evelyn Lincoln, which lies open at the JFK Library for the first week in October 1962. It records an insane schedule of appointments allocated in three-minute segments starting at 5:19 A.M. McGeorge Bundy, the national security adviser, was in twice on this particular morning—the first time at 6:18 A.M., for seven minutes; then, after the president had face time with Secretary of State Dean Rusk and Ted Kennedy, Bundy was back at 6:31 for another three minutes.

Bill Clinton had seen the Kennedy, Carter, and Johnson Oval Office replicas and wasn't impressed. He told his architect, James Stewart Polshek, that for his library in Little Rock, "if you can't do it exactly right, don't do it at all." That meant genuine sunshine through actual windows. "He was adamant about the need for real daylight," says Polshek. "The real Oval Office has a south orientation. Ours has flipped 180 degrees, so the west side is seen as the front, surrounded by borrowed light." Alone of the libraries, Clinton's Oval has become a real part of the building, rather than a piece of scenery. It stands on the second floor within an oval-shaped column that rises the full height of the building, with the entrance lobby underneath it.

Bush's museum cannot quite make up its mind about tone. Should it reveal Bush as the WASP patrician son of privilege that he was, growing up on a family estate in Kennebunkport, the product of Phillips Academy (motto *Non Sibi*) and Yale? Or does it portray him as the self-made Texan he always claims to be, to demonstrate his populist roots in his adopted state? In the end it opts for the latter. Bush—captain of the baseball team at Phillips—presents the art of politics and public service as a game for regular folks. "The adrenaline factor in politics is identical to the adrenaline factor in sports. The extra last throw of a horseshoe is similar to a debate situation or a crisis in the legislature," he says. And the Studebaker of the type in which he crossed the continent, clearly there to add color to the display, is accompanied by a claim that "to celebrate his new life George Bush stopped for lunch outside Abilene, ordered a local beer and chicken fried steak, a dish he had never heard of before, but which was to become his favorite meal." The display offers such precious insights as Bush's words that "my mother taught me the fundamental things. 'Don't brag. Think of the other guy. Be kind to people.' The things they have taught me have stood me in good stead."

The exhibition layout shuffles its way through Bush's career, marking the highlights by constructing a series of landmarks. There is a giant plywood model of the dome of Congress and a mock-up of the White House. His time in China is signaled by a pagoda, which looks much like the kind of thing you might find in an upmarket but somewhat old-fashioned Chinese restaurant. Nixon's library does something similar—not surprising, since both were designed by the same firm. There is the bicycle Bush was given when he was America's ambassador to China, but which shows no signs of ever having been used. Deng Xiaoping is portrayed meeting Bush in 1985 in tapestry form. The moment was captured by two artists from the Shanghai Red Star Tapestry Factory, who spent fifty-three days weaving it, kindred spirits of Ms. Goodnight and her galloping horses outside. Bush's time as ambassador to the United Nations is encapsulated, daringly in the context of the limited worldview of the Texas backwoods, by a row of U.N. flags. Lots of photographs of Bush in dinner jackets are displayed, although none that record the evening in Tokyo when he threw up, practically in his host's lap.

Visitors also have a chance to sit inside a replica of the president's cabin on *Air Force One* and to fasten an actual seat belt. The first Gulf War is signaled by an hourglass in which the sands of time are energetically running out. Visitors can reset it as Bush gets ready to draw his line in the sand. Mannequins dressed in military uniforms have been spray-painted silver and white, in an attempt to humanize the hardware. Visitors can get a glimpse of the Kuwaiti desert through night-vision goggles. On the way out is a less than understated cigarette boat that Bush acquired in the 1970s to boost his sporty image, and the offer of a customized letter for each visitor signed by the former president and his first lady.

EVER SINCE CONGRESS VOTED TO TAKE OVER THE LIBRARY THAT Franklin Roosevelt designed next to his house at Hyde Park in upstate New York, every president has built a presidential library. Hyde Park is the personification of modest domesticity: a U-shaped range of clapboard-covered barnlike structures organized around a garden. It's on two floors but looks lower because of the steep shingled roof. Yet it reflects the extraordinary life of a president who had to deal with the key events of the twentieth century while confronting the difficulties of a life in a wheelchair. Over time it has sometimes seemed as if the more lackluster the president, the larger the library—a phenomenon that culminated with Gerald Ford, who has split his library in two, with a building to his name at either end of Michigan. Congress finally moved to limit competitive attempts by ex-presidents to erect ever larger monuments to themselves by passing legislation insisting that a president raise the funds to pay not just for the building but also for an endowment equal to 20 percent of the cost before a presidential library is adopted by the federal government. Those libraries larger than 70,000 square feet require a larger endowment. It's a measure that has not been entirely successful in curbing the growth in size of these libraries: Roosevelt's library is just 30,000 sqare feet, while Kennedy's is 95,000 square feet, and Clinton's 125,000 square feet.

Roosevelt notwithstanding, classicism of one kind or another has been the model for almost every presidential library. But when Gordon Bunshaft, the dominant force at Skidmore, Owings and Merrill, America's biggest architectural practice in the 1960s, was asked to design Lyndon Johnson's library in Austin, he used a Greek rather than a Roman model. The LBJ Library rises over Red River Street like a Texan acropolis as conceived by NASA, a complex of three related, strictly symmetrical structures that step down a hillside by way of a series of ramps, overlooking the university lawn. The main library is an all but windowless box, faced inside and out with six bands of travertine, which were imported from Italy in the teeth of bitter opposition from protectionist American quarry owners. The stone dazzles in the sun against the deep blue Texas sky. A series of reflecting pools leave rippling water patterns on the blank walls so intensely white that they hurt the eyes even in winter. To one side, the LBJ School of Public Affairs is faced in distressed concrete rather than travertine, to make it clear that respectful tribute is being paid to the mother ship holy of holies, rather than trying to upstage it. The complex sits on top of a podium that contains a thousand-seat auditorium. Its sloping walls look like the ramparts below the

Parthenon, and are faced in more travertine, in a careful pattern that uses three vertical slabs of stone to each horizontal slab. A deep cornice throws the top of the wall into shadow. Chrome-plated steel discs stud its underside, recalling the triglyph and metope pattern of the Doric order, a classical detail that might seem calculated to let Bunshaft's fellow architects know that he can navigate his way around classical architecture. But in fact, under the impression that he was a modernist of the most hard-line kind, Bunshaft claimed the arrangement was simply the product of functional necessity rather than history. The concrete roof beams have eight steel cables threaded through them to boost their strength. Each of the cables has a metal disc to cap the anchor point, to which Bunshaft added a ninth in the interests of symmetry. Or at least that's what he said he did.

Look at the library head-on, and you see that the sidewalls curve out as they approach the ground, tapering toward the middle, and then flair out again at the top, suggesting a classical column, with all the sharp edges rounded off. It's not strictly a part of the classical repertoire, but close enough to be a reminder of the idea of entasis.

It's not pretty or engaging, but then neither was Lyndon Johnson. Bunshaft recalled his first meeting with the president, driving to the Johnson ranch to look at the cows: "Johnson was building a prefab on his property, and we went in there and he was proposing to put a window in one wall of a bedroom. I said, If you do that, you won't have any place for a bed. You ought to put it there. He said, 'No.' I thought to myself, He's trying to figure out whether I'm some pansy decorator, or a real man."

The library suggests either a mausoleum or the final assembly building for the Saturn rocket program. In fact Bunshaft's co-architects on the project, Brooks, Graeber and White, in addition to designing Johnson's ranch and his family-owned radio station, had designed the manned spacecraft center in Houston.

Bunshaft described Johnson as "an aggressive, big man, who had helped make great social changes into law. You would not think of

Lyndon Johnson if you went to Roosevelt's library. It seemed to call for a building of some virility." Despite its roots in the architecture of Athenian democracy, the LBJ Library feels unmistakably imperial, if only in that it is manifestly more competent in its architecture than the usual run of presidential libraries.

The library's position on one end of the campus's central axis drove Bunshaft to inflate the scale of the project: "It would have to be massive, even if it were made to hold rubber bands."

Bunshaft had designed a library before—Yale University's Beinecke Rare Books Library—and he put the lessons he learned there to good use in Austin. Treated mechanically, a library could become simply a storeroom for books. Bunshaft managed to create a space of sullen grandeur at the heart of the building that is undeniably a work of architecture rather than of stagecraft or display. It rises a full eight stories and accommodates a flowing marble double staircase, rising under a giant carved presidential seal, in a way that cannot fail to impress. "It's a monumental building, because a presidential library should express the importance of a president and his papers," felt Bunshaft.

The great hall of the library is dominated by books—one entire wall glows with them, or at least with the scarlet buckram-covered boxes that contain Johnson's papers, behind a regular grid of marble-framed glass windows, each with an individually spotlit gold presidential seal. They make it instantly clear what this building is without having to spell it out in words or signs. The hall makes a lasting impression, one that Jimmy Carter's architect feebly attempted to replicate in Atlanta by offering a perfunctory flash of file boxes through a glass porthole. Bunshaft clearly had no interest in allowing the exhibition to distract visitors from the magnificence of the space he had created. The exhibits are squashed into a semibasement, apparently as perfunctory afterthought.

Although Johnson and Bunshaft clashed over the Oval Office replica, there could have been no architectural practice more appropriate than Skidmore, Owings and Merrill to design this particular president's library. The firm represented both the ascendancy and the decline of a certain kind of America. The office established by Louis Skidmore and Nathaniel Owings that Bunshaft first joined in 1937 was to expand into the world's largest architectural practice as America itself grew into an unchallenged superpower. SOM created the uniform of modern capitalism in America. In Manhattan it designed Lever House on Park Avenue, the first glass and steel skyscraper anywhere. It built Chase's headquarters for the Rockefellers, occupying two full downtown blocks, as well as towers for Marine Midland and U.S. Steel. In Chicago SOM built the Sears and Hancock towers. These swaggering skyscrapers may have owed their aesthetic expression to Mies van der Rohe, but it was SOM that used his vocabulary to create the American downtown in the 1950s and 1960s. They also exported the physical image of America around the world. Everywhere they went, they created a certain kind of steel and marble modernity for governments or corporations struggling to look up-to-date. They built airports and office towers, convention centers and hotels, that had the effect of making every ambitious city in the world look the same. Inside those towers, SOM designed open-plan white-collar factories, equipped with sheep pens and five-wheeled chairs for the clerical classes. For the masters of the universe, they created offices with handcrafted one-off desks, flanked by specially woven tapestries, flattered by spotlights, and guarded by Chinese carved figures and glossy hardwood fittings. The carpets were ankle deep, the leather upholstery was dyed in primary colors, and the chrome-plated furniture came from the Bauhaus. The embodiment of corporate power must have impressed the young Jacques Attali, encouraging his ambitions for the scale of the EBRD.

SOM's work was entirely lacking in self-doubt; it seemed to represent the faithful and undiluted expression of an America born to rule. And when the Vietnam tragedy, the burning of the ghettos of the 1960s, and the assassinations destroyed the self-confidence and unassailability of that America, SOM's confidence evaporated with it. Financially, SOM was battered and bruised by the post-Vietnam economic slump and the oil shock, but its real trauma was philosophical. It was no longer possible to build the way that Bunshaft had done. His generation had invested heavily in the aesthetic of swaggering restraint. It was more than a mannerism: he and his contemporaries had believed in it, regarded it as a moral imperative. In the 1970s, when modernism began to be viewed not as a progressive force, but as a deeply reactionary tendency unpopular with both CEOs wanting to make a mark and radical opponents of urban redevelopment, SOM simply did not know how to respond.

Just as LBJ decided not to seek reelection in 1968, so SOM, at the end of the 1970s, set up a series of conversations with the postmodernists to see where to go next. Bunshaft lived long enough to scorn his successors at the firm he once dominated: "In my book, David Childs [who runs SOM's New York office] isn't an architect at all. He's just a planner who gives everything a pomo skin."

Bunshaft's library was almost the last act of certainty in a career that never considered the possibility of doubt, while the library's exhibits portray an America that has already lost its optimism and confidence and is beginning to understand the need to demonstrate humility. Johnson himself was hardly conspicuously blessed with that quality. But the events of his years in office were so manifestly traumatic for America that the relentlessly positive tone that Bush's library takes was simply not possible in Austin. The Bible that had belonged to Jack Kennedy, on which Johnson took the oath of office on the plane taking him back to Washington from Dallas, sits in one glass case. In another is an MK-82 500-pound general-purpose bomb of the type dropped in ever larger numbers on North Vietnam starting in 1964. Almost as chilling are the photographs in the display on civil rights that show the whites-only ladies' restroom of a Mississippi courthouse—they could belong to the nineteenth century. But in this setting we are forcibly reminded that they are part of our own times. To his credit, LBJ's library can also display the collection of pens used to sign into law the bills that created his Great Society program.

At several levels the LBJ Library reveals a conflict between the taste of the architect—and perhaps even more that of Arthur Drexler, the Museum of Modern Art's director of architecture, who curated the original museum display—and that of President Johnson. The dignified restraint of the original library has been subverted by an attempt to appeal to a different America, energetically abetted by Cranstoun, the designer of the green gunk fountain, and his ubiquitous silver-sprayed mannequins posing as American soldiers. The stately, if slightly camp, bifurcated staircase at the heart of the library atrium, with its sweeping travertine curves, now has a 1968 stretch Lincoln Continental parked awkwardly underneath it. Not far away is an animatronic figure of Johnson—donated by Neiman Marcus—in a Stetson with one western boot lodged on the hitching-post rail dispensing wit and wisdom at the touch of a button. A pair of Mies van der Rohe's Barcelona chairs, clearly a relic of the previous design regime, have been drawn up as resentful captives in front of this spectacle, as if to suggest the enforced submission of the elite taste of the Volvo-driving classes to the popular will.

ALTHOUGH PLANNING STARTED ON THE KENNEDY LIBRARY FIVE years before Johnson commissioned Bunshaft, I. M. Pei's building did not open until long after Austin had been completed. In fact it was fifteen years, two sites, and three different designs between the announcement of Pei's appointment and the endlessly delayed opening of the library on Columbia Point, a spit of artificial land overlooking the sea south of downtown Boston. Given the tortuously slow rate of progress, it's hardly surprising that it did not turn out to be one of Pei's more impressive designs. But it was to prove a decisive project for him. It consolidated the transformation of a former student of the Bauhaus refugees

Marcel Breuer and Walter Gropius from house designer for the piratical New York property developer William Zeckendorf into the preferred architect of presidents with imperial pretensions. Pei worked for Mitterrand at the Louvre and for Helmut Kohl on Berlin's historical museum. The Kennedy Library allowed Pei to explore his fascination with the pyramid, a form he was later to use for Mitterrand. Here he designed the only presidential library before Clinton's that militantly rejects the classical model.

The glamour of Kennedy's life and the tragic circumstances of his death made the competition for the design of the library as vigorously fought as that for the reconstruction plan for Ground Zero. The president's widow was introduced to a wide range of architects through an elaborate process of conversations that involved flying Alvar Aalto from Helsinki, Kenzo Tange from Tokyo, Franco Albini from Milan, and even Basil Spence from England to a Boston hotel for a weekend of awkward silences. Were the participants meant to be offering advice and condolences, or to pitch for the job? Spence reported that the whole room was moved to tears when they were read a note from Kennedy instructing an architect in the design of a federal building in which he quoted Pericles: "Let us not imitate, for we must inspire others." Jacqueline Kennedy was initially taken with Louis Kahn, but, according to Pei's biographer Carter Wiseman, Bobby Kennedy wouldn't treat Kahn—who was given to asking bricks what they wanted to be—and his flights of poetic fancy seriously. Mies van der Rohe was so reserved in their conversations that she didn't believe he really wanted the job.

In the end, Jacqueline Kennedy opted for Pei, then not yet fifty, after a carefully stage-managed interview in his office, specially painted white and emptied of clutter for the occasion. Just before his death, Kennedy himself had looked at a site for the library on the Charles River that would form part of the Harvard campus. But with Pei appointed, the university offered a second site that avoided the problems involved in clearing the railway freight depot that occupied the original choice.

After an excruciating delay, and growing opposition from those who described the project as a Kennedy Disneyland that would flood Harvard with two million visitors a year, the university changed its mind and withdrew its offer.

Those attendance figures were, of course, utterly fantastic. The most visited presidential library is Johnson's, a fact that is certainly connected with its refusal, unique among the libraries, to charge for admission. And even LBJ never racks up more than a trickle of 200,000 supplicants in a year.

The University of Massachusetts offered an alternative site on an isolated waterfront point overlooking a sewage outlet. Like Bunshaft's work for Johnson, the Kennedy Library uses architectural space, more than exhibits, to engage the visitor. As you arrive, the view out over the water is hidden from sight, to be revealed only as you enter the vast, empty ten-story-high glass extrusion that is at the center of the complex. Chopin plays tastefully over the speakers, and from the entrance terrace, with its black granite floor, there is a view to the sea across a soaring space with its huge American flag hanging like a waterfall from the steel truss roof. In the distance you can see the skyscrapers of Boston, and the jets on their way down into Logan. This is a memorial as well as a library, "dedicated to the memory of John F. Kennedy, thirty-fifth president of the U.S.A. and to all those who through the art of politics seek a better world."

By the time it was finished in 1979, Pei's design had lost its initial clarity. Worse, by then it looked simply dated. The balance between architecture and content had shifted decisively. Bunshaft could batter his way through all opposition and build a presidential library that really was a library. Pei, working with the designer Ivan Chermayeff, a contemporary of Kennedy at Harvard, had to incorporate the narrative, storytelling aspects of a presidential library. And in this way, the JFK Library has set the pattern for all the subsequent presidential libraries. On the way to the cinema that begins the tour, visitors get a glimpse through gray-tinted glass of the twenty-six-foot sloop that was given to Kennedy by his parents as a fifteenth birthday present. The library is less than thirty years old but seems far older—even if not as ancient as Pei's pharaonic geometry, with its black glass prism, white cube and cylinder, would imply. But its restless shapes and its position against the sky somehow recall those heroic black-and-white photographs of the landmarks of the modern movement.

On the November Saturday that I am there, forty years to the day after the assassination, the boat is stored on Cape Cod, its regular winter home. Three signal flags spelling out JFK barely move in the biting cold as geese fly overhead. There are just a handful of visitors inside the library itself. Outside, a Somali taxi driver sits listening to his radio, blaring about the lockdown by the air cavalry of an Iraqi town on the Syrian border.

The world this building evokes seems impossibly remote. Its television sets show blurred images of the 1960 presidential campaign, when politicians still made speeches that were worth listening to, and when Frank Sinatra sang "Everybody's Voting for Jack." It was a time when the Kennedy brothers wore silk top hats for the presidential inauguration. And the matter-of-fact documents displayed on the wall carried bulletins from a world on the edge of being vaporized. The words "Eyes Only, Reproduction Prohibited Unless Declassified" are stamped across a series of pieces of paper displayed in one of the exhibition rooms. I look at one, and am jolted to find myself reading a letter from Nikita Khrushchev that has been written apparently from the heart:

> Just imagine Mr. President that we had presented you with
> the conditions of an ultimatum which you have presented us
> by your action in presenting us with these. You Mr. President
> have flung a challenge at us. Who asked you to do this? By
> what right do you do this? You are no longer appealing to rea-
> son, but wish to intimidate us. No Mr. President, I cannot

agree to this and I think in your own head you recognize that I am correct. We will not simply be bystanders with regard to piratical acts by American ships on the high seas. We will then be forced on our part to take the measures we consider necessary and adequate in order to protect our rights. We have everything necessary to do it.

In the same case, dated just six days later, a second document reproduces the verbatim text of the translation of another, more despairing message from Khrushchev to Kennedy, relayed via the U.S. embassy in Moscow. Declassified by the CIA only in 1968, it begins:

I think you will understand that if you are really concerned about the welfare of the world everyone needs peace. Both capitalists, if they have not lost their reason and still more we Communists, people who know how to value not only their own lives, but more than anyone the lives of their people. I see Mr. President that you are not devoid of a sense of anxiety for the fate of the world. I have participated in two wars and know that war ends only when it has rolled through cities and villages everywhere sowing death and destruction.

The exhibition ends as it can only end, with the black walls of a room marked "November 22, 1963," which shows images of the funeral, but not the assassination. You exit, past the images of Charles de Gaulle and Harold Macmillan in black, and past the image of the memorial stone at Runnymede, witnessing the gift of an acre of England to the United States of America. Finally you emerge from the black room into the ten-story-high void looking at the sky, the water, and the Boston skyline, a process that feels like the moment of release after a funeral service. You turn to see words from Kennedy's inaugural address: "All this will not be finished in the first 100 days, nor will it be finished in the first

1000 days, nor in the lifetime of this administration nor even perhaps in our lifetime of this planet. But let us begin."

Since designing the Getty villa, the firm of Langdon Wilson, whose recent achievements include the Taco Bell building in Irvine, seem to have lost their touch. For the Nixon Library they paraphrased the Getty layout, complete with a reflecting pool, respectfully wrapped around the little suburban house in which Nixon was born, standing in the midst of a particularly lurid thicket of yellow and purple flowers. If you want, in the library shop you can buy a three-by-five-foot, embroidered, 100 percent acrylic, made-in-the-U.S.A. American flag, which has flown over the Nixon house for a day, for forty dollars. The shop throws in a certificate of authenticity, and "if you want a certain date for that special person just call us."

Nixon's library is staffed by volunteers in blazers who rather alarmingly call themselves docents, a term used for guides in the tonier kind of art museum. But they go out of their way to be genuinely nice to every visitor who passes through the doors. They tell you all about the presidential Lincoln parked in one room, and how it was shipped to Moscow so that when Nixon and Henry Kissinger were there negotiating with Leonid Brezhnev, they could talk without worrying about the electronic eavesdroppers that plagued the U.S. embassy. "We had a Russian gentleman here who was involved with security for the KGB at the time," one docent informs me, "and he told us that they knew they were up to something, but that they couldn't figure it out." The docents point out the hall of world leaders at the center of the library, a group of plaster dummies milling about awkwardly, looking more as if they were trapped in an elevator lobby than in the waiting room for eternity. Nixon wrote the guest list himself, selecting the statesmen who impressed him most. De Gaulle, with his military kepi on his head, is the tallest, towering over Churchill in a bowler. Mao stands with his back to Konrad Adenauer and Golda Meir, who is clutching a handbag. The docents eagerly identify the less familiar figures—these days, that's just about all of them—and explain how each one was carved life-size in plaster, dressed in "actual clothing," and sprayed bronze.

More moving is the case full of keepsakes from American POWs, acquired during their time in Vietnam. On display are threadbare prison uniforms, with strange flashes of color stitched into them that look like the work of an advanced Japanese fashion designer, and cardboard toothpaste boxes and cigarette packets with the Stalinist graphics favored by the Vietnamese, from the Red Cross. The museum goes on to chart Nixon's tortured, even sadomasochistic relationship with the press, culminating in a wall display that shows all fifty-four of the issues of *Time* magazine during the course of his life that put him on the cover. "More than anyone else," says the caption with not a little trace of pride, despite the humiliating headlines on so many of them. Another case contains a tiny piece of moon rock and a NASA space suit. The matching pair of boots look as if they come from the local hardware store and have been sprayed silver, as if for a theatrical production.

The most enlightening exhibit at the library, however, offers a particularly chilling reminder of Nixon's continuing interest in spin. A copy of a memo to H. R. Haldeman, Nixon's chief of staff, outlining the procedures to be adopted by the president in the event of a disaster during the first moon landing hangs behind glass. It includes the script written for the television address that Nixon could have given: "These brave men, Neil Armstrong and Edwin Aldrin, know that there is no hope for their recovery. But they also know there is hope for mankind in their sacrifice." Prior to the statement, the president would have telephoned each of the widows. "A clergyman should then adopt the same procedure as a burial at sea, commending their souls to the deepest of the deep, concluding with the Lord's Prayer."

These insights aside, the primary objective of the whole enterprise is to prove that there never was a smoking gun at the Watergate. "The president knew nothing about the break-in. Some of his aides became involved in the cover-up," is as far as the library will go in conceding that

anything went wrong during Nixon's watch. It is, however, only too willing to level charges of rampant vote rigging in Illinois and Texas against
the Kennedy campaign in 1960. Nixon contended that he actually won
that election but, as he has it, magnanimously chose not to contest the result in court, to save the country from the agony of endless recounts. The
exhibition ends with a black tunnel leading inexorably to a photograph
of the helicopter rising from the White House lawn, and that grim
"I have never been a quitter" speech, the one that goes on to suggest that
"the greatness comes when you are really tested."

Compared with Bush the Elder's library, Nixon's is a shrill and
slightly down-at-heel shrine for true believers. The slickness of the Bush
building reflects a smoother, more socially secure character, still in command of a political machine that presents the presidential story in bite-
size chunks designed not to test the patience of its audience.

AS A PIECE OF PLANNING, THE CARTER LIBRARY DOES MUCH
better than Bush's, but its architecture is glum to the point of catatonia.
It occupies a suburban site in a leafy residential neighborhood full of big
comfortable houses with landscaped grounds, where middle-class soccer
moms take the dog for a walk on a Saturday. It's in sight of Atlanta's
downtown, not far from the World of Coke and the Martin Luther King
Jr. historic site. Landscaping took a higher priority than architecture. Car
parking is screened out of sight, and visitors walk to the entrance
through the formal symmetry of a garden arranged around a series of
pools of water, flanked on both sides by white park benches and pergolas,
like the country retreat of a retired Caesar. The illusion is somewhat undermined by the sign warning visitors that a shirt and shoes are required. But behind this dignified approach, the design breaks down into
a banal series of circular pavilions that betray the faintest of faint echoes
of Frank Lloyd Wright's style, no more than the cosmic hum left after
the Big Bang. The two large pavilions on the left are the library and the

museum. On the right are five smaller interlinked circles that house Carter's offices. Straight ahead, a series of landscaped gardens and lakes look out over Atlanta's skyscrapers in the distance. But inside the layout is inept, and the exhibits unfortunate. Access is through one of two 250-seat cinemas placed back-to-back and designed to show the introductory film continuously, an inflated provision that is the product of euphoric overoptimism about visitor numbers. On the wall that proclaims the former president to be a peacemaker and protector of human rights, Carter invites the nonexistent crowds "to consider some of these decisions that I had to make, and as you visit with us today, to ask yourself what importance they have and then to come to the town meeting to discuss them with me." The town meeting turns out to be a dismal space under a rotunda less convincing even than Bush's, with five people sitting on the benches, and Carter's blotchy orange image playing to the camera on a flickering TV screen.

There are no mannequins dressed as soldiers here and no rock music playing over the public address system—just a reminder of the Nobel Peace Prize awarded Carter in 2002 in the form of a particularly hideous painting on velvet by Vald Jensen, as well as a lunch table laid for Deng Xiaoping's state visit in 1979 (well, actually, only half of it, with a mirror in the middle). In another corner is a hefty automatic voting machine of the hanging chad era. It's configured for the Carter-Reagan election. There are places on the ballot for endless state and county offices, for the Libertarian party, and for Angela Davis. With perhaps unnecessary frankness it seems to have been set by someone who was not planning to vote for Carter.

RONALD REAGAN'S LIBRARY HAS NO PRETENSIONS TO PATRICIAN values. Reagan had initially wanted to build it on the Palo Alto campus at Stanford. A site was chosen and a design was drawn up, but the university rebuffed him, just as Harvard eventually turned down Kennedy's library. Instead Reagan decided to slum it, and accepted the gift of a site from a house builder on a ridge at the outer edge of Los Angeles in Simi Valley. In California there is certainly no such thing as a free lunch, and this was one land donation that came with a price. An hour's drive north from Santa Monica, where the suburbs begin to thin out and even the strip malls and the motels are built in what passes for mission style, the streets suddenly begin to take on the names of former presidents. As you wind up Presidential Drive to the library, you pass homes on Roosevelt Drive and Eisenhower Drive, streets so new that they look as if they haven't yet had their shrink-wrapping removed. At the top of the hill, the land falls away to reveal fresh subdivisions ready for the next explosion of tract houses down in the adjacent valley and the sites being cleared for the bigger, more opulent houses up on the neighboring hillsides.

On the outside, Reagan's library is a hacienda—all Roman pantiles, chimneys, pink stucco, and a loggia built around a handsome open court-yard dotted with folksy benches. On the way in, you encounter a bronze statue of the late president in his denims and cowboy boots. His glossy black Lincoln is parked in a corner of the courtyard. The entrance hall is lined with what looks like plastic wood. The clay tiles on the floor make it feel like a generic Mexican restaurant. Inside the museum, gimcrack ceiling tiles and blue carpet tiles crackling with static lovingly evoke the ambience of the convention room of an airport hotel. There are *Bedtime for Bonzo* posters on the wall, and a replica of the diner booth in which Ronnie first met Nancy—with not so much as a photograph of his first wife, Jane Wyman, in sight. The *General Electric Theater* shows excerpts from the Great Gipper's movie hits.

Reagan's library is much less artful than Bush's, and somehow more engaging too. The copy of the Alzheimer's letter that Reagan wrote in 1994 after his diagnosis with the disease silences even the most ferocious of his critics for a moment. The authenticity of the library's re-creation of the White House situation room may be thrown into question by the photograph of the real thing included in the caption that highlights the glaring discrepancies between the mock-up and the original. Nevertheless, it is a mismatch that feels almost endearing in its naïveté.

The exhibits also have a disarmingly homespun quality. Many look like junk salvaged from the attic. You can find Reagan's letter sweater from college days, as well as the one he wore back to the White House from the hospital after the attempt on his life, and a bulletproof vest, one of several sent to the White House by well-wishers after the shooting. Alongside it is a copy of an X ray showing the bullet still lodged in his chest. A cruise missile is casually propped up in a corner behind the TV set on which Reagan talks warmly about Gorbachev. On one table is an array of dummy prototypes made by the Hughes Aircraft Corporation as part of the Shield in the Sky program, otherwise known as Star Wars. One is a miniature vehicle sensor, the other is an antisatellite infrared sensor designed for use on the space shuttle. Models of an M1 Abrams tank and a Bradley fighting vehicle serve to demonstrate Reagan's enthusiasm for re-equipping America's armed forces on the ground as well. Thankfully, the museum resisted the temptation to accept the full-size versions that their grateful manufacturers would no doubt have been only too eager to donate.

When it was finished, the library had a certain unpretentious architectural charm, benefiting from a beautiful setting and a well-chosen site. But encroaching housing, and the decision to extend the library by creating the first mission-style aircraft hangar to accommodate *Air Force One,* have done much to dissipate that charm. The customized Boeing 707 that flew Reagan and several other presidents around the world is almost as big as the library itself, and its presence gives the impression that this is the contemporary equivalent of the burial site of a Saxon warrior, entombed with his longship and chariot. And indeed this is Reagan's chosen burial place, just as Dwight Eisenhower built his mausoleum in his presidential library in Kansas.

IN 1998, TO MARK THE TWENTIETH ANNIVERSARY OF PHILIP Johnson picking up the first Henry Moore trophy and check that come with the Pritzker Prize for Architecture, the Pritzker family prevailed upon the White House to host the ceremony. Bill Clinton complied, making the presentation to Renzo Piano. It has certainly done Piano's subsequent career in the United States no harm.

As it happened, architecture was very much on the president's mind that year. With the end of his second term in sight, he was beginning to think about life after the Oval Office, and in particular about his presidential library. He had been one of the guests at the opening ceremony of the Bush Library when it opened. Deeply unimpressed by its architecture, he left vowing to do something very different when his turn came.

"I want," said Clinton a few months later, "something that is welcoming, but has a sense of grandeur." Two Pritzker winners had already designed a presidential library: Gordon Bunshaft, who died in 1990, was no longer available; the other was I. M. Pei.

Clinton had of course seen both buildings. He thought that the best modern building in Washington was Pei's addition to the National Gallery, and that the best presidential library was the Kennedy. But to hire the same architect as Jackie Kennedy would have seemed perhaps too much like self-aggrandizement. He looked at the other Pritzker winners as possible architects for his library. The non-American winners were clearly not an option for such a symbolically charged project. By all accounts, neither Robert Venturi nor Philip Johnson nor Richard Meier nor even Frank Gehry, the other American recipients, managed to hit it off with Clinton. What, the president was in the habit of asking, do you think of that museum in Bilbao? And how do you think that titanium will look in twenty years? There was a certain amount of lobbying. Steven Spielberg, who had recently had a house designed for him in the Hamptons by Charles Gwathmey, suggested that he might be just the architect for the job. Disney's Michael Eisner, who had transformed the Mouse Kingdom with buildings by Michael Graves, Frank Gehry, Robert Stern, Antoine Predock, and Arata Isozaki, offered some names. But in the end it was the Clintons' decorator who suggested that they talk to James Polshek, a New York architect who had recently completed the new planetarium at the American Museum of Natural History, and a man with no known Republican sympathies. Clinton had definite ideas about what he wanted. He was looking to use his library, as Jimmy Carter had done, as the springboard for the next step in his career: that of a freelance international elder statesman.

Clinton wanted the same combination of library and offices. It's hard to imagine him entirely turning his back on his new base in Harlem for Little Rock, the city that came up with $17 million to persuade him to set up there. But he has ended up with a piece of architecture as impressive as that of any of the presidents, one of the few that addresses an urban context and that plays its part in the renewal of a run-down area of the city. It takes the form of a glass bridge cantilevered out over the river with a spectacular view of the city.

"We were invited to the White House in 1999," says Polshek. "We got ninety minutes in the Oval Office. We took an associate partner from Little Rock with us and they got on right away. Clinton said, 'Will you do one of those napkin sketches you architects do?'" Polshek told him they are apocryphal, "but we do them sometimes, Mr. President."

Polshek wasn't going to risk letting the job slip out of his hands by limiting himself to just one sketch. He and his partner worked on three different designs, drew them up, and built three detailed models to explain them at the next meeting to an audience unfamiliar with architectural drawings.

"We presented on the night of the Columbine massacre. He was late, which was unusual. He came in very agitated and red eyed. His first words: 'Here as we speak, they are killing our children.' He gave us forty-five minutes in the map room."

Polshek advised against the greenfield site the city had offered. It was too obvious and too easy. "We ended up on brownfield railroad land that could act as a catalyst for development." It's a site littered with industrial history: the Union Pacific and the Rock Island lines both crossed the Arkansas River here. And the hundred-year-old Choctaw Bridge across the river, no longer used, provided a handsome fragment of industrial archaeology. It also turned out to be immediately next to the offices of the local newspaper, the *Arkansas Democratic Gazette*, which was violently opposed to the building of the library. Polshek offered Clinton three conceptual strategies for the library. Did the president see it as a villa in a park, a campus, or a single major building? Then there was the question of how to realize the strategy. The first version was to align the library along the river frontage, but that didn't seem to be making the most of the site. "We had a joint epiphany, when we realized that if we made the building perpendicular to the river, its principal views would be to the west and downtown. You could look up and down, see six bridges, and so become fully aware of the city."

As well as the museum, the building includes a big meeting hall and a suite of offices for the Clinton foundation. The form of the building, a glass cantilevered structure, came from the bridges. It can be read as a contextual gesture, but also as a metaphor that Clinton could identify with. As the detailed design evolved, Clinton kept coming back to the idea of the glass bridge. "In a political way, and for reasons that have never been explicitly stated, he is very concerned about openness, which is why he wanted there to be so much daylight," says Polshek. "The National Archives and Records Association expected a blank box for the library, but Clinton was clear that the staff shouldn't live like moles. So we put the people up in light in a pavilion on the roof, and the books in the vault."

Despite their painfully obvious limitations, the presidential libraries belong to a long line of would-be architectural monuments, stretching all the way back to the great library of Alexandria and beyond. In their gestures toward making an enduring mark, they can be understood as being driven by the same impulses that motivated Imhotep and Augustus, Louis XIV and Napoleon III, to say nothing of François Mitterrand. All of them have attempted to put architecture to work to defy the inevitability of death, to dignify their own lives, to shape a city, and to find the consolation of a sense of meaning in an orderless world. The Bush and Reagan libraries are perhaps more limited in ambition than their predecessors, but they are still as much political as architectural statements.

With their display cases of tributes accumulated over the decades, their accounts of valor in battle, service, and the celebration of a leader's triumph over the enemies of the state, they have uncomfortable parallels with the practices of those later Roman emperors who had themselves deified. If there were ever going to be a cult of president worship, the libraries are where it would start. But, unlike their predecessors, the presidential libraries belong to a period that is agnostic about the possibility of making a lasting mark. Perhaps we have simply seen too much history and too many ruins to believe in architecture as a manifestation of a state religion anymore. Despite their ambitions, the libraries—Bunshaft's acropolis in Austin excepted—mostly seem flimsy enough to blow away at any moment, leaving nothing behind. Most are simply not up to the architectural part that they are intended to play.

CHAPTER 10

A TOMB AT THE DRIVE-IN

GIVEN THAT IT HAS A BEST-SEATS-IN-THE-HOUSE VIEW OF AN Orange County freeway, Richard Meier's new visitor center for the Crystal Cathedral in Garden Grove is finished in a particularly appropriate shade of BMW dealership silver. It takes the form of a five-story-high cylindrical drum, part of a cluster of religious buildings that makes up the Reverend Robert Schuller's personal version of Vatican City. To the right is the Crystal Cathedral itself, designed by Philip Johnson. It has the shape of a slender glass iceberg, its razor-sharp edges rising one hundred feet in the air, supported on an intricate steel grid.

The cathedral faces the Tower of Hope, a stubby cream-colored block designed twenty years earlier by Richard Neutra that contains Schuller's offices and is topped by a chapel and an outsize cross. Meier's visitor center is the most recent addition to the complex. It floats midway between Neutra and Johnson in a sea of parking lots and gardens.

On the second floor of Meier's building, a piece of construction debris has been left behind by the contractors and is still waiting to be tidied away. It is only after a second or even a third look that you notice that the shriveled and blistered strip of tarmac, the bitumen-patched tar-paper damp proofing, and the rough-sawn timber joists supporting them have all been lovingly laid to rest on a cube of polished travertine, signaling that they are to be understood as sacred relics and not garbage. And on this tarmac in ancient time those feet did indeed walk. This is, according to the caption (printed on a piece of paper that is already peeling away), an original section of the roof from the now demolished snack bar at the Orange County Drive-in Theater, on which Schuller took up his stand one March Sunday in 1955, to conduct what he describes as his very first worship service.

For musical accompaniment, Schuller and his wife had bought a church organ on easy terms. They towed it to the drive-in behind their station wagon that morning. Schuller preached to a congregation of fifty, attracted by his advertisements in the local paper. Sitting in their Plymouths and their Buick coupes with the tops down, they listened respectfully to his sunny message of blithe can-do optimism crackling out on the public address system over the fan-shaped parking lot. Next to the marble cube is a Plexiglas box sitting on a plinth. It contains a collecting plate, piled up with $83.75 in 1955 vintage quarters, pennies, and dollars, and the occasional five-dollar bill, the exact sum raised by that first collection.

In a small way, Schuller has done for architecture what Oprah Winfrey did for American literature. Like Winfrey's on-air championing of new writing, Schuller has brought contemporary architecture to an audience that would never previously have considered it as part of their world. When he set up in Garden Grove, Schuller was creating a new version of Christianity and, like so many clergymen before him, part of his strategy was to attract attention with the architecture of his church. That is to say that he wanted to retain enough of the traditional signals to reflect that this was still a Christian church—bell tower, cross, altar, and so on—but to put them together in a different configuration that would make his organization look impressive and, at the same time, modern and forward-looking.

Religious architecture is a question of continuity, interspersed with brief periods of rapid change. The purpose of a religious building is to send signals that are intended to tie worshippers together over long periods of history and across huge distances. When a new religion, or a new sect of an old one, seeks to establish itself or reinvigorate itself, it develops a new architectural language.

The orientation of religious buildings and their interaction with natural phenomena—especially daylight, but also the stars—reflect the earliest attempts of sacred architecture to frame the heavens. It's done to produce recognizable building types that in their fabric carry the imprinted message of the sacred. The Crystal Cathedral tries to do all of those things, in the bleakest of settings.

Religion has continually used architecture as a propaganda vehicle and to create a shared sense of identity. A religious building is devised to make the individual worshipper feel a sense of belonging to the larger body of the faithful—and in some sense to play a part in revealing sacred truths. Thus the particular concern with orientation common to the major religions. Every mosque must face in the same direction. For early Christian churches there was a presumption in favor of placing the altar at the east end, facing toward Jerusalem, and the rising sun. The cruciform plan was equally inspired by the body of Christ on the cross. Certain architectural languages have become associated with certain religious movements. In the nineteenth century some reformers equated the pointed gothic style with truly Christian architecture and found classical architecture, with the pagan associations of the temples of the Greeks and Romans, distasteful.

In many religions there is a recurring need to replicate a founding church or temple. Sikh and Hindu migrants to Western Europe, for example, have made literal re-creations of temples that follow their originals precisely in form and detail. They have in some cases imported specialist craftsmen from the subcontinent with the high levels of skill needed to build them.

There are parallels between the design of a place of worship and that of a theater. In a traditional nave, with rows of parallel pews arranged on either side of an aisle, facing directly toward a pulpit, the congregation's awareness of its own presence is limited. A series of tiers facing one another, as in a theater in the round, does more to make the members of a congregation aware of each other's presence. And like the abolition of the proscenium arch in the theater, this arrangement makes a congregation feel more like an active participant in a religious ceremony rather than a passive spectator.

But there is also a level on which architecture is used to define a mood: to create a sense of space and expectation, of reverence, that serves to make individuals feel that they have been transported out of the everyday world, and are for a moment open to the sacred.

Nevertheless, there are limits to what an architect can do to a church. When faith is invoked by what can be seen as artificial or manipulative means, it is counterproductive; it is not just traditionalists who put a premium on maintaining forms sanctioned by precedent who are repelled. For an architect to consciously set out to create the atmosphere of sanctity is to reveal the underpinnings of the process. Hence, the importance of tradition over innovation in church architecture. And yet the mechanical repetition of traditional patterns in the end becomes deadening and ineffective.

Religious architecture must follow a careful path if it is not to become a form of stagecraft and to reveal the mechanism by which the atmosphere has been created. Religious faith cannot be seen to be reduced to a conjuring trick.

Some worshippers still listen to the Reverend Schuller's sermons in their cars, but his ministry has expanded enormously, thanks in part to his weakness for collecting famous architects, and exploiting them for their publicity potential. Ten years after that 1955 sermon, Schuller moved up the road from the Orange Drive-in to Garden Grove, where, with Richard Neutra, the Viennese-born architect who brought modernism to Los Angeles, as his designer, he built what he called the world's first walk-in, drive-in church. Schuller's congregation went on growing, to the point that, after a series of additions to the first building, he decided that he needed a second church on an adjacent site. This was what became the Crystal Cathedral, completed at the end of the 1970s. And now Richard Meier has added his steel drum to offer visitors something to do when services are over.

The gardeners and the maintenance men tending the Crystal Cathedral's grounds in the summer heat murmur quietly to one another in Spanish. But the church seems to cater to a different audience. The improving, upbeat biblical messages scattered everywhere are all in determinedly monoglot English. At the entrance to the cathedral is a Holy Family grouping, equipped with donkey, and carved with such startling, lifeless banality that it is hard to understand how it can share the same universe as Johnson's svelte and knowing architecture. But it is just one of scores of artworks of equally numbing mindlessness distributed all over the site. Under the bell tower in a special circular chamber lined with a stockade of multicolored marble columns and equipped with a glass door, is a rotating Christ, easily mistaken for a hologram, but actually hollowed out of a clear Plexiglas cube.

How is it possible that the same man who took such a sophisticated approach to commissioning architecture and used it as an effective propaganda weapon for his church could believe that this was art?

Schuller is a cleric untroubled by false humility. Indeed, at every stage in his career, he has taken a special pride in coaxing his congregations to reach deeper and deeper into their pockets to build churches that are bigger and more ambitious than the barns that were expected of him and his kind. "I am an Iowa farm boy. Where did my passion for great art and architecture come from?" he asks himself with cloying immodesty in his autobiography. "I cannot build just anything. It has to glorify God so qualifying as a thing of beauty that will be a joy forever."

But Schuller does confess to having been deeply hurt when he read the parable that the Reverend Wendell Karsen, a missionary in Hong Kong, wrote about his church in *The Church Herald* magazine. Karsen, as Schuller tells it, imagined the wretched of the earth converging on Garden Grove for a glimpse of the Crystal Cathedral, only to see their reflections in the mirror glass, and reeling back, shocked at the image of their misery. "One of them picks up a rock, and throws it at his own image. Others follow suit, until the cathedral is reduced to rubble, then ransacked by the starving in search of food and raw materials to ease their suffering."

Schuller consoled himself with the thought that he had been misunderstood. All the money spent on the building had actually gone to a good cause, feeding the families of its builders, and he seems to have shrugged off the hurt easily enough. "For whatever reason, critics such as the Reverend Karsen failed to see the role played by great monuments throughout the history of the church. The cathedrals at Chartres and Notre Dame, along with Westminster Abbey and St. Peter's in Rome, continue to inspire us centuries after the last workers set the last stone in place, and inlaid the last stained glass window"—which is true, but it's a somewhat self-regarding comparison with the warped space frame structure and its liver-colored marble podium that he commissioned from Philip Johnson.

Sitting in Richard Meier's snowdrift-white office in Manhattan, where the workers are corralled in little cattle pens to make space for an exhibition of his work, I ask him if he ever discussed art with Schuller.

"No." He smiles a little weakly. "No."

So how did he get to meet his client?

"I was elected to the American Academy of Achievement, for their Man of the Year Award. When I went to the dinner in Jackson Hole, he was there. And we talked. People are put off by his exuberance and passion. But I like him."

Schuller is a Christian, but his theology is concentrated, as he puts it, on individual responsibility and self-improvement. There is a lot more focus on his homilies than there is on Christ's suffering in his agony on the cross, or in the more challenging aspects of spiritual insight. Schuller's message is inscribed in foot-high chrome-plated steel letters pinned to the walls. They promise "inch by inch, and everything is a cinch" and "tough times never last, but tough people do."

Meier is not a Christian and the visitor center is not, so he says, a religious building. Its purpose is to provide a public space that offers visitors a place to spend time before and after services, filling the spiritual void between the parking lot and the pews. There is a chapel on the top floor. It's a sunlit white space without an altar, but it is equipped with some uplifting paragraphs from the Epistle to the Philippians inscribed on the wall, as well as a few dozen office chairs arranged in a horseshoe, and a view of the cemetery. But the chapel is so small and so modest that it hardly registers set against the far more dramatic spaces below it that serve to define the building's purpose. In the middle of a great circular drum, banks of stairs rise three and four floors high, taking visitors on an erratic journey through Schuller's view of the world.

It is not a view that Meier's architecture appears to share. Its light-filled elegance sits uncomfortably with much of its content. Even Meier's soberly tasteful carpets seem to be shrinking away in alarm from the burden of sickly sentiment that they are expected to carry. In the exhibition space, next to the fragment of the snack bar roof, is a dismaying procession of larger-than-life-size bronze representations of a selection of the preachers who have visited Garden Grove over the years. They show a wildly ecumenical taste in their costumes. Billy Graham is in a western suit and stacked heels. Bishop Fulton J. Sheen, the first television evangelist, is resplendent in full episcopal regalia, complete with cap, cape, and ring, alongside a somewhat alarming statue of Schuller himself, suggesting that the eventual purpose of the visitor center might also be to provide a tomb for its founder. There is a jarring mismatch between the objects and their museumlike context. Look at the objects in isolation, and you see them as overwhelmingly kitsch. Against the background of the white walls and the subdued palette of materials, your preconceptions try to wrench your brain into understanding the kitsch in a different way. Two Americas that very seldom meet have come face to uncomprehending face here.

This is, Schuller says several times, a "museum that motivates." All visitors are handed a leaflet that tells them, "You are standing in the middle of a sermon that has been lived."

To the agnostic eye, this could be the standard off-the-shelf Richard Meier museum atrium, as seen in Atlanta, Frankfurt, Barcelona, and half a dozen other cities: a soaring space, shaped by heroic architectural gestures and a Corbusian-inspired geometry. We have become so accustomed to museums that take on the role of the sacred spaces in the modern world that it should be no surprise to see a semireligious space attempting, not entirely convincingly, to look like a museum. The east wall of the visitor center is a great sail of glass that forms the backdrop against which a white steel ramp zigzags back and forth on its journey to the roof. Since this is a Richard Meier design, there are inevitably a lot of external staircases and elaborately cantilevered balconies etched against the sky, the kind of things that he has perfected over the years and can now build in his sleep.

The doors at the entrance slide out of sight to open up most of the ground floor to the sunshine and the gardens. But instead of the predictable black leather and tubular steel Le Corbusier armchairs that you would expect to find in such a space, it is furnished with the kind of reproduction antique furniture and generic sofas that you can see over tea and cucumber sandwiches in the lobby of the Kuala Lumpur Shangri-la Hotel. The cut flowers on the low tables are "lovingly donated by the Sterling family." Instead of the installations by Christian Boltansky, the canvases by Francesco Clemente, and the inevitable Richard Serra sculpture that are the conventional background to Meier's architecture, there is only a portrait of Robert H. Schuller, a gift of Lyt and Venita Harris. Schuller is depicted as a luxuriantly silver-haired red-faced patriarch in his pastor's robes, which would look as if they had been borrowed from one of America's more conservative university deans were it not for the two-tone purple and violet color scheme. His gown, worn over a conventional collar and tie, is exactly the same as the outfits adopted by the rest of his priesthood, but for the two additional patches of imperial purple on the collar.

There are other elements of the contemporary museum in this space, but all of them have been subtly distorted. There is a museum café, of course, except that here it is designated as the food court and called the Miracle Café: "We serve Starbucks with pride." And there is a shop, but rather than the usual collection of impressionist postcards and miniature versions of iconic modern movement furniture, it sells *God's Health Plan*, which, according to the cover of the booklet, "adds years to your life"; blue and pink velour Crystal Cathedral leisure suits; Crystal Cathedral mints in tins inscribed "God loves you, and so do I"; and Richard Meier– designed glassware. A red-jacketed guide sets off with a group of visitors every half hour on a tour of the art collection in the grounds and the architectural highlights of the cathedral campus. There is a ticket counter too, where you can make reservations for the services at the Crystal Cathedral just across the plaza. And of course there is a donor wall, just like the one in every museum in America—except that for once there is no coyness with naming names about money. Next to the shop is a white granite wall on which the names of "the pillars of this construction project" have been etched. According to the inscription, which radiates a degree of social insecurity that seems curious in an organization that is otherwise so sure of itself and its faith, "The founders of this international center for possibility thinking," as the visitor center is called by everybody except its architect, "are the first people to step forward and embrace the dream of this world class structure. Each committed a gift of $1000 or more to provide funds to retain one of the greatest world recognized architects of the twenty-first century, Richard Meier, commissioning him to capture the dream and design a timeless physical frame for this ministry to see the home site of the crystal cathedral." It does seem uncomfortably important to the Reverend Schuller to suggest that the eyes of the world, as well as God's, are on Garden Grove.

For those pillars of the church who weren't quite so quick off the mark with their checkbooks, beyond the wall there is still the promise of the incomplete transparent crystal brick wall glowing with light tinged the palest of pink. Visitors are invited to "gaze at its glistening majesty, each name engraved for the ages, by a donor who made a $500 gift possible to help construct this magnificent structure. Add your name here." As another of those stainless-steel sentences distributed throughout the building blithely proclaims, "There is never a money problem, only an idea problem." But to judge by the exposed roof trusses, and the air-conditioning ducts visible in the exhibition space, there is still room for a few more donations to finish off the museum that motivates.

Overhead, at the top of the atrium, three huge light collectors are intended perhaps to convey the only subliminal religious message contained in the entire structure—they may, or may not, be hinting at the concept of the trinity. For Meier, light is the acceptable face of the sacred. But everything else in the way of a religious message in the building has been reduced to the blindingly obvious by his client. For almost two thousand years, even the simplest and the humblest Christian churches have been loaded with iconography and an imagery explicit enough to allow the faithful to read a religious message in their architecture and the art that they contain. But they have been capable of being interpreted on a variety of different levels, from overt symbolism to more occult readings, through orientation, plan, and detail.

Schuller has built a church for the age of large-print books for the visually impaired. It leaves no room for doubt, personal interpretation, or subtlety. It reduces the consolations of religion to an Esperanto cartoon, a subtitle, or, in the case of the suggestion "If you can dream it, you can do it," an advertising jingle.

Visitors are handed a leaflet from Schuller, inviting them to experience what he calls a structure with a sermon. "Every structure makes a

statement, but this exciting new building is the first structure ever designed to preach a life-affirming, dream-building, possibility-thinking
sermon. Check them off as you go. First of all, the sermon starts with a
BIBLE VERSE. In the glorious Grand Lobby of this elegant new
Richard Meier structure, stand in the center of the lobby and look up at
the glistening stainless steel letters to read the timeless words of Jesus
Christ."

And when the self-guided tour sprinkled with an abundance of capital letters and exclamation marks and glistening adjectives is over, the
leaflet suggests that, as they do after every good sermon, people go and
have something to eat, and maybe go shopping. That's all at hand in the
food court and the store.

Schuller was born into a Dutch Reformed family in rural Iowa. He
felt his calling as a young man, and set out to take religion from the farm
to the godless suburbs. His ministry began in Chicago, and for a time he
broke with the National Council of Churches because he felt it was too
soft on communism. The Soviet Union repaid the compliment by featuring him in Leningrad's St. Isaac's Cathedral, which had been converted
into a museum of atheism, as a wicked exploiter of the gullibility of the
masses by soaking them of their savings to pay for his churches. He
evolved into a freeway evangelist with a much sunnier disposition, prepared to take a more ecumenical view than most of his peers. He dropped
the downbeat paranoia, and started meeting popes and grand muftis,
rabbis, and Communists. There is even an image of a somewhat bemused
Mikhail Gorbachev at the Crystal Cathedral.

"Don't call yourself a Dutch Reform, or a Methodist church," he once
advised aspiring pastors and ministers planning their first move into the
exploding and unchurched new suburbs of Southern California. "Drop
the labels, and call yourself a community church." It's a formula that has
certainly been successful. Every Sunday Schuller's congregation comes
from all over the Los Angeles sprawl pouring into Garden Grove in the
car-pool lane. They fill the seats of the Crystal Cathedral for a service—

or perhaps "performance" is a better word—that is broadcast around the world as *The Hour of Power* on Christian cable channels and seen, Schuller claims, by twenty million people every week.

The Crystal Cathedral delivers an audience that Americans on the stump with a political ax to grind, or a book to sell, have been almost as eager to cultivate as Oprah Winfrey's. *The Hour of Power* has featured Gerald Ford and Dan Quayle, Charlton Heston and Ray Kroc, Norman Schwarzkopf and even Philip Johnson claiming, with a nod and a wink, divine inspiration for his design for the church.

The campus has grown continually over the years, relentlessly swallowing up orange groves, walnut trees, and the tract houses that used to surround it, in plots ten acres at a time. In his hunger for more land, Schuller has even outbid the local shopping center. To record the scale of the giving that has made it all possible, Garden Grove's pavements are embossed with the names of donors, each one set in a framed border shaped like the Crystal Cathedral's floor plan. The effect is very much like the Walk of the Stars on the pavement outside Grauman's Chinese Theater in Hollywood.

On Easter Sunday, such is the demand for seats for "The Glory of Easter," a service that promises live animals, flying angels, and professional actors, that no fewer than eight performances are offered during the day. Big for Schuller is better. Larger and larger congregations are the way to reach ever more people, by creating the sense of a shared civic occasion that only religion and sport can now offer in the suburbs. And they provide a bigger pool of donors for funding yet bigger churches. The Crystal Cathedral says it has the fifth largest organ in the world and claims to have the biggest cross and the longest stone wall in architectural history—unaccountably, the well-traveled pastor, who could teach Donald Trump a thing or two about self-promotion, seems not yet to have encountered the Great Wall of China.

The view of the cathedral from the freeway is a critical part of Schuller's strategy for attracting the congregations that are needed to fill the steadily increasing number of seats and parking places. As you drive through Orange County, the ivy-decked noise barriers that edge both sides of the freeways hide most of the landscape, rendering any building without a tower invisible. All you see are the very tops of things. Bits of shopping centers, inspired at considerable distance by Daniel Libeskind and Frank Gehry, bob up and down in the aimless flotsam of multiplexes and malls that come swimming into view as you head south. Then there is a Sheraton Hotel, disguised as a Disney castle, to be followed soon after by the "real" thing: Disney's towers picked out in a palette of pastel colors, which warn you that you are getting closer to Schuller's Vatican. Gliding past Anaheim you glimpse fragments of the Mouse Kingdom's helter-skelters. The freeways themselves are developing their own version of white-knuckle rides, terrifying linguini-thin concrete viaducts exploding in starbursts above the cloverleaf intersections. Then on the left you can see the Angel Stadium, fronted by a pair of giant orange baseball caps. On the right, the Crystal Cathedral comes into view. Slightly detached from the main building, Johnson's chrome-plated paraphrase of a campanile marks out the presence of the complex on the Orange County flatlands, just like the turrets of Disneyland a mile away. There is no danger of actually hearing the bells from the freeway, but Schuller wanted the tower anyway. It's both a signpost and a billboard. The diffuse scale of Los Angeles makes the bell tower an essential response to its context, providing an updated version of a very traditional element on the urban skyline.

WHEN SCHULLER FIRST BEGAN BUILDING UP HIS CHURCH, HE realized instinctively that he needed something to make him stand out from the competition. The Orange Drive-in was all very well as a base for the early days of the movement, but the area was rapidly turning into a new type of city rather than a suburb, and Schuller wanted to build a church with the appropriate civic presence to match his maturing audience.

Just like the Mormons, who defined themselves with their massive complex of temples in Salt Lake City; the Seventh-Day Adventists, whose sub–Frank Lloyd Wright–style churches span the globe like gas stations; or for that matter the Cistercians, who had defined the distinctive ornament-free form of their churches and monasteries eight hundred years ago, Schuller needed an architect to help him get his message across in the most memorable way possible. His permanent church was meant to embody the open-air origins of his ministry; that meant lots of glass, and creating the sense of the outdoors, even when the congregation was indoors. And an expanding new congregation could use the reassuring endorsement of hiring a big-name architect to design its church, just as America's small-town banks have always tried to strike a balance between looking imposing enough to suggest that your money was secure, yet not so overendowed with marble and Corinthian columns as to look as if it was being squandered.

Richard Neutra's picture had recently been on the cover of *Time;* in the article inside, he talked about his interest in nature and the outdoors, a combination of celebrity and hokey philosophizing that was enough to arouse the clergyman's interest. Schuller drove up to Neutra's office to see him, with his own sketch for the "walk-in, drive-in cathedral." As Schuller tells it, his opening gambit was to ask Neutra why he should hire him. Schuller was duly impressed by the Austrian-born Neutra's immediate reply: "Hire me, and your buildings will never go out of style."

Over the years, Neutra ended up working on four projects at Garden Grove: the glass-walled church itself, a meeting room, a bell frame, and finally the office tower with its huge cross on the roof. These were not Neutra's best works. He was reaching the end of his creative life when he worked on them. But in their context, they have a certain dignity that is still apparent. Certainly they were the nearest thing to architectural high culture anywhere in Orange County at the time.

Schuller insists on claiming at least part of the credit for designing them. According to the exhibition in the Meier building, Schuller "was acquainted with Richard Neutra, one of the great architects of the time, whose philosophy was called biorealism. The two men are a team, and bring to the world a new and different kind of church building, marrying the outside with the inside." That the church has no stained glass was the result of Neutra successfully persuading Schuller that he should keep the lines of the church "clean, sharp, and vertical." This was not how Schuller had envisaged his church would look. But the result impressed Schuller enough for him to insist that the Johnson church ended up with no stained glass either.

With rubble stone walls laid in vertical bands, and the surrealistic tricks that Neutra plays with cutouts at the foot of the masonry to make it look as if the church is floating, this is a highly mannered form of religious architecture. Schuller was unconcerned by Neutra's lack of commitment to his religion. He was happy enough with his architect's enthusiastic embrace of sunshine and nature, and his fame. Transparency was to supply the leitmotif for all Schuller's buildings. He kept coming back to the idea of preaching in the open air, just as he had done on the roof of that snack bar in the original drive-in site, and he asked his architects to interpret that spirit in their buildings.

Transparency was certainly the basis of Philip Johnson's work at Garden Grove. According to the exhibition's commentary, the brief for the design was the product of Schuller's prayers: "Lord, if we must build a new sanctuary, let it have glass walls and a glass roof. Let me see again the blue skies and the trees." The white-painted structural steel of the Crystal Cathedral, invisible from the outside, makes you feel as if you are in the middle of a cloud when you go inside. Johnson was a shrewd choice on the part of Schuller in the 1970s. He was at just the point in his career when he would start to achieve his highest visibility. And Schuller knew how to get what he needed out of Johnson. The architect's first design was a relatively conventional church; Schuller's response was lukewarm. What he needed was something spectacular, and Johnson got the message. The cathedral turned out to be one of his most photogenic projects, an advertisement for both Johnson and for Schuller's church, a building that was constantly being photographed and published. And the association with as established a figure as Johnson helped shift the church away from the perception that it was a marginalized sect.

When Schuller first appeared in Johnson's office with his sketches, and his tales of working with Neutra, Johnson was apparently under the impression that Schuller was himself an architect looking for a job. Then the preacher told Johnson what he really wanted: there had to be seating for a congregation of three thousand and the building must blend and not compete with the Neutra office block, bell frame, or sanctuary. Then he explained that there was no money to build it, but the Lord would obviously provide. In the meantime, Schuller took out a bank loan to pay Johnson his fee. Shortly after, at the celebration of his twentieth anniversary at the drive-in, Schuller set about the process of raising the cash. He stood before an audience of seven thousand people to talk about the future, and elevated the host—or, rather, he held up a little model of Johnson's building high over his head. "I believe that this project will be validated by a $1 million gift, soon," Schuller declared. The money duly materialized on time. Building the church, however, was more expensive, and more technically demanding, than he had hoped.

Schuller wanted an all-glass structure, which would be risky in an earthquake zone. To complicate things further, California was just beginning to think about enforcing energy-saving building codes, and glass is not the most obvious energy-efficient material. But he managed it, raising the money and dealing with the complex nature of the construction process. At one bound the Crystal Cathedral leapfrogged Schuller over the heads of his rivals in the increasingly competitive world of televangelism. The zigzag space frames left exposed inside the building and the elegantly fabricated glass exterior made Schuller's congregation look like the confident face of the future—it's a "world-class building," as Schuller would and does say, over and over again, not a dim provincial also-ran. The low-rent preachers, the Swaggarts and the Bakkers, were in trouble already, but the Crystal Cathedral left them for dead, like greasy spoons trying to compete against the confidence of the McDonald's-style fast-faith corporate steamroller. Johnson had given Schuller's ministry a draw that made even Neutra's buildings look a little flat.

The Garden Grove Vatican has grown and grown, just like a museum—except that here the decisions are all taken by the Reverend Schuller, in consultation with the Almighty rather than a boardroom of quarrelsome trustees. It's easy to scoff at the Crystal Cathedral mints, the copies of *The God Diet* piled high in the book section, the little shopping bags with a silver-embossed representation of the Crystal Cathedral (just like something from Bloomingdale's), and the message on the cathedral's director of communications' answering machine that assures you, out of the blue, that "God loves you." But the buildings are something else. As Richard Meier says, without architecture, what would there be at Garden Grove?

ON THE SURFACE, THE CRYSTAL CATHEDRAL HAS THE CHARISMA and the confidence to make you think that it represents religion in a form to be reckoned with. But even the most cursory trip around Los Angeles's newly built Cathedral of Our Lady of the Angels shows just how far any newly established denomination has to go to catch up with the Bishop of Rome. The city's new cathedral, a replacement for the earthquake-damaged nineteenth-century structure of St. Vibiana, overlooks the freeways, just across the street from Frank Gehry's Walt Disney Concert Hall, but it feels as if it has all the weight and authority and wealth of a two-thousand-year-old organization behind every detail. It was designed by Rafael Moneo, an architect who began his career with Jørn Utzon working on the design of the Sydney Opera House, and it says a lot about the continuing role of architecture in religion. Like the Crystal Cathedral, where Schuller's architects were self-consciously innovating, Moneo was equally self-consciously designing within the Catholic tradition. The Cathedral of Our Lady of the Angels attempts to create an example of one of the oldest urban institutions in the center of a very new kind of ultradecentralized city. It hints at the increasingly Hispanic character of Los Angeles but, in Rupert Murdoch's financial support for the project, it also reflects the contemporary restlessneess of power in the city. And like the Crystal Cathedral, it has attracted bitter criticism from those who see it as money squandered on vanity and self-promotion, rather than put to work by the church in serving the pressing needs of the poor.

This is a cathedral designed by a European architect in a manner that struggles to reconcile a traditional idea of what a cathedral should be with the realities of life in California. It sits on top of four levels of parking; the faithful make their way here by taking the elevator. Moneo has given the cathedral a pedestrian square, but it is marooned and isolated from the streets around it, hanging over the edge of the Hollywood Freeway. Moneo optimistically describes the highway's twelve lanes of melting asphalt as the contemporary equivalent of a river but, as if unconvinced by the metaphor, has tried to screen and protect the cathedral from its impact as much as possible. The effect is closer to a walled monastery, with a sense of enclosure and retreat from the world outside, than a cathedral as the focus for a religion that is engaged with the city around it.

Like Schuller's church, Our Lady of the Angels can seat three thousand people. It is part of a complex that includes a rectory for the archbishop and his resident priests. There is a businesslike conference center and offices planned around a cloister garden. The two-level plaza is overshadowed by the 150-foot-high campanile.

Moneo deliberately avoided making an entrance that opened directly from the street. Instead, pedestrians enter at the lower level of the walled plaza and move up a grand staircase to the upper plaza. From there they are pulled up and on into the church, and toward pews and the altar. It is a route that is designed to give worshippers the sense of the spiritual journey of the individual, moving gradually from the profane to the sacred, a journey that takes them upward into the light as their feet tread the Spanish limestone floor.

The liturgical content of the church is a mix of the comfortably familiar and the safely innovative. Rather than having an entrance at the west end, directly facing the altar, the church is designed with two ambulatories: one takes visitors past a series of side chapels, and the other provides access to the crypt.

Moneo veers between evoking the massive masonry structures of gothic Europe and responding to the context of California and its own complex traditions. The massive yellow ocher concrete walls of the structure refer to the mission architecture of the earliest Spanish colonial settlements in Los Angeles. But the result is flabby and puffy rather than the highly crafted piece of architectural sculpture that Moneo had clearly intended it to be. The interior, with its zigzag route to the body of the church, is clearly intended to orchestrate a mounting sense of expectation. The main entrance is to one side of the altar and forms the beginning of a processional route upward that requires a sharp turn. Once negotiated, it reveals the altar only when visitors have had time to adjust to the solemnity of their surroundings, picked out in sunlight that has been carefully filtered through veined alabaster. From the north ambulatory, a staircase provides access down into the crypt, embellished by stained-glass windows made in Germany in the 1920s and salvaged from the old cathedral of St. Vibiana that Moneo's building replaces. Niches and tombs here are marketed like apartments in a new condominium tower: a few well-placed leaks about who has been looking over them for space, and the bookings just come flooding in. The emotional resonances of the routine religious art in Moneo's cathedral are no more convincing than the banality of the work at the Crystal Cathedral.

RELIGIOUS ART MAY HAVE DECLINED INTO THE MINDLESS PRODUCTION of the routine and the lifeless, characterized by crucifixes turned out on an industrial scale and lacking in aesthetic ambition or conviction. But familiar banality can still seem less threatening than objects that have been touched by a genuinely creative, but potentially disturbing vision. The vacuousness of so much contemporary religious art is an issue that has seriously exercised Christian intellectuals for at least a century. Alain Couturier, a French Dominican priest, believed that part of the responsibility for the decline of the church's appeal in the second half of the twentieth century was its loss of a link with the creative arts. The sculpture associated with the church, and religious art in general, had become a hermetic category lacking in any freshness or conviction. More cautious Catholics could see this, but were worried by the risk of losing control the church would be taking in commissioning contemporary creative art. Couturier tried to overcome their anxiety by setting an example, showing what was possible with a series of demonstrations. He was responsible for Henri Matisse's being commissioned by the church to decorate the interior of the chapel of St. Paul de Vence in the hills behind Nice and to design the vestments for its priests. Matisse's work set a precedent that was followed around the world, from England to Brazil. And it was Couturier who promoted Le Corbusier's name for the two great religious commissions of his career: the pilgrimage church of Ronchamp, in southeastern France, and the Dominican Monastery of La Tourette not far away. Together, they served to set a new model for contemporary religious architecture, with strongly sculptural forms and a sense of sanctuary and enclosure, as well as the appropriation of natural light to reveal and conceal these architectural forms, creating a sense of dematerialization and mystery.

Couturier's commissions were highly influential in encouraging Catholic dioceses around the world to experiment with more challenging architects. And the Catholic church has shown continuing interest in attempting to present itself as part of the contemporary world in architectural terms.

It's an impulse that can be seen in the Vatican's celebration of the third millennium with Richard Meier's Dio Padre Misericordioso jubilee church in suburban Rome, after an international competition. The monks of Novy Dvur, in the Czech Republic, who commissioned John Pawson to build Eastern Europe's first new monastery in a century, were equally committed to making the most of contemporary architecture.

"Light is the means by which we are able to experience what we call sacred," says Meier, with a telling use of euphemism for the spiritual. The three shells of Meier's jubilee church create an enveloping atmosphere, in which the light from the skylights above creates what he calls "a luminous spatial experience" in which "rays of sunlight serve as a mystic metamorphosis of the presence of God."

For Meier, "the jubilee church will show the true modernity of the Catholic church's efforts to adapt to the revolutionary time we live in." However, he found that the process of designing the church in Rome was much more opaque than that of working with Schuller in Garden Grove. "Schuller's participation was very evident at the beginning and the end of the design process. He might change his mind, but you know where you are. With the Vatican it's never so clear."

Meier's only argument in Rome was about the cross over the altar. "I wanted simple geometry," the architect says. "The church insisted on a representation of Christ on the Cross. So I said I am sure we can find something from the sixteenth century in the Vatican's basements. Well, we ended up with a nineteenth-century cross that turned out to be papier-mâché."

All architecture has its origins in sacred building. Its techniques, intellectual as well as material, have shaped architecture's contemporary role and given us our understanding of an architectural language with a temporal as well as a spiritual content. Meier and Moneo, as much as their clients Schuller and the Vatican, represent the two poles of religious architecture—violent innovation and continuity. But they are also both using architecture in the same way, as a means to create an aura around their churches, to demonstrate their continuing vigor and relevance. If Schuller's ministry outlasts him and his family, and continues to grow, then it's not hard to imagine a version of Meier's and Johnson's buildings exported around the world as part of the missionary effort of the church, in just the way that so many religions have done throughout the centuries.

CHAPTER 11

THE USES OF CULTURE

THERE CAN NEVER HAVE BEEN A MOMENT WHEN QUITE SO MUCH high-visibility architecture has been designed by so few people. Sometimes it seems as if there are just thirty architects in the world, a flying circus of the perpetually jet-lagged that consists of the twenty who take one another seriously enough to acknowledge the presence of another member of the magic circle when they meet in the first-class lounge at Heathrow and another ten running on empty——the others are on to them, but for the time being they can still pull in the clients on the strength of past glories. Taken together, they make up the group that provides the names that come up again and again when yet another sadly deluded city finds itself laboring under the mistaken impression that it is going to trump the Bilbao Guggenheim with an art gallery that looks like a flying saucer, or a hotel in the form of a twenty-story-high meteorite. They are, with just two exceptions, all men. You see them in New York and in Tokyo; they are on the plane to Guadalajara and Seattle, searching for work in Amsterdam, and all over Barcelona, of course. And now they are converging on Beijing. They cross and recross one another's paths, taking part in the same invited competitions, on the platform at the Pritzker Prize ceremonies, and on the juries that select the victors in the design competitions that they do not enter themselves.

Why has this happened? Mainly, it's because architecture has managed to make a mark in a way that it never has before. Every ambitious city wants an architect to do for them what they think Jørn Utzon's Opera House did for Sydney and Frank Gehry and the Guggenheim did for Bilbao. When the Gehry-designed Disney Concert Hall finally opened in Los Angeles, most of the speeches at the opening ceremony talked more about what this new concert hall was going to do for the city's image than about its acoustics. Everybody wants an icon now.

But given the sheer weirdness of so much contemporary architecture, how can would-be icon builders be confident that their particular meteorite or flying saucer is going to turn out to be the landmark they are looking for, rather than the pile of junk that they half suspect it might be?

The answer is that they can't. So they rely on that list of thirty names drawn from the ranks of those architects who have done it before. They are the ones licensed to be weird. Commission one of them and you can be confident that nobody is going to laugh at you. Just like buying a suit with the right label when you know nothing about fashion. But it's a self-defeating process. The more that those few names vacuum up all the high-profile projects, the fewer there are to choose from the next time around. This has the effect of turning architecture into a brutally divided business, caught between famine and glut. Architects either have too much work to concentrate on any of it properly and destroy their reputations by parodying themselves, or so little that a kitchen extension can turn into a life's work and they starve.

All the relentless attention and hype has a worrying effect on some of the more suggestible members of the flying circus. They start believing it. They can't help that little hint of amused disdain for any architect outside the charmed circle who isn't actually in the room at the time. But there is also the constant anxiety not to be upstaged for fear that their membership will prove only temporary.

This state of mind is the entirely predictable outcome of the bizarre quest for the icon that has swept architecture and has become the most ubiquitous theme of contemporary design. To stand out from an endless procession of economic basket cases equally determined to build an icon of their own to bring the world beating a path to their doors, an ambitious city must come up with something really attention-grabbing. One Bilbao can shock its way into the headlines, but repeating the trick is the way to an architecture of diminishing returns, in which every sensational new building must attempt to eclipse the last one. It leads to a kind of hyperinflation, the architectural equivalent of the Weimar Republic's debauching of its currency.

As a result, form no longer follows function—it follows image. The starting point for a museum used to be the shape and size of the collection that it would contain, or the technical demands of filtering daylight into the galleries. But many architects' first thought now is how to create an instantly recognizable silhouette for their buildings. This is no way to produce architecture that lasts, or of quality.

Sensationalism has produced egg-shaped airport terminals, opera houses in the form of giant crustaceans, and skyscrapers equipped with integral Ferris wheels. But the museum has been the most vulnerable building type to fall to this tendency. Given the loose nature of the layout and the budget, it's the easiest for architects to manipulate into curious shapes. And no museum has gone further in that direction than the Guggenheim, along with its troupe of architects, led by Frank Gehry.

The Guggenheim sold 320,000 tickets for its 2002 exhibition celebrating Gehry's architecture, more than for any other show in the fifty-year history of the Frank Lloyd Wright–designed building in New York. The museum called the show a retrospective, but the reality, stretching all the way up the seasickness-inducing spiral at the heart of the museum, was nothing less than Gehry's coronation by Thomas Krens, the Guggenheim's director, as "the most important architect of our time." With an uneasy mixture of the folksy and the self-regarding, Krens simultaneously compared Gehry to Michael Jordan and to Wright himself— comparisons that were perhaps calculated to say as much about Krens as they did about Gehry. If Gehry really was the most important architect in the world, that would clearly make Krens, who commissioned Gehry's most important building, the Bilbao Guggenheim, the world's most important architectural patron.

In thirteen years at the Guggenheim, Krens had turned a modestly scaled museum with an endowment and a collection a fraction the size of much less well-known institutions into a global art circus, positioned conceptually somewhere between the Bellagio Casino and Louis Vuitton, thanks in large part to the drawing power of sensationalist architecture. Krens had made Gehry a star and in return Gehry made Krens the most talked-about museum director in the world. No museum had come to embody the role of culture in the contemporary economy, and the uses to which it could be put, more than the Guggenheim.

Krens had behind him not only the startlingly successful establishment of the Guggenheim's colony in Bilbao, but also the launch of outposts, albeit not quite so impressively, in Berlin and New York's SoHo, just five miles south of the Wright mother ship. Oblivious to the implosion of the dot-com bubble, Krens had presided over the $20 million launch of Guggenheim.com earlier in the year. With *Martha Stewart Living*'s former homes editor to help, it was a commercial Web site that was meant to make the museum rich. The synchronized opening of two more Guggenheims in a Las Vegas casino, representing a collision between high and popular culture beyond parody, was imminent. And Krens was already talking about building yet more franchises in Tokyo, Taiwan, Rio, Salzburg, St. Petersburg, and Edinburgh. In every case, how the building was going to look came ahead of what it would contain. He had moved on from Gehry to Rem Koolhaas, Zaha Hadid, and Jean Nouvel to add to his architectural firepower.

But Krens's ability to defy the laws of gravity would never be quite the same after the Gehry show. The Las Vegas Guggenheim, in its Koolhaas-designed rusty red steel box in the bowels of the Venetian Casino, never paid its way, and was forced to shut after a humiliatingly short life. The SoHo Guggenheim was swallowed up by a new Prada store, and Guggenheim.com vanished in a flash of very expensive pixels. Even Bilbao had trouble maintaining its popularity. From a high of 1.3 million visitors, the total fell dramatically, before recovering to around 900,000 a year.

The usual explanation for this catastrophic sequence of reverses is to suggest that the Guggenheim was somehow just another victim of the tragic aftermath of the attacks on the Twin Towers, which took place just ten days after the Gehry show closed. But the museum was already in trouble without any help from Al Qaeda. All the signs were there in the Gehry exhibition. In its hubris and its narcissistic self-obsession, the show revealed an institution in the grip of an ego-fueled thirst for glory. Its director and his trustees were bringing out the bombastic worst in one another.

Like an aggressive young fashion designer brought in to rescue a fading couture house, Krens's first move as director had been to purge the Guggenheim's product line of the dated and the safely familiar in favor of the up-to-the-minute. He sold works by Chagall and Modigliani and bought Panza di Buma's collection of conceptual art. And he signed up a new architect to make a big splash with his flagship boutiques.

Gehry, who has the rumpled affability of a Californian Woody Allen, makes an unlikely Frank Lloyd Wright, and an even less likely icon builder. He has a self-deprecating irony of a kind not usually associated with American architects. Nor does he show much interest in the opaque language that plagues so much of what passes for contemporary architectural discourse. Gehry is apparently at his happiest messing around in a workshop with a soft black pencil and some yellow drafting paper. But not very far below his amused affability is a more complex personality, offering material that Gehry has mined for some of his most interesting work.

Gehry was born Frank Owen Goldberg in Toronto in 1929. He moved to Los Angeles as a teenager to become an American. Like many architects, he changed his name. But it wasn't a suggestion from their mother-in-law that transformed Charles-Edouard Jeanneret into Le Corbusier, or Ludwig Mies into Mies van der Rohe. Goldberg, who became Gehry when he married his first wife, has since said that it was a decision that he regrets, but it is too late to reverse. He did, however, accept the invitation of Jean Chrétien, Canada's prime minister—issued, so Gehry says, in the middle of a long-distance telephone conversation about ice hockey—to take up Canadian citizenship again.

Like that of Louis Kahn or I. M. Pei, Gehry's early architectural career revealed few clues of what was to come. In between designing apartment buildings, jewelry stores, and shopping centers for Victor Gruen, in what can only be called a commercial vernacular, Gehry started experimenting with cardboard furniture. His obsession with fish imagery in the 1980s, which included building a restaurant in Japan in the shape of a giant carp and creating a fish out of a cloud of steel mesh on the Barcelona waterfront, seemed to suggest that something Jungian and out of the ordinary was about to emerge. But it wasn't until he reached fifty that he built anything of real power. He developed an artist's wariness of offering too many apologies for his work. Why make a building look like a fish? "Oh I don't know, I just kind of liked it." But at other times he would talk about childhood memories, and playing with the live carp that his mother would bring home each week for Friday night supper.

Los Angeles was Gehry's other important source. With its seemingly random urban landscape of colliding shapes and odd juxtapositions, Gehry's architecture reflects the context in which it was born. When you are surrounded by freeways, giant advertising signs, and drive-in restaurants in the shape of giant bowler hats or hot dogs, there is not much point trying to create chaste, well-mannered buildings. Gehry began to explore a loose, unbuttoned approach to architecture. Rather than look for formal perfection, Gehry made architecture from untidy fragments, and apparently chaotic geometry. Influenced by such artist friends as Claes Oldenburg, he was ready to collage shapes and forms that didn't seem to belong together, and made no apologies for putting cheap materials, such as sheetrock and metal mesh, on show. It was too much for many potential clients in Los Angeles, who still felt more comfortable with safely established architects and a less challenging approach. Only much later did the city's power brokers begin to see a Gehry house, a colorful piece of giant sculpture, as a more conspicuous measure of success than the usual art collection or charitable foundation could ever be. In L.A., a Gehry house has come to rank so far ahead in the infinitely competitive game of social status that a Warhol portrait, even with a certificate of authenticity, hardly registers in comparison. A Gehry house is cheaper than a Lear jet but is way ahead not just on rarity grounds, but also in terms of the time and effort and respect that it implies. The tycoon who already has everything and still needs reassurance can console himself with the thought that here was a man, spoken of in the same breath as Frank Lloyd Wright by no less an authority than the director of the Guggenheim, who was ready to spend his precious time planning *my* bathroom, and manipulating the spatial relationship of *my* swimming pool with *my* living room.

Despite the commissions to design houses that started to come thicker and faster after Gehry won the competition to build the Disney Hall in 1991, it clearly rankled that it had taken him so long to win a major civic project in his home city and that so few others followed. Arata Isozaki designed Los Angeles's Museum of Contemporary Art, and Gehry regrets that he even entered the competition that he wasn't meant to win. The Getty went to Richard Meier. And when Gehry finally did get a serious project in his hometown, construction stopped on the concert hall almost as soon as the foundations had been dug, when the trustees ran out of money.

Gehry was beaten in the competition to design Los Angeles's Catholic cathedral by Rafael Moneo. He was passed over again when the Los Angeles County Museum of Art (LACMA) went looking for an architect. By this time he was claiming that he didn't do competitions. More of a problem was the fact that the architect whom LACMA director Andrea Rich appointed was going to have Eli Broad as his real client. Gehry had already had a series of unhappy experiences with the billionaire patron.

The Bilbao Guggenheim catapulted Gehry into an orbit far beyond the limits of Los Angeles. His design was a sensation because it looked nothing like an art gallery—or, for that matter, not much like a piece of architecture, at least not as architecture had previously been understood. With its puckered titanium-skinned roof, swooping and soaring through the bridges and embankments that line Bilbao's river, the Guggenheim was more like a train crash than a building, a homemade mutant version of the Sydney Opera House.

Its biggest achievement was seen as its part in the transformation of Bilbao from a grimy and run-down industrial backwater plagued by terrorism, with just a couple of international flights a day. Bilbao became the sort of place where affluent Americans might spend a weekend, and which could figure in the opening sequences of a Bond movie—not, it has to be said, universally regarded as the essential measure of urban civilization. Gehry had also succeeded in unleashing a wave of exhibitionistic architecture, motivated as much by materialistic as by cultural concerns.

The economic calculations behind the Bilbao Guggenheim stripped away a lot of the alibis for building museums, revealing the egotism and showmanship beneath the rhetoric of self-improvement and scholarship.

Yet Bilbao is hardly the first place to use a spectacular building housing a collection of objects to transform its economic fortunes. The practice goes back to the trade in holy relics by all faiths, from Shias to Catholics, which saw cities snatching sacred bones away from one another, and the construction of elaborate shrines to accommodate them in order to encourage a lucrative pilgrimage trade. When Germany's finance minister attempted to hold down spending on the rebuilding of Berlin in the 1930s, Hitler told Albert Speer to ignore him: "If the finance minister could realize what a source of income to the state my buildings will be in fifty years. Remember what happened with Ludwig II. Everyone said he was mad because of the cost of his palaces. But today most tourists go to upper Bavaria solely to see them. The entrance fees alone have long since paid for the building costs. The whole world will come to Berlin to see our buildings. All we need do is tell the Americans how much the Great Hall cost. Maybe we'll exaggerate a bit and say a billion and a half instead of a billion. Then they'll be wild to see the most expensive building in the world." Evidently, the Führer has a claim to having invented the Bilbao effect.

What made the Gehry show at the New York Guggenheim so revealing was the way that you could pick away below the surface and find traces of just about all of the preoccupations of a particularly gaudy decade congealed within it, even as the conditions that had brought them into being were about to be transformed forever. The show appeared to be about architecture, but it was really about the excess, egotism, and greed of the 1990s. Here was a selection of the urban icons pursued with quixotic abandon by ambitious cities all over the world. Here were the trophy houses of the egotistical robber barons of the new economy. And here was the newly awkward relationship between architecture and art revealed at its most raw and painfully exposed. No wonder that Richard Serra was getting so piqued about the way that Gehry, his former friend and collaborator, was being talked about—as much as an artist as an architect. "We are in a time now when the architect kind of rules," he said at the time on TV. "I draw better in my sculpture than

Frank Gehry draws in his architecture. Frank is parading right now, and so are all those mouthpiece critics that you know, support him as an artist. Hogwash." Serra's generation of sculptors had reversed the centuries-old status hierarchy that had put architects ahead. And now the tables were being turned again. No wonder sculptors are getting so touchy about this uncomfortable piece of scar tissue.

ARCHITECTURE OCCUPIES A CURIOUS POSITION IN THE CULTURAL landscape. It is the most visible expression of cultural and civic values. It has a history of being at the very heart of statecraft. And yet for most of the second half of the last century it was marginalized in a high culture dominated by writers and artists. This happened not least because the architectural elite withdrew into an ever smaller ghetto, erecting barriers of incomprehensibility against the world. The language they used to describe what they were doing often seemed calculated to be as impenetrable to outsiders as possible. And the buildings they designed were often somber and difficult.

Gehry by contrast brought a flamboyance to his work that appealed over the heads of his peers to a wider audience. He is an architect who can build a gallery and pack in an audience as well, without the need to fill it with art. What is that going to do to the prices of Gehry's architectural models?

What was not immediately visible in the Guggenheim was the fragility of the bubble on which all this architectural exhibitionism was based. In a distillation of the zeitgeist that was almost too neat to be true, the major sponsor for the Gehry show was Enron, indulging in a last gesture of cultural largesse just before it went down in history as one of the greatest corporate fraudsters of all time. Enron's president and CEO, Jeff Skilling, wrote in all his pomp, months before the company imploded, an introduction to the catalog so embarrassing that you would have expected the Guggenheim to pulp every surviving copy: "Enron shares Mr.

Gehry's ongoing search for the moment of truth, the moment when the functional approach to a problem becomes infused with the artistry that produces a truly innovative solution. This is the search that produces a truly innovative solution. This is the search Enron embarks on every day, by questioning the conventional to change business paradigms and create new markets that will shape the new economy. It is this shared sense of challenge that we admire most in Frank Gehry. We hope it will bring you as much inspiration as it has brought us."

Skilling and several of his executives eventually faced their own prolonged moment of truth when they surrendered to justice in Houston, having destroyed the jobs of thousands of employees and robbed countless shareholders of their savings.

Dominating the Guggenheim's retrospective was Gehry's bravura plan for yet another new Guggenheim museum in Manhattan, this time a huge 572,000-square-foot structure designed to sit on stilts over the East River at the end of Wall Street. Mayor Rudolph Giuliani had just offered Krens the land as a gift and promised some cash to go with it, suggesting that the project was about to take on the solidity that marks the turning point between a speculative fantasy and a serious possibility. But the downtown Guggenheim was not the only one of the procession of models beneath the cascade of perforated metal ribbons that Gehry had dangled over visitors' heads with revealing things to say about the nature of contemporary architectural culture and its incestuous relationship with power.

These were not the icily perfect white models of an architect attempting to impose his own sense of order on a reluctant world. They had the purposeful roughness of the cardboard furniture that Gehry was making in the sixties when he was first involved with Claes Oldenburg and Richard Serra. That roughness moved them imperceptibly away from the status of working tools, or sales aids, toward the expressive quality of objects infused with artistic ambition.

The model for what the catalog called the Lewis residence—"house" was much too modest a word for it—included a shiny blue plastic fish, a pointed Moorish dome, folds of red cloth, and strips of metal foil, which had been collaged together. This particular project began as an invitation to remodel an existing house in Lyndhurst, Ohio. The plan was eventually abandoned, ten years later, after the design had ballooned into an all-new fantasy palace sprawling over no less than 42,000 square feet. The unbuilt house gets twelve pages in the catalog, second only to the Guggenheim in Bilbao with fourteen. Gehry tactfully suggests that the forms and materials developed in the Lewis project allowed him to explore the sculptural themes and the materials that have shaped his work ever since.

People who commission Frank Gehry to design houses for them are a group unlike any other. Among their characteristics, self-doubt is conspicuous by its absence. The client for the Lewis house, Peter Benjamin Lewis, became chairman of the Guggenheim's board of trustees in 1998. He had personally contributed $77 million to the museum before he resigned at the beginning of 2005, in frustration at his inability to curb Krens's Edifice Complex.

Lewis is certainly a flamboyant figure. He has a 255-foot boat, *The Lone Ranger*, which is big enough for an on-board swimming pool and a crew of eighteen. He has made no secret of his taste for marijuana, a predilection that brought him a night in a New Zealand jail when the sniffer dogs at the Auckland airport got excited about the contents of his briefcase. He even suggested to his employees at Progressive Insurance that he would go on working until what he called "the Rockefeller event," as he described Nelson Rockefeller's fatal in-flagrante heart attack. After his left leg was amputated below the knee as the result of a vascular disease, Lewis developed a habit of removing his prosthetic limb during interviews and clasping it in his lap. But all these eccentricities could perhaps be seen as following in the example set by the museum's founder. Solomon Guggenheim was persuaded to collect contemporary art by his mistress, Hilla Rebay, a German baroness who was herself a painter. She encouraged Guggenheim to take an interest in radical art. But apart from her interest in Kandinsky and Max Ernst, she had an unshakable belief that drastic dentistry was the gateway to spiritual health. Indeed she attempted, unsuccessfully, to persuade Frank Lloyd Wright to have his teeth extracted while he was designing the original Guggenheim.

Lewis made his money—$1.4 billion of it, according to *Forbes* magazine—by turning the car insurance business started by his father from a company with 100 employees and revenues of $6 million in 1965 into a giant with 14,000 employees and revenues of $4.8 billion in 2003.

According to the catalog, "the plan to renovate the original house was quickly abandoned in the face of mounting needs that overwhelmed the structure." It's an interesting use of the word "needs," suggesting that a team of dour engineers had been wrestling with a series of sober, functional imperatives driving the design as if they were the inexorable laws of physics.

Gehry is much less guarded about the story of architectural obsession that the Lewis house represents: "Peter kept adding to the program." Lewis asked for a ten-car garage, and Gehry designed it. Then he said he needed storage for his art collection, and the design changed again. Then he needed a private museum. Later that expanded when Lewis said he needed space for a director for the museum, and space for a curator, and for a library. And of course for a state-of-the-art security system, including panic rooms and an escape tunnel, and somewhere for a collection of Persian rugs. . . . And still the program kept changing.

Gehry was dealing with that very special form of indecision associated with an excess of wealth, the kind that makes a grown man unable to make up his mind whether he needs one guesthouse or two, or whether he would rather keep the garage out of sight of his front door than get wet walking to the house from his car after parking—and all the other vanities and neuroses and insecurities that even a great architect cannot always keep from looking absurd.

In Lewis's eyes, at least part of the point of the house was to get his own back at what he regarded as the Cleveland establishment. He wanted to put a seventy-five-foot-high Claes Oldenburg golf bag in his garden that would have been clearly visible from the grounds of the neighboring Mayfield Country Club, an institution that he felt had humiliated him as a twelve-year-old half a century earlier. "I was taken for a swim there by a school friend who told me the following day that he had been taken to task for being kind to a Jew." It is perhaps as well that Lewis met Philip Johnson, whom he asked to design a guesthouse for him, and who was brought up in Cleveland himself, only long after his Gray Shirt years.

Presentations turned into circus performances. "Every time I went to see him he'd have a film crew in tow. On one of his birthdays he flew back the model and he invited the governor of Ohio and many other guests to a big party," says Gehry. "I had to make a presentation of his house to this party." Gehry responded by making a model the size of a playpen.

The project kept being canceled when Lewis took fright at the cost. Then he would go back to Gehry to try to convince him that he was serious about getting the house built, and that the most important thing in his life was to get his architect to go back to work. The budget kept rising from $5 million, to $20 million, $65 million, and even $80 million. Then Lewis's son got involved: "He spent three weeks working in our office, and he decided that we were scamming him."

Lewis is divorced, and his children are all adults. It's hard to imagine how all of those rooms would have been used simultaneously and the sheer effort and choreography that would have been needed to make them come alive as anything but museum pieces. America's obesity epidemic had evidently hit its domestic architecture as well as its waistline.

The film crew did, however, manage to complete their film on the nonbuilding of the Lewis house. Jeremy Irons contributed a reverential voice-over.

By this time, Gehry was used to working for billionaires. Paul Allen, Bill Gates's onetime partner at Microsoft, for example, indulged his passion for Jimi Hendrix by having Gehry design the $240 million Experience Music Project soap bubble in Seattle. But the only project he actually finished with Lewis was the Peter B. Lewis Weatherhead School of Management at Case Western Reserve University in Cleveland.

It's not as colorful or as expensive as the house would have been, but it is still explosive enough in its disdain for orthogonal geometry. The building carries Lewis's name because he contributed $36.9 million to the cost. It was not, apparently, an entirely happy experience for him. Lewis's original contribution was to have been $15 million, but he was persuaded to more than double his donation after building costs escalated from $25 million to $61.7 million, a cost overrun that apparently he did not begrudge Gehry, but that caused a violent falling-out between Lewis and the university. He told the Cleveland *Plain Dealer,* just after the Guggenheim's exhibition closed, that Case Western is "a diseased university that is collapsing and sucking Cleveland into a hole with it." He demanded that the university trustees restructure their board and cut their numbers in half. Until they did, he would be boycotting every charity in Cleveland.

But then Lewis isn't very keen on Cleveland anyway. As his view of the golf club would suggest, Lewis has long had an uneasy relationship with the city. In the 1980s he wanted Gehry to build a fifty-story tower there for his company. He unveiled a model of the design, curiously missing from the Guggenheim show, in his apartment in the city. Donald Judd, Richard Serra, and Claes Oldenburg were involved with the design, and one version looked as if the skyscraper were reading a giant version of the local newspaper. It never got built, at least in part, Lewis suggests, because he felt so insulted by what he took as a personally slighting remark made by one of the guests at the unveiling. "I have felt marginalized, disdained, excluded, laughed at," he said and took his building away. Years later, Lewis told a journalist that he was so angry that he wanted to throw the man, whose offense had apparently been not to have recognized him, down the stairs.

As chairman of the Guggenheim's trustees, Lewis should have focused on finding a way to deal with the fact that the museum's economic model of constant growth simply didn't work. Krens had gambled that a worldwide network of museums would allow him to spread exhibition costs across his (increasingly restive) colonial subjects in Berlin and Bilbao and wherever else he planted the Guggenheim flag. But touring the kind of blockbuster shows needed to pack in the crowds and balance the budgets does not work that way. A museum is not the same as a publisher packaging international co-editions to boost print runs and bring down costs. Lenders don't like lengthy tours, and the savings from shared costs turned out to be far smaller than Krens had assumed.

Despite all its frenetic activity, the Guggenheim could not generate enough revenue to stabilize its budget. It was forced into a constant search for new sources of cash. The $15 million that Krens extracted from Giorgio Armani in exchange for his use of the rotunda for an exhibition of his clothes and the sponsorship money from BMW for using the same space for a display of its motorcycles were widely seen as surrendering the museum's dignity. These windfalls did no more than temporarily stave off the prospect of financial disaster.

Opening the Bilbao Guggenheim netted the museum a one-off $20 million fee from the Basque government, which also took care of the salaries, the running costs, and the acquisitions budget. But the Guggenheim was forced to dip into its endowment to meet its New York running costs in 2001 and 2002. In the two previous years it had sold $14 million worth of art to pay its bills. And it was relying on Ron Perelman, the president of the Guggenheim, for a further cash injection of $20 million. Las Vegas didn't bring in the profits or the visitors that Krens had predicted. The curators couldn't afford to mount their exhibitions program as planned, but all that Krens could focus on was how to find the money to pay for the next big architectural model to ship to the Far East to tempt a new partner into yet another new Guggenheim, like Ludwig of Bavaria madly stripping his treasury to build castle after castle.

After clinging on with grim determination to the wreckage of his relentless expansion plans and continuing to talk up increasingly fantastic schemes for new outposts for the Guggenheim, Krens finally alienated his chairman. Lewis saw the proposed budget for 2003 and issued Krens with an ultimatum: "Either you go away and come back with a real plan, or we will have to talk about your leaving," is how he explained his position. Lewis sweetened the pill by giving the Guggenheim yet another $12 million to clear its outstanding debts, but tried to make it clear that the price was no more fancy architecture: "If Frank Gehry designs a public-service building," as Lewis was by now calling the proposed new museum, "that gets built in downtown New York, I am willing to contribute the last 25 percent. But there are conditions; no energy is to be diverted from the museum to new building."

The threat was lost on Krens, perhaps because, as he claims, "it's easier to raise money for a building than a show. A building is permanent. The people who give money have a sense of confidence about the worth of a building." His thoughts were echoed by Frank Stella, who believes that architecture appeals to donors because "they know they are not being cheated. They don't want to spend $60 million on a van Gogh because, secretly, they think the real estate is worth it, and the painting is not."

Even after the downtown Guggenheim was finally abandoned, Krens was still hopelessly addicted to airports, architects, models, and contracts with ambitious mayors. He signed one in Rio for a Brazilian Guggenheim museum designed by Jean Nouvel that would be mainly underwater (Gehry couldn't agree on a fee with Krens to work on the project). It was budgeted at $250 million, and Krens hinted unwisely in public that it would make the Guggenheim a $40 million fee. But the project quickly got bogged down in recriminations in Rio about the morality of spending so much public money in a city ringed by shantytowns—especially one that, unlike Bilbao, already had an architecturally distinguished Museum of Modern Art and a thriving tourist industry.

A similar deal with Taiwan, involving a building designed by Zaha Hadid for the provincial city of Taichung, stalled. Local councillors mutinied against what they saw as a fundamental flaw in the scheme to open a branch of the Guggenheim. How could they hope to attract Japanese tourists when there was no international airport for them to use?

Despite Krens's relentless optimism, the Guggenheim was under severe financial strain, raising the possibility either that the cash crunch was so bad that Krens had no choice other than to roam the world in pursuit of more quick-fix financial deals to keep the creditors at bay, or that he simply couldn't help himself but keep playing at architecture to distract himself from impending disaster. Either way, the Guggenheim's critics were starting to ask difficult questions about what would happen if the museum defaulted on its bond issues. Was the collection itself ultimately at risk?

Lewis himself began to become alarmed. "If doing all these feasibility studies for new branches is such a good idea, why isn't the Metropolitan doing it? Why isn't MoMA doing it?" he mused in public. The chairman tried to rally the board against Krens. Matters came to a head at the beginning of 2005. Lewis lost his attempt to discipline Krens when a majority of members refused to back him, and resigned immediately.

UNLIKE LEWIS, ELI BROAD HAS ACTUALLY BUILT A HOUSE DE-signed by Frank Gehry. It's on a three-acre hillside site in Bel Air. Like Lewis, Broad has a taste for conspicuous art. In place of the seventy-five-foot golf bag that Lewis wanted, Broad had a sixty-ton Richard Serra piece called *No Problem* fabricated on the East Coast and shipped to California on flatbed trucks. But Broad's house wasn't in the Guggenheim retrospective because Gehry found his client's style of micromanagement intolerable. If there is ever a Gehry foundation established to rule on the provenance of his surviving work in the manner of the Warhol Foundation, the Broad house would be the most problematic case that it could face.

Broad, the richest man in Los Angeles, made his money by carpeting three states with tract houses designed down to the last nail and screw to be as economical to build as possible. He knew exactly what he wanted in his own house, except of course that he couldn't design it for himself. But he couldn't wait for Gehry to complete the working drawings either. Gehry disowned the project when his client went ahead anyway, and built the house without him. That didn't stop Broad from preening for photographers in his new house.

"Most large American companies are run by managers who preside over the status quo," he boasted. "They are apt to live in traditional homes and be interested in art from previous eras. But if one is an aggressive entrepreneur, he's drawn to new thoughts. And probably to contemporary art and architecture. It's innovative and energetic."

Broad is much richer than Lewis. *Forbes* estimates his fortune at $3.4 billion, the result of two distinct business successes: the house building, with the KB Home Corporation, and Sun America, Inc., a pension company. Others put his wealth at $5 billion. Broad now describes himself as a venture philanthropist—that is to say, he uses his money and his friendship with Los Angeles's former mayor, Richard Riordan, to bend the city to his will. He backed a successful campaign to persuade the voters of the L.A. unified school district to approve a bond issue to build the first new schools in the city for three decades. He was involved in the construction of the Museum of Contemporary Art (MoCA), where he survived the resignation of a major fund-raiser from the board, and his lawsuit against the museum for the return of his $1 million donation when his fellow trustees refused to fire Arata Isozaki, the architect he had appointed in the first place. Broad was instrumental in attracting

Pontus Hulten, the respected Swedish curator, as the museum's director, and also implicated in his rapid departure. Now he wants to make Grand Avenue, the downtown boulevard on which the Contemporary sits, into the Champs-Elysées of Los Angeles.

If Lewis is the type whom wealth leaves paralyzed with the kind of indecision demonstrated by the saga of the house that was never built, Broad knows exactly what he wants. And what Broad wants to do is to put his name on buildings. There is already an Eli Broad College of Business and Graduate School of Management at Michigan State University. There is a Broad Art Center at UCLA. The California Institute of the Arts has the Edythe and Eli Broad Center and Broad Hall, and there is also a Broad Center for Biological Sciences. The Broad Art Foundation has no permanent gallery of its own for its holdings of more than 700 works by 100 contemporary artists, with Jeff Koons, Jean-Michel Basquiat, Andy Warhol, Cindy Sherman, Jenny Holzer, and David Salle particularly well represented. And he is using that collection to command the attention of the world's museums, a process that he is clearly enjoying hugely.

According to the Broad Foundation's own Web site, "*Art News* recognized the Broads as among the top ten collectors of art worldwide." But it is Broad's money, rather than his eye for art, that drives the collection. The *Los Angeles Times* waspishly described his policy of accumulating work by artists who already have substantial reputations as "shopping not collecting." He has been involved with the boards of MoMA and MoCA; those of the Whitney, Hammer, and High Museums in New York, L.A., and Atlanta, respectively; and most recently, with LACMA. Each time, Broad flirted with the idea of construction, looking for the chance to make a landmark in his own image, decided that he wasn't going to get his way, and moved on.

Broad was involved with fund-raising for the Disney Hall and attempted to take command of the construction process out of Gehry's hands; this provoked the architect to threaten to quit if he lost control of the design. It's hard not to see Broad's loan of part of his collection directly to the Guggenheim in Bilbao for a temporary exhibition without going through New York as a deliberate twisting of Krens's tail (shows in Bilbao that originate in New York allow Krens to charge a fee; those that don't earn him nothing). Broad flew to Bilbao accompanied by ex-Mayor Riordan and another wealthy friend with a Gehry-designed house in L.A., Rockwell Schnabel, America's former ambassador to the European Union.

Certainly it was Eli Broad's attention that Rem Koolhaas was attempting to engage on the day at the end of 2001 when he made his presentation to the board of the Los Angeles County Museum of Art, with its sprawling and unsatisfactory collection of pavilions. Koolhaas knows how to make a memorable presentation. This time it was punctuated by a series of words, flashed up one at a time—most notably, "Disobey," to suggest that he was not following the carefully crafted brief. And "LACMAX" encapsulated his maximalist strategy of demolishing all of LACMA's existing buildings and replacing them with a single new structure.

This would, Koolhaas said with a straight face, be the most economical solution to the museum's problems. It was of course just the kind of bold gesture that was calculated to appeal to a man like Broad, approaching seventy and determined to build a landmark before it was too late for him to be able to enjoy the pleasure of walking around it. But after a year of negotiations, LACMA dispensed with Koolhaas's services. Even Broad's arm-twisting abilities were not enough to unlock the donations needed to build it and, wealthy though he was, he would not put up all the cash needed. Broad had donated $1.2 million to prime the money pump, and he loaned LACMA $1 million to put a ballot measure to the county's voters that would have raised $98 million for the Koolhaas design under the pretext of earthquake and fire-safety improvements. Three donors, a couple of foundations, and the state's money would add up to $250 million—enough, he calculated, to get the project under way. But the bond issue was defeated, there was no cash from taxpayers, and Broad started talking instead to Renzo Piano about adding a Broad pavilion to the LACMA campus.

Koolhaas's design had transgressed one of the fundamental rules of fund-raising for museum building. All those LACMA pavilions, some of them no more than twenty years old, that Koolhaas wanted to demolish had their own donors, with their names inscribed over the doors. Koolhaas was providing a brutal reminder to every potential donor of the transience of all things, even money and museums.

Broad celebrated his seventieth birthday by announcing a $60 million gift to LACMA. There would be $50 million to build a freestanding new building designed by Piano, and the rest would go toward acquiring new works. Broad is clearly more adept at having his way with recalcitrant museum directors than Peter Lewis has been. The Guggenheim spends money on what Thomas Krens sees fit. Broad had LACMA's Andrea Rich in a corner, especially after she had invested so much personal prestige into the abortive Koolhaas project. Broad is too coy to promise his collection to LACMA, or even to make a long-term financial commitment. Although the new building will be called the Broad Contemporary Art Museum at LACMA—presumably on the basis that a "museum" has a better chance of survival than a mere "gallery"—the running costs will be the responsibility of LACMA.

Painted into a corner, Rich resigned in April 2005.

RENZO PIANO HAS BECOME THE FAVORED ARCHITECT NOT JUST OF rich people seeking immortality, but also of American cultural institutions. Before Broad, he worked for Dominique De Menil in Houston and for Ray Nasher on his private museum in Dallas. Piano supplanted Rem Koolhaas not just in Los Angeles, but also as the architect for the expansion of Manhattan's Whitney Museum. He is remodeling the High Museum in Atlanta, originally designed by Richard Meier, and the Morgan Library in New York.

Broad has demonstrated with brutal clarity the essential nature of the balance of power between rich men and museums in a way that seems to be repeated every couple of decades. He is following the example of the Lehman family, which as part of the price of making a donation of their collection to New York's Metropolitan Museum insisted on the reconstruction of their living room within the museum, as if following the funeral rites of the ancient Egyptians. They also stipulated that there would never be loans from the collection, and nothing but Lehman works could be shown in the gallery without the approval of their own set of trustees.

The roots of the modern museum, for all its espousal of humanist values, lie in two of the most fundamental of human impulses: to defy death and to glorify power. The museum is the synthesis of the shrine and the monument; it has become a variety of national icon. From the very beginning, loot has had a key role to play in its evolution. Napoleon determined to make Paris's position as the capital of Europe clear by systematically relieving his conquered subjects of their art treasures and putting them on show in the Louvre. His attempt to take the Rosetta stone to France from Alexandria failed when it fell into British hands. But he did have the bronze horses of St. Mark's Square removed from Venice and paraded around Paris in his victory celebrations for his Italian campaign. With Napoleon's exile, the horses eventually returned to Venice, which of course never even considered passing them back to their former owners in Constantinople—from where, in the midst of an orgy of rape and pillage that passed for a crusade at the start of the thirteenth century, La Serenissima had grabbed them in the first place. But Byzantium was not the original owner either. Some scholars suggest that the horses may have been brought from Chios; others think that they came from Rome. Should they be returned once again, along with all the other classical sculpture that adorns Venice, and the lions that sit outside its Arsenale?

The horses at least went back to Italy; not all of the flood of art seized by Napoleon made it back home across the Alps. There is of course something genuinely shocking about the brutal simplicity of Napoleon's version of connoisseurship; acquiring the national treasures of others by force is an uncomfortable throwback to barbarism, even if it did lead to the creation of one of Europe's greatest museums. It's a reminder of the days when victorious generals got the chance to drag captured enemies from their chariot wheels, of Mussolini's collecting obelisks during his Abyssinian campaign, or Hitler's plans for a gigantic art museum in Linz, to be filled with loot from all over Europe and designed for him by Hermann Giesler, Speer's rival.

We have come to understand the museum as the repository of disinterested scholarship and civilized values, but it has always had a highly political role. And its rise has been fueled by a potent blend of vanity and economic and national policy. The fate of the Elgin Marbles in the British Museum, or the Parthenon Marbles, as most now call them, is a clear case in point. You don't have to work very hard to understand what the Greek government was trying to tell the world about itself when in 2000 it appointed Bernard Tschumi as the architect for a new museum to house the marbles in Athens. Never mind for a moment what Tschumi's new Acropolis Museum would look like. From the point of view of Greece's Socialist government of the time, he was the ideal architect to design it. Not only was Tschumi not Greek—and could therefore be presumed to be neutral in the struggle for the marbles—but he is also moderately fashionable. So his appointment could be presented as a confident, open-minded gesture of cultural maturity rather than the more predictable selection of a favored local son. He may not quite have lived up to the dazzling promise of his first major built commission—the pioneering urban park at La Villette in Paris—but the marbles demand to be treated with extreme politeness rather than be subjected to an aggressive architectural statement.

That is why Tschumi, both politically and aesthetically acceptable, won the second competition to design the museum in ten years, after the first collapsed in chaos. He brought credibility to the whole process. Small wonder, then, that the Greek culture minister invited Tschumi to accompany him on his charm offensive to London in an attempt to embarrass the marbles out of Britain in the run-up to the Athens Olympics. Hiring a fashionable Swiss American to build a glass-walled museum is not just Greece's way of reminding us of its claim to the marbles. It's also trying to say that it is a sophisticated modern state. One Athens newspaper went so far as to contrast Tschumi's light-filled design, allegedly typifying the new Greece, with what it called "the grim and depressing British Museum." But it's the unconscious message that is more interesting. Creating a half-empty museum to house sculptures it is never likely to obtain suggests a gesture of impotent anger rather than confidence.

Tschumi's plans showed how the marbles could be reunited with the monument from which they parted company almost two centuries ago. Not that they would actually go back on Ictinus's frieze, where there would be nothing to protect them from the corrosive atmosphere of modern Athens. Tschumi's strategy was to create a museum at the foot of the Acropolis, overlooking the Makriyanni excavations and partly extending over them. Visitors will enter through a solid base and wind their way gradually up through a series of double-height galleries displaying the museum's collections in chronological order, telling the story of the site from the archaic period and moving through to the Roman Empire.

Along the way, they will encounter the inevitable shops and restaurants. Finally, in a theatrical climax to the careful sequence of displays, visitors come blinking up into the sunshine, climbing into a giant glass box to see the marbles, against the backdrop of the temple itself, attached to a set of internal walls aligned precisely on the Parthenon. Tschumi maintains that the glass walls will be designed to protect both sculptures and visitors from the climate, but it's hard to believe that the furnacelike heat of the Athenian summer can be handled without a daunting amount of air-conditioning, sunshades, and tinting, which would have the effect of shutting out the views and the light that were the object of the exercise in the first place.

Britain said no—not for architectural reasons, but because the British Museum resolutely refuses to contemplate existence without the marbles. But there are serious questions—more than simply its glass walls—that could be asked about Tschumi's design. It suffers from being the product of a brief that, like his appointment, is as political as it is cultural.

Much of the logic of the Greek case for the return of the marbles rests on establishing a visual link between them and the temple. But to achieve it, Tschumi was pushed into building on a site that Greek archaeologists fear has been irreparably damaged by the disturbance of the construction process. There were protests against the preliminary site works, which have, it is claimed, destroyed Christian and classical remains. The Socialist government ignored them and continued to maintain it was committed to opening at least part of the museum in time for the Olympics, lest it be left looking weak and incompetent. In fact construction had only just started at the time of the Greek elections in March 2004 that saw the Socialists ejected from power. A new culture minister briefly threatened to cancel the project once and for all, and to pursue his predecessor in the courts for ignoring legal rulings against the project and the archaeological damage it would do.

The building of the museum could be seen as the continuation of the transformation of the physical remains of the Parthenon into a monument to a very particular view of Greek identity that has been going on for almost two centuries. This process presents the Acropolis today as an isolated, ethnically pure moment of history—cleansed of all the later additions, which were in themselves of enormous historic interest.

A mosque, a Venetian fortress, and a series of Roman and Renaissance remains have all been excised to create the iconic view that Athens now projects to lay its claim to the most glorious moments of classical Greece. In the same way Tschumi's Acropolis Museum is alleged to have destroyed layers of priceless archaeology yards deep in the interests of making a political gesture. In the event, there was nothing to see of the museum during Greece's moment of Olympic glory.

Every country uses its museums as part of a repertoire of instruments with which to define themselves. In Britain, at the same time that Tschumi was trying to construct an idea of Greece, both the Tate Gallery and the Victoria and Albert Museum were reshuffling themselves and the images and objects that have served to construct a notion of Britishness ever since they opened in the nineteenth century. Both institutions share an ambiguity toward those objects. It's an ambiguity that can be read as much the deconstruction of an identity as a celebration of it. Both the newly renovated galleries at Tate Britain and the V&A's British Galleries are bigger than the Acropolis Museum would be. But they are invisible to the outside world. Britain prefers to express itself in transformations of old buildings, rather than in showy new ones. Tate Britain has become the nation's mantelpiece. A sequence of William Blake's drawings share a wall with the poet Thomas Chatterton portrayed on his deathbed, while J. M. W. Turner's curious image of a forlorn vanquished Bonaparte hangs opposite. It's still an art gallery, but it is also a repository of the nation's favorite keepsakes and souvenirs. Meanwhile, at the V&A, you get to see the mantelpiece as well as what is on it. You move from four-poster beds upholstered in gorgeous crimson Genoa velvet, past gilded carriages, and an oak bookcase as big as a house. There are magnificent marble fireplaces under Adam ceilings, the willfully bloody-minded furniture of the nineteenth-century cabinetmakers that Thomas Hope collected, and a cabinet that appears to have been designed by the gothic revival architect William Burges while under the influence of laudanum.

The egocentric, as opposed to the nationalist, tradition from which the museum springs is perhaps best represented by Peter Eisenman's prodigious City of Culture taking shape on the outskirts of the Galician city of Santiago de Compostela. An opera house, a library, a museum, and a complex of academic buildings are being built in one huge gesture, in the form of a hillside. The purpose is ostensibly to provide a new economic resource for the city, which once prospered on the pilgrims drawn by the saintly relics that the Galicians had managed to acquire. But the City of Culture is only possible because Manuel Fraga, a politician who began his career in the Franco era and who commissioned it in his late seventies, is clinging to power to see it finished as a means of immortalizing himself. Santiago depends on huge subsidies from Madrid and from the European Union in Brussels and, soon, on a grandiloquent refusal to face up to the practical problems of running an opera house in a city with no tradition of opera.

Not long after the collapse of Koolhaas's LACMAX project, a previously obscure body known as the East of England Development Agency launched what it called with almost comic bathos an international competition to find a "visionary plan for a landmark, or series of landmarks." The agency said it was looking for "an icon that will foster a sense of identity for the region as a whole." It was part of its strategy to present the East of England as "a region of ideas," and a measure of how far the mania for exhibitionistic architecture had spread. No site was specified, nor had any money been committed, which hardly inspired confidence, but one board member claimed that this piece of wishful thinking was "a fantastic opportunity for us to come together as a region and decide how to present ourselves to the rest of the world." Setting aside the wounding likelihood that the rest of the world would continue to treat the East of England with the same indifference that it had adopted ever since the decline of the wool trade in the fifteenth century, it's not hard to guess the kind of thing that they had in mind: an opera house with the titanium fish scales designed by Frank Gehry as a free-form blob, or a gratuitously eccentric footbridge by Santiago Calatrava. Competitions such as this have become ubiquitous, leading all but inevitably to the kind of architecture that looks designed to form the backdrop for car commercials, or one of those Eiffel-Tower-in-a-snow-globe paperweights.

Santiago Calatrava, the kitsch dark side to Gehry's playful, free invention, still calls himself an architect. But in fact he has given up designing buildings to concentrate on producing icons. There is the mass transit station at Ground Zero, with its soaring glass wings pointing skyward, and its steel beak touching the ground in an uncomfortably close resemblance to the American Airlines logo. His opera house in Valencia looks like the bleached skeleton of a long-dead sea creature, inflated to giant scale. Calatrava is constantly unveiling new footbridges to add to a collection that already includes specimens in Bilbao, Barcelona, and Mérida, and, outside Spain, in Manchester and Venice. Touchingly, he continues to cling to a functional alibi. Closely examine one of his drawings and, although it might look like a proposal to inflate a lobster to the scale of a skyscraper and construct it out of reinforced concrete, you will find a helpful, descriptive label: for instance, "opera house." Or in the case of the whale's tail that he has actually built in Milwaukee, it says with equally surreal economy of means: "art gallery." Of course there is hardly any gallery space inside this Calatrava addition; it's there simply to attract attention to Wisconsin, to remind the world that the gallery exists. It was seven months late in opening and cost so much to build that the museum struggled for years to make up the shortfall. The director left soon after the extension opened, and staff members were cut.

You could see Calatrava as either the greatest beneficiary or the primary victim of the sudden mania for icon building. He began his career designing beautifully crafted structures with great economy of means. But his ever more eager clients have condemned him to keep repeating himself, with ever noisier special effects to distract us. Calatrava designed what is called a concert hall in Santa Cruz, a city of 200,000 people on Tenerife. Officially the white concrete shells are described as resembling a wave breaking over the seafront. The less sympathetic would interpret it as a gigantic representation of a nun's veil, or even something of a steal from far-off Sydney. Either way it is the classic "iconic" project: a cultural building, designed with a heavy subsidy from public funds, with the express purpose of getting previously obscure cities into the pages of in-flight magazines.

Calatrava is one of a kind, famously trained as both an architect and an engineer. It's a combination that has allowed him to create the suggestion of a sense of inner logic around his work, providing an alibi for what could otherwise be seen as blatant exhibitionism. Calatrava has about him a whiff of the otherworldly vision that lingers around those who profess to find a hidden order in blades of grass, snowflakes, and rock crystals. From it he has concocted a kind of genetically modified gothic that is now the main theme of his work—or perhaps it is prefabricated Gaudí, squeezed by the yard, like toothpaste from a tube. Its bravura visual quality is enough of a diversion to prevent his patrons from asking why exactly his extension to Milwaukee's art gallery should look like a whale's tail or his Valencia opera house has a structure reminiscent of a mollusk, as well as to prevent his having to justify them in terms of functional performance. Or why his roof for the Athens Olympic Stadium was so complex that it was completed only days before the opening ceremony for the games.

THE MORE CLIENTS CONTINUE TO ASK FOR ICONS, THE LESS INclined is a new generation of architects to oblige. Shallow, garish, showoffy buildings suffer from the law of diminishing returns. The smart response from younger architects taking a strategic view, such as the firm Foreign Office Architects, is to design buildings, like their ferry terminal in Yokohama, that can't be reduced to logos. And the most successful new museum to open in America—the Dia, in Beacon, New York—is an old cardboard-box factory on the Hudson River, which is completely free of self-conscious monumentalism. Perhaps, like art nouveau, which flourished briefly at the end of the nineteenth century, the icon has become ubiquitous just as it is about to vanish.

CHAPTER 12

HIGH-RISE SYNDROME

A STRANGE AND MOVING PHOTOGRAPH OF MINORU YAMASAKI PIC-
tures him looking as vulnerable as a child, standing tentatively in front
of the World Trade Center, holding a tiny model of the Twin Towers in
the palm of his hand, as if it were a toy. He was in late middle age when
the picture was taken, but in the image he is a slight, diminutive, and,
above all, touchingly sad-looking figure. If you didn't know that he was
the architect of the two gigantic obelisks soaring skyward behind him,
he could be Charlie Chaplin trapped in the machinery of *Modern Times*,
or a simple-minded clown trying to hold back the Great Dictator's army
with a water pistol. Or he could be conducting some obscure magic rite,
with a propitiatory offering in his hand.

The strangest thing about the picture is that there is no sense of triumph, or even of achievement, in Yamasaki's downcast, anxious eyes.
This Nisei child, born into poverty to Japanese emigrants in America, appears to take no pride in the immensity of the mark that he made on the
swaggering skyline of the richest city in the world.

You can't help but try to scour the image for clues to find some kind
of meaning beneath the surface, to see if there is any precognition in it
of the appalling events of September 11, 2001. It's an idle exercise. Maybe

Yamasaki had a hangover on the day that the picture was taken, maybe the photographer was annoying him, or maybe he was worried about the troubled state of his marriage—any or all of which would have been likely possibilities, to judge by his autobiography. Maybe he was weighed down by the hostile response of his peers to the design of the towers. They were described as pieces of minimal sculpture inflated to an absurdly monstrous scale. They were said to be dehumanizing because they reduced the individual to visual insignificance. They gave no clue as to the kind of activities that took place inside them. The very idea of ultra-tall buildings was seen as a primitive throwback by some.

In his palpable anxiety, Yamasaki does not look like a man who is comfortable about having designed the tallest building in the world. The impression is strengthened by the passage in his architectural autobiography in which he explains why all but a handful of the tens of thousands of windows in the Twin Towers were just twenty-two inches wide: "These windows are narrower than one's shoulders. I have often gone to a high floor, and comfortably placed my nose against the glass to view the plaza below. I can't do this in a building with floor-to-ceiling glass and mullions, say five feet apart, because, experienced as I am in high rise buildings, I still have a strong feeling of acrophobia." Nevertheless, the picture also suggests some of the reasons for the continuing grip very tall buildings have had on the imagination of the world.

For Minoru Yamasaki, who in his own person represented a link between the lost golden age of New York's skyscrapers of the 1930s and the modern world, to be prepared to admit that he is scared of heights is like hearing the pope confess his doubts about the existence of original sin. Before he set up on his own in Michigan, Yamasaki had worked for the two architectural offices that between them did more to define the American skyscraper in the 1930s than anyone else. For six years he was with Shreve, Lamb and Harmon, the firm that designed the Empire State Building. Then he worked for Wallace Harrison and the firm that led the consortium responsible for designing Rockefeller Center.

The World Trade Center was always meant to be big and imposing, but Yamasaki suggested transforming the concept of a complex of new buildings into the tallest structure in the world, with a design that finally overtook the Empire State Building when it topped out in 1972. Yamasaki was also the one who had the idea of concentrating almost all the office space proposed for the site into just two identical towers—a pattern that he used again in the twin triangular towers of Century City in Los Angeles. Yet, when Yamasaki died in 1986, he was well on the way to professional obscurity. He was all but forgotten in America, where his early promise seemed to have been irretrievably eclipsed by the notorious demolition in 1972 of his huge Pruitt Igoe housing project in St. Louis, less than a decade after it was completed. This was a scheme built as a bold attempt to bring the best of modern architecture to American public housing, designed by a still idealistic young architect convinced that he could transform ordinary people's lives with good design. But neither Yamasaki's idealism nor an AIA Award for the apartments could save Pruitt Igoe from inadequate construction standards, or absolve it from the near total absence of a maintenance budget as well as a concentration of desperately poor occupants. The sad history of that project was transformed from a local disaster into an emblematic event signifying a wider crisis not only in America's public housing policies but also in its cultural life.

The photograph that caught the moment when dynamite charges exploded across the front of the stricken hulk of the abandoned apartment blocks, sending them collapsing in a cloud of dust, was endlessly reprinted. It came to be seen as a symbol of the vanishing confidence of a generation of architects that no longer believed that they could construct a more civilized version of the world as they found it.

Pruitt Igoe certainly wasn't the first architectural project that failed to live up to the promises of its designers and builders. But it was clearly a traumatic experience for Yamasaki. One such episode would overshadow almost any career. Yamasaki suffered two of them, the second, posthumous disaster immeasurably worse than the first.

Yamasaki was a difficult man, with apparently no gift for guile or self-preservation. He was anxious enough about his reputation to expunge any image of the Pruitt Igoe project from his autobiography. But the book raises other questions about his aesthetic judgment. Did Yamasaki genuinely believe that the questionable watercolor landscape he had made shortly after starting his own office—used by a client as a Christmas card, as he proudly boasts—was good enough to publish? And if he did, what does that say about the quality of his architectural decisions?

He tells you more about his marriages—there were four, the first and the last to the same woman—than is comfortable in a conventional professional monograph. He was brought up in the kind of poverty that made him determined to escape from it. But when Yamasaki, sitting in his provincial Michigan office, opened the letter from New York's Port Authority inviting him to discuss the idea of designing a major office complex in Manhattan budgeted at $280 million, his immediate response was to suggest that there was an accidental zero too many. If there wasn't, he said, then his office was too inexperienced to handle the job.

During Yamasaki's lifetime, the World Trade Center was bitterly criticized for its antiurban qualities. The five-acre public space at its center, which the architect fondly compared to Siena's Campo and St. Mark's in Venice, was regarded by many as a poor substitute for the scruffy vitality of the fourteen blocks, with their radio stores, tailors, and bars, that were demolished to build it. The sheer bulk of the Twin Towers seemed to run entirely counter to the porcelainlike decorative delicacy of the Seattle World's Fair structures that, for a while, put Yamasaki in the same league as Eero Saarinen and Philip Johnson.

The design took a terrible drubbing from Yamasaki's peers, especially from the generation who saw themselves as young radicals at the time, and who later turned out to be just the people who were in the running to rebuild the complex when it was destroyed. But the generation that came after them had a different perspective, rediscovering the grandeur of its heroic proportions and coming to an understanding of the extent to which the Twin Towers had become part of New York's popular identity.

There is no doubt that there were practical problems with the World Trade Center. The raised plaza was a particular bête noire of planners: it was seen as driving out life and urbanity, creating an isolated and forbidding enclave, while the shopping space was driven underground into labyrinthine malls. Yamasaki's one moment of brilliance in the design is its duality. He established the idea of Twin Towers as an element in the typology of high-rise building.

Yamasaki's office remained busy until his death, but it was in demand mainly outside the United States—and even then, only for the kind of buildings that failed to give him a chance to shine. For an architect to build commercial projects in unfashionable parts of the world in his later years, as he did in Saudi Arabia, has never been a good move for those interested in building a lasting critical reputation.

THE CATASTROPHIC DESTRUCTION OF THE TOWERS JUST AT THE moment when the critical view of them was beginning to become more positive transformed the meaning of Yamasaki's professional life. Yamasaki not only had a link with the early days of the skyscraper, he also seemed to have a direct connection with the tower's nemesis. A persistent legend linked the construction firm that Osama bin Laden's father owned with two projects that Yamasaki built in Saudi Arabia: the airport terminal at Dhahran, whose arcades joltingly recall the World Trade Center, and the Saudi Arabian Monetary Authority building in Riyadh, one of the last projects of Yamasaki's career.

Anwar Ali, governor of the Saudi Arabian Monetary Authority, called Yamasaki in 1970 to ask him to design his new headquarters in Riyadh. Yamasaki replied that he was too busy with the Twin Towers to take it on. As he tells it, Ali told him that he didn't mind waiting and called him back three years later, when the World Trade Center was finished. Was Ali willing to wait because he appreciated the sensitivity of Yamasaki's concrete vaults at Dhahran airport, with their delicate synthesis of Arab traditions and modern materials built ten years previously, or was it because he was determined to use the architect of what was the biggest tower in the world at the time to build his own office?

There have been specious suggestions that the World Trade Center was designed as a conscious evocation of the center of Mecca. In fact, the arrangement of low-slab blocks on top of arcades forming a perimeter around a plaza that Yamasaki devised for the World Trade Center is an almost exact replica of what he had done in Seattle, his native city, for the Federal Science Pavilion at the 1962 World's Fair. That project had attracted the Port Authority to Yamasaki in the first place. His gothic pavilions are still intact, marching through Seattle's biggest park like Martian monsters on the loose from *The War of the Worlds*. They are a ghostly echo of the Twin Towers' two ground floors, rendered in concrete and grouped around stagnant ponds, under the shadow of the panting, wheezing elevator that clatters up and down the shaft of the Space Needle, topped by a giant Frisbee that is Seattle's most famous landmark.

The difference in Seattle was that the pavilions were designed to be an oasis from the crowds that swarmed around the competing attractions of the fair. In New York the bulk of the towers exerted an overwhelming physical and psychological impact on the plaza and its less than inspired arrangement of circular pool and second-rate sculpture. Yamasaki stripped away every decorative detail, suppressing the doors and the windows, so that all that registered on the exterior was the extreme verticality of the structure rising from the ground like an uninterrupted cliff for 110 floors. The vertical fins made the towers appear solid, reducing architecture to an idealized platonic form. Despite Yamasaki's self-deluding belief to the contrary, he had made the towers so enigmatic and so stripped of any sign of humanity that they appeared entirely otherworldly, removed from any connection with time and place. They seemed closer to Stanley Kubrick's alien monolith from *2001* than to any of their architectural contemporaries.

Yet Yamasaki betrayed the conventional attitudes toward the city of an architect of his time. He thought it fortunate that there was not a single building worth saving on the tiny irregular blocks that made up the World Trade Center site, which he regarded as obsolescent and inconvenient: "The tremendous number of intersections make it impossible to walk or drive; this area was planned for horse and carriage days."

But Yamasaki had enough insight to realize that it would only be a matter of time before another building was declared the tallest in the world, and that his design needed to do more than break records. He had also considered the objections to the enormous street-crushing bulk of the towers, and the way they threatened to turn people into ants. He spent a lot of time walking around the Empire State Building, trying to get a sense of what his towers would be like, and he convinced himself that they would be beautiful. "There was no diminution of the soul," he claimed. "No antlike feelings in the face of such a large object. Man had made it, and he could comprehend it. I am happy I was able to design these very buildings with the proper scale relationship so necessary to man. They are intended to give him a soaring feeling, imparting pride and a sense of nobility in his environment."

Apart from its impact on the skyline of Manhattan, the most memorable physical aspect of the World Trade Center was the sheer weight of all those stories pressing down on you as you tried to negotiate the plaza between the two towers. To do it required a measure of determination. Standing on the World Trade Center's plaza, you could feel the pressure of two enormously massive towers rising up into the sky on either side of you. To move across the plaza was like passing through a narrow gap in the thickness of a monolithic wall. Their mute bulk was enough to put the air between them into compression, and to force your muscles to push back against them.

Moving toward the entrance of the North Tower, you could feel the pressure build up as you came closer and closer. The weight above you grew more and more intense, even as the building itself appeared to become more transparent as your point of view shifted to look head-on at the shining aluminum fins rising the height of the towers. Negotiating the threshold required the greatest psychological effort of all. The door seemed to carry the weight of the entire building. It trapped you for a moment as you summoned up your courage. Walking through, you experienced a sense of release into the soaring space of the double-height lobby, for a moment denying the presence of the 110 floors stacked up over your head. After that came the thrill of riding the elevators; the air-pressure buildup as you accelerated skyward made your ears pop, pressing your feet to the floor. Emerging out into the rarefied atmosphere 1320 feet above the ground brought with it an uncomfortable sensation of anxiety, as you waited to see if the tower really did sway in the wind as you had always heard it would. It did, but not that much. The shock absorbers—needed to restrain a building with nothing heavier than an aluminum skin to hold it down—kept the sway to just 8 inches in a 100-mile-per-hour wind.

We have tamed ultra-tall buildings and made them part of the invisible background to daily life by denying their extraordinary qualities. Once the skin is in place, a high-rise building is no longer the preserve of nonchalant steel riggers taking their lunch on huge I beams jutting into the void. It becomes a banal cocoon for watercoolers, dress-down Fridays, and going-away parties. But Yamasaki was still ready to confess to the possibility of fear of what he had created.

San Francisco's Golden Gate Bridge exerts such a powerful pull on would-be suicides that there are documented cases of the desperate driving across the Oakland Bay Bridge, ignoring the many and varied possibilities it offers for putting an end to themselves, just in order to reach the other span. The Golden Gate is a lightning rod, one that seems to create the weightlessness that triggers feelings of vertigo, as if there is nothing to hold you down anymore, nothing to stop you floating upward, no reason not to let go and fall. The effect has to do with the investment of all the energy needed to span such a long distance, to move so high over water to do it. And perhaps the sense that a big bridge has turned the placeless into somewhere unique, signaling the presence of the ambition of making a mark on the Earth, the most fundamental impulse of mankind. Very tall buildings can induce similar feelings. They exert a real physical impact on us. They shape the landscape.

By the time that I made it up to the Windows on the World, the restaurant on top of the North Tower, the World Trade Center was no longer the tallest building in the world. The Sears Tower in Chicago, designed by SOM, eclipsed it in 1974, and yet this was still a complex of extraordinary force. The Twin Towers erupted from the midst of a cluster of lower towers, and somehow managed to impose a sense of order and discipline on them. They created a skyline that was instantly recognizable from any angle as New York, unlike the anonymous silhouette of so many cities that use the same vertical elements without managing to achieve a sense of identity. How many people can immediately tell from a photograph whether a cluster of towers is Atlanta, Los Angeles, or Seattle? The World Trade Center had a personality, and that persona was what gave them their impact, as much as their height.

The towers were interpreted as a signal of power and authority by those who wanted to challenge America's hold on the world. They were, it was insinuated, the personification of the evils of capitalism. The idea of building them was first put forward by David Rockefeller, as part of an urban renewal proposal that would have the effect of safeguarding his investment in the area. But the Twin Towers were actually built by a group of public officials in a bid to revitalize the local economy, which had been badly damaged by the loss of traditional employers as shipping and manufacturing operations in Manhattan vanished in the 1950s. The buildings were filled, initially at least, not by the heartless masters of the universe, but by white-collar workers, clerks, cleaners, and civil servants.

The World Trade Center was meant to be a demonstration of confidence in New York, a city that experienced a loss of direction in the 1960s and would face worsening budgetary crises in the 1970s. The complex was conceived as a gigantic urban life-support machine, an iron lung intended to resuscitate the city, and an unmistakable and extraordinarily visible signal that New York was still a force to be reckoned with. Outside America, of course, the nuances of one city jockeying with another became blurred. The World Trade Center came to be seen as an American icon, rather than a reflection of New York's nervousness about the jobs it was losing to the suburbs and the Sun Belt.

Something remarkable happened to the global balance of cultural power at the beginning of February 1996. Competing teams of Korean and Japanese contractors, working continuously by swelteringly humid tropical day and arc-lit night for three years, finally topped out the twin towers of the Petronas Center in Kuala Lumpur. With their Bangladeshi workforce earning just a few dollars a day, collapsing exhausted to sleep on beds in huts on the site that had just been vacated by the next shift, directed by Australian foremen and German engineers, they had done it at last.

For the first time since the gothic cathedrals were built, the world's tallest structure was no longer in the West. From the center of what was once a torpid colonial city, the Petronas Towers erupt skyward, like fireworks, leaving a trail eighty-eight floors high that dominates every view of the horizon from Kuala Lumpur's elevated highways, where rainstorms leave cars ankle deep in red mud. With heavy nods to Islamic geometry, the towers look uncomfortably like a couple of giant extruded pineapples, tempered by a spidery bridge at the forty-first floor that seems to come straight from a sword-and-sorcery epic.

The design is the work of Cesar Pelli, the Argentine-born American architect who built Britain's tallest tower at Canary Wharf, Manhattan's World Financial Center, and, more recently, the tallest tower in Hong Kong. But the towers are not, however, primarily an exercise in architecture. They are an assertion of political will in steel, marble, and glass. The Petronas Center eclipsed Chicago's Sears Tower as the world's tallest building for the express purpose of demonstrating the determination of Mohamad Mahathir, the Malaysian prime minister at the time, to be taken seriously as a figure on the world stage.

In the process, the development swallowed up a colonial-era race-course at the heart of a city that is frantically reconfiguring itself as a metropolis. It also provoked serious worries among international bankers that Mahathir's buildings would signal that Malaysia's decade-long boom was turning to bust. Exactly who was going to occupy all those millions of square feet of office space? For America, which invented the art of skyscraper building, the prospect of Malaysian hubris was little compensation for being overtaken by an upstart Asian nation of just 21 million people.

For years the Americans alone claimed the secret of building high. They had the sense of conviction to make towers that look like more than giant refrigerators. By comparison most European attempts at building high are as unconvincing as East German efforts to copy American consumer goods.

The Petronas Towers were conceived in a shroud of deceptive vagueness. In an attempt not to alert any of the dozen or more competitors around the world when the designs were first published, Pelli would say only that the towers were going to be big, but never spell out exactly how big. Something very similar had happened in New York back in 1929, when William Van Alen did not reveal the full truth about his design for the Chrysler Building until its nearest competitor for the title of New York's tallest skyscraper, the Bank of the Manhattan Company Building, designed by an ex-partner, was safely completed. Then he had the spire that forms the Chrysler's final flourish assembled inside the tower and installed overnight in a stunning conjuring trick to shoot effortlessly past its rival. In the event, the Chrysler Building was eclipsed the very next year by the Empire State Building.

There is of course something ludicrously childish about the irrational urge to build high, simply for the sake of being the world's highest. But the idea of extreme height shows no sign of relaxing its grip on the world's imagination. The kind of people who present themselves as hardheaded, rational, infinitely cautious businessmen rush headlong into attempts to build ever taller structures.

These are, moreover, structures that often make dubious economic sense. Extreme height inevitably carries cost penalties and creates buildings that are hard to use efficiently. You cannot let out a single square foot until they are entirely finished, so large sections remain empty, earning no revenue. And extreme height means that a much larger percentage of each floor is being devoted to elevators and structure than in more modest buildings.

But that doesn't stop people doing it. Before he was exposed as a crook, Robert Maxwell claimed to be serious about buying the Sears Tower, but only if the purchase price included the right to rename it the Maxwell Tower.

The Prince of Wales once asked Cesar Pelli why Canary Wharf had to be so tall. The answer that Pelli was too polite to give was that the Docklands development needed a skyscraper as its centerpiece for the entirely irrational and yet essential purpose of impressing the skeptics. A huge tower makes nowhere suddenly into somewhere.

And yet, despite its transparently childish ambition, the Petronas Towers are so readily identifiable that Kuala Lumpur is no longer just another anonymous Asian city. For a few years, it could claim to have the world's tallest building, and that brought with it the kind of kudos produced by staging the Olympics.

With so much at stake, a curiously elaborate set of rules has been drawn up to measure and compare the height of skyscrapers that allows no possibility of cheating. Donald Trump's trick, first used at Trump Tower, of simply numbering the floors and omitting the first ten from the elevator buttons to make a tower seem taller than it really is has been used all over the world. The tallest inhabited floor, the tallest enclosed space, and the tallest projection are all recorded and documented now with the zealousness of schoolboy enthusiasts collecting aircraft registration numbers to ensure that like is compared with like. But it seems scarcely possible that the Council on Tall Buildings and Urban Habitat, which records all this data, has actually been out there to measure and independently verify the claims that building owners make.

Within six years Malaysia's competitors caught up with the Petronas Towers. The 101 Tower, a skyscraper in Taipei, is almost 200 feet taller than the Petronas. And Kohn Pedersen Fox's Shanghai World Financial Center, with 94 floors, topped by a Ferris wheel, will turn out to be even taller. The tallest towers in the world are now being built in cities that few in the West could place on the map: Pusan in South Korea, Tianjin and Guangzhou in China.

The attack on New York came precisely at a moment when, after decades of skepticism about building high, the world had embarked on a particularly feverish bout of skyscraper building. In London, Norman Foster had just finished building his second tower for the Hong Kong and Shanghai Bank, this time at Canary Wharf, and was starting work on the unmistakable cone-shaped Swiss Re tower in the city center. Renzo Piano had secured the commission to design a tower for *The New York Times* and got involved with a quixotic project to put the tallest building in Europe on top of London Bridge Station. Jean Nouvel was planning a tower just as phallic as Foster's Swiss Re for Barcelona. In Asia every burgeoning metropolis was looking to establish its presence with a crop of ever taller structures. Clusters of towers were under way in Vienna and Milan. Melbourne and Sydney were competing to build the tallest apartment tower in the world. Dubai was trying to establish itself as a resort center with what it claimed was the tallest hotel in the world, even though Shanghai had built much higher hotel rooms by putting a hotel on top of fifty stories of offices.

It had all been so different just a couple of years earlier. After the revolt against the lumpish high rises of the 1970s, in most European cities both architectural and public sentiment determined that nothing else should be allowed to break through a strict but unstated height limit. Then, equally suddenly, the received wisdom was turned on its head. Building tall became an obsession for architects not just in Asia and America, but in Europe too.

When Asia's cities are building towers as fast as they can in a deliberate effort to modernize themselves, those western cities that don't follow suit begin to look somehow quaintly old-fashioned and fossilized. At their best, high-rise towers are elegant and technologically sophisticated, and they represent the future of the city. Yet they get built as the by-product of a primitive, unsubtle battle of egos. Politicians are fascinated by the image of the high-rise city, whether it is the Mori Corporation in Shanghai or Ken Livingstone's London. As mayor, Livingstone has been doing his best to bring new towers to London. This is ostensibly because it is what the multinationals want to stop them moving to Frankfurt or New York, but the reality owes more to the unsubtle symbolism of being the biggest or the tallest and so the most important.

The timing of the attacks on the Twin Towers certainly suggested the terrorists had been listening to the debate and had gotten the message about the symbolic significance of high-rise architecture. There is a particularly uncomfortable resonance to the fact that one of the hijackers who led the 9/11 attacks, Mohammed Atta, was himself a graduate of Cairo's school of architecture and a postgraduate planning student in Hamburg. If he had been a lawyer, an engineer, or a software designer, his background would simply have suggested that this was another disaffected middle-class radical. But the architectural connection seemed to suggest that Atta had recognized that the opposite side of the will to build is the attempt to delete.

Mohammed Atta was born in 1968 into a middle-class Egyptian family. He had enrolled at Cairo University in 1985 in the engineering school, whose four-year architecture syllabus allowed him to explore the history of architecture in both the Arab and the European worlds. It taught him to draw and how to analyze a design problem. His education taught him to think about how buildings worked, what made them stand up, and how they were made.

In a period of rapid political and social change, architecture represents a cultural confrontation. The Middle East has been importing it from the West for decades. It appeals to wealthy regimes because they are interested in representing themselves as part of the modern world, just as they would go shopping at Boeing or Airbus to equip a national airline or an air force. But the transformation of a city with new buildings that seem like insensitive transplants from another world, with different values, can be seen as not just a by-product of imperialism, but imperialism itself. Architecture is a painful and continuing reminder of the tension between modernity and tradition.

For those who study architecture in the Arab world, the acquisition of these apparently alien skills can be interpreted as a humiliating acknowledgment of technical and cultural weakness. It does not need to be understood in this way. Atta studied at the oldest architecture school in the Arab world. Hassan Fathy, Egypt's most distinguished architect, remains its most famous student. Fathy pioneered the rediscovery of Egypt's vernacular building techniques and devised an architecture sensitively attuned to the particularities of climate and indigenous skills, with an awareness of the fundamental cultural traditions that shape the way that buildings are used. With his philosophy of an architecture of the poor, Fathy focused on the needs of the country's dispossessed, rather than Egypt's westernized elite. If Atta's concerns had been genuinely to use his professional skills to effect social change, Fathy offered an inspiring role model for him. Instead, Atta left the country for Europe.

The Technical University of Hamburg Harburg is one of Germany's newest universities, having been established only in 1982. Its suburban campus is close to the River Elbe. It sits in a complex of mainly new buildings that have at their heart an approximation of an ancient Greek public space. An agora stepped into semicircular tiers for Socratic dialogue, it's a reflection of the belief of the dean of the town planning department, Dittmar Machule, in the virtues of traditional urban forms. Machule received a grant from the German Vibrant Cities Foundation to conduct a research program to determine what makes a city center lively. But it was more likely that it was Machule's work in Aleppo, the 5000-year-old Syrian city, funded by the German government's technical assistance program for conservation and rehabilitation, that attracted Atta to Hamburg in 1992.

Atta's time in Germany seems not to have been entirely financed by Osama bin Laden. He earned money working as a draftsman for Plankontor, a planning consultancy in Hamburg, for a couple of years. He enrolled in the postgraduate planning course and, after spending time in Syria, he wrote a thesis that explored the conflicts between traditional Islamic urbanism and modernity. His examiners found a dedication on the flyleaf of words taken from the Koran: "My sacrifice and my life and my death are all for Allah the lord of the world."

Machule gave him the highest marks for the thesis.

WATCHING THOSE MONSTROUS TELEVISION IMAGES OF THE TWIN Towers collapsing, a lot of architects found themselves speculating not so much about the unknowable question of why this horrific event was unfolding unstoppably in front of them, but how. And then, almost immediately afterward, asking themselves what it would mean for them as professionals. It's a response that might be seen as the ultimate in self-absorption. To focus on the technical in the midst of such a crisis is, perhaps, to find some sort of psychological comfort in the midst of seemingly limitless anxieties.

But three months later, when the Max Protetech Gallery opened its exhibition of speculations—"proposals" would be too strong a word—from architects on how best to rebuild the Twin Towers, technicalities were the last thing on their minds. For once, architects were not talking merely to themselves—they had the whole of New York looking over their shoulder.

Deciding whether or not to take part in the Protetech show wasn't easy. Zaha Hadid and Will Alsop both said yes, but Peter Eisenman, the New York architect who designed Berlin's monument to the Jewish victims of the Nazis, declined. So did Richard Meier. It was too soon; it was going to look like tacky self-promotion; it was plain ghoulish. And, in any case, it was all going to be pointless. It was obvious to anybody who thought about it for a moment that the future of the site was going to be shaped not by the imaginations of the dozens of architects who did take part in the show, but by the roomful of developers, insurance loss adjusters, and politicians carving up the area among themselves. Yet that is not to say that the exercise was not worth trying. It forced architects to grapple simultaneously with both the everyday and the horrifying.

How, on the one hand, do you deal with a relic of an approach to planning seen by many planners as hopelessly outmoded—one that created a monoculture of office space, cut off from the surrounding streets by an elevated pedestrian plaza—and, on the other, address the fact that this site is a mass grave?

Part of the dilemma is the time scale that architects must try to deal with. Ground Zero's meaning has changed already. One day it will be a place where people go to meet their accountants, have keys cut, pick up their dry cleaning, and sit on park benches. The emotional charge will still be there, especially for those who have lost children or partners, but it won't be there all the time. A successful rebuilding of Ground Zero will make the area an everyday slice of the city again. To this end, the creation of a memorial of more or less power is not the real issue. The essential question facing New York is exploring how to make a city. And not just any city. New York is *the* city, a city that is the product of a ruthless confrontation of a grid plan with geography and money. Such a city cannot be treated as if it were a suburb or a village. Despite the sentimental view that has helped us talk ourselves into believing that cities should be fluffy little villages like backdrops to Frank Capra movies, the essential quality of "cityness" demands a more robust view, as well as the creation of a city that can support diversity and anonymity simultaneously with a sense of community.

In retrospect, the idea of asking a single firm of architects to produce no less than six different ways of rebuilding the World Trade Center, then whittling them down to three preferred options, and finally incorporating their least unpopular features into a single master plan was not the best way to deal with Ground Zero. Things started badly enough when the Lower Manhattan Development Corporation (LMDC) held a competition to find an architect for the job, not on the basis of their design ideas, but on the strength of a credentials pitch. They picked Beyer Blinder Belle, a firm best known for its restoration of such nineteenth-century New York landmarks as Grand Central Terminal, but without much of a track record in new thinking. Beyer Blinder Belle were paid $3 million and expected to come up with six different ways of dealing with Ground Zero in a matter of weeks. The task would have defeated a Le Corbusier, never mind a businesslike but uncharismatic professional office. The results were not, claimed LMDC, meant to be taken literally as architectural designs. Rather, Beyer Blinder Belle's diagrams were intended to show nothing more ambitious than where new towers might be built and what could be left as open space.

Even if this was the right way to go forward, the presentation did nothing to make the case. The firm's leaden drawings were taken literally and were universally condemned as not being up to the job. The renderings seemed to portray a generic provincial city, not the skyline of the most dynamic metropolis in the world.

The results went on show in Wall Street in the spring of 2003. Like glib salesmen, Beyer Blinder Belle had brought out their sample case to offer passersby any kind of memorial they liked. One was a memorial "plaza," another a memorial "square." There was also a memorial triangle, a memorial garden, a memorial park, and even a memorial promenade (as if the sense of loss could be dealt with by a banal multiple-choice test). The reaction came down to two mutually irreconcilable views. On one side, there was a sense that none of the proposals matched the massively impressive quality of Yamasaki's lost towers, and on the other, that if the city was to heal it must build something to match the impact of what had been destroyed. A consensus also formed that the site is a mass grave and should be treated as such.

Just four weeks after unveiling Beyer Blinder Belle's six schemes, LMDC started again. Admitting none of the options put forward was right, the development corporation announced "a worldwide development competition," and asked contenders for designs with more "excitement, creativity and energy."

But the confused issue of who would actually get to select a design was never addressed. It was an ambiguity that was to prove disastrous for Daniel Libeskind.

When Libeskind first unveiled his plans to rebuild the World Trade Center, he was regarded as a serious-minded architectural intellectual, locked into the most arcane kind of private professional discourse, the kind that is understood only by its initiates. But from the moment he began to talk about his designs live on CNN, he was transformed. "Like so many others, I arrived by ship in New York harbor as a teenager and as an immigrant," he began, looking and sounding like a turbocharged Woody Allen. "The Statue of Liberty and the Manhattan skyline made an unforgettable impression, and this scheme is all about that."

For an architect to talk like this might have sounded hollow at any other time or place. It certainly sounds hollow after all the jockeying for position and the lawsuits that followed Libeskind's Pyrrhic victory in the competition. But in the glass-vaulted Winter Garden of the World Financial Center, from which the open wound in the rock and mud that was all that was left of the Twin Towers was clearly visible, the impact of his words, as Libeskind obviously knew, could not be anything but electric. He drew a round of applause as he finished speaking, ringingly declaring that rebuilding was an assertion of life in the face of tragedy.

For a moment he had stopped being an architect altogether. Libeskind was offering an emotional response to a collective tragedy. He had become a charismatic public figure, as if this particular issue was too much for architecture by itself to handle. For the cynics (and their numbers swelled rapidly as Libeskind's design developed), he was becoming a therapist as much as an architect. But for Libeskind his presentation was a highly personal and completely uncalculated response. He had put everything into the project, suspending the skepticism that many architects felt about the flawed competition process. Frank Gehry won few friends by refusing to take part, suggesting that the $40,000 fee for participants was demeaning.

"I know people say that the competition was window dressing, and that the real decisions are being taken somewhere else. But I couldn't feel cynical," says Libeskind. "At one level you have a civic responsibility; you are not just an architect, you are also a member of the public." However, by the summer of 2004, Libeskind's lawyers were looking for $1 million from Larry Silverstein for his work on the project, and the architect could be forgiven a certain amount of skepticism.

Of all the architects taking part, Libeskind was the only one not afraid of using the word "I." Strangely enough for a profession that cannot be anything but egotistical, the first-person singular personal pronoun is almost always finessed away. It's always "we" did this, when an architect means "I." But not Libeskind: "I went to look at the site," he said, "to see and feel what it is like to be standing in it, to see people, to feel its power, and to listen to its voices, and this is what I heard, felt and saw."

His competitors took a very different tone. Even though Stephen Holl, a prominent member of one team, actually saw the destruction as it happened from his office windows and Norman Foster was in a New York hotel on September 11, they used a more distanced, neutral voice.

Libeskind designed a ring of boldly sculptured blocks to deal with the 11 million square feet of office space that have to be accommodated on the site and gave them hints of an architectural language that those who have seen his Jewish Museum in Berlin will recognize as distinctively his own. But what really counted were the multiple layers of symbolic meaning he tried to give the project. He identified the bedrock seventy feet below ground, on which the towers once stood, as their most moving memorial: "The great slurry walls are an engineering wonder, designed to hold back the Hudson River. They withstood the unimaginable trauma of the destruction, and stand as eloquent as the Constitution itself, asserting the durability of democracy, and the value of individual life." Libeskind's original design left this raw wall as a silent monument. As things turned out, Libeskind won a competition staged by a public body that had neither the money to rebuild the towers nor control of the land on which they stood.

THERE ARE TWO UTTERLY DIFFERENT LIBESKINDS. ONE IS THE deeply serious architectural intellectual. His drawings are ink and pencil explosions that look more like an obscure form of musical notation than conventional architectural images. They came spattered with fragments of concrete poetry and Dadaist texts. This Libeskind is an architect who would rather not build at all than not build things his way.

And there is the opportunist Libeskind, prepared to do anything it takes to get the job—and that includes simultaneously hiring two different public relations firms in New York and discussing the finer points of his cowboy boots and his spectacles in the Style section of *The New York Times*. He was certainly the first candidate for dean of Columbia University's School of Architecture ever to have appeared on *Oprah*. More troubling to some in New York was the enthusiasm with which he played the patriotic card in the race to secure the World Trade Center commission. He took to wearing a Stars and Stripes pin in his lapel. He wouldn't stop talking about his first glimpse of the Statue of Liberty from the ship that brought him to the land of the free as a teenage immigrant. And even though he hadn't actually lived in the city for twenty years, he told every interviewer, "I am a New Yorker, and an American."

In fact, architecture can never insulate itself from the pursuit of politics. It is a game that can be played with more or less sophistication, but sitting the game out altogether is not an option. What is in question is the extent to which an architectural vision can survive intact once it has been subjected to the demands of a political strategy. The surprise with Libeskind was the confidence with which the intellectual changed gear to become the populist.

The schizophrenic combination of both these Daniel Libeskinds— the intellectually credible populist and the supersalesman—probably accounted for his anointment by Mayor Michael Bloomberg and Governor George Pataki as the architect of the reconstruction of the World Trade Center. The political skills of Libeskind's wife, Nina, a Canadian whose niece is, she tells you, Naomi "No Logo" Klein—driving her husband, lobbying behind the scenes, and devising a media strategy—were certainly also a major factor. No wonder that some observers have been more than a little confused about the emergence of this new Libeskind, whose existence they previously never suspected. Herbert Muschamp, then the *New York Times* architecture critic, was particularly confused. From having greeted Libeskind's short-listing as inspiring and his initial submission as "marvelous," Muschamp suddenly decided that it was in fact "manipulative kitsch." When the competition came down to a straight fight between Libeskind and his Argentine rival Rafael Viñoly, Muschamp attacked Libeskind's emotional symbolism as the embodiment of Cold War propaganda. It was not just the tower 1776 feet high, conspicuously echoing the Statue of Liberty's torch, that he interpreted in this way. There was also the "wedge of light," which would not in fact ensure that there are no shadows cast on the site between 8:46 A.M. and

10:28 A.M. every September 11, as Libeskind promised, and the Park of Heroes, tracing in the ground the paths taken by New York's firemen as they rushed into the Twin Towers.

The Libeskind camp was predictably outraged. Libeskind's executive assistant started an e-mail campaign urging sympathizers to write to *The New York Times* demanding that it sack Muschamp. The hapless assistant quickly had to issue a shamed-faced apology, saying that it was done "without the approval or the knowledge of Daniel or Nina Libeskind."

In the event he need not have bothered. The chances of Muschamp's favorite, Viñoly, were effectively torpedoed by a report in *The Wall Street Journal* on the eve of the closely run race that, contrary to Viñoly's hints about fleeing Argentina as a political exile escaping persecution by the military dictatorship, he had actually built his career thanks to the patronage of the junta and its generals.

Despite his intensity about architecture, Libeskind is clearly not afraid to take the gloves off if the going gets rough. When Viñoly shamelessly started describing Libeskind's design as "the Wailing Wall," Libeskind called Viñoly's design "two skeletons in the sky," and suggested that for Viñoly to name it the World Cultural Center smacked of the Stalinist Palace of Culture in Warsaw.

The troubling issue for Libeskind now is whether he is an architect, in the widest sense, or one who has focused entirely on the idea of commemorating tragedy in one form or another. After Berlin, he was once asked if he could build another Jewish museum. "I can't be a professional Jewish museum builder," he replied. But then he went on to accept a commission to build a Holocaust museum in San Francisco and also designed the Imperial War Museum North in Manchester.

In the months that followed the competition, an increasingly bitter dialogue between Libeskind and David Childs, working for developer Larry Silverstein (whose leases with the Port Authority gave him ownership of the project), ended with Childs taking control of the so-called Freedom Tower, and a series of other architects, including Norman Foster and Jean Nouvel, being appointed to take on other parts of the development. The big tower retained the height of 1776 feet—the tallest in the world—but otherwise it is all SOM's work.

THE TROUBLE WITH SKYSCRAPERS IS THAT WE CANNOT MAKE UP our minds about them. We lurch from celebrating them as the primitive signals of virile economic health to deploring their brutal impact on the fragile skyline of historic cities.

Norman Foster's striking new tower in the City of London—on the site of the Baltic Exchange, which was devastated by an IRA bomb in 1992—is a representation of that duality. Although the building is huge, it seems to insinuate itself into the landscape by stealth. We are not even meant to call it the Swiss Re tower. That would smack too much of a cult of personality for its careful insurance company owners.

According to the agents struggling to rent the empty upper half of its forty floors, the gherkin, as it has been nicknamed, is actually 30 St. Mary Axe. It's the kind of blandly discreet name that could suggest almost anything—a Georgian rectory perhaps, or a dignified stone-faced banking hall. Anything, in fact, except what it really is: the most conspicuous eruption on London's skyline in a quarter of a century, a single building that is as big as a small town, with 500,000 square feet of space able to accommodate four thousand people with ease. Whatever it's called, this is the tower that ignited London's current preoccupation with the skyscraper. It broke the 600-foot barrier in the Square Mile for the first time since 1979, when Tower 42—Richard Seifert's brash, steel-lined rolling pin, originally the home of the NatWest bank—opened the field to the rush of tall buildings that followed.

Most towers have all the charisma of an upended loaf of sliced white bread. We are expected to get excited about skyscrapers simply on the basis of their height, an attribute that is supposed to make us overlook the fact that everything else about them is banal and exceptionally uninteresting: a slick skin (if you are lucky), a marble-lined elevator lobby with a couple of black leather and chrome chairs, followed by a stack of identical floors, one on top of the other. The architecture, if there is any, is confined to a foot-deep zone around the outer wall. Norman Foster's tower is not like that. Despite its obvious phallic shape, it is more than the one-liner you might initially expect.

Foster has always been interested in subverting the conventional filing-cabinet repetitiveness of the office building. In the case of the Hong Kong and Shanghai Bank, with its exoskeleton structure and its hollowed-out interior atrium, which allowed the public to swarm all over the ground beneath, he succeeded to an extent that has never been equaled.

But that was a one-off, a handmade Bugatti. Swiss Re is more like a suave, polished, factory-engineered BMW. The structure is a muscular steel basket sheathed in a smooth glass skin. At the sidewalk, it emerges from the diamond-pattern glass to create an arcade of shops at street level. The argument against the tower during the controversy over its planning application was that it would look too dominant on the skyline; not only would it be excessively tall, the circular plan and shape would make it even more prominent. In fact, although the gherkin is visible from long distances, it can't be seen from everywhere. As you move around the City, it slips in and out of view. Clearly this is an effect that is beyond the control of the architect. But Foster has been careful to create a civilized dialogue between the tower and its nearest neighbors. The result is an intimate new plaza, where the sun casts reflections of the diamond pattern of Foster's building over its neighbors, like tattoos or the logos on Louis Vuitton luggage. Close up, it's impossible to see the top of the tower, which curves out of sight like a balloon.

Farther away, especially from the east, the tower erupts over the City's fringes like a colossus, a King Kong that, thanks to the diamond-shaped windows, looks as if it is wearing giant argyle socks. The pattern even suggests an affinity with a Tudor casement window. As important as the exterior is the fact that the tower is not conceived as a single mono-lith but has been designed to function as a stack of grouped floors.

Cloyingly, the architects call these stacks "villages." Each group of six floors is linked by a spiraling open atrium that twists around the building, opening up the structure and offering a sense of belonging to a wider entity than merely the floor on which you happen to be sitting. The result is a disruption of the oppressive flat ceiling that is the most universal and negative aspect of deep-plan, aircraft-hangar-size office floors.

Once, when you went up one of the few isolated towers, you were alone in the clouds. Now you find yourself up on the thirtieth floor, eye-ball to eyeball with people looking back at you from the thirtieth floor on the other side of the road. The fabric of the city is being squeezed up-ward, into the sky. The Swiss Re's pièce de résistance is the last two floors in the nose cone of the tower, what Foster calls "the mountain top," and you can see what he means. The peak is a glass bubble, with a 360-degree, uninterrupted view. This is, for once, an interior that justifies the word "sensational." There is nothing to get in the way of an awesomely dramatic view. You have left the solid, dependable pavements of the City of London and climbed into the stratosphere to look down on the capital as if you were a mountaineer. Emerge from the elevators and you are suddenly transported into Doctor Evil's lair. The view, from Windsor to the Thames estuary, is magnificent, fit for a master of the universe; the place radiates a sense of power over the human ants below.

All this is too much for a Swiss insurance company which is so dedi-cated to egalitarianism that it has not a single corporate parking place in the basement. Even senior executives are expected to travel by public transport (a taxi is still a form of public transport). There is no way that the chairman of such an organization could possibly have his desk up here. As a result this top level is a communal dining facility, somewhere for tenants to take their guests for a corporate lunch and to look down over Europe's financial heart. They can glimpse the jets taking off from Heathrow, twenty miles away, as well as the glinting river wrapping itself around the Tate Modern, the Tower of London, and Canary Wharf in a series of tight serpentine coils. And it's also a place to reflect on the paradox of a structure that seems so ordinary at street level, and so out of the ordinary up here in the clouds.

CHAPTER 13

AN INCURABLE CONDITION

ENOUGH EMPIRES HAVE COLLAPSED IMMEDIATELY AFTER THEIR rulers have finished building a sumptuous capital city—ostensibly for the national good, but more likely to personify and glorify their regimes—to suggest that architecture is not always a particularly effective political tool. Haussmann's brand-new boulevards did not stop the Parisian mob from burning down the Tuileries in 1870 after Napoleon III's ignominious end, or the bloodshed of the Commune and the appalling violence of its suppression that followed. The Prussians may have been impressed by the splendors of Paris, yet the trappings of a superior urban civilization were not enough to deter them from their invasion of France.

But Haussmann's Paris was not simply the product of imperial megalomania. Without it, France would have been a poorer and less commanding state. In the long term, Haussmann did indeed have a lasting impact in shaping the world's view of France, and its place in the international order. And the fact that Hitler did his best to have Paris destroyed in 1944 would suggest that architectural symbolism has an essential part to play in great power conflicts.

The British left New Delhi just twenty years after Edwin Lutyens and Herbert Baker completed an imperial capital intended to last for centuries. The city looked and felt authoritative enough for India to adopt it for its own use. That achievement was not, however, a sufficiently convincing demonstration of the superiority of European civilization to dissuade Indians from demanding their independence from the power that built it.

As demonstrated by the Shah of Iran's ill-fated attempt to rebuild Tehran as a modern western city, and Ferdinand and Imelda Marcos's compulsion for dropping monumental concrete cubes all over Manila, architecture has on occasion actually speeded up the process of regime change. Such projects have seemed more like the follies of the advanced stages of monomania than rational development. But just because the will to build is not always effective does not mean that it is unconnected with statecraft. After the facile identification of modernism with progressive politics, and classicism with authoritarianism, was discredited, it became common among architectural critics such as Leon Krier to suggest that there was no connection between architecture and power. Or else to suggest that if there was, then it was less than effective. However, military force seldom achieves its objectives either, but no historian would suggest that its disposition is irrelevant to the fate of nations, or that it is possible fully to understand history without it.

Buildings last a long time, but their political role may be relevant only at the moment of their initial creation. A moment of relevance may come again in quite a different context. Britain's House of Commons meant one thing when it was built, something very different when it was destroyed by enemy action in World War II, and something different again in the daily grind of political life at the start of the twenty-first century.

Germany's Reichstag became the symbol of Nazi Germany's defeat when the Red Army occupied it in 1945, even though it had played little part in the direction of Hitler's regime. Half a century later, the Bonn parliament's decision to move the seat of the reunited Germany to Berlin, and then to commission a British architect to restore the Reichstag for its new purpose, was an explicit use of architecture with a political purpose on a number of different levels. The move expressed a newfound sense of national identity. At the same time, choosing Norman Foster was a conciliatory gesture to demonstrate the rejection of overheated nationalism. Foster's glass-domed roof, with its spiraling ramp directly above the parliamentary chamber, is open to the public. The design, which allows the German electorate the freedom to wander over the heads of their representatives, is another deliberate signal of the regime's intentions. It is as much a rhetorical statement about the reunited country's progressive values as Foster's provision of an air-conditioning system for the parliament that does not depend on fossil fuels.

Building is not just about the practical provision of shelter or the construction of the modern infrastructure of a state. Although architecture may appear to be rooted in pragmatism, it is a powerful and extraordinarily revealing expression of human psychology. It has a significance both at the largest scale and at the most personal. It is a means for inflating the individual ego to the scale of a landscape, a city, or even a nation. It also reflects the ambitions and insecurities and motivations of those who build; because of that, it offers a faithful reflection of the nature of power, its strategies, its consolations, and its impact on those who wield it.

What architecture does as no other cultural form can is to glorify and magnify autocrats and suppress the individual into the mass. Architecture can be seen as the first form of mass communication; it is still one of the most powerful. That is why architecture has flourished under so many autocratic political systems. And it is why it has a way of appealing to powerful individuals looking to make their mark. It has both an intellectual and a material impact.

There is hardly a single twentieth-century autocrat who achieved power who didn't embark on a campaign of building: from Hitler and Mussolini, to Stalin, Mao, Saddam Hussein, and Kim Il Sung. Indeed it has been argued that for Hitler, architecture was not simply a tool for the creation of the Nazi regime, but that he saw things the other way around. Establishing the Nazi regime was a means for realizing his architectural ambitions.

That closeness between totalitarianism and architecture is what gives monumental building the sinister undertone that George Orwell was thinking of in an essay that he wrote about politics and culture shortly before his death. Orwell suggested that while poetry might survive in a totalitarian age and "that certain arts or half arts, such as architecture, might even find tyranny beneficial," the prose writer "would have no choice between silence and death." That sardonic observation is the product of one of the keenest literary intelligences ever to emerge from British culture. From the first, Orwell had understood the nature of Stalinism, its determination to co-opt cultural life as an essential part of its strategy for maintaining its grip on power, and its corruption of everything and everyone it touched. The cultural elite, provided that they played their parts as expected in the apparatus of the state, were loaded with honors and privileges. And even the dissidents were persecuted rather than ignored, a situation that the intelligentsia of the West, assailed by the nagging sense of its impotence and irrelevance, has always quietly envied.

Orwell had understood Stalin's buildings and the monuments of Hitler's Germany for what they actually were. Despite the lordly disdain of the prose writer *de haut* for the *en bas* of the architect, his was an acidly perceptive view. It's one that should shape an understanding of architecture as it is practiced not just by the hacks ready to blow with any political wind, or the reactionary and the deluded, but also those who might be called the practitioners of high architecture. Le Corbusier and Mies van der Rohe, Rem Koolhaas and Renzo Piano, Wallace Harrison and Frank Gehry are not free agents. Their work depends on their engagement with the political context of the world. And in that world the totalitarians and the egotists and the monomaniacs offer architects, whatever their personal political views, more opportunities for "important" work than the liberal democracies. They are the kind of projects that illuminate the nature of the compromises that architects find themselves making. Strongly centralized states, such as Mitterrand's France, or outright dictatorships, such as the Shah's Iran, have been more typical models of architectural patronage than the liberal regimes with their policies of benign neglect. Post-Franco Barcelona and the Netherlands of the 1990s are exceptions, following in the tradition of small states that have used modernism as an architectural language to demonstrate their visibility or to make a break with an unhappy past.

Architecture has always been used to give those who build it the sense that they are able to escape the transience of existence, and to give it some sense of coherence. To place man-made architectural objects in the landscape is one way to try to give them meaning; it is suggesting that they belong to a system. The landscape lasts far longer than mankind. Trying to make our objects part of that time scale offers the consolation of a sense of connectedness with a version of eternity. Architecture searches for meaning at a wide range of scales. Some architects look to the landscape and to the stars as their reference points. Others try to find solace in the idea that naturally occurring forms, such as crystal structures, skeletal forms, or molecular plant cells, can be used as the starting point for architectural form. Doing so, they believe, allows a building to reflect some kind of inner harmony—for example, by achieving maximum strength for the most minimal use of resources. In mimicking such forms in their own structures, the initiates evidently believe that their designs will achieve the same sense of balance and order as the naturally occurring world with its patterns and harmonic structure.

Beyond these clues in the natural landscape and the characteristics of organic matter, architects have looked to find ways of creating their own intellectual definitions of architectural meaning, based on a philosophy of design, rather than looking at naturally observable phenomena. Such definitions are based on the construction of a set of principles that determine all of the choices and decisions that an architect makes in designing a building. The classical orders of architecture find that determination in a precise set of rules that define the composition of each column, from the nature of the decorative detail around its capital, to the proportion of its height, to its width. The rules serve also to define the ways in which those columns are grouped, and what happens at each corner of a building, how the building touches the ground, how it meets the sky, and how those columns and their proportions relate to their place in an overall composition. Symmetry is part of the conceptual kit of parts; so is the idea of a sense of harmony and rhythm, which seems to be a metaphor for finding a place in the world.

Other architectural approaches are less explicitly codified than classicism, because they are much more recent and less universally understood. Often they depend on analogy, or the creation of a set of rules that can acquire the sense of a moral force. Such rules, which are perhaps the definition of architecture itself, are the route into a world with a sense of purpose. Perhaps the secret is to be found in using as few materials as possible, which implies a whole set of decisions that will determine what happens when one of these materials meets another. In Victorian houses, plaster walls meet stone floors, but the meeting point between the two was hidden behind an elaborately patterned skirting board. In certain kinds of modern houses, the architect insists on removing the skirting board and making a shadow gap, an indentation between plaster wall and stone floor. It looks much simpler, but is actually much more difficult for the contractor. Celebrating the joint by embellishing it looks difficult, but actually allows for less exacting standards of craftsmanship, and offers a chance to hide mistakes. But the decision to hide a joint or to put it on show is given the character of a moral issue by those who claim to see design as a question of "honesty." Some of these approaches are transparently nothing more than arbitrary and self-imposed. There is no real reason to believe that windows should line up at the top, rather than at the bottom. But such rules become the means of defining the angle that a handrail should make with the banisters on a staircase, or how a window is placed in a wall to demonstrate that each element is part of a larger architectural whole. What the system is matters much less than the fact of its existence.

Objectively, there is no right answer to the question of where to put a window. Or rather there are a lot of right answers, depending on the internal logic that the architect has constructed for an architectural system—or even the lack of logic if, as often happens, the logic is deliberately based on randomness.

Avant-garde architectural narratives begin as personal fantasies, and then through constant repetition become more plausible with the passing of time. As they become more widely accepted, they are taken up by larger and larger groups of designers, before eventually being replaced with another narrative. The idea that architects should design buildings to look as if they were made by machines, rather than the laborious and often messy process of handcraft that is actually involved, was a narrative current throughout the 1920s and 1930s; it produced something called functionalism. The white, smooth walls and the flat roofs of the Bauhaus style were presented as logical, rational solutions to technical problems. In fact, they were the result of aesthetic decisions.

When Richard Rogers and Renzo Piano designed the Pompidou Center in such a way that the ducts and pipes servicing the building, as well as the structure holding it up, were made visible—legible, as Rogers put it—they devised a system for design. The system is based on frankness, showing the constituent parts, and again it has an apparent logic. It serves to create a fragment of existence in which if you suspend disbelief and don't ask too many questions; you find yourself in a world in which reason and logic appear to exist. They even came up with a logic for its color-coded exterior, adopting the standard colors used on engineers' drawings to show electrical circuits. But it is actually an aesthetic system, just as the Doric order is such a system. The architect has invented a set of rules that, if followed carefully enough, produce a coherent build-ing—provided that you accept the fundamental premises of the system.

These systems can appear to be material, or ethereal and spiritual. Architecture spans both these poles in a way that few other disciplines can. Such systems can take many forms, including the belief in the power of numbers—an occult preoccupation that has consumed archi-tects from every period, from the classical to Le Corbusier, with his "modulor" dimensional system and his vain pursuit of logic, order, and harmony through the hardly comprehensible proportional rules that he devised. There is the mysticism of a Christopher Alexander, or the pur-suit of an architecture based on ecological imperatives—the latter sig-naled by turf roofs and triple glazing.

On one level, architecture never changes. Despite the veneer of the contemporary, architecture is intimately concerned with the primal is-sues confronting us in our attempts to come to terms with who we are, and where we are and what life is. Architecture is constantly about the same things: power, glory, spectacle. And yet it always looks different. The processes, the materials, the time scales that shape building have shifted. No one can co-opt a particular architectural language forever.

Architects have given up trying to persuade us that buildings have the power to make our lives better or worse. Of course architecture can do that, in the sense that leaking roofs make us wet and weather-tight ones keep us warm, but that is not what interests most architects. Per-haps that is why architects are now so keen to pose as artists, liberating themselves from the alibi of function. Architecture does trigger emo-tional responses at a personal level, as well as for a society at large. Architecture reflects our vanities and our aspirations, our weaknesses and our ambitions and our complexes. But it is more often the product of a strong and ruthless individual than of a collective vision.

An understanding of what it is that motivates us to build, and the na-ture of the elusive relationship between architecture and power, is a key insight into our existence and can allow us to free ourselves from the most pernicious aspects of the manipulative uses of architecture.

Architecture exerts an abiding fascination on the most egotistical of individuals, desperate to use it to glorify themselves: the billionaire museum trustees, the skyscraper builders, and the mansion owners. Equally, it can be put to work by reforming mayors looking to transform their cities for the better. Whatever the architects' intentions, in the end they find themselves being defined not by their own rhetoric, but by the impulses that have driven the rich and the powerful to employ architects and to seek to shape the world.

BIBLIOGRAPHY

First a few words about sources, some of which the reader who wants to explore the subject more deeply would be well advised to consult. Specific bibliographic information regarding these titles is included in the listing that follows these comments.

Writing this book has reminded me of how few architects have been the subject of a biography as personal or psychological in its interpretations as those which we have come to expect for the great artists of the twentieth century, let alone the writers, soldiers, and politicians. Such bibliographies of architects are so rare that when a portrait as colorfully realized as that painted by Jane Ridley's life of Edwin Lutyens, *The Architect and His Wife: A Life of Edwin Lutyens*, is published, it comes as something of a jolt to find the architect's sex life implicated in his architecture. The balance is almost invariably tipped in the other direction. And even Lutyens's role in the creation of New Delhi is treated in the book in a way that seems to detach the motivations and impulses of the architect from the political role that his work is playing. Le Corbusier and, in particular, Mies van der Rohe are the subjects of a vast amount of specialist literature that dwells exclusively on their work, without any sense of the passions and motivations that shaped it. Charles Jencks tries in his *Le Corbusier and the Tragic View of Architecture*. But there is still so much to know about this remarkable architect, his equally remarkable life, and his dealings with notable individuals ranging from Josephine Baker to Stalin.

Philip Johnson's political career, revealed through a series of magazine articles—notably Michael Sorkin's in *The Village Voice*—has its fullest exposure in Franz Schulze's impressively detailed and revealing biography, *Philip Johnson: Life and Work*. It has a degree of frankness that makes it read as if Johnson's cooperation with the author had been given on the assumption that it would be published only posthumously. In his book Schulze describes Peter Eisenman's abandoning an attempt at a biography of Johnson when his subject became aware of just how much of his enthusiasm for extreme right-wing politics would be featured. But to judge by the papers that Johnson himself lodged with the research library at the Getty Research Institute while he was still alive, it's hard to imagine what else Eisenman could have found to reveal.

Mies van der Rohe was also the subject of a study by Schulze that is rather less revealing: *Mies: A Critical Biography*. Mies's compromises with Nazi Germany, long dismissed as hearsay and rumors spread by surviving Bauhaus faculty in America, were documented beyond doubt in Elaine S. Hochman's detailed and not unsympathetic account in *Architects of Fortune: Mies van der Rohe and the Third Reich*.

The literature on Albert Speer is extensive, but most of it concentrates on his political life rather than his architecture, and it ranges from the ambivalence of Gitta Sereny in *Albert Speer: His Battle with Truth* to the angry Matthias Schmidt, clearly incensed at Speer's manipulation of his history, in *Albert Speer: The End of a Myth*. Speer's own diaries written with Joachim Fest, *Speer: The Final Verdict*, are hardly great works of literature, and if it is possible to infer architectural skill from literary style, which it isn't, they would support the reading of Speer's classicism as the routine assembly of detail into a massive but unconvincing whole.

The plans for the rebuilding of Berlin as Germania, which Speer led, are documented in a series of books, such as Lars Olof Larsson's *Albert Speer: Le Plan de Berlin*, that have the air of dusty partisan tracts rather than objective expositions.

But the greatest gap is the life of Boris Iofan, an architect with a tantalizingly undocumented relationship with Stalin that one can infer had something of the closeness of that of Speer with Hitler. He appears only as a walk-on figure in accounts of the competition for the Palace of the Soviets, as if he were Rosencrantz or Guildenstern, rather than the Hamlet that he so clearly was.

Victoria Newhouse's *Wallace K. Harrison, Architect*, with its sober, carefully documented account of the relationship between Harrison and Nelson Rockefeller, is a model for what still remains to be done on Iofan.

As far as the men—Imelda Marcos and Farah Pahlavi apart, they are always men—who commissioned these projects, and the other architects who have served their purposes, Frederic Spotts's *Hitler and the Power of Aesthetics* provided a compelling account of the dictator's self-image as an artist, and Kanan Makiya's *The Monument: Art and Vulgarity in Saddam Hussein's Iraq* attempts rather less compellingly to do the same for Saddam Hussein. But there is still a lot of work to be done on Atatürk, Mussolini, and Stalin and their passion for building.

Timothy J. Colton's *Moscow: Governing the Socialist Metropolis* demonstrates what is to be gained from an understanding of the political manifestations of building.

For the account of the relationship between Peter Lewis and the Guggenheim, the archives of *The New York Times* and the Cleveland *Plain Dealer* have been invaluable.

Berlin, alone of the major cities that I went to, has a substantial literature connecting history, politics, architecture, and space, including, in English, Alan Balfour's *Berlin: The Politics of Order* and Brian Ladd's *The Ghosts of Berlin: Confronting German History in the German Landscape.*

As a journalist rather than a scholar, I have relied as much on my own eyes and ears, and on the first draft of history in the media, as on published sources in this book. Architects from Richard Meier to Norman Foster have talked to me about the nature of their work. In the case of the work of the dead, there is no substitute for pacing the wide-open spaces of Tiananmen and Red Squares, and EUR, or Lyndon Johnson's library in Austin, to understand what was driving their builders.

I list below only the writings that have been of use in making this book. This bibliography is by no means a complete record of all the works and sources I have consulted. It indicates the substance and range of reading upon which I have based my ideas, provided for those who might wish to pursue further reading.

ADES, DAWN, TIM BENTON, DAVID ELLIOTT, and IAIN BOYD WHYTE. *Art and Power: Europe under the Dictators 1930–45.* London: Thames & Hudson, 1996.

ALLEN, MICHAEL THAD. *The Business of Genocide: The SS, Slave Labor and the Concentration Camps.* Chapel Hill: University of North Carolina Press, 2002.

AMAN, ANDERS. *Architecture and Ideology in Eastern Europe during the Stalin Era: An Aspect of Cold War History.* Cambridge and London: MIT Press, 1992.

BALFOUR, ALAN. *Berlin: The Politics of Order.* New York: Rizzoli, 1990.

Berthet Pochy: Interior Design. London: Wordsearch, 1994.

BOSWORTH, RICHARD. *Mussolini.* London: Hodder Arnold, 2002.

BUNSHAFT, GORDON. Interview for Chicago Oral History Project, April 1989, www.artic.edu/aic/libraries/caohp/bunshaft.

CARO, ROBERT. *The Power Broker: Robert Moses and the Fall of New York.* New York: Random House, 1975.

COHEN, JEAN LOUIS. *Le Corbusier and the Mystique of the USSR: Theories and Projects for Moscow, 1928–36.* Princeton, N.J.: Princeton University Press, 1992.

COLTON, TIMOTHY J. *Moscow: Governing the Socialist Metropolis.* Cambridge and London: Harvard University Press, 1995.

DARTON, ERIC. *Divided We Stand: A Biography of New York's World Trade Center.* New York: Basic Books, 1999.

DAVIES, PHILIP. *The Splendours of the Raj: British India, 1660–1947.* London: John Murray, 1985.

FARRELL, NICHOLAS. *Mussolini: A New Life.* London: Weidenfeld & Nicolson, 2003.

FEST, JOACHIM. *Speer: The Final Verdict.* London: Weidenfeld & Nicolson, 2002.

FITCH, ROBERT. *The Assassination of New York.* London and New York: Verso, 1993.

FRASER, VALERIE. *Building the New World: Studies in the Modern Architecture of Latin America.* London and New York: Verso, 2000.

GOLDBERGER, PAUL. *Up from Zero: Politics, Architecture and the Rebuilding of New York.* New York: Random House, 2004.

HINES, THOMAS S. *Richard Neutra and the Search for Modern Architecture.* Oxford: Oxford University Press, 1982.

HITLER, ADOLF. *Mein Kampf.* Translated by Ralph Manheim. New York: Mariner, 1999.

HOBSBAWM, ERIC, and TERENCE RANGER, eds. *The Invention of Tradition.* Cambridge: Cambridge University Press, 1983.

HOCHMAN, ELAINE S. *Architects of Fortune: Mies van der Rohe and the Third Reich.* New York: Fromm, 1990.

———. *Bauhaus: Crucible of Modernism.* New York: Fromm, 1997.

HUGHES, ROBERT. "Of Gods and Monsters." *Guardian,* 1 February 2003.

JENCKS, CHARLES. *Le Corbusier and the Tragic View of Architecture.* London: Allen Lane, 1973.

JONES, LINDSAY. *The Hermeneutics of Sacred Architecture.* Cambridge: Harvard University Press, 2000.

KINROSS, PATRICK. *Atatürk: The Rebirth of a Nation.* London: Weidenfeld & Nicolson, 1993.

LADD, BRIAN. *The Ghosts of Berlin: Confronting German History in the Urban Landscape.* London and Chicago: University of Chicago Press, 1998.

LANE, BARBARA. *Architecture and Politics in Germany, 1918–45.* Cambridge: Harvard University Press, 1985.

LARSSON, LARS OLOF. *Albert Speer: Le Plan de Berlin, 1937–1943.* Brussels: Archives d'Architecture Moderne, 1983.

LEONARD, MARK. Interview with Rem Koolhaas. *Financial Times,* 6 March 2004.

LEYS, SIMON. *Broken Images: Essays on Chinese Culture and Politics.* London: Allison & Busby, 1979.

———. *The Emperor's New Clothes: Mao and the Cultural Revolution.* London: Allison & Busby, 1977.

MAKIYA, KANAN. *The Monument: Art and Vulgarity in Saddam Hussein's Iraq.* New York: I.B. Tauris, 2002.

MONTEFIORE, SIMON SEBAG. *Stalin, the Court of the Red Tsar.* London: Weidenfeld & Nicolson, 2004.

NEWHOUSE, VICTORIA. *Wallace K. Harrison, Architect.* New York: Rizzoli, 1989.

NOBEL, PHILIP. *Sixteen Acres: The Rebuilding of the World Trade Center Site.* London: Granta, 2005.

PAHLAVI, FARAH. *An Enduring Love: My Life with the Shah.* New York: Miramax, 2004.

RAGHEB, J. FIONA, ed. *Frank Gehry, Architect.* New York: Abrams, 2001.

RIDLEY, JANE. *The Architect and His Wife: A Life of Edwin Lutyens.* London: Pimlico, 2002.

ROWE, PETER G. *Seng Kuan: Architectural Encounters with Essence and Form in Modern China.* London: MIT Press, 2002.

RUSSO, ANTONELLA. *Il Fascismo in mostra.* Rome: Rivniti, 1992.

SALISBURY, HARRISON. *The New Emperors: Mao and Deng.* London: HarperCollins, 1992.

SCARROCCHIA, SANDRO. *Albert Speer e Marcello Piacentini: L'Architettura del totalitarismo negli anni trenti.* Milan: Electa, 1999.

SCHMIDT, MATTHIAS. *Albert Speer: The End of a Myth.* London: Harrap, 1984.

SCHULLER, ROBERT H. *My Journey.* San Francisco: HarperSanFrancisco, 2001.

SCHULZE, FRANZ. *Philip Johnson: Life and Work.* New York: Knopf, 1996.

————. *Mies: A Critical Biography.* Chicago and London: University of Chicago Press, 1985.

SCOOBIE, ALEX. *Hitler's State Architecture: The Impact of Classical Antiquity.* London: Pennsylvania State University Press, 1990.

SERENY, GITTA. *Albert Speer: His Battle with Truth.* London: Picador, 1995.

SHIRER, WILLIAM L. *Berlin Diary, 1934–41.* New York: Galahad, 1941.

SHORT, PHILIP. *Mao: A Life.* London: Hodder, 1999.

SPAETH, DAVID. *Mies van der Rohe.* New York: Rizzoli, 1985.

SPEER, ALBERT. *Inside the Third Reich.* New York: Galahad, 1970.

SPOTTS, FREDERIC. *Hitler and the Power of Aesthetics.* London: Pimlico, 2003.

SUDJIC, DEYAN, and HELEN JONES. *Architecture and Democracy.* Glasgow: Laurence King, 1999.

TAYLOR, ROBERT R. *The Word in Stone: The Role of Architecture in the National Socialist Ideology.* Berkeley, Calif., and London: University of California Press, 1974.

VALE, LAWRENCE. *Architecture, Power and National Identity.* New Haven: Yale University Press, 1992.

WISE, MICHAEL Z. *Capital Dilemma.* New York: Princeton Architectural Press, 1998.

WISEMAN, CARTER. *The Architecture of I. M. Pei.* London: Thames & Hudson, 1990.

YAMASAKI, MINORU. *A Life in Architecture.* New York: Weatherhill, 1979.

INDEX

FOR THE BEST IN PAPERBACKS, LOOK FOR THE (🐧)

In every corner of the world, on every subject under the sun, Penguin represents quality and variety—the very best in publishing today.

For complete information about books available from Penguin—including Penguin Classics, Penguin Compass, and Puffins—and how to order them, write to us at the appropriate address below. Please note that for copyright reasons the selection of books varies from country to country.

In the United States: Please write to *Penguin Group (USA), P.O. Box 12289 Dept. B, Newark, New Jersey 07101-5289* or call 1-800-788-6262.

In the United Kingdom: Please write to *Dept. EP, Penguin Books Ltd, Bath Road, Harmondsworth, West Drayton, Middlesex UB7 0DA.*

In Canada: Please write to *Penguin Books Canada Ltd, 90 Eglinton Avenue East, Suite 700, Toronto, Ontario M4P 2Y3.*

In Australia: Please write to *Penguin Books Australia Ltd, P.O. Box 257, Ringwood, Victoria 3134.*

In New Zealand: Please write to *Penguin Books (NZ) Ltd, Private Bag 102902, North Shore Mail Centre, Auckland 10.*

In India: Please write to *Penguin Books India Pvt Ltd, 11 Panchsheel Shopping Centre, Panchsheel Park, New Delhi 110 017.*

In the Netherlands: Please write to *Penguin Books Netherlands bv, Postbus 3507, NL-1001 AH Amsterdam.*

In Germany: Please write to *Penguin Books Deutschland GmbH, Metzlerstrasse 26, 60594 Frankfurt am Main.*

In Spain: Please write to *Penguin Books S. A., Bravo Murillo 19, 1° B, 28015 Madrid.*

In Italy: Please write to *Penguin Italia s.r.l., Via Benedetto Croce 2, 20094 Corsico, Milano.*

In France: Please write to *Penguin France, Le Carré Wilson, 62 rue Benjamin Baillaud, 31500 Toulouse.*

In Japan: Please write to *Penguin Books Japan Ltd, Kaneko Building, 2-3-25 Koraku, Bunkyo-Ku, Tokyo 112.*

In South Africa: Please write to *Penguin Books South Africa (Pty) Ltd, Private Bag X14, Parkview, 2122 Johannesburg.*